959.70434
Nolan, Keith William, 1964-
Search and destroy : the story of an
armored cavalry squadron in Vietnam :
1-1 Cav, 1967-1968
c2010

Discarded by
Santa Maria Library

SANTA MARIA PUBLIC LIBRARY

Search and Destroy

Books by Keith W. Nolan

House to House: Playing the Enemy's Game in Saigon, May 1968
Ripcord: Screaming Eagles Under Siege, Vietnam 1970
The Battle for Saigon: Tet 1968
Sappers in the Wire: The Life and Death of Firebase Mary Ann
A Hundred Miles of Bad Road: An Armored Cavalryman in Vietnam, 1967–68 (with Dwight W. Birdwell)
The Magnificent Bastards: The Joint Army-Marine Defense of Dong Ha, 1968
Operation Buffalo: USMC Fight for the DMZ
Into Cambodia: Spring Campaign, Summer Offensive, 1970
Into Laos: The Story of Dewey Canyon II/Lam Son 719, Vietnam 1971
Death Valley: The Summer Offensive, I Corps, August 1969
Battle for Hue: Tet 1968

Search and Destroy

The Story of an Armored Cavalry Squadron in Vietnam:
1-1 Cav, 1967–1968

Keith W. Nolan

ZENITH PRESS

First published in 2010 by Zenith Press, an imprint of MBI Publishing Company, 400 First Avenue North, Suite 300, Minneapolis, MN 55401 USA

Copyright © 2010 by Keith W. Nolan

All rights reserved. With the exception of quoting brief passages for the purposes of review, no part of this publication may be reproduced without prior written permission from the Publisher. The information in this book is true and complete to the best of our knowledge.

Zenith Press titles are also available at discounts in bulk quantity for industrial or sales-promotional use. For details write to Special Sales Manager at MBI Publishing Company, 400 First Avenue North, Suite 300, Minneapolis, MN 55401 USA.

To find out more about our books, join us online at www.zenithpress.com.

Library of Congress Cataloging-in-Publication Data

Nolan, Keith W., 1964-2009
  Search and destroy : the story of an armored cavalry squadron in Vietnam : 1-1 Cav, 1967-1968 / Keith W. Nolan.
     p. cm.
  Includes bibliographical references and index.
  ISBN 978-0-7603-3312-9 (hbk. w/jkt)
  1. United States. Army. Armored Cavalry Regiment, 1st. Squadron, 1st. 2. Vietnam War, 1961-1975--Regimental histories--United States. 3. United States. Army. Armored Cavalry Regiment, 1st. Squadron, 1st--Biography. 4. Soldiers--United States--Biography. I. Title.
  DS558.4.N66 2010
  959.704'342--dc22
                                   2009053301

Designed by: Helena Shimizu
Cover by: Matthew Simmons
Maps and charts by: Richard Brummett; produced with Mapdiva's Ortelius™ software
On the cover: *Official Department of Defense photo*
On the back cover: Crewmen from A-30 and A-35 enjoy the morning sun atop A-35 near LZ Goat. *John Guzik III*
Author photo by: Richard Brummett

Printed in the United States of America

For Britt, of course, of whom I could not be more proud . . . and Kristin Lynn Halbert, to whom I could not be more thankful . . .

*Yea, though I walk through the valley of the shadow of death,
I shall fear no evil, for I am the meanest motherfucker in the valley.*

Charles Nathan Boyd
1st Armored Division
Việt Nam, 1967–1968

You got arms and legs on that one, Three Five.

David Earl Roesler
1st Armored Division
Việt Nam, 1967–1968

Contents

Introduction 1
Notes 5

PART ONE—1967

Saddling Up: January–May 1967 11
Hurry Up and Wait: June–August 1967 23
Bound for Foreign Shores: August 9–27, 1967 27
The Advance Party: August 14–28, 1967 35
Getting Situated: August 28–September 4, 1967 43
First Blood: September 4–5, 1967 49
On the Go-Go: September 1967 53
Finally, Solid Contact: September 24–30, 1967 63
Cigar Island: October 7–13, 1967 71
End of the Line: October 1967 75
The Real Face of War:
   October 20–November 1, 1967 81
Meanwhile, Charlie Troop:
   October–November 1967 93
Into the Valley of Death: November 6–14, 1967 95
The View from Above: October–December 1967 111
The Daily Grind: November–December 1967 113
The Pineapple Forest: November–December 1967 123
The Best Defense Is a Strong Offense:
   December 1967 133
The Turning of the Screw: December 1967 137

PART TWO—1968

Changing of the Guard: January 2 and 7, 1968 147
Like Nothing that Had Come Before:
   January 3–16, 1968 149

Sorry 'Bout That: January 1968 167
Good Hunting: January 1968 169
Skirmishes: January 1968 175
Tết: January–February 1968 177
The Tết Counteroffensive: February–April 1968 185
The Road to Tiên Phước: April 1968 225
One of the New Guys: April–May 1968 229
The Mayor of Fat City: May 1968 233
LZ Goat: May–June 1968 239
Another Patton: July–August 1968 247
The Battle of Tam Kỳ—Day One: August 24, 1968 ...259
The Battle of Tam Kỳ—Day Two: August 25, 1968 ...267
The Battle of Tam Kỳ—Days Three, Four, and Five:
   August 26–28, 1968 277
Seeing the Elephant: Summer and Fall 1968 285
Finale to the Third General Offensive:
   September 1968 301
A Dull, Gray Time: October–November 1968 323
Operation Daring Endeavor:
   November 10–20, 1968 329
End of an Era: November–December 1968 337

Epilogue: Home from War 343
Appendices 377
Glossary 415
Bibliography 423
In Memoriam 427
Index 429

Introduction

FORTY YEARS REMOVED FROM the events in question, a certain amnesia, bordering on whitewashing, has developed regarding the realities of General William Westmoreland's search-and-destroy war in South Việt Nam.

A vivid reminder seems in order. One unit intimately involved in the search-and-destroy war, the 1st Squadron of the 1st Cavalry Regiment, originally arrived in Việt Nam during the summer of '67. The squadron, which made war from tanks and armored assault vehicles known as tracks, reinforced the ongoing campaign in I Corps, the most northern of the four tactical zones into which South Việt Nam had been divided. High casualties were the price of admission for units that operated in I Corps, and, indeed, most members of the squadron not killed or seriously wounded accumulated at least one or two flesh wounds during their tours of duty. The allies faced two implacable foes in I Corps: Việt Cộng guerrillas who planted mines amid the villages of the coastal lowlands and the light infantrymen of the North Vietnamese Army, who ventured from the mountains to the west to make conventional war, resupplied and replenished as they were through Laos.

Tough troopers for a tough war, the young men of the 1-1 Cavalry gave as good as they got. Mostly draftees, they had little use for the army and played by their own rules, loading coolers of beer into their tanks and tracks along with the ammunition. Led by professionals, however, and confident in their firepower, they were ferocious in battle, routinely racking up lopsided body counts—ten to one, fifty to one, a hundred to one—over the VC and NVA.

Veterans of the 1-1 Cavalry, a tight bunch indeed, remain immensely proud to have known such good men as those they fought beside at places like Cigar Island, the Pineapple Forest, and the Quế Sơn Valley. If you ask, they will tell you of the young trooper who walked down a line of enemy entrenchments, methodically killing NVA in their spider holes until felled by a grenade, the platoon sergeant who took on a trenchful of VC with his pistol, the pugnacious lieutenant who waited for the medevac with a cigar and beer after losing an arm, or the sergeant and medic who raced headlong into a fatal crossfire while attempting to rescue a wounded infantryman from a different unit. Such was the bond between American GIs in Việt Nam.

In old photographs, the battlefields appear beautiful: beaches as white as paper, vibrant green meadows and rice paddies, mountains on the horizon, and oasis-like islands rising from the farmland upon which villagers built thatch hootches under palm trees. The enemy transformed these islands into bunker complexes. When contact was made, the tanks and tracks would "bring smoke"—that is, line up and pour on the firepower—before advancing relentlessly into the trees, ignoring the tracers zipping past and the rounds ricocheting off gun shields and turrets. After the bunkers had been silenced, dismounted cavalrymen would root diehards from tunnels with grenades and plastic explosives, while helicopter gunships fell like birds of prey upon those battered enemy still alive and trying to escape. The officers and men of the 1-1 Cavalry were rewarded for the aggressive conduct of their operations with fistfuls of Bronze and Silver Stars, plus three Distinguished Service Crosses during the period covered here, and a Congressional Medal of Honor.

That is the war most veterans want preserved in print. Press a little deeper, however, ask uncomfortable questions about what search-and-destroy really meant at the ground level, and the picture begins to smudge around the edges. These men had been sent to fight a war in which the enemy, originally nicknamed Charlie—as in Victor Charlie, the VC—had since been dehumanized as Gooks, Dinks, Slopes, and Zips. The same epithets came to be applied to all things Vietnamese, whether friend, foe, or civilian. If some veterans speak openly about this reality, most acknowledge the dark side of their memories only reluctantly, for an outsider couldn't possibly understand the accumulation of frustrations that led otherwise normal young men to run people off the road for fun or use water buffalo for target practice. That was just the beginning: there were also the villagers who were beaten, the hamlets that were torched, the prisoners who never made it back to the rear. Most disturbingly, there were the troopers who came to enjoy killing; unmoored from the real world, convinced that they were dead men walking, they operated in a fugue state in which it seemed somehow right and normal to toss grenades into shelters occupied by women and children, or use a machete to hack the head from a slain Việt Cộng.

Explanations don't suffice. Realities shift. Consider these stories from different angles, and you can find justification in them for any view you prefer about the conduct of the United States Army in Việt Nam.

It's all here, and it all happened.

UNITED STATES ARMY AND UNITED STATES MARINE CORPS REGIMENTS, BRIGADES AND DIVISIONS

1st Cavalry

7th Cavalry　　8th Cavalry　　9th Cavalry　　11th Cavalry　　12th Cavalry　　17th Cavalry

1st Infantry　　21st Infantry　　31st Infantry　　35th Infantry　　52nd Infantry　　7th Marines

11th Armored Cavalry Regiment　　11th Light Infantry Brigade　　196th Light Infantry Brigade　　198th Light Infantry Brigade

1st Armored Division　　1st Cavalry Division　　4th Infantry Division　　23rd Infantry Division　　1st Marine Division

ARMY OF THE REPUBLIC OF VIỆT NAM REGIMENTS, DIVISION, SPECIAL AND MILITIA UNITS

4th Cavalry　　4th Infantry　　2nd Infantry Division　　Popular Forces　　Regional Forces　　Provincial Recon Units

Notes

Vietnam or Việt Nam?
Throughout this book the reader will see Vietnamese names and places with the Việt diacritical marks. This is to honor the people of Việt Nam, who were so afflicted by the many years of war in their countryside and cities.

In addition, in Vietnamese, every syllable is written as a separate word. Thus, Saigon or Hanoi for us but Sài Gòn or Hà Nội for them.

When Việt words are seen inside quotes of American soldiers, however, they are written in the American style.

1st Cavalry or 1st Cavalry?
It has been mildly annoying to many former dragoons of the 1st Cavalry Regiment to be confused with the infantrymen of the 1st Cavalry Division. This is especially vexing when encountering veterans who may have had a bad experience with that division during the war.

Accepted military shorthand is to imply the regiment but to state all other units: army, corps, division, brigade, or battalion. Thus the 1st Infantry and the 1st Infantry Division or the 3rd Marines and the 3rd Marine Division.

While the Marine Corps has its regiments intact, the Army long ago broke up its regiments of cavalry, infantry, and artillery into the constituent squadrons and battalions for tactical flexibility while keeping the regimental crests and history for historical continuity. The only exceptions during the Việt Nam era were the intact 2nd, 3rd, 6th, 11th, and 14th Armored Cavalry Regiments.

To the further confusion of the civilian reader, the Army assembled a new type of airmobile (helicopter-borne) division for the war in Việt

Nam and called it the 1st Cavalry Division. Its maneuver elements had the names of old cavalry regiments but were called battalions, not squadrons, and were composed entirely of infantrymen—or, in Department of the Army parlance, they were cavalry organized as infantry. Thus the 1st and 2nd Battalions of the 12th Cavalry were infantrymen in the 1st Cavalry Division although the 3rd and 4th Squadrons of the same 12th Cavalry were actual cavalry in the 3rd Armored Division and 5th Infantry Division respectively.

So, 1st Cavalry refers to the dragoons and tanks you will meet in this book, not the infantrymen and helicopters of the 1st Cavalry Division. (Although elements of that division do make an appearance.)

Gasoline or Diesel?

Early in the war, the lessons of World War II and Korea unlearned, the tanks and tracks were gasoline powered. This was done as a dollar-saving measure, since diesel engines are more expensive than those powered by gasoline. The human cost was, however, great. In a combat environment, the merest tickle of a rocket-propelled grenade could ignite the gasoline fuel to the disadvantage of the crew. Many unneccesary severe burns and deaths were suffered by our troops before a belated change to diesel was effected.

A-15 or Alpha One Five?

Tanks and tracks were identified by troop, platoon, and individual vehicle for clarity in radio communication. "A" is for A Troop, "1" is for the 1st Platoon, and "5" is for the fifth of ten vehicles in that platoon. Written, it is the former; spoken, it is the latter.

LZ Goat or FSB Young?

The reader will not find *LZ Goat* on any list of U.S. Army installations in Việt Nam. For some reason, its official name was unknown to both officers and men of the 1-1 Cav in 1968. It was only last year that they found out it was officially called *FSB Young* and was so named after the assistant commander of the 23rd Infantry Division.

Goat it was to the Cav in 1968, and Goat it shall be in this book.

Quảng Tín or Quảng Nam?

North and South, which disagreed about so much, also saw the names and boundaries of provinces differently. The reader will search in vain on contemporary maps for Quảng Tín Province, since it was erased after the war by the victorious North and absorbed into Quảng Nam Province.

Tam Kỳ, the provincial capital of Quảng Tín during the war, is today the capital of the enlarged Quảng Nam.

Cigar Island or Barrier Island?

The low, sandy barrier island at the eastern edge of the 1-1 Cavalry area of operations does not have a Vietnamese name. This is because it does not "read" as an island to them. Since it is so large and delineated on its west by only a narrow and shallow stream, it is considered simply a part of the mainland.

Mậu Hoà or Mâu Hoà?

The alert map reader might protest there are two sets of hamlets in Quảng Nam Province named Mau Hoa. To the Vietnamese it is obvious this is not so, since they are not spelled alike. That simple dot below the first "a" makes all the difference.

Likewise, the reader might discover two sets of hamlets named Thôn Hai in Quảng Nam. This would be true except that in 1968 those hamlets were in Quảng Nam and Quảng Tín Provinces. Much like our Camden, New Jersey, and Camden, Delaware.

Hill 29 or Hawk Hill?

There were different names for the home of the 1-1 Cavalry for different groups of soldiers. The line troops thought of it as Hill 29, while the officers and rear echelon troops called it Hawk Hill. A mild clash between the utilitarian and romantic view of war, perhaps.

Dragoons or Hussars?

Finally, a historic conundrum. Although the members of the 1st Squadron, 1st Cavalry bill themselves relentlessly as being a force of dragoons, they are not. In the pre-industrial era, dragoons were soldiers who rode to battle on horses but then dismounted and fought on foot. The name was derived from the French *dragon*, the type of short musket the French carried. In 1968 terms, the battalions of mechanized infantry would more properly be called dragoons. The troops of cavalry attached to the light infantry brigades in Việt Nam lacked tanks in their ranks, so one might call them light cavalry. The M48A3 tanks were, if anything, heavy, so the 1-1 Cavalry of 1968 could reasonably be called heavy cavalry or hussars.

Arguing against the hussar label are the facts that the constitution of various European hussars changed over time from light to heavy and back again and that the U.S. Army never used the term.

However, one could assert that the 1st U.S. Cavalry in this book does hark back most strikingly to the famous heavy Hussars of King John III's Polish-Lithuanian Commonwealth. Astride their massive horses, big armor-clad Slavic troopers bearing seven-foot lances with swords and pistols at their sides swooped down upon the Turks outside the walls of Vienna in 1683. John, one of the last kings to lead men personally into battle, was at the head of the largest cavalry charge in history as he saved Vienna and all of Europe from Ottoman oppression.

However, *dragoon* is a romantic term long in American usage, and its faintly ominous sound lends itself to the image cultivated by the hard-charging officers and men depicted in this work.

So, dragoons they shall continue to be.

PART ONE
1967

ARMORED CAVALRY PLATOON
Table of Organization and Equipment
1st Platoon A Troop 1-1 Cavalry
1967 – 1968

Platoon Sergeant   Tank Section

Platoon Leader   1st Scout Squad

Infantry Squad

2nd Scout Squad   Mortar Section
Scout Section

Armored Cavalry Platoon Personnel

Soldiers		MOS
12	Tank Section	11E
24	Scout Section	11D
5	Mortar Section	11C
11	Infantry Squad	11B
1	Platoon Leader	1204
1	Field Medic from HQ Troop	91A
1	Field Mechanic from HQ Platoon	63C
55	Total Soldiers	

Armored Cavalry Platoon Armaments

3	M48A3 medium tanks
6	M113A1 armored personnel carriers
1	M125A1 armored mortar carrier
10	M2 .50-cal machine guns
14	M60 7.62mm machine guns
3	M73 7.62mm machine guns
3	M41 90mm direct fire cannon
1	M29 81mm indirect fire mortar
10	M79 40mm grenade launchers

Three line platoons per troop; three line troops per squadron;
multiply this force nine times to arrive at the firepower of the
1-1 Cavalry of 1967 – 1968

Saddling Up

JANUARY–MAY 1967

LIEUTENANT COLONEL RICHARD H. Harrington, commanding officer of the 1-1 Cavalry at Fort Hood, Texas, was dispatched in January 1967 to participate in an on-the-scene study of armor tactics and weapons in Việt Nam. Harrington's departure was an obvious clue, and by the time he returned ninety days later, the word was official: the squadron was to be brought to full strength, then, after several months of intensive training, detached from the 1st Armored Division, and shipped as a separate unit to the Republic of Việt Nam.

Lieutenant Colonel Harrington so informed his troop commanders, of whom there were four—Headquarters, plus A, B, and C—cautioning them that their destination remained classified. Such precautions succeeded only in producing a classic bit of military comedy: holding closed meetings in their orderly rooms, the captains no sooner advised their lieutenants and sergeants that the squadron had been alerted for deployment to an undisclosed location than troopers began shouting from barracks windows: "We're goin' to Vietnam!"

The regiment through which the squadron traced its lineage had been to war many times in the past. Those presently assigned were well versed, in fact, on the storied history of their predecessors. That history had begun with the organization in 1832 of a battalion of mounted rangers to fight Chief Black Hawk during an Indian uprising in Illinois. In 1833, the commander and other officers from the disbanded rangers raised the U.S. Regiment of Dragoons, soon renamed the First Regiment of Dragoons, at Jefferson Barracks, Missouri. Nearly a century and a half later, members of the unit were still known as dragoons—soldiers able to fight on foot and horseback—and the ebony-colored hawk that adorned their regimental crest represented the rangers of the Black Hawk War.

The dragoons fought in Mexico, then, rechristened as cavalry, galloped through the Civil War with pistol and saber, campaigned against Apaches and other hostiles, landed in Cuba during the Spanish-American War, tracked guerrillas across Luzon during the Philippine Insurrection, and patrolled the Texas border against Pancho Villa. Horses retired, the outfit fought in North Africa and Italy during World War II as the 1st Tank Battalion, 1st Armored Division, then joined the occupation forces in Germany as the 1st Constabulary Squadron. In the course of five wars and innumerable expeditions, this complement of dragoons-turned-cavalrymen-turned-tankers, reactivated most recently as the famed 1st Cavalry Regiment, had earned sixty-seven campaign streamers and was heralded as the most battle-honored unit in the U.S. Army.

Both squadrons went to Việt Nam determined to fulfill expectations and write a new and glorious chapter in the history of the First Regiment of Dragoons.

While in garrison, Harrington's troop commanders had gotten by with a lieutenant or two and perhaps a platoon's worth of enlisted men, who lived in two-story cinderblock barracks on a bleak and arid post that was half empty because of the war. The squadron's mission at the time had been to maintain its equipment and conduct enough training to put the requisite fifty miles a month on its M60 tanks and M114 scout vehicles, a pint-sized seven-ton toy used primarily by cavalry units patrolling the border between East and West Germany.

To get the squadron ready for war, the army replaced the M114 with the eleven-ton M113A1 armored personnel carrier (APC), which was shaped like a shoebox except for its sloped front. The personnel carriers—nicknamed "tracks" after the treads, or tracks, that propelled them—were made of aircraft-quality aluminum, which was not as strong as steel but was lighter, a distinct advantage in a war being fought in muddy rice paddies.

To be a young soldier looking down on the world from atop a track was an inherently powerful experience: the command cupola was mounted with a hard-hitting .50-caliber machine gun (Ma Duce), and there rumbled under the engine panel a 212-horsepower V-8 Detroit Diesel.

In the cavalry, a track was not used to carry an infantry squad to battle, as originally designed, but to literally charge the enemy. As such, the APCs were refashioned as ACAVs—armored cavalry assault vehicles—with a circular gun tub, made of steel, around the command cupola; a flat steel panel was welded to the front of the tub, the barrel of the .50 extending through a slot. Finally, two M60 light machine guns were mounted behind the command cupola, one to either side of the vehicle. The two gunners stood waist-deep, and back-to-back, in the square-shaped cargo hatch, protected by their own gun shields.

In addition to a headquarters element, each troop fielded three platoons, six ACAVs per platoon, plus a mortar track. Each platoon also acquired three M48A3 tanks, fifty-two-ton monsters with a 90mm main gun and a 750-horsepower V-12 Continental diesel engine. The M60 tanks were replaced because they were so new that a canister round had not yet been developed for their larger main gun, and canister—each round of which was packed with a thousand cylindrical steel pellets—was among the most effective munitions in Việt Nam.

Each vehicle was identified by its fender number; using the 1st Platoon of A Troop as an example, the following system was used in the 1-1 Cavalry:

A-10: scout track
A-11: scout track
A-12: scout track
A-13: scout track
A-14: tank
A-15: platoon sergeant's tank
A-16: platoon leader's track
A-17: infantry track
A-18: mortar track
A-19: tank

Five subordinate leaders reported to the platoon leader: a tank-section leader and two scout-section leaders; the mortar squad leader; and the infantry squad leader, whose troops presently turned in their obsolete M14 rifles for M16s.

Each tank had a four-man crew—commander, driver, gunner, loader—and each scout track had a commander, driver, two gunners, and a grenadier who sat on the back deck, facing backward with an M79 grenade launcher, lest a threat appear from behind. The tankers, as well as the track drivers and commanders, were issued the combat-vehicle-crewman (CVC) helmet, better known as a communications, or commo, helmet because of the built-in earphones and microphone that snapped down in front of the mouth.

So many warm bodies poured in that Captains J. Christopher Conrad, David H. Staley, and Ralph P. Brown, commanders, respectively, of A, B, and C Troops, soon had four lieutenants each, a full complement of non-commissioned officers (NCOs), and enough troopers to form seventy-five-man platoons. They would actually be going to war with about fifty men per platoon. The platoons had been beefed up so that "we could get rid of the duds and deadwood before we deployed, and still be at full strength," notes James A. Dickens, then a platoon leader in Bravo Troop. Most of the troops were fresh from basic training and underwent their advanced individual training with the 1-1 Cav as infantrymen, mortar men, armored reconnaissance scouts, or tank crewmen. They studied vehicle maintenance, conducted gunnery practice, and participated in field exercises, by which time many had fallen in love with their fearsome war machines the way a teenage boy would his hot rod. The expansive training grounds at Fort Hood were part mesa, part forest, and were inhabited by scorpions, rattlesnakes, deer, and armadillos. There, the troops learned to rough it in the field, conduct mounted and dismounted operations, and "herringbone" whenever a column halted, meaning that vehicles alternately pivoted forty-five degrees left or right so as to place all weapons outward in case of attack. At sunset, they established night laagers with the tanks and tracks facing outward in a wagon-train circle, command vehicles in the center. When helicopters reported an imaginary enemy in this wooded area or that, mock assaults were launched "into the wool," a phrase to be carried over and applied to the jungles of Việt Nam. "We were very cohesive because of the training," notes Dickens. "We had drilled and drilled and drilled, so that when we finally went into combat,

I would start to give an order and the guys would already be doing what I was going to tell them to do."

In addition to quality troops, there was also an ample supply of good leaders, to include Captains Conrad, Staley, and Brown. The lieutenants were a mixed bag. There were a handful of West Pointers, including gung-ho, ranger-trained Lieutenant Dickens, Class of '66, who'd been serving in a tank battalion at Fort Hood when he heard talk about the dragoons going to Việt Nam and requested immediate reassignment to the 1-1 Cav. Several of the lieutenants were university graduates commissioned through the Reserve Officer Training Corps (ROTC). The rest were either ambitious ex-sergeants or ex-privates who, because they had some college, scored well on the military aptitude tests, or otherwise exhibited leadership potential, and qualified for Officer Candidate School (OCS).

Some of the lieutenants were naturals, some unfit. Most were green but motivated, and all had a safety net, for the squadron was infused from top to bottom with Regular Army NCOs. These included old-time first sergeants who started the day with a beer and cigar, plus the sergeants, staff sergeants, platoon sergeants, and sergeants first class who filled the tank-commander and section-leader slots in the line platoons. The squadron was so rich in sergeants because the army had cleaned out the armor school at Fort Knox, Kentucky. Having settled in with wife and kids after doing their part in World War II or Korea, some of the Fort Knox NCOs took early retirement rather than accept duty with the combat-bound 1-1 Cav. Those who remained were the "cream of the crop," notes Staley. "These were guys who had been instructors in the tactics, weapons, and maintenance departments, so I can't begin to tell you what a professional group of NCOs we took with us to Vietnam."

Reflecting a growing trend, a good percentage of the noncoms were black. As a group, they were self-assured professionals who easily won the confidence of their mostly white troopers, no small feat given the prejudices of the day. Platoon Sergeant Herman R. Jessie of A Troop, a native Texan and perhaps the best of the noncoms of any race, was poised and sophisticated, demanding without being overbearing, and coached his lieutenant in a manner that did not make the man feel that his authority was being challenged. To no one's surprise, Jessie would prove fearless when the squadron got to Việt Nam.

The acknowledged leader among all the noncoms was Platoon Sgt. Charles Nathan Boyd, who had originally joined the army at seventeen after dropping out of school to get in on the fight in Korea. The big farm boy from Ohio ended up carrying a BAR—Browning automatic rifle—with Easy Company of the 21st Infantry, 24th Infantry Division. Sick of hunkering in trenches under Chinese mortar fire, young Nate Boyd volunteered for the regimental reconnaissance platoon, and, being a crack shot, went out on one-man sniper patrols. The platoon also conducted recon patrols, ambush patrols, and behind-the-lines strike patrols. One memorable mission involved a pair of 100mm howitzers that fired from a railroad tunnel immune to air strikes. The recon men killed the guards at the tunnel entrance, rigged the interior with plastic explosives, ignited a ten-minute fuse, and took off for friendly lines. The blast ignited the howitzer ammunition, collapsing the tunnel and bowling over the recon men, who had made scant progress as they tried to run through snow up to their knees.

Platoon Sergeant Boyd, serving exclusively in the armored cav after Korea and marrying a German girl along the way, had been assigned to the 1st Platoon of A Troop, 1-1 Cavalry, in December 1965. As the squadron prepared for war, Boyd suddenly had fifty new men, including two tough guys with no time for lifers. Boyd picked out the bigger of the two when they acted up in formation, marched him behind the barracks, then doffed his shirt in preparation for a fistfight. The private scoffed: "Sarge, ain't you a little old for this?"

"Naw, I don't think so," growled Boyd, who looked older than his thirty-five years. "But I think you're a little young to be pullin' this shit of yours."

The kid swung at Boyd, who ducked, grabbed his opponent's arm, twisted it behind his back, and, using his other hand to grip the tough guy by the hair, asked him which building he wanted to be hurled through. The kid went limp, then wordlessly returned to his place in the platoon formation. "That got all our discipline problems squared away," notes Boyd, allowing him to get down to business. "I told these kids, you're going in a combat zone, and if you're smart enough to listen to me, most of you are going to come back alive."

Boyd advised his troops that he'd been to war and knew they were going to be scared when their time came, and that they needed to train hard "because when the shit starts flying, your training needs to be so drummed into you that it takes over and you don't even have to think about what to do—you just do it." The infantry might operate at two and a half miles an hour, said Boyd, but a cavalryman had to be able to think at thirty miles an hour. "You're moving," he explains, "and you've got to be able to read maps, you've got to know radios, you've got to know your weapons, you've got to be able to evaluate terrain. It's something you can learn. I said we're a team. Just like a football team or basketball team, you're only as good as the weakest link. They got the message, they really did. They turned into damned good soldiers."

Thomas M. Bursott recalls, "Sergeant Boyd instilled a real esprit de corps in our platoon. We worked hard and played hard. If we did good out in the field, we partied when we got back. We had a lieutenant, but I can't remember his name. It was Sergeant Boyd's platoon. We were Boyd's Bastards."

Captain Conrad of A Troop and Captain Brown of C Troop, career men both, were well regarded for their low-key professionalism. Brown was a West Pointer, while Chris Conrad, possessed of a particularly sharp intellect, had graduated from the ROTC program at the University of California at Berkeley.

Captain Staley of B Troop, also a career man, came from a broken, working-class home and had been raised by his grandmother in Oceanside, California. He had no college degree but was instead a twenty-seven-year-old ex-cop and ex-sergeant commissioned through National Guard OCS. He was also an expert in martial arts and hand-to-hand combat, as demonstrated while a platoon leader with the 10th Cav at Camp Kaiser, Korea. While making a late-night check of an enlisted men's club, Staley was "jumped by some goon from an infantry unit," recalls his former troop commander. "Before the guy knew what happened, Dave had broken both his arms and dislocated a shoulder. The goon was a pretty pathetic sight at his court-martial. Dave just sat there and smiled at him."

The funny thing was that Dave Staley stood but five-foot-five and, prematurely balding, was generally wimpy in appearance. "He was the meanest guy on two feet that I've ever met in my life," jokes James S.

Lindsey, former platoon leader in B Troop, "but he looked like a druggist from Poughkeepsie." Lindsey was himself a cool and loquacious Southern boy with a degree in marketing and advertising from the University of Kentucky. Drafted after getting married and landing a good job, the only silver lining was that fate had put Lindsey in the care of a pro like Capt. David H. Staley: "The day I reported in, he was lying under a track with a maintenance officer, pulling out an oil line. He was a hands-on officer, and a phenomenal troop commander."

Despite such kudos, Captain Staley was the black sheep of the 1-1 Cav. The problem was partly a matter of Staley's National Guard background in a unit full of West Pointers. More than that, Staley was his own man. He was not part of the team. Based on conversations with NCOs who had already pulled tours in Việt Nam, he was contemptuous of all the confident talk in the officer corps about trouncing those little raggedy-ass VC. He was also genetically incapable of kowtowing to curry favor with his superiors. "Staley just would not play the game," says Lindsey. "He was a real hard-ass. He was a grungy, down-and-dirty, get-it-fixed, get-it-right, work-all-night, do-it-over-and-over-and-over-and-over-until-it's-perfect kind of officer. The only thing he gave a damn about was getting his unit ready for combat. We trained six and a half days a week because we were gonna keep those troopers alive in Vietnam."

The rest of the squadron was not impressed, contending that B Troop worked hard but not smart. Charles W. Donaldson, then the executive officer of A Troop, recalls that when the squadron received new track for its tanks, Captain Staley "announced that they were going to work all weekend to get them on. They did." Meanwhile, Captain Conrad advised his troopers "that they were going to work on the project until it was done and done right. We finished late Saturday evening and took Sunday off. The officers bought a few cases of beer for the troops to celebrate the end of the task."

There were no beer parties under Captain Staley. While soldiers in A and C Troops received weekend passes, those of B Troop were kept busy cleaning and maintaining weapons and vehicles when not actually in the field. "I was tough on 'em," says Staley. "They hated my guts." Indeed, semi-serious grumbling could eventually be heard about putting a bounty on

Staley's head to be collected by whoever took advantage of the confusion of a firefight to shoot the captain after they got to Việt Nam. During a final pre-deployment meeting, Staley dryly noted that he knew about the bounty. "Now I got 'em where I want 'em," he announced. "They hate me so much that when we get to Vietnam, they're gonna kill Charlie just to get their frustrations out."

Harrington originally met Capt. John L. Barovetto, a Berkeley graduate and key figure in training the squadron, during his fact-finding mission to Việt Nam. Barovetto was still a lieutenant then, but one so charismatic and highly recommended that Harrington asked him to join the dragoons. His expertise would be invaluable: not only had Barovetto been through the deployment drill before with the 3-4 Cav of the 25th Division, but his unit operated in the same area near Sài Gòn to which the 1-1 Cav was to be sent. Barovetto accepted the transfer offer on the condition that Harrington give him the first troop command that opened up in the squadron. Assigned as the squadron intelligence officer, Barovetto impressed the rest of the dragoons as much as he had Harrington. The man was rugged and gregarious, an expert on the opposite sex, and an officer whose enthusiasm brought out the best in soldiers. He was also a walking primer on armored operations in Việt Nam. In an army where turf was jealously guarded, Staley paid Barovetto the ultimate compliment: "If he decided something was so screwed up that he had to stop my guys and tell 'em what they were doing wrong, I had given him that authority."

While an enlisted man, Dick Harrington had served as a waist-gunner on a B-17 bomber in the U.S. Army Air Forces of World War II. After the war, Harrington completed his education and received a reserve commission. Soon thereafter, his older brother, Tracy B. Harrington, a West Pointer and commander of a cavalry squadron in the war, secured for him an active-duty assignment in the armor branch. Tracy Harrington kept tabs on his brother's career and, while a colonel at the Pentagon, pulled the strings necessary to bestow upon him command of the 1-1 Cavalry. Tracy Harrington continued to pull strings when the dragoons were alerted for deployment, reviewing the records of armor officers, for example, and ensuring that only the most highly rated were sent to fill out the squadron. He also arranged for many of the newly assigned officers to attend the excellent Jungle Operations Course in Panamá.

Dick Harrington had proven himself in combat in his youth and had since matured into a devoted family man and courteous old soldier. The squadron officers generally liked their agreeable old colonel. Taking note of his worrywart ways, they had nicknamed him Grandma Harrington, more in affectionate jest than derision. They did not, however, "find very much to fear or respect about him," to quote Chuck Donaldson. "He was out of touch, out of mind, and out of the loop." Simply put, the squadron commander had no dash, no drive, and no particular expertise in ground combat. "He was one of those guys who hung on a long time and finally got a command," reflects Donaldson, adding that nobody expected much from garrison commanders in those days: "They were just supposed to go in their office and smoke their pipe."

Harrington leaned on his executive officer, Maj. Donald Lundquist, and his operations officer, Maj. Crosbie E. "Butch" Saint, an academy graduate young for his rank at thirty and handpicked for the 1-1 Cavalry. "Harrington was not suited for the job he had," says Saint. "I'll tell you one thing, though, he could have been a hell of a lot worse. He was a good guy—fair, high principles, good values—and he worked hard, he wanted to do well, but he just did not have the troop experience he needed. He was not up on war fighting."

In contrast, Majors Lundquist and Saint had spent the majority of their service with operational units, and Conrad notes that if Harrington managed not to "make any major blunders, it was because Lundquist and Saint wouldn't let him. They were essentially in charge of the squadron." Fortunately, the two co-rulers clicked well. "They were a Hollywood version of an executive officer and an operations officer," muses Conrad. "Lundquist was bluster and bullshit. Saint was cerebral and smooth. Both were extremely ambitious."

Saint was second-generation West Point, the son of a lieutenant colonel who perished in Japanese hands after the fall of the Philippines. The younger Saint was Class of '58, and he had his eyes on general's stars from the time he was a platoon leader in his first armored cavalry squadron. His ambition burned so brightly as to be off-putting at times. "Butch Saint took care of Butch Saint," confides a peer who was otherwise a friend and admirer. Saint was friendly, if not particularly outgoing, possessed of a wry wit, and obviously highly talented. "When you've got a Butch Saint, if you're smart, you'll just stay out of his way," says George E. Norton III, then a West Point lieutenant on the squadron staff. Saint had high standards, and his ass-chewings were memorable, but after rebuking a junior officer who screwed up, the major would generously remark, "No hard feelings—let's move on and do it right."

Donald Lundquist, born and raised in Germany and fourteen years old when the war ended, had joined the U.S. Army when he came of age, fought in Korea, made master sergeant, and subsequently attended OCS. Handsome and smugly confident at age thirty-six, Lundquist was "an old-time soldier," says Saint, meaning the major "drank hard, played hard, worked hard." Saint was much impressed with Lundquist's ceaseless efforts to prepare the squadron for Việt Nam. "Lundquist was determined that we would leave no stone unturned in making sure we were ready," notes Saint. "Nothing got in his way when we needed something. He could be brutal—but he got the job done."

Major Lundquist enjoyed nights of poker and two-fisted drinking, often in the company of hard-charging Lieutenant Dickens and 1st Lt. James A. Taylor, the ex-sergeant assigned as B Troop's executive officer. Saint thought Lundquist blunt and effective. Dickens and Taylor thought him the ideal officer, someone who knew the army and soldiering inside and out, and possessed a heart of gold under his tough-as-nails exterior. The rest of the squadron despised the man. "Lundquist was just a phony bullshit artist trying to further his career," according to Clifton L. Dunn, then a chief warrant officer at squadron headquarters. "Lundquist was an arrogant, sadistic asshole," states Chuck Donaldson. "He ruthlessly bullied and abused soldiers and junior officers. Worse, he provided no help to the troop executive officers who should have been able to look to the squadron executive officer for assistance."

Like his peers, Major Lundquist hoped to use the war as a career springboard. Like some, he said as much. He also said things that raised questions about how far he was willing to go to build the kind of combat record that would garner him silver oak leaves and a battalion of his own, and from there, he would muse, the eagles he wanted before he retired. "Lundquist told me he had lost out in Korea because [his superiors] neglected their troops and didn't give them any medals," says Staley, "but that he expected to come back from Vietnam with a bunch of 'em." The implication was that Lundquist didn't care how he got the medals, as long as he got them, and as squadron executive officer, he could indeed make sure he got a chestful. "I never knew when Lundquist was telling me the truth," writes Conrad, summing up the problem. "I don't think he did, either."

For the record, Capt. Walter R. Reed, the squadron maintenance officer, formed a favorable impression of Major Lundquist after an incident involving the vehicle lockers—one per crew, and made of ammunition crates—stored in the troop maintenance sheds. Lundquist instructed Reed to have the lockers opened after lunch one day so that he could inspect the contents and decide which items they should take overseas and what could be left behind. Reed passed the word, only to find half the lockers still padlocked at the appointed time. Lundquist asked Reed why he had not complied with his instructions. Reed explained that the sergeant with the key to this locker could not be located, while the sergeant with the key to that locker had taken his wife to the doctor, and so on. Lundquist stalked off without a word, then reappeared with a sledgehammer that he used to bust open every padlocked footlocker. Lundquist told Reed to have all the lockers torn apart and thrown away by the end of the day: "We are getting ready to go to war. We will not be taking a lot of excess crap with us. If it can't be stored on the tracks, we don't need it!"

The lockers were reduced to scrap wood, as ordered. "It was the right thing to do," writes Reed, "and Major Lundquist did it with flair."

One final, fun note about squadron headquarters: to instill the spirit of the old horse cavalry, officers and noncoms at headquarters turned in their .45 semi-automatics for .38-caliber revolvers, issued with a black holster and leather belt studded with extra cartridges. "Some of the officers drove around the outlying areas of Hood," recalls Karl Steinmetz, then the squadron logistics officer, "taking pot shots at road signs and anything else to get the feel of the new pistol."

Hurry Up and Wait

JUNE–AUGUST 1967

THE TRAINING CYCLE COMPLETE, Lieutenant Colonel Harrington and the hundred tanks and tracks of the 1st Squadron, 1st Cavalry, passed in review for the commanding general of the 1st Armored Division. The reviewing stands were filled with wives who already lived off-post and family members who'd made the trip to Fort Hood. The pass-in-review was followed by a squadron picnic with bratwurst and kegs of beer. Mothers took snapshots of short-haired sons in starched fatigues who seemed newly confident and mature, and fathers pumped the hands of the officers and noncoms who had made men of their boys, perhaps sharing an anecdote about their days in World War II. "Dumbass me, I didn't know any better than to meet the wives and parents of my guys," says Nate Boyd. "I should've never done that. It's okay to know your men, but I don't think you ought to know their families. I found that out after we went over. You get a guy killed, you got to write a letter, and that's hard under any circumstances—but it just tears you up even worse when you can see the faces of his family in your mind."

Not everyone who'd begun the training cycle remained at the end. "We hand-picked the guys we wanted to take," notes Staley. To get the units down to size, troop commanders were forced to transfer completely competent soldiers. "It got rough at the end," says Staley. "I had people come into the orderly room, almost in tears, saying, 'Why did you cut me—I want to go with the squadron!'"

§

The troops took their pre-embarkation leaves in staggered groups through June and July. In the meantime, they also attended to the multitudinous tasks involved in relocating a thousand-man unit to a combat zone on the other side of the world. Orientation lectures had to be endured, personnel records organized, inoculations for tropical diseases administered assembly-line style. Items of issue not needed in the jungle had to be stored away, the rest packed for travel. "[T]hing[s] have been real fouled up," wrote Tom Bursott. "[L]ike we will pack something one way and then they will turn around and tell us do it another [way] and by the end of the day it is the same way we had it the first time."

Flak jackets were issued, and standard footgear and utilities traded for jungle boots and jungle fatigues with big cargo pockets on the trouser legs. "Got my new clothes and not a bad fit," Spc. 4th Class John Max Pryor of C Troop wrote his wife. "[S]ure was lucky[,] you should see some of these guys."

"Well the army is really teaching me to be a happy housewife for somebody," wrote Private Bursott. "I have been sewing on patches and name tags on my jungle fatigue[s]. Also went and dyed all of my white under clothes green."

In case the infantry to whom the dragoons would be attached could not provide adequate logistical support, "we robbed Fort Hood blind," recalls then-Lieutenant Norton. In addition, Chief Dunn made several trips to Bergstrom Air Force Base in Austin, "and returned with truck loads of furniture, beds, mattresses, refrigerators, etc.," notes Steinmetz. "I remember our warehouse got so full we were walking on top of the items because we could not see the floor." Captain Steinmetz's crew packed everything into a hundred steel conexes, each the size of an office cubicle. The containers were lined up in the squadron motor pool. Harrington told Steinmetz that they had to be marked in some way, noting that he had seen too many lost shipping containers during his trip to Việt Nam. As such, Steinmetz's guys used a stencil to paint the Black Hawk insignia on the top of all the conexes, where someone in a helicopter looking for lost or stolen squadron property could see it. The conexes were shipped by train to Galveston, Texas, then loaded aboard a freighter bound for Việt Nam.

The squadron's tanks and tracks followed the conexes to Galveston after being driven aboard flat cars at the direction of impatient, foul-tempered railroad men who gave the impression of being retired drill sergeants. It took the unfortunate working party some forty hours to get every last vehicle perfectly positioned and lashed down before the train finally pulled out of the depot on July 18. Equipment and vehicles packed and gone, there followed for the dragoons three idle weeks of waiting for the word to mount up. "We ain't doing a damn thing," Max Pryor wrote his wife, "except cooling it and laying around."

The troops occupied the dull hours writing letters or going to the movies: *The Dirty Dozen* with Lee Marvin and Jim Brown was popular. They also got into trouble. These young soldiers had had all the training they could stand and were primed, ready to get the show on the road. The men of B Troop were wound the tightest, and as they began acting out—ignoring orders, disappearing into town when they should have been on duty—the roll call at morning formation became something of a running joke: "Headquarters Troop, all present or accounted for . . . A Troop, all present or accounted for . . . B Troop, twenty-three absent without leave . . . C Troop, all present or accounted for . . ."

Captain Staley kept his men busy with make-work. The resulting bitching reached such a volume that Staley remarked to a trooper: "If I walked into that barracks right now, I'd probably get punched in the nose, wouldn't I?"

"Yes, sir, you probably would."

"That's fine—I don't want a bunch of nice guys where we're going."

Two members of Staff Sgt. Kenneth L. Bouche's infantry squad reached the point of mutiny. Lieutenant Taylor wanted to court-martial the pair; Bouche changed the exec's mind, arguing that his troublemakers "will be completely different when we get over there and get in the shit—and besides, what worse penalty could you give a guy but to take him to Nam?"

Tom Bursott was crossing a small field to return to his barracks, after a phone call to his parents, when he "noticed that everybody was coming out of the [nearby] beer hall, at first I thought they were closing it down, then the stuff hit me[,] it was tear gas." Someone had chucked a CS tear gas grenade into the beer hall. "[B]oy that stuff burned[,] even what little I got in that field," wrote Bursott. "I [went] on up to the barracks after getting something to eat. Some [of] the guys came back a little later and said that they [the M.P.s] had close[d] every beer hall on Hood because all had to[o] much no[i]se and going's [*sic*] on."

§

On August 8, the squadron held one last pass in review "for some dam[n] Genral [*sic*]," as Max Pryor put it in a letter. "Hot[t]er than Hell out side to[o]. Had to stand for about [an] hour. I[t] sucked." But, afterward, the word was passed that the squadron would finally depart Fort Hood the next morning, bound for Việt Nam. Wrote Pryor: "[W]e're off to Charlie Vill[e] country."

Bound for Foreign Shores

AUGUST 9–27, 1967

AN ADVANCE PARTY LED by Lieutenant Colonel Harrington and Major Saint, and including Captains Conrad, Staley, and Brown, was to precede the squadron overseas, present itself to the infantry unit to which the dragoons were being attached, and after organizing a staging area, welcome the 1-1 Cav to Việt Nam.

Because the advance party was to fly while the squadron went by ship, the troops actually left first with Major Lundquist and the troop executive officers in acting command. Dressed for battle but carrying unloaded weapons, the dragoons flew from Fort Hood to San Francisco on August 9 aboard 727 Boeings from Frontier Air Lines. They were then bused to the naval docks in nearby Oakland. The weather was chilly and the sky hazy as the boarding of the troopship began by way of a narrow gangway descending from a hatchway in the hull. The name of the vessel into which disappeared this single-file, duffel-bag-over-the-shoulder procession of GIs from the 1-1 Cavalry, the 2-1 Cavalry, and various support units: the USNS *General Nelson M. Walker*.

Officers and NCOs were quartered six to a cabin on the main deck. The enlisted men were packed sardine-style on the three lower decks where steel-framed, white-canvas hammocks were stacked three or four high in the troop compartments, and wherever else they fit amid the gleaming-white piping, wiring, and interior architecture of an ocean-going vessel.

There was, noted the dragoons, an antique feel to their new lodgings. The *General Walker* was, in fact, an old World War II troopship formerly named the USS *Admiral H. T. Mayo*, retired after Korea only to be brought out of mothballs for Việt Nam. The ship's officers were U.S. Navy, the grease-stained crew merchant seamen employed by the Maritime Sea Transportation Service.

The weather was still chilly and overcast when the *General Walker* set sail on August 10. The troopship sailed under the Bay Bridge, past San Francisco and Alcatraz Island, and then under the Golden Gate Bridge, beyond which beckoned the blue expanse of the Pacific Ocean. The troopers crowding the railing realized as they cheered, and waved at every vessel they passed, that they were recreating a scene from old war movies and could not help but feel a proud link with the GIs of World War II and Korea who had also passed under the Golden Gate Bridge.

The ship sailed through several dreary mornings of rain as many troopers, not yet accustomed to the rolling pitch of the ship, succumbed to seasickness. The merchant seamen, meanwhile, explained the layout and routines of the ship, conducted abandon-ship drills for the troops, each of whom was issued a life jacket, and then generally ignored the GIs swarming all over their ship as they went about their duties. When the weather cleared, the dragoons marveled at a world split between sea and sky, and excitedly took note of flying fish and shark fins, distant whales, and the families of dolphins that sometimes swam alongside the hull. The sunsets were gorgeous and the nights awe-inspiring, the sky a jet-black pallet sprinkled with diamond dust. Private First Class Lawrence W. Graham of A Troop wrote to his wife: "This is truly God's creation."

The view eventually ceased to dazzle. Ultimately, the voyage was tedious, physically uncomfortable, and accompanied always by an uneasy buzz in the pit of a soldier's stomach about what was waiting for them in Việt Nam. The hammocks produced aching backs, and the anti-malarial pills the troops were now required to take gave everyone the runs. There being a small town's worth of humanity crammed aboard the troopship, meals, using the head, buying cigarettes at the ship's store, and every other activity involved long lines. A two-hour shuffle through the galley "wasn't worth it," wrote Graham. "[The meal] was by far the most horrible food I have ever eaten." The lines at the head were almost as bad, and "whooo on your young ass if you half [sic] to take a shit between 8:30 AM and 11 AM," wrote Max Pryor, noting that the facilities were off limits at that time while being cleaned. "Just hold it until you turn red."

The ship ran low on fresh water. By the time the *General Walker* crossed the International Date Line, water rationing had begun. The troops dripped sweat in the wilting equatorial heat. There was no relief below decks, even at night, noted Graham: "I can't seem to sleep worth a shit! No body can. It's like a damn oven in our compartment."

The troops shaved in salt water and took salt-water showers. They tried to wash their fatigues, which would be tied to the railing to dry, but a bar of soap won't lather in a basin of cold salt water. "Things are getting pretty crummy in our compartment," Graham wrote. "[E]veryone is out of clean clothes . . . and the ventilation is bad. [The compartment] smell[s] like a gymnasium."

To keep occupied, the troops exercised on the main deck, posed for photographs against the railing, or played checkers, bingo, rummy, and hearts in the rec rooms. Major Lundquist retired to his cabin with several lieutenants for a two-week poker marathon. The merchant seamen, meanwhile, ran blackjack-for-a-dollar games, liberating some soldier boys of as much as twenty greenbacks, big bucks on a private's pay. Few had thought to bring books to pass the time, and a coveted copy of *Valley of the Dolls* was passed from GI to GI. Movies like *McClintock*, *The Slender Thread*, and *The Second Best Secret Agent in the World* were shown on the fantail. The crowds were standing room only.

Such diversions were not enough. Eventually, guys stopped smiling and joking. They took Darvon painkillers for their sore backs and tried to sleep as much as they could to blot out time. Napping during the day only resulted in insomnia at night, further aggravating the situation. Graham described the growing sense of ennui to his wife: "I miss you so much darling, this is almost unbearable. It seems as though we are the only ones in the world out here. There are no newspapers, radio, or anything to keep in touch with the outside world . . .The days here seem to last forever, at times I think we are standing still and the water is just going by us."

Homesickness aside, Larry Graham was proud to be wearing the uniform and heading into battle. The son of a lawyer and a housewife, he had grown up in Broomfield, New Jersey. He had been married two years and had a good job in sales and marketing when drafted at the age of twenty-four. He accepted his draft notice without complaint. "I was a real hawk about the Vietnam War," he recalls. "This was to be my war. Didn't each generation get theirs? It was my turn to step up to the plate like the older generation had during World War II."

Tom Bursott felt the same way as Graham, a fellow member of Boyd's Bastards. Bursott's mother had been an army nurse and his father a lieutenant in the quartermaster corps when they met during World War II. They had since made a solid, middle-class life for themselves in Olney, Illinois, where the father sold oil-drilling equipment. Bursott's parents "had instilled in me the belief that there was a price for living in America," notes Bursott. "If your country calls, you went." Having flunked out of junior college and not sure what to do next, this young fan of war comics and war movies wasn't particularly unhappy when the selective service put him in uniform. Nineteen when drafted, going on twenty-one when he boarded the *General Walker*, Bursott felt that "I was all grown up and a man, however naïve that sounds now. I had been out drinking and smoking and all that, and I thought going off to war was another manly thing to do. As far as Vietnam, well, that's where the war was."

Whatever the generally hawkish attitude of these soldiers, they were all individuals, each a character to himself inside his uniform. Sergeant Richard P. Rensi was from Hopedale, Ohio. Married five years and working as a truck mechanic, all his workaday worries about paying the mortgage and such evaporated the day he found an induction notice in his mailbox. Private First Class Wayne L. Byrd, also of A Troop, had grown up on a chicken farm in Asheboro, North Carolina. "My daddy worked in the mill, and my mother managed the farm," notes Byrd, who was drafted after flunking out of North Carolina State. "I went from the smallest high school in the state to the largest college. I wasn't ready for it," recalls Byrd, who, determined to return to college after the service, spent his spare time memorizing his Bible and the manual for the M48A3. "I figured my life depended upon both of them. I learned how to study in Vietnam."

Private First Class Arvin W. Schoep hailed from a family of fourteen children living a hardscrabble, make-every-penny-count life on a

Minnesota farm. His parents belonged to a strict Protestant sect that forbid smoking and drinking. Neither did they read newspapers or own a television. Schoep was drafted a year after receiving a diploma that didn't really mean much considering all the days he'd spent helping on the farm instead of sitting in class. Away from home for the first time, Schoep drank his first and only beer at Fort Hood and immediately puked. Quiet and unworldly, Schoep was also a good soldier who calmly took things as they came when the unit went into combat. Schoep's still waters ran deep: because of what he was to see in the war, the unassuming farm boy would dramatically change the course of his life after Việt Nam.

Specialist Fourth Class Dick L. Taskey was a small, pugnacious-looking guy, his reddish hair receding at age twenty-five, and like Bursott, Graham, and Schoep, another of Boyd's Bastards. Loyal friend and gutsy soldier, Taskey was also an alcoholic: from his teenage years until drafted, he had sipped apple-jack to keep warm while working as a lumberjack with his father's small logging company in northern Michigan. Bursott had caught Taskey, out of money for beer, straining Sterno through a loaf of bread in their squad bay at Fort Hood. Bursott gave his buddy his last two dollars and sent him to the beer hall. There was no beer hall on the *General Walker*, and a desperate Taskey spent the latter part of the trip in the ship dispensary, having indeed downed some Sterno. Once in-country, Taskey obtained sugar and raisins from the mess section, and fermented raisin wine, lest the beer ration not arrive. The guys enjoyed hoisting a cup after a patrol—it packed a wallop—but the wicked combination of booze and killing was to drive Taskey a bit mad in Việt Nam.

Specialist Fourth Class Max Pryor was from Tuscumbia, Missouri. He was twenty and his high-school sweetheart seventeen when they wed, and he bumped along for several years thereafter, working odd jobs, taking college classes, and raising hell in smoke-filled roadhouses. His brother had served as a Navy Seabee in Việt Nam, and he knew his turn was coming, too. Being married no longer rated a deferment as the war heated up. "If you didn't have any kids, you were screwed," notes Pryor. Preparing for the inevitable, he moved his wife—a cute brunette who would keep his morale up with indelicate Polaroids while he was overseas—into a trailer on his parents' property in Tuscumbia. Pryor detested the press, the protesters, and the burn-baby-burn types, and thought the government should keep a lid on things with tear gas and live ammo. On the other hand, he had sized up Việt Nam as a no-win political war and was suspicious of anything that came out of the mouth of a snake-oil salesman like LBJ. Still, Pryor, a track commander, was to perform so well under fire as to earn three stripes and then the rocker of a staff sergeant. He liked the weapons and things mechanical that one got to play with in the army. To quote from one of his early letters from Việt Nam: "Today the Lt [lieutenant] got all the scout T.C.'s [track commanders] together and now each track has a [S]tar Light Scope on it. [This night-vision device] is one of the most amazing things I've ever seen . . . I just took it out and looked through it and you wouldn't believe how far you can see and everything is so clear. It has a 7 power scope on it so you can imagine how good it would be for deer hunting at night."

Private First Class David L. Eady, an amiable, laid-back track gunner in A Troop, had been working at General Electric, where his father was also employed, when drafted at age nineteen. "I thought, what a bummer, because I just got a good job and bought a car," he recalls. "Once I got into it, though, I kind of enjoyed the army. I thought it was a neat experience." Part of the fun was "hooking up with all these guys from the East Coast," says Eady. "They were from Rhode Island, New Jersey, Philadelphia—and a little more worldly than a kid like me from Decatur, Indiana. Matter of fact, I got introduced to pot by those guys during a weekend pass when we were still at Fort Hood."

The character of characters among the northeasterners was Spc. 4th Class John Guzik III, a tall, tow-headed Polish-American from a row house in Camden, New Jersey. Guzik had been driving a bread truck when drafted at nineteen, and going to night school at Temple University. Bidding good-bye to his parents, four sisters, and fiancée, he took to soldiering without missing a beat. Thoroughly irreverent, and definitely on the hip side of the marijuana question, Guzik was also so good at his job that he was selected as gunner on A-35 under Platoon Sergeant Jessie. "I'd never met anybody like Guzik," recalls Eady. "He was very funny, very outgoing. It was like, wow!"

There was certainly a share of colorful wise guys in the unit, including some blacks, Hispanics, and ethnic whites who were alumni of "street clubs" from the rougher sections of New York, Chicago, Detroit, or Los Angeles.

Nonetheless, many of the city boys were really just "everyday kids straight out of *American Graffiti*," notes Richard J. Sears of Danvers, Massachusetts. Sears was one of those kids. Michael D. Esmond was another. Sears came from a conservative, middle-class family of diehard Yankees. He played football and hockey in school and, after graduating, had a ball surfing and otherwise bumming around with some buddies in Hawaii. Nailed by the selective service soon thereafter, he decided to take his chances as a two-year draftee rather than sign up, as had been arranged, for six years in the guard. Meanwhile, Esmond, son of a milkman and product of the Catholic school system, completed an apprenticeship for a defense-related job at the Philadelphia Navy Yard. He had barely drawn his first paycheck, however, when the base commander surrendered two hundred worker deferments for the war effort. Esmond was drafted two weeks later. His father, a veteran, hugged him the last day of his pre-deployment leave and said with tears in his eyes: "I went to war. You were never supposed to go to war."

Sears was a tanker in B Troop, Esmond a medic. Both were twenty years old. Both would be highly decorated. One was to be medevacked with devastating injuries. "We weren't heroes," says Sears. "We didn't want to be in the army—but when your country calls, you go. Those smug damn protesters never understood that you can't pick and chose your responsibilities to America."

Needing to refuel and take aboard potable water, the *General Walker* dropped anchor at White Beach Naval Facility, Okinawa, on August 24. Having donned clean khakis, the pent-up troopers aboard the *General Walker* were given shore leave at one in the afternoon. Entertainment in the overcrowded clubs included go-go dancers and Japanese bands that sang Beatles songs, plus inebriated naval aviators who conducted practice carrier landings—meaning that they lined up their tables, took a running start, and dived down the improvised runway on their bellies with arms outstretched. If an aviator came to a stop at the last table, he had made a good landing. If he crashed to the floor, he had to do it again.

Locals appeared on the high ground behind the base, beckoning the GIs to their off-limits village, which was crowded with sleazy bars, massage parlors, and houses of prostitution. "After visiting the village," says Alfred V. Cognetti, part of A Troop, "I don't remember how we got back to the ship!"

Max Pryor was in charge of a fifty-man detachment tasked, he wrote, with keeping the GIs "from tearing hell out of White Beach." The detachment broke up numerous brawls and hauled "the drunks back to the boat in the truck the navey [sic] let us use." Some of those so apprehended went to the far side of the ship, jumped overboard, and swam back to shore. Following midnight curfew and the wretched procession of booze-sick troopers up the gangway, a bar-to-bar search was conducted for stragglers. Panning his flashlight across the interior of one whorehouse, Pryor saw rows of beds divided by curtains, a regular assembly line to service GIs. A few overlooked troopers made it to the ship only just before it departed in the morning, including a bruised regular army sergeant wearing the ripped remnants of a shirt and escorted by two MPs. When the ship put out to sea again, notes Bursott, "everybody was hung over. They fed us hardboiled eggs and greasy bacon, and the proverbial shit on a shingle [creamed beef on toast] which nobody felt like eating."

Those edgy days and nights crossing the salt provided time for much anxious thought. One A Trooper pondered the symbolism of being led into the heart of darkness by Joseph Conrad himself. Perhaps, thought the trooper, that was why Captain Conrad went by his middle name. Creepier still, was being in the cavalry and having a platoon leader, George Wallace, with the same name as one of Custer's second lieutenants. At least the earlier George Wallace had been lucky, since Custer had sent him to be with Major Reno the day before his squadron of the 7th Cavalry had met its end at Little Big Horn. Maybe this one would be equally lucky.

Captain George Wallace's number did come up fourteen years later when he was the only officer to die at Wounded Knee.

There were only three days of sailing time between Okinawa and Việt Nam. The war was coming at these soldiers very fast now, and, looking inward, they leaned against the railing at night, each a solitary sentinel as he agonized about how he would react under fire. Sergeants and platoon leaders asked themselves if they really knew what they were doing. *What if I screw up and get myself killed?* Or worse: *What if I screw up and get my guys killed?*

Christ, let's get this over with . . .

The Advance Party

AUGUST 14–28, 1967

LIEUTENANT COLONEL HARRINGTON'S ADVANCE party flew out of Bergstrom Air Force Base aboard a C-130 cargo plane on August 14. Harrington's group had spent the previous five days signing buildings and other property back to the post commander at Fort Hood. During that time, a disappointed Captain Steinmetz had been reassigned, despite the fine job he had done, to assist the newly formed 3-1 Cav in taking the 1-1 Cav's place in the 1st Armored Division.

There were fourteen men in the advance party: Lieutenant Colonel Harrington and his jeep driver; Major Saint and two lieutenants from the operations section; Captain Reed, the maintenance officer; Capt. David E. Roesler, the new logistics officer; Captains Conrad, Staley, and Brown; and, finally, the supply sergeants from A, B, C, and Headquarters Troop.

The advance party landed at Travis Air Force Base near San Francisco, then took off again for a fifty-hour flight across the Pacific with refueling stops in Hawaii, Wake Island, Guam, and the Philippines. Harrington and his people catnapped on supply pallets, or otherwise sat alone with their thoughts, the interior of a four-engine C-130 Hercules being too noisy to carry on a normal conversation. Harrington anticipated rendezvousing with his vehicles, supplies, and troops at the port city of Vũng Tàu in III Corps, then launching operations northwest of Sài Gòn with the 25th Division. Instead, Harrington learned en route that the dragoons were to join Task Force Oregon, a provisional division formed to reinforce the marines in southern I Corps. Task Force Oregon was headquartered in Chu Lai, a marine air base on the coast, and controlled three brigades sent from II and III Corps: the 196th Light Infantry Brigade; the 3rd Brigade, 4th Infantry Division; and the 1st Brigade, 101st Airborne Division.

Harrington made anxious calls at each refueling stop to ensure that troopship and freighters understood their new destination was Đà Nẵng, the base with a port facility nearest Chu Lai. Having lost a day upon crossing the International Date Line, the advance party landed at Đà Nẵng before dawn on August 18. After a delay of nine or ten hours, the group caught another cargo plane for the flight south to Chu Lai. For all the confusion, a liaison team was waiting from the 2nd Squadron, 11th Armored Cavalry Regiment, which the dragoons were to replace. Maps were opened as Harrington's hosts explained the lay of the land. Task Force Oregon's AO (area of operations) included southern Quảng Tin Province and all of Quảng Ngãi Province, which lay across an invisible line south of Chu Lai. Despite the occasional rocket attack, the living was good at Chu Lai, what with the cookouts on the beautiful beach and easy access to vice thanks to all the civilian workers. The base was squeezed between the ocean and Highway 1, which, paralleled by a single-track railway built by the French, followed the coast all the way from Sài Gòn to Hà Nội and on into China.

The host squadron's rear detachment was located at Fat City, aka Hill 35, as measured in meters above sea level, a logistics base seven klicks (kilometers) northwest of Chu Lai on Highway 1. The next link in the chain, Hill 54, was six klicks farther along the highway. To reach the 2/11 ACR's most forward position, one traveled the fourteen klicks from Hill 54 to Tam Kỳ, provincial capital of Quảng Tin, and then another twelve to the access road leading west from Highway 1 to Hill 29. Highway and railway veered three kilometers apart at that point, and the base camp sat in the middle between them. To the north were the marines; ten klicks east, the ocean. Green foothills grew from the paddies to the south and west. The hills ascended step-like into the mile-high, jungle-covered mountains that belonged to the North Vietnamese Army.

While a staging area was established near the airstrip, Captains Conrad, Staley, and Brown went out to observe operations with their counterparts in the 2/11 ACR. The experience was not encouraging. The squadron, whose tanks, tracks, and troopers looked decidedly beat-up, wanted nothing more than to pack up and return to its parent regiment near Sài Gòn. The unit had not been bested in battle. In fact, there had been no battles. Instead, morale had been rubbed raw by mines. The enemy around Chu Lai were farmers by day, guerrillas by night. They laid mines and disappeared. They fired a few sniper rounds and vanished. They scooped a hole in the sand to anchor a mortar tube, popped out two or three rounds, then grabbed their stuff and moved out. They were everywhere but nowhere, and they seemed to know everything, thanks in part to the children who waved at passing GIs, then reported their movements to the Việt Cộng.

Lieutenant Norton was sleeping in an aid station on a rise above the staging area when a casualty was brought in around midnight. The GI had been slipped ground glass or bamboo while eating in one of the little shops that crowded the highway outside the base. Before the man was rushed to an evacuation helicopter, he writhed on a litter in the aid station. "The moaning, the screaming, the wailing, the pleading—it was not good," recalls Norton, who had just learned lesson number one about Việt Nam: "You can't trust anybody."

The decision to commit troops to this strange war in this distant land had been long in coming. President Dwight D. Eisenhower had originally been encouraged to take that fateful step after the French defeat at Diện Biên Phu in 1954 but heeded the counsel of Gen. Matt Ridgway to keep the U.S. Army out of Indochina. Instead, advisors were dispatched to newly created South Việt Nam, to be followed by helicopters, fighter-bombers, and the vaunted Green Berets during the administration of John F. Kennedy.

Despite such measures, the communist insurgency in South Việt Nam steadily gained ground. The reasons were simple enough. The venal regime in Sài Gòn did nothing to win the allegiance of the peasant majority, and the Army of the Republic of Việt Nam was no match for the National Liberation Front. There were some good ARVN units, but in general its officer corps was corrupt, the troops unmotivated. In comparison, the cadre of the Front had come up through the ranks and shared the hardships of its guerrilla fighters. This cadre rallied the support of the peasantry through good works, propaganda about the better life offered them by communism, appeals to national unity and the end of foreign domination—and the use of selective, cold-blooded terror.

With disaster looming, the pressure inexorably built upon President Lyndon Johnson to either wash his hands of the whole mess or finally settle the issue with the military might of the United States. Unwilling to lose face or suffer the domestic political repercussions of appearing soft on communism, Johnson landed the marines at Đà Nẵng in March 1965. The conventional wisdom as the U.S. Army and Marine Corps shouldered the ARVN aside was that the war was as good as won. Few recalled Hồ Chí Minh's taunt to the French, or could have dreamed that it applied to the Americans, too: "You will kill ten of our men, and we will kill one of yours, and in the end it will be you who tire of it."

There stood in South Việt Nam, after the build-up of 1965–1966, a nearly half-million-man army under Gen. William C. Westmoreland, Commander, U.S. Military Assistance Command Vietnam (MACV). Westmoreland was a brisk, can-do type of general, his army well-trained, well-led, well-supplied, and highly mobile thanks to its fleets of helicopters: the young marines and infantrymen in the field, known as "grunts," more than proved their tenacity in jungle fighting as ferocious as the Pacific campaigns of World War II. To watch such a professional military machine in action was to inspire confidence, and as enemy body counts—the metric of success in Westmoreland's war of attrition—were tabulated in ever-increasing numbers, that confidence, in turn, inspired the faith that great progress was being made. The light could be seen at the end of the tunnel.

General Westmoreland's army, trained to fight a conventional war, used shot and shell without counting to minimize its own losses and maximize those of the enemy during an aggressive continuum of search-and-destroy missions in the rural areas of South Việt Nam. As a result, those of the innocents caught in the middle matched enemy casualties. Despite the communist tactics of assassinating government officials and rampaging through uncooperative villages, Martha Gellhorn reported in 1966 that "we, unintentionally, are killing and wounding three or four times more people than the Việt Cộng . . . We are not maniacs and monsters, but our planes range the sky all day and all night, and our artillery is lavish and we have much more deadly stuff to kill with." Gellhorn likened the tactic of bombing villages from which a single sniper had fired, or into which a squad of guerrillas might have slipped, to "destroying your friend's home and family because you have heard there is a snake in the cellar . . . This is indeed a new kind of war, as the indoctrination lecture stated, and we had better find a new way to fight it. Hearts and minds, after all, live in bodies."

Firepower and the courage of the grunts won many battles. The war was not won, however. Westmoreland had intended to eliminate enemy soldiers at a rate that Hà Nội could not sustain, but such a strategy was confounded when it was the enemy—hidden by the jungle, aided by the rural peasantry—who initiated most firefights, then slipped away when the price of battle became too high. In sum, the communists could not be forced to expend more men than could be replaced. If battered, the VC and NVA could withdraw to Cambodia to regroup, and despite an intense bombing campaign, supplies and reinforcements were forever coming down the Hồ Chí Minh Trail, that network of hidden roadways running from North Việt Nam to South Việt Nam by way of Laos.

In frustration, General Westmoreland finally made war on the peasants in enemy-controlled "liberated zones" to use the communist lexicon. "People and their homes were dehumanized into grid coordinates on a target map," wrote Neil Sheehan of the New York Times. In order to drive the peasants off their ancestral lands and into government-controlled resettlement camps, hamlets were bombed and crops wilted by chemical defoliants sprayed from modified transport planes. The tactic of collective retribution was not new: it had led to the defeat of the American Indian and the excesses of the Philippine Insurrection. In a private conversation with Westmoreland, Douglas MacArthur himself had suggested a scorched-earth policy in Việt Nam. Television news footage of American boys putting Zippo lighters to thatch hootches might have shocked the public, but there was a method to the brutality. "If you destroyed the rural society," noted Sheehan, explaining a tactic he thought criminal and counterproductive, "you destroyed the resources the enemy needed to fight. You deprived him of recruits . . . [and] food and the intelligence the peasantry provided; you reversed Mao Tse-tung's axiom by drying up the sea . . . in which the guerrillas swam."

The area in which Task Force Oregon operated had been a bastion of resistance for a hundred years, first against the French and then Sài Gòn. On Westmoreland's watch, it was decided to create a desert and call it peace. When journalists Jonathan and Orville Schell flew over Quảng Ngãi Province in August 1967—the same month the dragoons were steaming *across the Pacific*—they saw that two-thirds of the hamlets indicated on the map no longer existed. *The destruction had begun when the 1st Marine Division originally battled its way through hamlets transformed into enemy strong points with bunkers and interconnecting trenches. Those hamlets not destroyed in battle were burned to discourage the enemy from returning and the villagers from staying.*

Young soldiers told the Schell brothers of dark deeds being committed out there on the edge of civilization, to include captured VC being hurled from helicopters. "Maybe when I go home I'll just crawl inside myself, and not say a word," *one trooper confided.* "Things are so violent nobody would believe it." *Another GI took up the same theme:* "You wouldn't believe the things that go on in this war . . . No one's ever going to find out about some things, and after this war is over, and we've gone home, no one is ever going to know."

Over thirty years would pass before an internal investigation was made public, exposing how renegade members of the Tiger Force of the 1-327 Infantry, 101st Airborne Division, had taken ears and scalps from their kills, shot prisoners, and picked off farmers in their fields for sport while attached to Task Force Oregon during the Fall of '67. Such atrocities were inevitable, given the need to avenge dead buddies in what had essentially become a race war, and the outrage among the troops that those they had come to save were in league with those they had come to fight. Throw in, too, a pressure for body counts that produced the catchphrase, "If it's dead, it must be VC."

Atrocities were also a signal of an utter lack of progress: no matter how many communists were killed, more appeared, and no matter how lavishly the ARVN were equipped, they remained incompetent, apathetic, and intimidated by the VC and NVA. As for Sài Gòn, there was no stability, only corruption. For these reasons, the war could never have been won. Believing, however, that the military might of the greatest nation on earth was the primary factor in determining victory or defeat, the grunts complained bitterly that they were fighting with one arm tied behind their backs. They wanted to march on Hà Nội, thinking through neither what it would mean if the Chinese intervened, nor the horrors—friendly casualty rates included—of the nearly genocidal war that would have been required to crush a people as fanatically opposed to foreign domination as the Vietnamese. To quote one fed-up GI sent to fight this no-win, damned-if-you-do-damned-if-you-don't mess of a war: "The only thing to do is to kill everybody in the country over five years old."

And there the war stood as the dragoons arrived.

On August 26, Harrington's advance party greeted a U.S. Navy LST (landing ship, tank), which had taken aboard the squadron's conex shipping containers at Đà Nẵng before heading south for Chu Lai. Soon thereafter, other LSTs arrived, bearing the tanks and tracks. Each of the flat-bottomed, football-field-sized vessels opened its twin bay doors and dropped a loading ramp upon beaching, whereupon the captains and lieutenants of the advance party backed out all of the M48A3s and M113A1s, along with the M88 tank retrievers, M125 81mm mortar tracks, and M577 command tracks belonging to Headquarters Troop. From there, the vehicles were driven to the staging area and lined up across the sand dunes, platoon by platoon, troop by troop. The job lasted two and a half days and was completed only the evening before another LST was due to arrive with the men of the 1st Squadron, 1st Cavalry, 1st Armored Division.

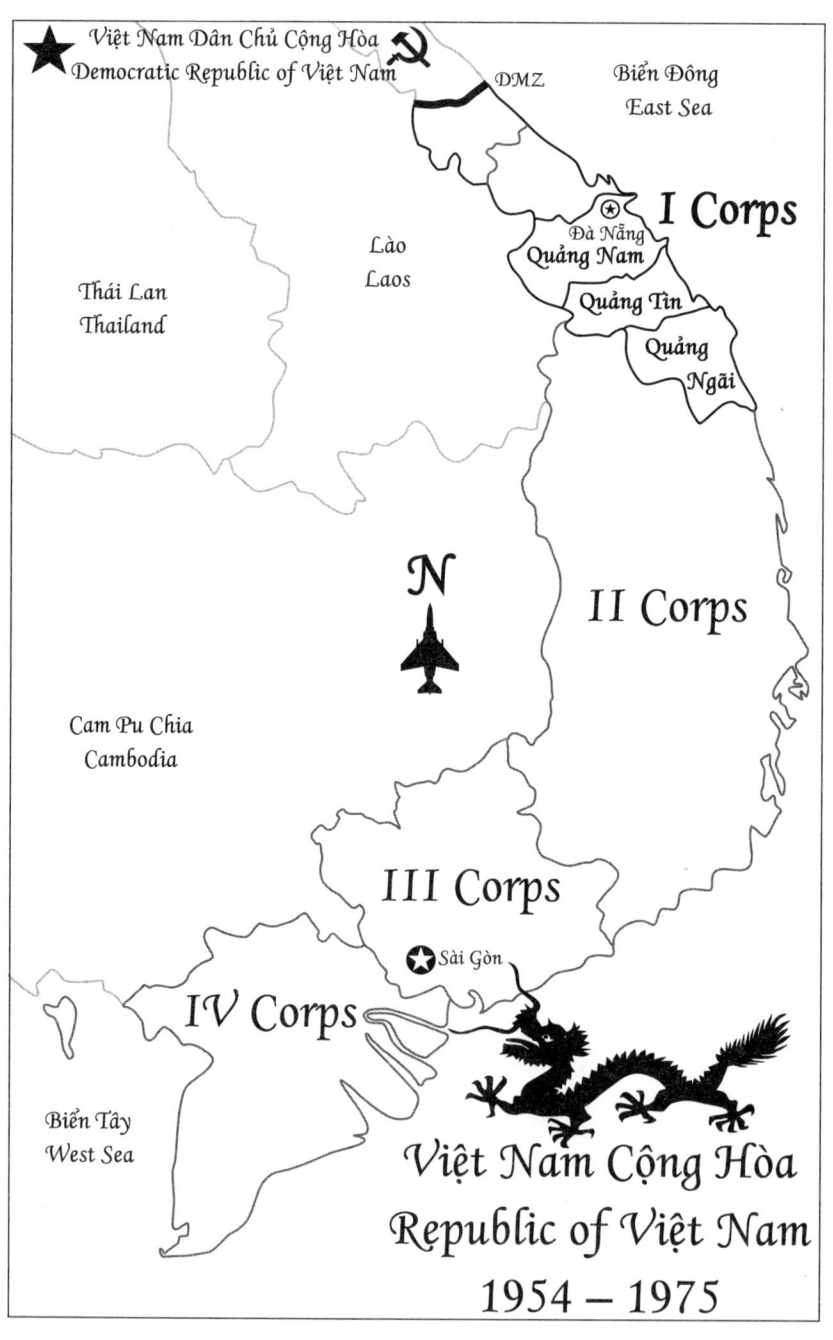

Getting Situated

AUGUST 28–SEPTEMBER 4, 1967

AFTER EIGHTEEN DAYS AT sea, all of which counted on a dragoon's one-year combat tour, the *General Walker* reached Đà Nẵng before dawn on August 28 and anchored five hundred meters offshore. Awakened by an announcement over the ship's public-address system, groggy troopers lined the rails, anxious for their first glimpse of Việt Nam. The scene was definitely attention grabbing. There was a battle in progress, complete with tracers and illumination rounds that floated down like small, smoke-streaming stars under their parachutes. One of the warships in the bay, a destroyer, fired its guns until dawn into the side of Marble Mountain, which overlooked the air base at Đà Nẵng.

The next day, ammunition was transferred from the ship's hold to an LST anchored alongside the *General Walker*. Downloading the ammo took longer than expected, leaving the dragoons to spend one last night aboard the *General Walker*. Final briefings were held in the crowded troop compartments. Noting that the enemy wore black pajamas like the locals, and sometimes even disguised themselves as government soldiers, one senior noncom warned: "If they aren't wearing a uniform like yours, they're the enemy."

"How 'bout the marines?" A joker called from the crowd.

Platoon Sergeant Boyd reminded his guys that they were a team and that they needed to keep their heads and remember their training when the platoon went into combat. Boyd also noted the wild tales they'd heard of GIs who took ears from dead VC, "and he made it very plain," notes former track driver Ronnie Fortner, "that this kind of stuff was not going to happen in A Troop."

The squadron had been instructed to only fire when fired upon and to refrain from reconning-by-fire, a standard tactic to flush the enemy out of hiding. Boyd disagreed. "I'm not going to lose any people over this kind of bullshit," he growled. "If we see something, we'll shoot first and get in trouble later."

The troopers of the 1-1 Cav boarded the USS *Iredell County* at dawn, leaving the 2-1 Cav to join the 4th Division in II Corps. The dragoons still lacked ammo for their personal weapons, a situation that made everyone more uneasy than they already were as the landing ship slowly chugged south, following the coast. Those troopers unable to find shade under the pilothouse or the ship's crane were left to the mercy of the sun during the seven-hour trip. Lips blistered, faces and forearms turned lobster red. The view, at least, was exotic. "From what I could see off [sic] the country from the LST," wrote Tom Bursott, "it is very pretty."

The landing ship arrived at Chu Lai at 3 p.m. on August 29. The dragoons exited through the open bow—a marine band greeted them with rousing patriotic music—then drew up in columns on the beach, flags and guidons flying, Harrington at the head of the formation, as a general welcomed the 1-1 Cavalry to Task Force Oregon. Trucks next transported the troops to the staging area, where Donut Dollies, as female Red Cross volunteers were known, offered smiles and cups of Kool-Aid. Larry Graham wrote that chatting with the Donut Dollies "was kinda nice for us cause we're all pretty sick of each other."

The tracks had been stripped for seaborne shipment, and much effort was now required to reinstall radios, remount gun shields, and reassemble machine guns once the cosmoline-smeared parts had been dipped in jet fuel and scrubbed clean. All the while, marine jet fighters took off with ear-piercing shrieks from the nearby runway. There was no shelter, only blinding white sand and a merciless sun, which deepened sunburns and plastered sweaty shirts against backs as the cavalrymen went about their labors in the hundred-plus heat. Pallets of C-rations and beer had been delivered to the staging area. The beer was unrefrigerated, and off-brand to boot, but better than nothing, at least until the dragoons discovered that the resident support troops would trade cold sodas for warm beer. When a drenching storm swept in at dusk, a truck pulled up; the back ramp flopped down, a frame and huge, rolled-up tent were shoved out, and one of the soldiers inside the canvas-covered truck bed shouted, "There's your home, boys! The sooner you put it up, the sooner you get dry!"

Exhausted troopers sleeping inside vehicles, or the hastily erected tent, were jolted awake during the night by outgoing mortar fire. Nervous sentries stood watch over the vehicles, armed with .45s for which they had been issued a single clip. The task of getting the vehicles combat ready resumed the next day. Fuel tanks were topped off, and ammunition unloaded from trucks. The amounts involved were enormous: each tank, for example, carried sixty-two 90mm rounds in honeycomb-shaped ready racks inside the turret and hull. The seat in each vehicle's command cupola was removed—better to sit on a board thrown across the hatch—and the two benches inside the tracks stripped out, too. The floor was layered with sandbags to muffle the effect of a mine blast and then stacked with ammo cans, making a platform on which the gunners would stand. The basic load of an armored cavalry assault vehicle weighed two tons and included a case each of smoke, fragmentation, and white-phosphorus grenades, plus cases of Claymore mines, C-4 plastic explosives, 40mm rounds for the M79, and, finally, at least 15,000 rounds of ball ammunition for the .50-cal and M60s.

Most of the crews were still working on their vehicles when the squadron was given a mission during the late morning of August 30. Captain Staley proudly reported that B Troop was ready to go, and several of his tanks were dispatched north on Highway 1 to the intersection with the access road leading to Fat City. There had been reports of sniper fire in the area. The tanks waited at the crossroads, then, taking a round or two, trained their main guns on the tree line in which the sniper was apparently ensconced and unleashed a volley of canister—the first rounds fired with lethal intent by the 1-1 Cavalry.

The squadron departed Chu Lai on August 31, bound for Fat City by way of Highway 1. The scenery along the way was beautiful, the poverty of the roadside towns shocking. "I don[']t see how these people can live," reported Tom Bursott. Combat operations began that very afternoon as part of Operation Wheeler and under the auspices of the 196th Light Infantry Brigade. "We were just thrown into it," notes Alfred Cognetti. "It was on-the-job training." Working independently, the line platoons guarded bridges, protected marine engineers who swept the roads for mines every morning, and escorted supply convoys. They also conducted search-and-destroy missions during which those who passed out from the smothering heat were medevacked, deserted tunnels, bunkers, and trenches destroyed with plastique, and Polaroids of the first booby trap to be discovered snapped at the request of headquarters. B Troop seized seventy-five one-pound bags of corn in a small hamlet. The villagers said it belonged to them. The cavalrymen wondered if the corn would not end up feeding the enemy, and the decision was finally made to leave forty bags and confiscate the rest. The squadron's primary mission went unfulfilled, however. "We made no contact," wrote Larry Graham. "Better luck next time!"

Mounted patrols returned to base at dusk, and after a hot meal prepared by the troop mess sections, the men slept in their tracks or out under the stars on extra litters. Guards were rotated so that there was always a man behind the .50-cal on each tank and track. Boyd's Bastards took sniper fire one night—A Troop's first action—and while a grenadier returned the favor, Boyd activated the million-candlepower searchlight on the main gun of his tank. There was nothing to see, and nothing further developed. Because of the enemy's nocturnal ways, the 105mm and 155mm batteries at Fat City fired H&I missions (harassment-and-interdiction) throughout the night. The artillerymen took note of the location of friendly patrols and also refrained from shelling the local hamlets, since they were ostensibly under government control. Otherwise, anything in no-man's-land after dark was fair game—villagers had a dusk-to-dawn curfew—and the sky lit up every night like the Fourth of July.

Meaning to take back the night, the infantry squads conducted nerve-jangling ambush patrols. "Man, I don't even know what the fuck I'm doin'," the point man of one patrol was heard to mutter as he led his squad out the gate at Fat City. After cat-footing to the designated spot on the map, the would-be ambushers would divide up the watch—half awake, half asleep—smear on oily mosquito repellent, and pray for the dawn. "[L]ast night I went on my first [ambush] patrol," wrote Tom Bursott. "Boy[,] you talk about a mess." Bursott splashed into a creek when the log being using to step from one side to the other gave way. The squad moved into an overgrown shell crater. Before long, a heavy rain began to fall, and the depression filled with cold water. "We sat there all night," recalls Bursott. "I don't think my teeth ever chattered as much as they did that night. I swear I was about ready to freeze to death."

Lieutenant Dickens had been called to Captain Staley's track during a halt on the highway during the original road march to Fat City. Major Saint was waiting at the track, and he explained that Dickens was to be detached then and there for a special dismounted mission. Dickens was to take his rifle squad, and one from another platoon in B Troop, and interdict by way of ambush the waterways around one of the little islands in the intercoastal area along the South China Sea. Dickens and his group departed in a matter of moments atop a marine amphibious tractor—amtrac, for short—which turned off the highway some klicks past Fat City, rolled down an embankment, and ferried the cavalrymen across an inlet between the mainland and the little island.

The amtrac departed. Fifteen armed men soon approached along the beach. Lieutenant Dickens had his men form a hasty skirmish line. The unidentified group stopped, and a lone individual came forward to explain in English that he and his comrades were supposed to link up with the GIs. Dickens had been told nothing about such a rendezvous, and, glancing uneasily at these characters with their nondescript clothing, web gear, and old weapons, he wasn't sure if he was dealing with militiamen, bandits, or Việt Cộng. "I don't know who you are or where you came from," Dickens finally said, "but my advice to you is to take your people and leave because anything we see on this island or in the water after dark will be considered hostile—and engaged." After several fruitless days on the island—not a soul was seen, let alone ambushed—the detachment finally departed aboard a helicopter to rejoin Bravo Troop.

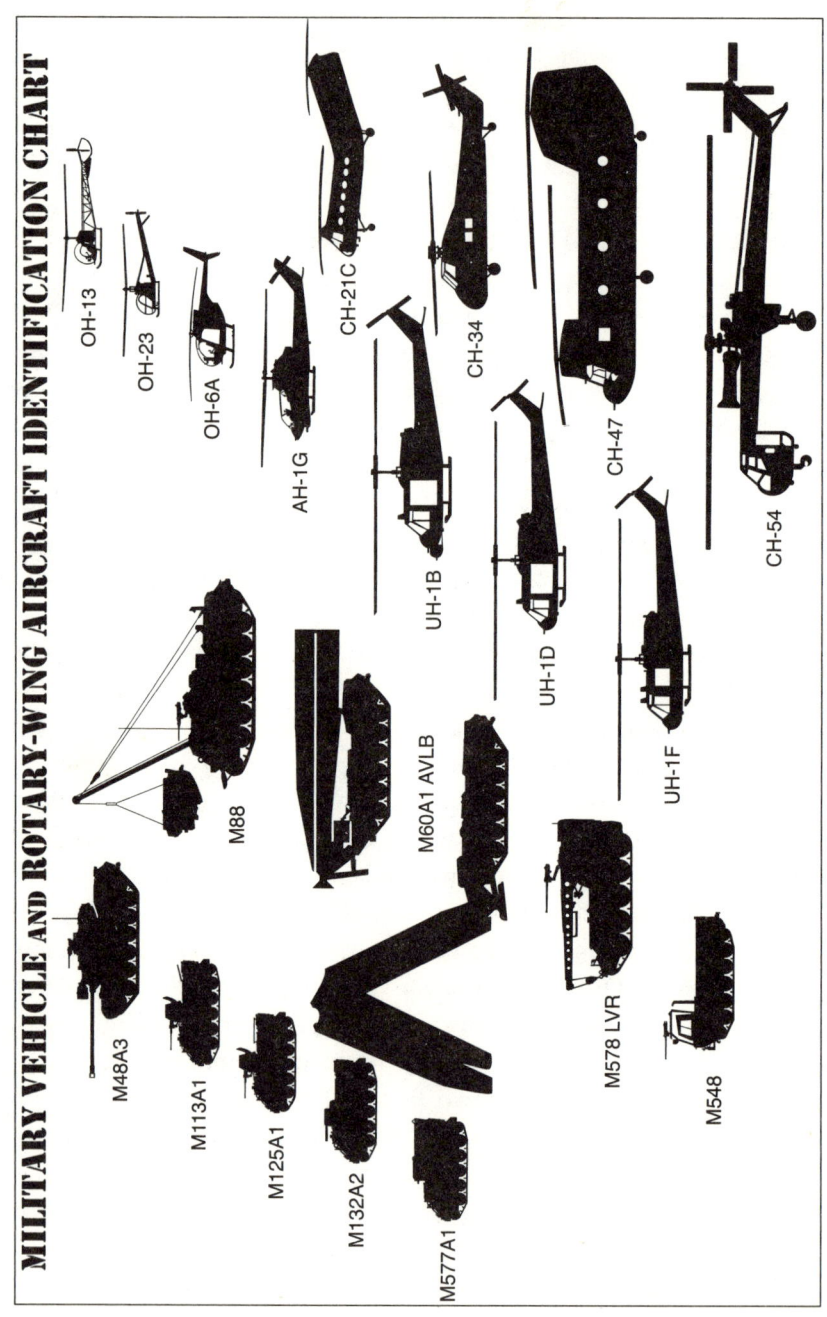

First Blood

SEPTEMBER 4–5, 1967

First Lieutenant Garland D. Whitmore and half of 2nd Platoon, A Troop, were laagered on a gently sloped hummock two klicks below Fat City when the sound of digging echoed across the paddies shortly before midnight. Reporting that he had activity of some kind a hundred meters south of his outpost, Whitmore requested permission to open fire. He was told instead to observe the area with the infrared light of the tank he had with him. Whitmore explained that the sounds had come from behind another hill, and though he was not allowed to shell the area with his mortar track, lest the target be an ambush patrol that had strayed off course, permission was granted to put up some illume.

The light revealed two figures. At that point, Whitmore was instructed to open fire and then dispatch a mounted patrol to count bodies or scoop up prisoners. The patrol returned empty-handed. Whitmore reported that the enemy had been "scared off." They had not. The digging began again some thirty minutes later. One of the tracks fired a burst. It drew no response. The tank flipped on its searchlight, but the beam of white light revealed nothing. Another thirty minutes passed, and then a flash of some sort was spotted. The outpost opened fire and popped more illume. Two tracks left to sweep the area without result. Given all the commotion, most of the guys joined those on watch atop the vehicles. Though they were alert, it did not sink in that they were in mortal danger. They thought they were in a "safe" area because, as Tom Bursott had written home, "They told us that the cong don[']t get any large[r] than 3–6 men in this area"—hardly enough to worry about.

An hour passed, then, without warning, there was a flash of sparks as two shells thumped in quick succession from a mortar tube. Both shells exploded inside the laager, one scoring a direct hit on the back ramp of the command track, which had been lowered, per routine, the better to be able to get in and out of the vehicle. The interior lights being on, the red glow, though dim, was thought to have provided the enemy a good reference point. Sergeant Charles H. Gobble, an FO (forward observer) attached from the 3-16 Field Artillery, was killed instantly. Lieutenant Whitmore's right leg was blown off, and because he had removed his flak jacket in the suffocating heat, he suffered a sucking chest wound too, meaning that his lung had been punctured and might collapse and suffocate him as his chest cavity filled with air. Ten other dragoons were injured, two of them seriously. The radio net filled with frantic voices.

Thirty long minutes later, a medical evacuation helicopter, better known as a dust-off, arrived from Chu Lai. Sergeant Rensi, track commander, would later note that "it was real hectic on the radio because nobody knew how to call in a dust-off." Fortunately, a sergeant on his second tour took over and controlled the medevac. Cursing himself for not having paid more attention during his training, Rensi was glad someone knew what the hell he was doing. "I didn't even know where we were. I was second-in-command at that outpost—and I didn't have a clue where we were except somewhere in Vietnam." Flares were stuck in the ground to mark an LZ (landing zone), and the medevac landed as the tracks laid down suppressive fire. The platoon leader and another badly wounded cavalryman were quickly loaded into the cargo bay. The night continued to reverberate with outgoing fire after the medevac departed. "We fired like hell at the VC," one dragoon wrote, "but checked the area this morning and apparently didn't get any of the little bastards."

Returning to base, the troops were informed that Lieutenant Whitmore had died on the medevac. "It knocked the props out from under us," says

Wayne Byrd. "He was an outstanding platoon leader. He always had a smile on his face. I mean, he would chew you out with a smile, and you knew he was chewin' you out with love because he wanted you to make it—and then he didn't make it."

The squadron chaplain held a memorial service during which a bamboo chapel was dedicated to 1st Lt. Garland D. "Skip" Whitmore II, age twenty-three, of Harrisonburg, Virginia. Fiercely anti-communist, Whitmore had left college to enlist when the war heated up, attended jump school and officer candidate school, spoke of making the military his career, and used to count cadence and jog circles around his guys during their early morning runs at Fort Hood. "He was very dedicated and loved his job," writes Larry Graham. "He was the kind of guy that you wouldn't want to let down."

Following the memorial service, nine of Lieutenant Whitmore's men received "impact awards" of the type approved before the paperwork was complete so to be pinned on immediately after an action to boost morale. The platoon medic was pinned with a Bronze Star Medal with "V" device—to indicate valor, as opposed to meritorious service—for aiding the casualties despite an injured leg. The medic also received the Purple Heart, as did the other eight troopers in the formation. "A couple of the guys didn't want the medals," recalls Rich Rensi. "They said nothing had happened to them. They were just trying to get down and cover their butt and got scratched in the process. The army is crazy at times: if a guy fell and stubbed his toe, they'd give him a Purple Heart."

Captain Conrad remarked that someone had to formally identify Skip Whitmore's body at the graves-registration detachment in Chu Lai. "I guess I should do that," muttered Chuck Donaldson. The executive officer was escorted into the morgue, where an aluminum cabinet was opened "just like you'd see on television," notes Donaldson, "and there he was: eyes open, mouth open, teeth showing. First unadorned dead person I'd ever seen, and I'll tell you, it scared the crap out of me. For a month or so after that, I slept inside a track every night. The notion of a sucking chest wound, which is what killed him, haunted me for my entire tour, and I became a very dedicated flak-jacket wearer."

On the Go-Go

SEPTEMBER 1967

PLATOON SERGEANT BOYD, VEXED by their losses, had an uncomplicated message for that night's ambush patrol: "Bring me back some fuckin' meat." The seven-man ambush moved a klick west of Fat City as dusk fell on September 7 and then assumed positions on one side of an open field to keep watch on the hamlet on the other side. Intelligence indicated that several guerrillas would leave the hamlet after dark. Hours passed in mosquito-plagued silence as the cavalrymen kept their starlight scope trained on the hamlet. Unexpectedly, their radio hissed: a tower guard back at Fat City, scanning the area with his own starlight scope, had detected approximately sixty guerrillas approaching the hamlet from behind the ambush patrol.

By the time the howitzers commenced firing, "the V.C. were practically on top of us," wrote Larry Graham, "so they had to drop it right in on us, too. That stuff sure packs a whallop [sic], it was just raining shrapnel all around us." The howitzer fire scattered the enemy. "We don't know how many it got, but there was a lot of flesh and blood out there this morning." The incident was great for morale. "We are going to try to get them to let us out there again tonite [sic] so we can finish the job," wrote an enthused Graham. "I can't say I enjoy being here but in a way I'm glad I am." He signed off with a cocky fillip to his peers back home: "I hope all the reservists and draft dodgers are enjoying themselves."

§

Captain Brown, commander of C Troop, laagered atop an overgrown hummock south of Fat City as night fell on September 9. Brown had called in his first medevac that afternoon when a sergeant stepped on a mine that shredded his leg and ended his war before it had really begun. Ambush patrols presently moved back downhill in the gathering darkness. Three mortar rounds dropped in around Sergeant Brooks' patrol from 1st Platoon. Major Saint called in artillery from his helicopter, then had Brown use his tank searchlights to illuminate the woods in which the mortar tube had coughed in order to guide the pair of gunships that had been scrambled. The gunships no sooner began their strafing run, however, than Saint had to shut everything down: the tanks were illuminating not only the enemy but a patrol from another unit, and the gunships had come perilously close to killing GIs instead of VC.

The enemy dropped two more rounds on Sergeant Brooks who, shouldering an M16 with a starlight scope, put a neat hole above the right eye of a VC walking at the edge of the woods. Unable to put a foot on the body, the dragoons recorded the downed guerrilla as a probable instead of a confirmed kill. Captain Brown, meanwhile, sent a tank and two tracks bouncing down the hill to rescue Brooks' patrol, but the tank broke down on the way back to the laager. Max Pryor and Staff Sgt. Donald W. Durst of the 2nd Platoon moved to the scene, as did an M88 VTR (vehicle, tracked, recovery). The recovery effort was not a success, noted Pryor: "[T]he V.t.R.'s driver jack knife[d] the tank on the tow bar on the way back[,] and we stay[ed] all night out side [the laager] with them." The enemy left them alone, but Pryor was nevertheless incensed that they had been stranded in no-man's-land because of a careless or incompetent tank-retriever driver: "I'll tell you one thing[,] if things don't change a[i]n't none of us going to get home alive. [T]hese people real[l]y have their heads up their ass."

More than a little hot, tired, and fed up, Pryor also vented in his letter that "[w]e do a lot of straight lage [leg] walking[,] why I don't know[,] every where I've walked a track could do it better and you'd have twice the fire power and 100 times the ammo with the P.C. [Personnel Carrier]." The root of their problems was squadron headquarters: "These dam[n] pincle [pencil] pushers set back [and] look at a map and think they can fix anything with there [sic] mouth over a raido [radio]. But they are the ones that should go with us and be their [sic] under fire and then see how effecty [effective] their map and mouth is if you half [have] to weight [wait] 35 min. on a fire mission and another 20 for a correction of one round . . . I'll never be so glad to get home in all my life."

On September 10, Lieutenant Colonel Harrington and Major Saint relocated their command post up the highway to Hill 54, leaving Major Lundquist to run the squadron rear at Fat City. The enemy was definitely out there around Hill 54: he jammed the squadron's tactical net with static and whistles, and disabled a tank during A Troop's first patrol in the new area of operations with a command-detonated mine that left a crater six feet deep and ten feet wide.

Captain Brown and C Troop arrived the next day. The 2nd Platoon and its West Point lieutenant set out the following morning, September 13, on the road leading to an old 2/11 ACR position. The road was embedded with spent brass and bottle caps, and the marine engineers leading the way had to stop each time their minesweeper beeped and gingerly probe the dirt with a bayonet. Based on which would better survive running over a mine, a tank, rather than a track, was first in line behind the marines. Because a tank's treads were set apart more widely than a track's, the lead track could put only one tread in the safe path made by the lead tank. The track drivers, who sat up front and to the left, head exposed above a circular hatch, had been trained to use their left tread when "tracking" a tank. Better to trigger a mine with the right tread, since the engine on that side would shield the driver and, if they were lucky, keep the vehicle from flipping.

Reaching the objective, the lieutenant sent Spec Four Pryor back to a hamlet they had passed on the way in to stand watch over the road while the rest of the platoon searched the abandoned base camp in the rain. Finally starting back toward Pryor—who was surrounded by villagers begging for candy, smokes, and soap—the lead tank was followed by a scout track, the command track, and then the rest of the platoon. Private First Class Lawrence M. Svobodny, the lieutenant's driver, became distracted while talking to the medic sitting behind his hatch and allowed the track to veer slightly from the safe path cleared by the tank and lead track. Pryor described the price of that moment of inattention:

> Boom! Scratch one p.c. and its driver[,] also 5 crewmembers wounded . . . [The mine] went off under the driver and you couldn't even tell who he was. He made one mastake [*sic*] and that was his last[,] he didn't track his left track in the tank[']s track for about 20 feet and that was it . . . My track couldn't have missed the mine more than 6" any of the two times that we passed it . . . that is the closest I ever want to come to getting killed. I shook like a dog shitting peach seads [*sic*] on a tin roof . . .

The explosion blasted the driver out of his hatch—he left a leg behind—and turned the track on its side, belching smoke. Pryor believed the engineers had missed the mine because the platoon leader, under pressure to reach and return from his objective before dark, had become exasperated by all the delays on the way to the outpost: "Lt. B was getting excited and hurr[y]ing the mine sweepers instead of listening to them & letting them probe for mines."

Pryor also wrote that he "saw a marine kill a man" but would later be unable to recall if the marine had shot a villager who made himself a target by running—the crowd around the track scattered, in fact, when the mine exploded—or pulled the trigger on the nearest military-age male to avenge the dead driver. The punch-drunk platoon leader was medevacked with a slice over one eye and subsequently awarded a Bronze Star and Purple Heart. The platoon laagered in place under its platoon sergeant. "[W]e had to stay all night," wrote Pryor. "And fired 140 rounds of M79 . . . It keep[s] the V.C. away from us. This morning[,] we pulled the 26 P.C. back with mine. Had to pull it about 2 miles."

Movement was heard that night around the troop laager, and after an exchange of fire, Captain Brown reported the squadron's first confirmed kills, four of them. Brown moved his troop, but the new position was also probed and two more guerrillas killed. In sum, two male and four female liberation fighters were slain; all were dressed in black peasant's garb and armed with old carbines and AK-47s, the favorite automatic weapon of the VC and NVA.

The next day, a tank was disabled by another mine in the area, and some days thereafter Charlie Troop returned to the roadside hamlet where its troubles had begun. The villagers were to be punished for playing deaf, dumb, and blind about the mines in their neighborhood. "[W]e blew the road where the [platoon leader's] track got blown up, and we also drove our tracks through their rice fields[,] tearing them all to hell," wrote Pryor. "Had a man in town telling them why we were doing it to them. You should have seen the people asking us not to ruin their rice crop. But it didn't do them any good. They all knew where the mine was and now must pay for it. However[,] I real[l]y don't think we did enough to them. I real[l]y wish we'd burn their homes."

The enemy might have razed the hamlet themselves had its inhabitants offered warning to the Americans. Pryor wished the dragoons could play by the same rules. "We should have been able to have shot hell out of that town and the people," he wrote in frustration. "Then told them if it happened again we'd kill every dam[n] one [of them]. I believe the next time you went thru you'd know if a boom [bomb] was their [sic] or not. All they understand is a heavy hand and barked orders that must be obeyed. It[']s enough to make you loose [sic] faith in our gover[n]ment to see how this war is being run." If the government would turn them loose, concluded Pryor, "we'd get this war over in 4 to 6 mo. for dam[n] sure. All you'd half to do is kick ass and take names."

The pace of operations increased in the new area of operations. "[We] have been on the go ever since [moving to Hill 54]," noted Tom Bursott, "and I mean on the go-go[.]" The days were spent on search-and-destroy missions, the nights on outposts and ambushes. "It's impossible to keep track of time," wrote Larry Graham. "We have been on 7 nite [sic] ambush patrols in about 10 days. We are plenty pooped . . . Whenever I get to sleep at nite [sic] it[']s usually for 3–4 hours and I'm so tired I don[']t even dream . . . [W]e can only carry enough water to drink, not wash or shave so we are pretty grubby . . . I've got one hell of a beard!"

There were no sustained firefights, not at first. Instead, the dragoons engaged snipers, ran over mines, and weathered mortar attacks, some of which produced casualties. "Boy[,] you talk about someone hitting the dirt and trying to get inside of a steel pot," wrote Tom Bursott after hearing incoming mortar shells whistle down upon him for the first time. During one bit of excitement, two tanks and two tracks from C Troop roared through the night to "help the marin[e]s out of a jam," wrote Specialist Fourth Class Pryor. "They sure were glad to see us to[o]. We shot hell out of a V.C.[, but did] not know who killed him though."

Being new, the squadron also engaged itself a number of times around Hill 54, to include the day the 2nd Platoon of B Troop shelled Lieutenant Dickens and 3rd Platoon while registering its mortar. Platoon Sergeant Boyd lost a tank to a mine one evening, and the platoon's hilltop laager was mortared after sundown just as the infantry squad moved out on ambush. "[I]t shook the shit out of me[,] there was no cover anywhere," wrote Graham. "Then later that nite [sic], 11:30[,] our platoon thought they saw something down the valley and started firing. No one told them we were out there and they damn near hit us with mortar and 50-cal. Won't it be a shame to get shot by your own men!"

If contact with the enemy was fleeting, fighting the terrain was battle enough at times, as Larry Graham wrote a week after moving to Hill 54:

> Sgt. Boyd[']s [tank] got stuck in a rice paddy and he had a big tank wrecker (VTR) come to tow him out. He got stuck too. [S]o all the APC's (7) hooked up to pull him out and all [but two] got stuck too . . . Well[,] we were only 50 yds from a pretty wide[,] deep stream at the time and it started raining. Well[,] the stream over flowed and by 5 P.M. the paddy was neck deep. We had to go under water to hook up tow cables. Well[,] eventually everyone got out, but not before we broke 25 tow hooks, 18 tow cables[,] and they ripped the door off our track[,] and almost every track needs transmission work . . . I got 4 of my knuckles mashed when a tow cable snapped and we ran into another track . . . Most of us spent the next A.M. getting . . . leaches [sic] off of us with cigarette butts.

Private First Class Schoep, driving the lead track in Boyd's Bastards, was streaking across a wet rice paddy when the terrain suddenly dropped, and he plunged headlong into a river. The track started going down nose first, and while the gunners dove for shore, Schoep was pinned in his driver's hatch by the weight of the onrushing water. Not until the track had filled with water and was sitting ten-feet deep could Schoep push out of his hatch—but then the cord to his commo helmet got tangled on something. He struggled to tear free, then finally kicked for the surface. The track commander, standing atop his cupola, grabbed Schoep. "Boy, am I glad to see you," the sergeant grinned. "I thought I was going to have to come down after you!"

The northern monsoon, which began in earnest about the middle of the month, included winds strong enough to bring down the tents at Hill 54. "[E]very day at 4 P.M. like clock work it pours til about 2–3 A.M.," wrote Graham. "Then next morning the sun comes out and it[s] back up in the 110s°–120s°[.]"

The tracks could handle the wet terrain better than the tanks. Lieutenant Lindsey of B Troop penned an "Ode to the M48A3" for the squadron yearbook:

> The broad backed Hippopotamus
> Rests on its belly in the mud,
> And having wrenched a time or two
> Lays helpless as flesh and blood.
>
> The keepers dismount the 'potamus,
> Stand off and look in fear,
> And having looked a time or two
> Remove their shirts and gear.
>
> Flesh and blood is weak and frail
> And the 'potamus is mired fast,
> But with dirty hands and broken nails
> The keepers sweat at their task.
>
> The mud is thick and heavy and bleak
> And the 'potamus humbles a man,
> The cables whine and strain and creak
> As the keepers offer a hand.
>
> The Hippo stirs. The keepers smile,
> The cables strain at the awesome feat,
> A trail in the mud is cut like an aisle
> And the 'potamus comes to his feet.
> They put on their shirts and curse the sun

> But now there is nothing to fear.
> They mount the 'potamus one by one
> And the Hippo is put into gear.
>
> Off it lumbers across the paddies
> Coated with slime to the top,
> And having stumbled a time or two
> Slowly it grinds to a stop.
>
> The broad backed Hippopotamus
> Rests on its belly in the mud,
> And having wrenched a time or two
> Lays helpless as flesh and blood.

Despite the hardships, frustrations, and all the attendant bitching, "there was a fantastic sense of esprit in the unit," recalls James O. Hammerbeck, then a staff sergeant in B Troop. "Morale had been pretty crummy at Fort Hood, but people really came alive when we started putting our training into practice in Vietnam." Larry Graham wrote home from Hill 54 that it was better to serve in combat than garrison: in the field, "[t]hey treat you like a man doing a man's job."

The overloaded tracks ran slow, had trouble climbing hills, and burned out numerous transmissions. The crews had to get rid of something to lighten the load. Since it wasn't going to be ammo, they removed the sandbag floors. The drivers, meanwhile, learned when bustin' bush to ease up on the trees in their path and push them over. They had originally rammed the trees. Not smart. The trees would not snap but would bend and bounce back, depositing onto the track a papier-mâché nest from which boiled thousands of ants whose painful bites sent crewmen into slapping fits while buddies sprayed them with insect repellent. Tank drivers learned that they could not simply turn the steering wheel and go in at an angle when entering a paddy. Such a maneuver would put a tank's fifty-two tons on the downhill tread, causing it to disengage from the sprockets and roll off the road wheels. Instead, the driver squared up with the paddy, then slowly descended until the belly of the tank met the lower ground, at which point he stood on the gas and roared ahead in a straight line. To change directions, the driver had to tweak the steering wheel in increments—turning locked and transferred all the weight to the inside tread of the turn, and if done too sharply that locked tread would cut into the mud. Once that happened, the tank could sink to the top of its road wheels, bringing a mission to a halt.

There was a lot of pride in driving a track, a dangerous job that required a deft touch. To either side of the driver's seat stood a three-foot-tall lever known as a lateral. The driver pulled back on the left one to lock the left tread and turn left, the right one to lock the right tread and turn right. To slow down or stop, he pulled back on both at the same time. Track drivers had to learn to negotiate hills, ravines, and paddy dikes without throwing tread, getting stuck, or pitching the gunners overboard by giving the vehicle too much power at the wrong time. The only member of the crew inside the track, the driver was the least likely to survive an encounter with a mine. The situation was particularly unnerving for those who drove the scout tracks. Because the roads were mined, the scouts had to go cross-country, "and the whole challenge for us," recalls Schoep, "was simply finding the best way through the terrain. We were always up front, jamming this way and that, and praying we wouldn't hit a mine."

When the line platoons returned to base to perform vehicle maintenance, the troops were allowed to visit the little town just down the road from Hill 54. Many acquired "girlfriends" among the prostitutes who'd originally greeted the arrival of the dragoons with shouts of "Boom-boom, GI!" The townspeople included not only teenage girls turned to whoring by the war but mamasans with their wide-brimmed conical hats who peddled black-market soda at ten cents a can, black-market beer at two dollars and forty cents a case, and black-market whiskey at ten dollars a quart. For another buck-fifty, a trooper could get a twenty-five-pound block of ice. The ice was dirty and full of sawdust but worked well enough in a cooler. Last but not least, for those so inclined, there was marijuana to be had. "The other day[,] one of the boys bought some pot down town," Max Pryor wrote soon after getting to Hill 54. He had never before dabbled with dope, but, "I tried one [joint] and it real[l]y makes you dizzy and feel good. Kind of like being drunk but not really."

Feeling good in a combat zone was not conducive to staying alive, and Pryor swore off the stuff. His father and wife were intrigued, however.

Pryor sent a baggy of marijuana home through the military postal system, and one cannot but smile at the image of an old country boy and his young daughter-in-law passing a pipe of Vietnamese weed in a trailer home in Tuscumbia, Missouri.

Some of the dragoons tried to reach out to the locals. "It's a shame they are so far behind in their ways but that's what we're here for I guess," noted Graham. Medics ran sick calls, and GIs gave extra rations to the skinny kids who flocked around them. The kids also wanted smokes. "There is one thing I can not get over," Tom Bursott informed his family, "and that is seeing kids... puffing away on a ciagarette [sic]." Bravo Troop adopted a seven-year-old orphan boy. "[H]is name is Sam and he is real[l]y smart," wrote Pryor. "Of co[u]rse[,] he can cuss from being around so many G.I.s[.] They use him on ochasion [sic] to translate for them." Pryor snapped a Polaroid of Sam. "He was real[l]y proud of the picture so I took one of him by him self holding a[n] M-79 with ammo all over him. This one I gave him. He says he goes to school. He knows all the raido [radio] freeks [frequencies] and can talk over one fairly well so when he is in the track you've got to keep an eye on him else he call up some one."

On September 20, Pvt. 1st Class David E. Gossard, a cook in C Troop, got up before dawn to make breakfast and was killed when his field stove exploded, engulfing him in flames. Gossard was listed as a non-hostile casualty: apparently, vaporized gasoline had been ignited when he fired up the burners. The troops, however, suspected that one of the locals hired to fill sandbags and burn latrine waste at Hill 54 had slipped a grenade into a fuel can in the mess tent, the idea being that the gasoline would eventually dissolve the rubber band used by the saboteur to hold down the safety spoon after pulling the pin.

Incident by incident, the hearts of the dragoons hardened. Max Pryor's scout section came under fire while securing a bridge one night late that month. Pryor returned the fire, either killing the sniper or putting him to flight. "I also shot hell out of a little village about 1000 yrds from where the shots came from," he wrote. "I figured they probely [sic] knew who it was that shot at us. I don't know if I hit anyone their [sic] or not . . . I'll tell you one thing[,] that village I shot at last night ain't the same today. I put 100 round[s] of 50 Cal in it."

Finally, Solid Contact

SEPTEMBER 24–30, 1967

CAPTAIN STALEY TOOK THE 2nd and 3rd Platoons of B Troop when sent into an area nine klicks west of Fat City known as Dink Valley. Staley was to join in the valley a certain Company C of the 196th Light Infantry Brigade. The dragoons had operated with these grunts before and found them wanting. They did not put out flank security. They did not dig in at night. Their noise and light discipline was atrocious. They were really no different than a lot of eleven-bravo draftees who'd lost their edge due to inaction and fatigue, but to highly motivated armored cavalrymen less than a month in the field, these grunts seemed to be shuffling along in search of disaster.

Captain Staley's force, minus its tanks, which could not have negotiated the terrain, pushed south into the valley, pausing along the way to medevac a booby-trap casualty. Moving on, the 2nd Platoon, under 2nd Lt. Ronald Peeler (a pseudonym), discovered a guerrilla base camp. Charlie Company, meanwhile, choppered into Dink Valley and, after establishing its night defensive position, took carbine and AK-47 fire from a squad of VC.

The next morning, the grunts fired on someone watching them from a tree. The figure dropped to the ground, but a patrol found nothing. The grunts and cavalrymen spent that day and the next working the ridges to either side of the valley. The patrols, harassed by snipers—one cavalryman suffered a gunshot wound—happened upon tunnels, spider holes, and hootches, around which chickens pecked and in which were stored rice, potatoes, dried fruit, tomatoes, salt, nuts, bunches of bananas, plus bags of tea and jugs of rainwater. Also captured: a flashlight, mosquito nets, garden tools, and bamboo ladders.

Lieutenant Dickens advanced on the hillside from which his platoon had taken carbine fire to find a still-smoldering campfire and two tripwires stretched across a trail. Each led to a grenade whose pin had been pulled before being slipped into a beer can with the top removed: tug a tripwire, and a grenade would pop from its can, releasing the safety spoon. Continuing after the snipers, the dragoons found a blood trail. Their tracks, however, could not make it to the top of the ridges along which the enemy moved. Running out of daylight, the cavalrymen retired to the low ground to set up laagers from which the mortar tracks fired H&I along the ridgelines.

Captain Staley received an urgent call on September 27, the fourth day of the mission, to ride to the rescue of Charlie Company, which had run into a hornet's nest. Staley's two-platoon force was rearming and refueling at that time, ammo and fuel bladders having been delivered by helicopter. The refueling site was under sniper fire, "but it was coming from some distance away and was more of a nuisance than a threat," writes Dickens. "In fact, I'm not sure we even realized we were being shot at until we heard a couple of rounds impact vehicles!"

Lieutenant Dickens' people, refueled and ready to go, took off at top speed, covering the fifteen hundred meters to Charlie Company in a matter of minutes. Staley tagged along with several topped-off 2nd Platoon tracks, leaving Lieutenant Peeler to catch up once he had finished refueling all his vehicles. Staley and Dickens took fire from a wooded ridge on their left before turning through a saddle in the ridge and breaking out into a large rice paddy flanked on either side by more high ground. The lead platoon of Charlie Company was pinned behind the paddy dikes, having walked into an ambush. "It was difficult to see where the infantrymen were because they were all down as low as they could get, and didn't seem to be returning much fire," recounts Dickens. The enemy was firing from both ridges. Staley veered to the right with his group, Dickens to the left. Hugging the trees at the base of the ridge to avoid running over any grunts, Dickens ordered his platoon to turn toward the VC and commence firing once the tracks were fully stretched out between the enemy and the infantry. Dickens, standing in the cargo hatch of his track, spotted a guerrilla manning a drum-fed RPD light machine gun. The gung-ho platoon leader loved hand grenades and always had a sandbagful within easy reach; he pitched one now but was so adrenaline-charged as to overthrow the Việt Cộng by thirty feet—"and then something else diverted me, and when I looked back, he was gone. I don't know whether somebody ate him up with a machine gun or what."

Lieutenant Peeler arrived to engage the enemy on the right flank. Several rounds thumped into the side of Staff Sergeant Hammerbeck's track, peppering him with fragments. Hammerbeck swung his .50 about and, "hitting the butterflies"—that is, depressing with his thumbs the butterfly-shaped trigger between the wooden handles in his fists—blasted the sniper out of the treetop perch. Peeler ordered him to cease fire, screaming that he was firing on the infantry. He wasn't. Peeler was disoriented, was, in fact, coming unglued. "Peeler wasn't a bad guy, but he was not a cav officer," notes Hammerbeck. "He didn't know what he was doing. He tried to get us killed that day."

Captain Staley instructed Lieutenants Dickens and Peeler to mark their positions for an impending air strike. To avoid any confusion, Dickens said he would instead mark the *enemy* position. The command track roared up the ridge, commander and gunners firing. Dickens shouted to halt and threw a red smoke grenade, but as the driver started backward, a guerrilla appeared from the dust and smoke that carpeted the ridge to throw a grenade of his own at the track. It bounced inside through the cargo hatch. Fortuitously, the grenade was a weak, potato-masher type, probably homemade, and Dickens was merely stung with little bits of shrapnel where not protected by his helmet and flak jacket. The left-gunner, wounded and stunned, let go of his machine gun, but Dickens immediately grabbed the weapon, leveled it on the guerrilla, and cut him down even as the track continued bouncing backward down the ridge.

Target marked, two jet fighters took turns punishing the ridge with automatic cannons and high-drag bombs. Gunships also flocked to the scene, and with the attendant pause in the enemy fire, Lieutenant Dickens looked back to realize that none of the grunts they'd come to rescue were moving to the cover of his tracks. Dickens dismounted and joined Mike Esmond, the platoon medic, who had already jumped from the command track to treat the wounded. "We had to physically get the infantrymen up and shove them towards the ACAVs," remembers Dickens. "They were completely out of it."

Captain Staley, who'd caught a bit of shrapnel, ordered 3rd Platoon after the retreating enemy. Lieutenant Dickens' boys pursued with gusto, switching on the police sirens wired to the front of the tracks—the platoon leader had previously obtained them from his father, a state trooper—as they roared down the valley in hot pursuit. Unexpectedly, a VC fired an RPG, or rocket-propelled grenade, into one of the tracks. The vehicle, damaged, came to a halt, and Esmond again grabbed his aid bag and rushed to help the next batch of wounded. The medic was running back when the guerrilla popped back up with the reloaded launcher on his shoulder. Dickens screamed to hit the dirt, and Esmond did so just as the second RPG exploded behind him, splattering his legs and buttocks with white-hot shrapnel. The VC was blasted into rags in the next instant by Dickens and every other cavalryman who had a clear shot. For moving so freely through the enemy fire to reach their casualties, Esmond, medevacked after contact was lost, was subsequently awarded the squadron's first Silver Star.

The infantry battalion commander running the show from his helicopter gave the word to check the area thoroughly: "Should be a good body count."

Actually, only a bloody shirt was found, along with ten sullen women and children. The cavalrymen burned one of their hootches after taking sniper fire from the very area in which the people had been discovered.

The hootch exploded, ammo having been hidden in the thatch.

Lieutenant Dickens moved into the hills east of the valley on September 28 and was passing through a clearing when one of his troopers was grazed across the skull by a single sniper shot. The casualty, in shock and bleeding badly, was rushed back to a larger clearing that would accommodate a medevac, two other tracks tagging along to provide security. Major Saint, meanwhile, told Staley to reinforce Charlie Company, in contact to the west, whereupon Dickens moved out with his three remaining tracks. Topping a rise, the tracks entered a cleared area under the canopy: figures darted frantically about, and Dickens realized that they'd busted right into an enemy base camp. The cavalrymen fired into the jungle after the VC while Saint got on the artillery net to call in blocking fire. While securing the base camp, the leader of Dickens' infantry squad was about to frag a hole—that is, toss in a fragmentation grenade—when an old woman popped up with her hands held high, and seventeen women and kids emerged from an underground bomb shelter. Seeing their family members, the guerrillas out in the jungle ceased fire. The detached tracks rejoined Dickens after the casualty was medevacked, whereupon the platoon destroyed the hootches, tunnels, and punji stakes in the base camp, and reported a body count after the dismembered remains of a guerrilla were unearthed from a fresh grave covered with leaves.

The platoon was finally moving out of the area with the detainees packed aboard a couple of tracks when the enemy in the hills opened fire again. Lieutenant Dickens knelt on the back deck of his track, radio handset in his fist as he gave the word to return fire. Looking over his left shoulder to the two tracks closest to his own, he pointed with the map in his left hand to where he thought the enemy fire was coming—and then, suddenly, he was hit by a sledgehammer, spun around, and left gulping for air, the wind knocked out of him. His left-gunner having previously been medevacked, the GI manning the M60 was actually an army photographer sent out that morning to get some good action shots of the operation. The photographer stared for a moment with eyes as big as saucers and then hauled Dickens down inside the vehicle. Sitting against the hull, Dickens gasped, "I'm shot in the lungs—lay me down, lay me down!"

Finally catching his breath, Dickens realized that he did not have the sucking chest wound he feared. Instead, a bullet had struck his left shoulder blade and zipped down his outstretched arm to exit above his elbow.

The photographer pressed a bandage against the wound to slow the bleeding, while the track driver used the lieutenant's line number as he cried for help: "Double-oh-deuce's been shot! Call a dust-off, call a dust-off!"

Forcing himself to calm down, Dickens physically grabbed the handset away from his overly excited driver. Informing the platoon that he was still functioning, he began giving directions to his men only to be interrupted by one of the officers from one of the battalion, squadron, brigade, and division C&Cs orbiting the battlefield. The officer wanted a status report. "This is Bandit 3-6," Dickens barked. "Some motherfucker just shot me—now get off my damn net!"

Captain Staley had secured a landing zone with Peeler's platoon, and Dickens was soon loaded onto a medevac. The enemy dropped in two mortar rounds just as the Huey lifted off, caring not about the Red Cross painted on the nose of the helicopter or the fact that medevacs had no door gunners in recognition of their life-saving role. The helicopter's oil lines were damaged, and the pilots quickly realized that they weren't going to make it back to Chu Lai.

Flat on his back and out of it, Dickens didn't know they were in trouble until the medic bandaging his wound leaned over and calmly shouted in his ear over the roar of the wind in the open cargo bay: "Sir, I hate to tell you this, but we got hit coming out of the LZ, and we're gonna have to crash land!"

I don't need to know this, thought Dickens, wanting only to lie still with his eyes closed, quietly breathing. *Why in the hell are you telling me this? There's not a damn thing I can do about it!* Making it to the next valley beyond the battle area, the pilot skillfully auto-rotated into a clearing, and all aboard were rescued moments later when another helicopter landed near the downed medevac.

Captain Staley's force continued shooting up the hillside as the top and rear of the ridge was worked with mortar and artillery fire, and helicopters landed to deliver ammunition. There was apparently some miscommunication regarding the flight paths the helicopters should use to avoid the firepower, and one of the resupply Hueys, blown out of the sky by a U.S. mortar round, crashed on the LZ. "I think the hills are crawling with VC," Staley warned Major Saint during a lull, as recorded in the squadron log. "They know we can't get to them."

The detainees and crew of the resupply ship were evacuated, then the chopper itself was lifted out under a CH-47 Chinook. The enemy resumed firing, but jet fighters arrived on cue, dropping bombs, one of which produced a satisfying secondary explosion. The grunts and cavalrymen ran out of daylight before getting set up for the night, and it was going on midnight before they managed to link up for their mutual protection. Several tracks had gotten stuck along the way, and two, which refused to budge after tow cables were hooked up, were left a hundred meters outside the perimeter. Three other tracks provided security, and H&I fires thundered all night to keep the enemy away.

The raid declared done, the grunts were lifted out the next day. B Troop spent a final night in the area, during which an error in reporting its position resulted in the outfit being shelled by the artillery battery putting a protective ring of fire around the laager. Late the next morning, September 30, an enemy sniper having popped off a few last rounds, B Troop departed Dink Valley. The men of Bravo Troop had performed well in their first significant encounter with the Việt Cộng. They credited their success to their grueling training program, and all talk of shooting their seemingly power-mad troop commander ceased then and there. Captain Staley had provided calm, decisive, and up-front leadership during the mission and, like Lieutenant Dickens, would be decorated with the Silver Star.

Not that Captain Staley did not continue to be a brutal taskmaster. Alerted by his noncoms that the thoroughly decent and likable 2nd Platoon leader, Lieutenant Peeler, had alternately frozen up and freaked out during the battle, Staley relieved the lieutenant of command. And when Staley discovered that Lieutenant Lindsey and his boys had painted slogans on their tracks while the rest of the troop had been fighting in Dink Valley, he saw red. "You haven't done shit!" Staley roared at Lindsey. "You haven't killed anybody, and until you do, you don't have the right to fuck around with your tracks. Get that shit off right now!"

Task Force Oregon was renamed the Americal Division on September 25. Major General Samuel W. Koster assumed command in October. The original Americal—technically, the 23rd Infantry Division—had been raised a year after Pearl Harbor from units on New Caledonia. Its name was formed by combining the words America *and* Caledonia, *and its shoulder patch—four white stars on a blue shield—represented the Southern Cross that graced the skies above the South Pacific. The Americal went into battle alongside the marines on Guadalcanal, fought next on Bougainville and in the Philippines, and was deactivated after occupation duty in Japan. The Army reactivated the division because Task Force Oregon's ad hoc organization had revisited that of the original Americal, as had its relationship with the U.S. Marine Corps.*

Cigar Island

OCTOBER 7–13, 1967

MAJOR SAINT BRIEFED CAPTAIN Conrad on the mission with which A Troop had been tasked: a precursor of bigger things to come, it involved a long and generally narrow strip of land along the coast known as Cigar Island. It doesn't resemble a cigar on a map, but rather an elongated funnel, seven kilometers wide at the top and stretching some seventy kilometers southeast until finally tapering to a thin and bony finger that points to Chu Lai. Separated from the mainland by a river, the Trường Giang, this landform does not read as an island to the Vietnamese, so they have no name for it. Although it looked like a tropical paradise of white sand and picture-postcard fishing villages, Saint warned Conrad that Cigar Island was sown with booby traps, honeycombed with tunnels and bunkers, and populated by villagers loyal to the VC.

Captain Conrad, Lieutenant Donaldson, and the 2nd and 3rd Platoons of A Troop, minus the tanks, were ferried two tracks at a time by landing craft from Chu Lai to the southeastern tip of Cigar Island. The movement took all day, and it was not until dusk that Conrad linked up, as planned, with a detachment of marine amtracs and militia troops known as Ruff Puffs. In the morning, as a light rain fell, the combined force began rolling up the length of the island. The fishing villages searched along the way were mostly deserted. "The people around here are hiding because they are afraid of us," reported Conrad, as noted in the squadron log. One group of women, children, and old men offered that four VC had indeed been in their village that very morning but had since departed. Saint asked how the Ruff Puffs were doing. "Real good," said Conrad; they were "good searchers" and "seem to be enjoying themselves."

Four mines were found and destroyed about ten klicks into the sweep. The Ruff Puffs pointed to a boat in the next village that was longer and heavier than the others lined up along the beach. Unusually, there was a military-age male among the villagers, and he claimed the boat as his own. The Ruff Puffs, however, were of the opinion that the twenty-foot craft was not a fishing boat. Accordingly, they blew it up. The villagers interrogated by the Ruff Puffs agreed that, yes, the boat *did* belong to the VC. By then, the man had disappeared. He was spotted running in the distance and brought down with a burst of .50-cal fire. Shot twice in the legs, the man was captured, along with a pack containing a camouflage shirt. Smoke was popped and a medevac brought in, not only for the prisoner, but also a child accidentally shot in the head.

The sweep continued as heavy rains and fifty-knot winds swept across the island, cutting visibility to a hundred and fifty meters. The 3rd Platoon came under sniper fire, and one of its tracks hit a tripwire connected to a booby-trapped 175mm artillery shell. No explosion. The marines on one of the amtracs were not so fortunate: running over a mine that blew off a tread, they had to medevac a crewman who'd been badly burned along the side of the face—an ongoing human cost of gasoline-powered combat vehicles. Fortunately, all the 1-1 Cav's tanks and tracks, except for the M88s, were diesels.

Lieutenant Donaldson, atop the troop's VTR, which had fallen behind but now roared across the sand to rejoin the sweep, announced his arrival with a touch of humor: "On your left, the Desert Fox!"

The VTR ran over another mine at that moment. "Fox, are you okay?" asked Conrad. "Yes, but we have definitely been jacked up," replied Donaldson, who would jokingly use the call sign Chicken 5 from then on instead of Hawk 5.

The dragoons took more sniper fire during the night, and still more that next morning after rain-beaded, plastic-covered maps were consulted and the sweep continued through what seemed to be a typhoon. Numerous vehicles bogged down with mechanical problems. At some point, Lieutenant Donaldson provided a bit of comic relief when, having been cooped up inside the VTR because of the drenching rain, he finally squatted behind the vehicle to answer nature's call at the same moment Conrad called for a marking round from a warship offshore: the unexpected crack and flash in the sky saw a startled Donaldson diving back inside with trousers twisted around his ankles.

On October 10, 3rd Platoon, Alpha Troop, found another 175mm round, which had been rigged for detonation with fishing line, plus a dud 250-pound bomb, which left a crater ten feet deep when blown. The platoon medevacked a trooper wounded by the blast, then moved on to a fishing village on the ocean side of the island. Eight military-age males were rounded up, one of whom "admitted [to] working for VC for 6 years," as recorded in the squadron log. "[H]e planted numerous [sic] mines in area[,] also Propaganda Leaflets."

One of the detainees, presumably the admitted guerrilla, bolted, running into the surf and trying to swim away. An amtrac gave chase but was swamped by an overarching wave that washed three men off the top: a marine crewman, a navy corpsman, and Pvt. 1st Class George H. Winkempleck of A Troop. They all drowned. Winkempleck, a Native American from Porterville, California, had told his buddies that he would not be coming home from Việt Nam. The man's mother, believing him, had been frantic in her efforts to have her son released from duty as a sole surviving son. Actually an only son for whom there were no exceptions, Winkempleck at first went over the hill—went AWOL—but, surrendering to fate, returned shortly before the 1-1 Cavalry departed for Việt Nam.

According to the squadron log, the detainee who bolted into the sea was shot, apparently by one of the helicopters buzzing around the area. The log also indicates that two other detainees attempted to escape and were killed as well. Not exactly, says David Eady. Instead, Staff Sgt. Beverly Martin—a hot-headed ex-marine to be twice wounded and twice decorated for valor in the months ahead—forced the remaining detainees to their knees, then "walked down the line with his .45, and popped 'em in the head: *bam-bam-bam.*" John Guzik recalls Eady, and others, describing the executions upon returning to Hill 29. Eady was dismayed by the incident, thinking those shot were simple fishermen—they seemed too old to be real guerrillas—and sardonically describes the staff sergeant as the kind of tough guy "who'd take his knife out when we were back on the hill and practice tossing it at a board."

Two more days were spent searching the island, after which, mission accomplished, the two platoons were ferried back to the mainland.

On the morning of October 10, the infantry squad of 1st Platoon, Alpha Troop, back from another miserable, waterlogged ambush, went into the town adjacent to Hill 54. After entering and buying a beer, the squad leader engaged the thirteen-year-old daughter of the mamasan who owned the laundry shack in a joking conversation. The girl indicated that she would have to find a new boyfriend when the squad leader left the base camp. The squad leader raised his clipless M16, pointed it at her, and said that if she found a new boyfriend he would kill her. He pulled the trigger and the round he'd forgotten in the chamber entered her back under her right shoulder blade and blew her chest out of her body.

"The medics got there very fast but there wasn't anything they could do," wrote Graham. "[S]he was just a damned kid and there wasn't a damned thing we could do for her[.]"

The squad leader, a Mexican-American on his second tour, was devastated: the girl he killed had been such a chipper little thing that the GIs used to give her their extra C-rations when they picked up their laundry. "The MPs took the squad leader in for questioning," notes Graham; the sergeant was given a general court-martial and spent five months in the Marine stockade at Đà Nẵng. "His weapon was still loaded cause we had been on an ambush patrol last nite [sic] and he forgot to clear it. He was at fault for keeping it loaded . . . When you see so much of this blood and death shit you wonder, 'what the hell are we proving and why[?]'"

Depressed by the senseless violence and endless rain, Graham finally wrote his wife, "I don't know if I'll be able to stand it for a full 12 months."

End of the Line

OCTOBER 1967

ON OCTOBER 13, LIEUTENANT Colonel Harrington and Major Saint relocated the squadron once more, this time to double-humped Hill 29, the most forward position held by the 2/11 ACR, which returned then to its parent regiment. The 1-1 Cavalry christened its new and permanent base camp Blackhawk Hill, soon to be shortened to Hawk Hill, though some troopers never called the place anything other than Hill 29. "I thought that the other base camps were bad[,] but this one did not have anything on it what so ever," noted Tom Bursott. "It is not so bad any more, we know what we have to do and we just go ahead and do it. You know[,] like one group builds the bunkers, another builts [sic] tent[s], etc."

From the air, the base camp was a brown lump in an otherwise picturesque sea of green rice paddies, railway to the west, highway to the east. Hill 29's only neighbor was the shantytown on the access road leading to Highway 1. The headquarters personnel put up tents and constructed a half-submerged, sandbag-encased TOC (tactical operations center) atop the southernmost hill, outside of which they parked their M113s and high-backed M577s. The operations center was marked by a forest of radio masts. Two flagpoles went up at the entranceway, one for the Stars and Stripes, the other the red-and-yellow banner of the Republic of Việt Nam. The sign mounted in between featured an inscription meant

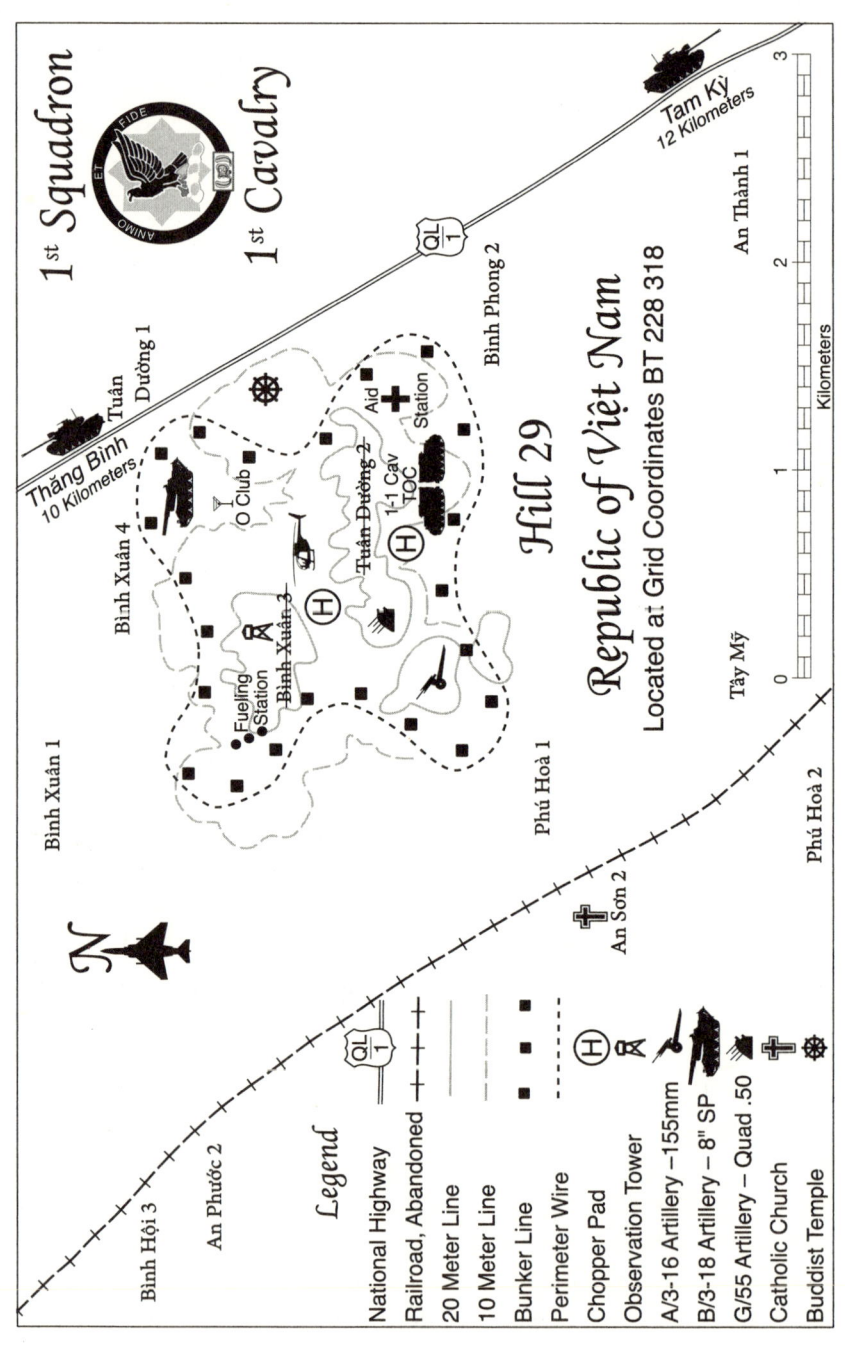

to let replacements and visitors know what the unit was all about. The inscription blazed red on a field of cavalry yellow:

> The U.S. Army's most battle honored unit
>
> FIRST
> SQUADRON
> FIRST CAVALRY
> ORGANIZED
> 1833
> AS THE
> UNITED STATES
> REGIMENT OF DRAGOONS

The perimeter wire was mostly for show. The dragoons immediately went to work with sledgehammers, engineer stakes, and spools of concertina wire. Five days later, Graham wrote that they'd "strung more than 12 miles of barbed wire (3 strands) around the perimeter, now we can sleep better (safer)."

The perimeter bunkers were manned during the day by headquarters personnel. When the line platoons returned at dusk from that day's mission, their tanks and tracks pulled into position on the perimeter. The crew of each vehicle, meanwhile, constructed a timber-sandbag-and-ammo-crate bunker, weatherproofed with tarpaper, in which to drink, play cards, read mail, and write letters by candlelight. Platoon Sergeant Boyd excavated the bunkers with a bulldozer previously found upside down and half submerged under a bridge being built by Navy Seabees. Boyd towed the bulldozer back to base behind his tank and tasked a trooper in his platoon, previously employed by the Caterpillar Tractor Company in Peoria, Illinois, to get it up and running. Soon thereafter, a party of Seabees arrived by jeep to retrieve the bulldozer. There was a tank undergoing repairs in the motor pool at the time, and when its commander got Boyd on the horn, the platoon sergeant gave him his orders: "You load that goddamn ninety-millimeter up and tell 'em they ain't takin' that dozer."

The dragoons discovered upon moving onto Hill 29 that a colony of rats lived under a big pile of concertina wire left by the 2/11 ACR. The rats were completely unafraid of people. "One afternoon, a wrecker moved all the wire, and we were left with this barren area full of rat holes," notes Chuck Donaldson. "Some enterprising soul decided to bring up the gasoline tanker. Large quantities of gas were poured down the holes and the whole thing was touched off. Following a loud but contained explosion, the rats began to emerge. Some were already on fire, while others, soaked in gasoline, caught fire on exit. What followed could only be described as both funny and macabre as soldiers chased flaming rats all over the top of the hill, killing them with shovels."

The squadron was supported by C Troop of the 7-17 Cav of the 1st Aviation Brigade, which sent a team of scouts and gunships each morning to Hill 29. The scout pilots flew nimble little light observation helicopters, egg-shaped and nicknamed Loaches. They screened the front and flanks of the ground units by buzzing low along tree lines, trying to draw fire. If they did, the Huey gunships, orbiting on high, would pounce. The dragoons much appreciated the Blue Ghosts, as the aviators were known (after their call sign), and would cheer passing Loaches from their M48s and ACAVs.

The dragoons came under sniper fire often in their new area of operations. They returned the fire, sometimes flushing the sniper, who was then pursued in coordination with the Blue Ghosts. Sometimes the snipers vanished, sometimes not: during one early patrol, B Troop pursued two guerrillas into a bunker, which they then blew up. During another patrol, two more VC who fired on B Troop were spotted as they made their getaway and brought down with M79 fire. One was captured, the other medevacked with a missing arm and a leg hanging by a strand. At the end of one sniper-plagued day, B Troop and its supporting gunships reported a body count of nine, including one guerrilla in whose pockets were discovered papers identifying him as a platoon leader.

The dragoons also searched the little hamlets on the high ground west of Hawk Hill. "It is kind of funny when you go into a village and there is nothing but old men, women, and children[,] and [yet] there is enough rice to feed a regiment," wrote Tom Bursott. The cavalrymen presumed the absent males to be guerrillas, the rest members of the communist infrastructure. "We've gone on 4 missions from this new base camp and the hunting is great," wrote Larry Graham. "We've found 5 V.C. villages and burned or confiscated over 4,000 [pounds] of V.C. rice." He added that they also shot the villagers' chickens, pigs, and water buffalo: "It seems cruel and it used to bother me[,] but they are feeding 'Charlie' and [Charlie is] shooting at us[,] so it evens out."

The Real Face of War

OCTOBER 20–NOVEMBER 1, 1967

*O*N OCTOBER 15, *A sky full of helicopters announced the arrival of the 3rd Brigade of the famed 1st Air Cavalry Division. The brigade established its command post at LZ Baldy, an artillery firebase fifteen kilometers up the road from Hill 29 at the intersection of Highway 1 and Route 535, which led southwest into the Quế Sơn Valley. The brigade, bringing with it an air-cavalry troop (B/1-9) and three battalions of airmobile infantry (the 1-7, 5-7 and 2-12 Cavalry), was placed under the operational control (opcon) of the Americal Division. In turn, the 1-1 Cavalry was tasked to support the airmobile brigade's thrust into the enemy-controlled Quế Sơn Valley and its clearing of Cigar Island. The ambitious campaign was codenamed Operation Wallowa.*

From the letter Tom Bursott wrote after A Troop joined the airmobile infantry in battle on October 20: "Yesterday I saw the real face of war and what I saw I pray to god [that] nobody in our family ever [has] to see." What had Bursott seen? For one, a hungry pig rooting in the chest cavity of a dead enemy soldier. More bodies were scattered across the sand dunes just short of the hamlet to which the enemy had attempted to flee when caught in the open by gunships. Those slain included not only guerrillas, but NVA, the first the dragoons had ever encountered, who wore web gear and khaki fatigues, and who were equipped with brand-new AK-47s and

RPGs. These men died a few helicopter minutes from LZ Baldy, near the Bàu Bàng between Highway 1 and the Trường Giang.

Captain Conrad and A Troop pursued the enemy with the 1st of the 7th Cav. The track on which Lieutenant Donaldson rode hit a mine during the running firefight. Donaldson was blown overboard, his commo helmet yanked from his head when it reached the end of its cord. Alpha Troop laagered at dusk. Several rounds cracked through the gloom, and Larry Graham spotted the sniper as he turned to run from the tree that had shielded him. "I got him in the back with my M79," Graham reported. "It really got him good. I hope I don't sound too blood thirsty, but this is our first big operation and he was sure trying to nail our assess . . . We killed a total of 31 V.C. (some were HARDCORE NORTH VIET Regulars) at last count . . . [W]e'll probably make the news with this."

Captain Conrad was amazed that the pursuit of the enemy did not begin the next morning until after the grunts had been provided a hot breakfast. Packed in insulated mermite cans, the meal was delivered by resupply helicopters, one of the perks of soldiering with the 1st Air Cavalry Division. Breakfast finished, the 1st of the 7th air assaulted onto Cigar Island. Conrad followed with A Troop, minus tanks, which would have been unable to ford the Trường Giang. The M113 was designed to float, and when crossing a blue line, the wooden trim vane on the front slope of the vehicle—also known as a splash board and painted olive-drab like everything else—was deployed to push the water to either side. Still, a combat-loaded ACAV "rode so low in the water," recalls Rich Rensi, "that it wouldn't have took but a half-inch of wave to flood them suckers."

The sweep began, the grunts on line across the island, the armored cavalry in line on the right flank. "[W]e rode on the beach about 20 ft from the surf," wrote Larry Graham. The weather was warm and sunny, the ocean inviting. "It really reminded me of home with the waves coming in and the salt air," continued Graham. "It was nice til 'Charlie' tore us up in an ambush."

Enemy soldiers ran up a low ridge to disappear on the other side. First Lieutenant Richard A. Haeme and the 2nd Platoon roared after them and right into the ambush: topping the embankment, the lead track was hit in the .50 shield by a rocket-propelled grenade that devastated the crew in a blaze of shrapnel. The rest of the platoon moved up the ridge to confront a lushly vegetated hamlet that stretched along the base of the next rise in the gently rolling terrain. The enemy were entrenched on the opposing high ground, and during the exchange of fire, Haeme was temporarily blinded by another RPG.

Captain Conrad had the 1st Platoon secure the rear, while the 3rd Platoon, under 2nd Lt. George N. Wallace III, hit the enemy's flank. Wallace was wounded in the process, probably by one of the RPGs shrieking downhill through the scrub pines growing along the ridge. One of Wallace's troopers was killed, wrote Larry Graham, when he "got off his track with [his M16 and] only 34 rounds [two magazines] instead of the normal 180 [ten magazines] and the gooks just waited til he ran out of ammo and [then] walked over and shot him."

Having lost two platoon leaders in fifteen minutes, Captain Conrad pulled his people back to regroup. Platoon Sergeant Boyd arrived on the scene then, having demanded that a helicopter pick up the outfit's platoon sergeants from where they sat with their tank sections on the quiet side of the Trường Giang. Listening to the engagement on the radio, these platoon sergeants had been frantic to rejoin their men. "I figured that's where in the hell we belonged. We'd trained those kids," states Boyd. "They left us behind, then got into a helluva firefight and got people killed," he continues. "They needed their NCOs. You've got to understand, the lieutenants out there, and the troop commander, they're green. They're good men, don't get me wrong, but training isn't like combat, and they really didn't know what they were getting into or what the hell they were doing yet. Only me and one other sergeant had combat experience from Korea."

Boyd accompanied Conrad on the command track, which moved to the disabled vehicle atop the embankment. They inspected the damage "while more or less under fire," as Conrad later put it, and determined that the disabled track could be driven out under its own power. The engine was still running. Unfortunately, the driver was still in his compartment, arm missing at the shoulder. Boyd ducked through the back hatch, dragged the unconscious trooper out of his seat, and got a pressure bandage in place. Then, taking the driver's place, he put the vehicle in gear and spun around to rejoin the troop. "I called 'em on the way in," recounts Boyd. "I told 'em to get dust-off 'cause the guy was pretty close. It was too late, though. He died. He'd lost too much blood."

Unable to get artillery support, Captain Conrad put his mortar squads into action and then ordered the tracks forward again. The second assault was greeted with more fire, and after one of the tracks took a recoilless-rifle round, Conrad pulled back again, his own track remaining in place to provide covering fire. Belatedly, artillery began exploding along the ridge. Medevacs touched down. Gunships unleashed salvos of rockets. Snipers fired from the rear, and the occasional mortar round burst among the sand dunes. "If you saw a muzzle flash, you'd shoot at it," recalls former track commander Rich Rensi. "If you saw what you thought was a flash from a mortar, you'd shoot at that, too."

The evening ended with the arrival of reinforcements, resupply, and air strikes. Come daylight, a sweep of the battlefield revealed three weapons and twelve enemy bodies. Against that, A Troop lost four KIA and seventeen WIA: killed and wounded by hostile action. To wit, another victory, rewarded in this case with Bronze Stars for Captain Conrad, Lieutenant Haeme, Platoon Sergeant Boyd, and others. One of those killed had gotten a letter from his wife the night before, informing him that she was pregnant. "I remember sitting on his track, talking to him about the letter," says ex-medic Larry L. Gaydon. "He was so excited that his wife was going to have a baby."

Having fled when the shooting started, the local villagers returned before the sweep was even finished, confirmation that the enemy had truly departed the scene. Later, a helicopter delivered to Captain Conrad a gaggle of reporters, one of whom, a television celebrity, wanted the troop to recreate the battle for the benefit of his camera crew by charging up the hill one more time and commencing fire. Alpha Troop rolled down the beach at the end of the day, leaving a double line of tread marks in the sand parallel to those made on the way in the day before. It was prudent to avoid old tread marks for fear that the enemy might plant a mine in them on the assumption that the Americans, having cleared a safe route, might use it again. As it turned out, the enemy *had* planted a mine, but having played it smart, the cavalrymen were able to spot and destroy it in place rather then run over it. There was little else about the mission to feel good about, as Larry Graham wrote home: "We lost quite a few guys for the few that we got."

§

Captain Staley of B Troop listened on the tactical net the next day, October 23, as a company from the 5th of the 7th Cav was ambushed on the west side of the Trường Giang. The radio traffic was desperate, and Staley didn't wait for orders before heading toward the sound of the guns. The infantry had pulled back by the time Bravo Troop arrived: unbelievably, fifteen grunts had been killed, including a lieutenant. Their bodies still lay where they had fallen.

Staley had his binoculars out. Those enemy positions that could be identified were marked with tracers for B Troop of the 1-9 Cav. "The gunships did a job on 'em," says Staley. "They just took those tree lines *out*."

Lieutenant Lindsey's platoon advanced with Staley and rescued several wounded grunts. They also recovered the dead, some of whom had been stripped by the enemy of their weapons, ammo, and jungle boots. "The most shocking thing is not seeing dinks," says Lindsey, "but seeing dead Americans lying on the ground as you go by 'em. That will tighten you up."

After laagering up for the night, Captain Staley put one of his gunners atop the dune overlooking the command track. "Next morning, this kid stood up to take a piss and noticed the sand was moving," recounts Staley. "He reached down—and there's this VC who'd been up there with him all night!" The guerrilla had been in a little burrow, breathing through a piece of bamboo. The Việt Cộng was relieved of his AK-47 and whisked away by helicopter after telling Staley's interpreter that he was part of a hundred-man company equipped with a mortar, recoilless-rifle, and two rocket-propelled grenade launchers. From the squadron log: "[The prisoner's] instructions were to stay behind & snipe. [His] unit is planning to move back a[f]ter we went through area."

The enemy, thought to be operating in battalion strength, ambushed and badly hurt the 1st of the 7th on October 24. Afterward, as best could be determined by aerial reconnaissance, the enemy moved to the upper and wider part of Cigar Island. Major Saint wanted to go after them with tanks, but requests for self-propelled bridge tanks went unheeded at division. Fortuitously, Captain Staley found a relatively shallow tidal inlet, and there the dragoons assembled at the crack of dawn on October 27. The plan for a hammer-and-anvil operation was hastily developed around the crossing point: after A and B Troops forded the Trường Giang and assumed blocking positions, the 1-7 Cavalry would land en masse and begin pressing toward the 1-1 Cavalry.

Staley determined a certain zigzag pattern the tanks needed to follow to avoid the deeper parts of the inlet and so informed A Troop, which was to lead the way across. The crossing was nevertheless a disaster, notes Staley: "They didn't follow our instructions, and they lost all their tanks in the channel."

Staff Sergeant Bouche had the impression that the commander of top-rated A Troop had been unwilling to listen to the black sheep of Bravo Troop. As a result, Captain Conrad's tanks sat helpless in the river, engines flooded. Bouche recalls Staley viewing the scene with a half-amused, half-disgusted grimace, and swears that one tank was totally submerged: "All you could see were the antennas. Tanks don't swim like the tracks. They sink real good, but they don't swim."

Captain Staley got all his tanks across the river—then lost all but two in the mud on the other shore. Conrad and Staley left their execs, Donaldson and Taylor, and their VTRs, to deal with the mess as Major Saint urged them on from the command ship in which he rode with Harrington. Saint put Staley in the lead because he still had those two tanks, and after the scout tracks found a good route through the sand dunes, B Troop pressed northeast to the ocean, then turned left and started up the beach. A Troop followed. Lieutenant Norton, an assistant operations officer, brought up the rear with two M113s and two M577s, a mobile command post from Headquarters Troop.

Eight klicks up the beach, the dragoons wheeled through a break in the dunes on their left flank and deployed across the flatlands so to face the slightly elevated fishing villages of Hà Tây and Bình Yên. Hà Tây sat against the ocean, Bình Yên to its west. At that point, the 1st of the 7th Cav air-assaulted into position north and west of the objective. The dragoons watched, impressed, as the infantrymen rode in on the skids of the Hueys and, alighting onto the sand, fanned out with well-practiced precision and advanced toward the brush and pines covering the village area. The enemy was waiting, and the grunts—nine of whom were killed—went to earth in front of bunkers all but impossible to see and returned fire, M16s, M60s, and M79s against AK-47s and RPDs.

Major Saint instructed Staley to advance on Hà Tây. Staley lost a tank when its drive sprocket broke while climbing a dune, leaving B Troop with a single M48. The line pressed on across the sand. The ambulance track in the center of the line, whose .50-cal and M60s belied the Red Cross painted on either side, suddenly took a smoke-trailing RPG from Hà Tây. Staley had eight medics, one with each platoon and five on the ambulance track. Three of them were badly wounded, if not in the initial blast then by the next RPG that slammed into their stalled and smoking vehicle. Meanwhile, the dismounted infantrymen scouting to the front of 3rd Platoon, now commanded by 1st Lt. William L. Wheeler, came under fire upon reaching the fringe of the fishing village. One of the infantrymen was shot in the stomach. "His buddy takes off running after him, and they nail him in the head, and he goes down, too," recounts Mike Esmond. "They shot the first guy again, and he's out there screamin'—and I'm the medic. I start crawling forward, and I'm taking rounds all around. I get up to sprint out to them, and this big black sergeant cracked me in the ankles with his M16 and knocked me to the ground." The sergeant told Esmond to stay down: "Those guys are just waitin' to blow you away!"

There was much excited chatter on the troop net as the line stopped in place and began returning fire. Captain Staley got on the horn: "This is Bravo 6, and I want to talk." Instant silence. Under Staley's direction, the enemy to the front was engaged while those who tried to get behind B Troop were driven back with short, controlled bursts. Fire nevertheless cracked from the rear, any number of spider holes having apparently been bypassed amid the brush and pines. Major Saint finally contacted Staley: "Are you aware of your situation?"

"In regards to what?"

"You are completely surrounded."

"That's affirmative," replied a laconic Staley. "Now I've got 'em where I want 'em. I can't help but shoot and hit 'em now."

Captain Staley instructed 2nd Platoon, now commanded by 2nd Lt. Raymond H. Mahoy, to silence a particular hootch with its one remaining tank. The driver literally rolled over the structure and ground it into the sand. An enemy soldier took the tank on with his AK-47. The turret traversed to train the 90mm main gun on the VC, who evaporated in the blast of a canister round and who, it was later speculated, must have been stoned to stand up and bounce bullets off a buttoned-up M48A3 medium tank.

Major Saint brought Conrad up on Staley's left flank, and A Troop engaged a platoon-sized force in Bình Yên. The cavalrymen were supported by artillery, gunships, and tactical air. Harrington and Saint marked targets with smoke grenades and fired on enemy soldiers from the door of their Huey. Captain Staley, meanwhile, rushed his wounded medics to the medevac point established by Lieutenant Norton's group from squadron headquarters. Lieutenant Wheeler also evacuated his two shot-up infantry troopers. "We put enough fire into that area that we were able to pull both of them back," recounts Mike Esmond. "The one guy, he was already dead. The other we loaded on a medevac chopper, but he didn't make it. They were the first guys to be killed in Bravo Troop."

Fire superiority having been gained, Captain Staley, Staff Sgt. Kenneth B. French, and Spc. 4th Class James Chamberlain dismounted and closed with the enemy, for which all received the Silver Star. According to the troop commander's citation, he fragged two bunkers and killed four NVA. Did he really do what he was cited for? "Something like that," he shrugs. In the process, Staley picked up multiple fragment wounds from an explosion of unknown origin. French eliminated several of the enemy before being wounded himself. Chamberlain silenced a bunker with his M16 and, ignoring a flesh wound, ran back to his track, tossed aside his empty rifle, and returned to the fray with an M60. He was credited with destroying two more positions and killing numerous NVA. Staley knew Chamberlain as a particularly alert and mature young soldier but could not have guessed that the kid would prove so nerveless in close combat. "Chamberlain was literally going along the tree line, and pulling these guys out of their spider holes." Chamberlain was finally put out of action when a grenade exploded at his feet. The sand absorbed much of the shrapnel, but "he was hurt, he was going home," notes Staley. "We took him back in my track to where the medevac ships were coming in."

The fighting sputtered out after dark. Staley reported a thirty-eight body count, plus ten prisoners. Before returning to base, Harrington dropped Saint off at Norton's medevac point, which had also become a resupply, radio-relay, and prisoner-collection point. Major Saint ignored heavy fire to coordinate supporting fires and supervise the medevacs that landed by strobe light, according to the citation for his Silver Star. The award was good for a man's career, but the hyperbole of the citation aside, "there really wasn't much fighting going on at that point," notes Saint; in any event, "the troop commanders did all the work. All I did was go around and talk to people and pump 'em up."

Major Saint and the commander of the 1st of the 7th meant to obliterate the enemy force trapped with its back against the ocean, infantry and cavalry arrayed on the other three sides of the box. To do so, they coordinated a night of artillery and awe-inspiring naval gunfire on the plateau and on likely routes of withdrawal, though an undetected escape seemed impossible given the huge flares being jettisoned from an orbiting flareship. "The plan was to close the noose the next morning," remembers Norton, "but the next morning—*they weren't there.* They were *gone.* We'd fought until dusk with an enemy force big enough to tie down two cavalry troops and an infantry battalion, then regrouped, called in the big guns, and swept in at dawn to find—*nothing."*

The morning was spent picking through the remains of the fishing villages, collecting enemy weapons, and counting additional bodies—some of which had been booby-trapped—in the bunkers torn open by the night's bombardment. Meanwhile, repairs began on that last tank lost on the way to Hà Tây. "Replacing a broken drive sprocket is usually a factory repair," recalls Richard Sears, "but those old-time Fort Knox NCOs put a tent over the left-rear of the tank, took the tank apart, had replacement parts flown in, then worked all night on the problem. They replaced the broken drive sprocket for a new one, and at the end of the day, the tank was all buttoned back up and running like new."

Captain Staley horseshoed his tracks against the beach and, with guards behind the .50s, allowed his men some time in the surf. Afterward, enemy soldiers and military-age males rounded up by the infantry were loaded aboard the tracks and transported to an area from which they were lifted out by chopper. Depending on the mood of the troops, "a military-age male could be anyone from ten to a hundred and ten," muses Gene R. Hotchkiss. An old man was escorted to his track by two grunts, one of whom thumped the detainee and barked ominously, "Get up on that APC, or you'll get what your buddies got." Hotchkiss could not blame the grunts for their attitude. "Those infantry guys had gotten their asses kicked, and they were not in a good mood," explains Hotchkiss, who nevertheless "reached down and lifted the old man up on the track and set him between me and the other gunner there. He was shaking like a leaf. He was just some poor old fart." The prevailing attitude was that the sullen villagers on Cigar Island were de facto VC. It did not seem improper then that the detainees, like the prisoners, had sandbags placed over their heads and their hands bound tightly behind their backs. Hotchkiss wasn't so sure. He thought that most of these fishing people were simply caught in the middle: "These VC and NVA slid into their village, and then here we come along, and the enemy starts shooting, and we return fire and shoot the hell out of the village 'cause the enemy's in the village. Put your own wife and family in that situation."

Riding a tank that had been pulled from the river, Lieutenant Donaldson caught up with A Troop the next day, October 29, and accompanied a sweep, which pushed eight klicks from the bombed-out fishing villages all the way to the upper end of Cigar Island. Not a trace was found of the enemy except the mine planted in a ravine the tank used to avoid some difficult terrain. As usual, the blast had the effect of a hiccup on those sitting atop a fifty-two-ton M48.

Unfortunately, Spc. 4th Class Ralph William Plummer III, having dismounted to ground-guide the driver through the narrow passage with hand signals, had yet to climb back aboard the tank when the mine exploded, blowing off the tread and a road wheel. The wheel slammed Bill Plummer against the side of the ravine, killing him instantly. Such a random, purposeless death was hard to accept, recalls Leon Palatas: "We were really shook up because we weren't in combat, yet our buddy lost his life."

Hours later, Lieutenant Norton's group, the mobile command post from squadron, recrossed the Trường Giang. "We were new in-country—dumb, stupid—and we went back exactly the same way we'd come in," admits Norton. The enemy waited in ambush on the high side of the dry creek bed the vehicles rumbled along after fording the river. Norton and Platoon Sgt. Jessie of A Troop, too ill that day to be on his tank, sat on the front of the lead vehicle, eyes peeled for mines. There was a sudden, jolting explosion: a guerrilla had just fired an RPG into the lead track, thus initiating the ambush but, having missed the engine, not shutting the vehicle down as planned and trapping the rest in the creek bed. Norton reached for a radio handset and, getting only an earful of static—the antenna had been sheared off—exited through the rear hatch "and went running like a fool from one vehicle to another, directing fire. It was like an out-of-body experience: holy smokes, they're shooting at me! Went for my pistol. No web gear. Learned the hard way, you never take your web gear off."

Platoon Sergeant Jessie, senior man by dint of experience, if not rank, was to receive the Bronze Star for taking charge and pushing through the kill zone. "It was just blind luck we were able to shoot our way out of the ambush," says Norton. It helped that the 1st Platoon of A Troop and a mine-sweep team had been moving toward Norton at the time, clearing the route back home for the command group. Hearing the shooting, Platoon Sergeant Boyd rushed forward, "and when the platoon swung around the corner," recounts Norton, "the lead tank blew the RPG gunner away with a canister round."

Platoon Sergeant Boyd won his second Bronze Star for breaking the ambush. Getting reorganized, Lieutenant Norton requested a medevac for two men who had suffered gunshot wounds, even as a team of gunships "happened along, dropped down on our push, and asked if we could use some help. As a matter of fact, we could. They hosed out the area." The enemy left a number of bodies behind. Back at base camp, the dings in the high-backed command tracks were examined by an enthused Lieutenant Colonel Harrington. The squadron commander instructed that the bullet gouges in the aluminum go unrepaired; as a result, explains Norton, "when the vehicles were parked behind the concertina in the squadron headquarters area, visitors to the unit could see all these battle scars on the command vehicles"—and never mind that the colonel never rode on a track himself. "Hell, no," scoffs Norton. "He was never in the field."

It took six days to recover all the tanks lost during the river crossing. Captain Reed, the squadron maintenance officer, coordinated the effort, which involved some "awesome feats of engineering," notes Chuck Donaldson. "Rescue eventually required the construction of a road out to each vehicle." The crews remained on their tanks the entire time, "and we had some very wide-eyed tankers when the first high tide crept up to the base of their turret rings. They looked like hurricane victims on top of houses every time the tide came up."

Platoon Sergeant Boyd built the roads across the tidal inlet with the bulldozer previously liberated from the Seabees, working from the west side of the river.

To reach the two tanks that had nearly made it to the east side, Captain Reed brought the squadron VTR from Hill 29 across the tidal inlet to Cigar Island, reaching the recovery site on November 1. With two VTRs, Captain Reed was able to reach the disabled tanks and, using several cases of C4, blew enough mud from the front of the tanks so that the operator could reach the tow hooks by diving under the water.

The tank retriever sank its forward blade into the earth as an anchor, whereupon "the operator released the winch, ran the cable out, pulled it into the water, and swam to our tank," recounts Wayne Byrd. "Somebody had to go underwater and find the hook on our tank, and hook that cable to it, then everybody buttoned up inside the turret because you don't know if the cable's going to snap when they take up the slack and start pulling. If it hits you, it's gonna hurt you."

Pulled to shore, both tanks were then towed across one of the roads to the west side of the river. Three mortar rounds landed just short of the area as the last tank was being towed across the inlet; the enemy adjusted his fire and dropped twelve rounds right on target. "They exploded exactly where we'd been sitting," notes Byrd. "They missed us by all of fifteen minutes."

Meanwhile, Charlie Troop

OCTOBER–NOVEMBER 1967

CAPTAIN BROWN AND C Troop continued to operate in the Hill 54 AO under brigade control until October 29, at which point they moved not to Hill 29 but to an area immediately northwest of Tam Kỳ known as the Pineapple Forest. The hamlets within the forest had long been home to local-force guerrillas. The area was finally to be cleared in a joint U.S.-ARVN operation whose spirit was defined by the government officer with whom Lieutenant Norton spoke when he traveled to Tam Kỳ to establish liaison between the ARVN and the 1-1 Cavalry: pointing to the irregular green blob that represented the Pineapple Forest on his map, the officer said, "All VC. Go kill all."

The dragoons had no intention of acting so wantonly, but what was planned was rough enough: the hamlets were to be razed, and the forest itself stripped to bare earth with bulldozers. The inhabitants of the Pineapple Forest were to be moved to the resettlement villages along Highway 1. Whether these refugees would arrive with anything other than the shirts on their backs was an open question because, "man, if anyone thought the Americans were bad," muses Norton, "they should have seen the ARVN go through an area: looting, burning, taking the chickens, taking the pigs, taking everything."

The operation commenced on Halloween. Specialist Fourth Class Pryor described the first day in a letter accompanied by Polaroids: "Here are three pictures of a village we burned to the ground today. The Arvins helped us do it . . . The tanks [also] shot [a church] down[,] the V.C. hide in it[,] so we are told. Around each of these houses is a maze of tunnels," Pryor continued. "We blew meby [sic] a dozen today . . . Some one must go into [each tunnel] and look. I went down one today after I threw two hand grenards [sic] into it. Was about 30 to 40 feet long and had t[w]o side tunnels where meby [sic] two men could hide in each one. We put 8lb of C-4 into it [and] blew it up." Pryor signed off by noting, "There were people living in the homes we burnt to day. They were told to move[,] to where I don't know and don't give a dam[n]."

Into the Valley of Death

NOVEMBER 6–14, 1967

*T*HE VALLEY, SHAPED LIKE *an arrowhead, pointed southwest from the coast into the Quế Sơn Mountains in southern Quảng Nam Province, along the border with Quảng Tin Province. Cleared for farming, the valley was one of the last densely populated areas below the mountains. The paddies were emerald green, the hillsides terraced for growing rice. Towering coconut palms grew above some of the hamlets. Comparatively prosperous, the area belonged to the enemy. The villages were governed by the National Liberation Front, and their rice crops, which the guerrillas helped harvest for a share, sustained the 2nd NVA Division up in the Quế Sơns. The ARVN knew better than to intrude.*

The marines struck into the Quế Sơn Valley for the first time in November 1965. They were still fighting there nearly two years later. The place was a meat grinder. Forced to fight an old-fashioned infantry war on ground of the enemy's choosing, the marines would sometimes lose seventy or a hundred dead in a matter of days. Given the grit of the marine rifleman, the NVA paid more heavily, but the communists could better absorb such sacrifices.

In October 1967, following the departure of the marines, elements of the 3rd Brigade, 1st Air Cavalry Division; the 3rd Brigade, 4th Infantry Division; and the 1st Brigade, 101st Airborne Division began operating in the Quế Sơns under the control of the Americal Division. The most forward element, the 2-12 Cavalry of the 1st Air Cavalry Division, inherited a marine firebase fifteen kilometers down the road from LZ Baldy near the southwestern end of the valley.

Dubbed LZ Ross by its new tenants, the firebase occupied two low, rocky plateaus linked by a shallow saddle on the south side of Route 535. The road forked at LZ Ross, one branch heading northwest into the Quế Sơn Mountains, the other southwest through a notch in a ridge into the adjacent Hiệp Đức Valley.

Unaware of the foreboding history of the area, B Troop of the 1-1 Cavalry had no sooner returned from Cigar Island but it was dispatched to LZ Ross.

Lieutenant Mahoy's platoon followed a mine-sweep team out of Baldy on the morning of November 6, bound for Ross by way of Route 535. Captain Staley moved out forty minutes behind Mahoy with Lieutenants Lindsey and Wheeler, escorting a section of 8-inch self-propelled howitzers. Three hours and four klicks later, one of the guns ran over a mine that blew off a tread, wounded two artillerymen, and left them begging the question: had the engineers missed an old mine amid all the false alarms from metallic debris, or had an alert enemy taken advantage of the gap between the two elements on the road to plant a new one?

The howitzer was hooked up to a tank retriever, and Staley's executive officer, Lieutenant Taylor, supervised its return to Baldy. Two tanks went along to provide security. Mahoy's platoon continued its slow creep down the road behind the mine-sweep team and did not reach Ross until dusk, eleven hours after departing Baldy. Three more hours elapsed before Lindsey closed into Ross with those tracks that had fallen behind with mechanical problems.

It was nearly midnight when Captain Staley presented himself to Lt. Col. M. Collier Ross, commanding officer of the 2-12 Cav, and namesake of LZ Ross. Staley recalls that Ross, sitting out in front of his quarters, was very much at ease at the time: the battalion commander was wearing a smoking jacket, puffing on a pipe, and chatting with the great war photographer Catherine Leroy. Staley told Ross that his people were exhausted after the intense operations of the last month: "I'd like to get 'em a good night's sleep, and then we need to do maintenance because my tracks have really been taking a beating, too."

Lieutenant Colonel Ross, a tall, lean, and very correct West Pointer, well-respected by his own officers, listened impassively, then told Captain Staley to take as much time as he needed with his tracks but that he expected B Troop to be moving out as of oh-six-thirty to conduct operations northwest of LZ Ross. Fuming, Staley asked Ross "if I could talk to his S2 [intelligence officer] or S3 [operations officer] so I could get a feel for what the hell we were going into. Ross hooked me up with his S2. The S2 said that they didn't really know what was out there, but that their patrols got shot up every time they went out there, and that's why they wanted us to go out there. I remember thinking: well, that's not very helpful." Staley was concerned enough to contact Harrington, who said the matter was out of his hands: Staley had been placed opcon to Ross. End of story. "We left at the crack of dawn the next morning, as ordered," notes Staley. "We were on our own. No maps, initially, and no better direction than: 'Just go out there and see what you can find, and keep us informed.'"

Rolling out of the firebase, Captain Staley and B Troop took the northwest fork of Route 535 to the base of the Qué Sons. Almost immediately, Lieutenant Lindsey's platoon was engaged by approximately thirty VC. Three prisoners were taken and a body count of eleven reported.

The following morning, November 8, Lieutenant Lindsey, moving south, came under sniper fire from the right. Turning into the fire, the platoon pushed through the brush, urged on by a scout pilot: "They're in front of you, fifty yards, keep going, keep going!" Breaking into a clearing, the platoon took heavy fire from the woods along a north–south stream. Captain Staley moved up on Lindsey's flank with Mahoy's platoon, and for forty-five minutes, the tanks methodically fired canister rounds to their front, and the tracks fired their machine guns. Gunships added to the mayhem. Finally, jet fighters made repeated passes, dropping their high-drag bombs one or two at a time over the course of another hour and fifteen minutes. "They're gettin' awful close," Lindsey informed Staley after one uncomfortably close explosion. Trusting the precision of the pilots, Staley replied, "Yeah, well, get your head down: here comes another one."

Lieutenant Lindsey's platoon advanced after the air strikes to report a body count of twelve and take possession of a training center hidden under the jungle canopy. The cavalrymen captured a tripod and a hundred-round link of .51-caliber ammunition, plus thatch-and-bamboo hootches in which were found "flip charts and big chalkboards," notes Lindsey. "They got out of there so fast they left behind all kinds of documents and boxes full of stuff."

Lindsey described the find to Staley. Instructed by the troop commander to "run it out," Lindsey sent his scouts after the retreating enemy. Crossing the stream, the scouts moved west across some two hundred meters of rice paddies toward a likely enemy sanctuary: an elevated hamlet, Thôn Hai 2, that was part of the larger village complex of Thôn Hai. Thumbing through captured documents in an enemy classroom, Lindsey was startled by the impact of high-caliber ordnance to the west and high-pitched radio calls from his scouts. Lindsey thought his men were being shelled by their own artillery and shouted as much on the radio to Staley after taking off in his command track. Catching up with his scouts at the edge of the ville, he saw that they were not under friendly fire but were engaged with a sizable enemy force firing not only AK-47s and RPDs but also 75mm recoilless rifles and 82mm mortars. Two tracks had already been damaged. "We pulled back and kind of licked our wounds a little bit," recalls Lindsey. "It was like: 'Goddamn! What the hell was up there?'"

Captain Staley wanted to know the same thing and, as requested, was soon picked up in a little OH-13 bubble helicopter so that he could make an aerial reconnaissance. Staley opened fire with an M60 on figures scuttling for cover below. Out of machine-gun ammo, he continued firing with the captured AK he had also brought along. "I know I got a couple of 'em," he says. "I mean, you could see them running around. There was a big outfit down there. I saw at least one recoilless-rifle position, and a lot of guys with RPGs." The pilot, following a stream, came around a bend and into the sights of three enemy soldiers—one stood in the stream, another on each bank—who opened fire with their AK-47s. Remembers Staley: "They had us cold."

The helicopter was riddled, and Captain Staley shot three times in the gut—the rounds came through the instrument panel—as the OH-13 hurtled past the trio of VC or NVA. Staley couldn't talk, couldn't breathe. He needed immediate medical attention to save his life. Nevertheless, this is the message B Troop received from the pilot: "Your 6 is hit, but he won't let me go off station until he marks the enemy targets he saw for you. He's drawing them on his map."

Captain David H. Staley, gasping for air and in terrible pain—one round had lodged in his stomach, another in his liver, the third had exited under his left arm after ripping through his intestines—marked areas on his map, then drew corresponding symbols on his notepad to indicate the type of weaponry visible in Thôn Hai 2. The pilot relayed the information. "We're gonna have to go, you're bleeding from everywhere," the pilot finally said. Staley could talk again. He rasped to hold on one more second and, getting Lieutenant Wheeler on the horn, told the only first lieutenant among his platoon leaders that he was now in command. With that, the pilot headed for Ross. Thanks to Staley's fortitude, "we had targets on a map," notes Lindsey, "and could get a sense of what we were up against." Six air strikes were subsequently directed onto Thôn Hai 2.

Lieutenant Colonel Robert G. Kimmel, commander of the 1st of the 35th Infantry, 4th Division, which had been placed opcon to the 1st Air Cav, was tasked as dusk approached with taking Thôn Hai 2. Kimmel instructed Capt. Charles W. Chaplinski, Jr., commander of Company A, to link up and take charge of B Troop, whereupon, said Kimmel, the combined force was to launch a night attack under a skyful of illume: "Roll right over their asses!"

Reaching the knoll along the stream where B Troop had regrouped, Captain Chaplinski conferred with Lieutenant Taylor, the acting troop commander, while his curious infantrymen inspected the M48s and ACAVs. One grunt who climbed behind the .50 on a track was suddenly shot by an unseen sniper, perhaps the same enemy marksman who had just earlier shot and killed Spc. 4th Class Thomas L. Scott of Bravo Troop.

Another shot rang out in the twilight gloom, "and all hell broke loose for a couple of minutes," recalls Chaplinski, as both infantry and cavalry sprayed the jungle around them. "We finally got everyone calmed down," continues Chaplinski; at that point, the grunts climbed aboard the tracks, which started down the knoll toward Thôn Hai 2. Captain Chaplinski rode on a command track, "and after about ten minutes of travel, the lieutenant informed me that one of the 113s had thrown a track. He was cussing and telling me that if we encountered the enemy, we'd be sitting ducks because of [blinding] muzzle flash, and confusion with tracks and infantry together."

Already dubious about the wisdom of what they were doing, Chaplinski contacted Kimmel on the cavalry lieutenant's advice: the colonel agreed to postpone the attack until morning. By then, the much-admired Captain

Barovetto had arrived to take command of B Troop. The command situation until Barovetto's arrival had been uneasy: Mahoy and Hammerbeck both heard that Wheeler had confronted Taylor when he'd originally choppered in to replace Staley, reluctant as he was to hand the reins to a staff officer who'd never been in combat. Taylor supposedly won the argument by right of his earlier date of rank. Taylor asserts that no such confrontation took place, but the anecdote, whatever its accuracy, speaks to the undeniable fact that 1st Lt. James A. Taylor was not well regarded by Bravo Troop of the 1-1 Cavalry.

For the record, Jim Taylor was from a big, hardscrabble family in the lumber business in rural Samoa, California. Following ten years of enlisted service, he had been selected for OCS in 1965 and the Armor School in 1966. Joining the 1-1 Cavalry at Fort Hood, Taylor made a most favorable impression on Major Lundquist, Captain Reed, and Lieutenant Dickens. "Jim Taylor was sort of the 'old man' of all the lieutenants," says Dickens. Though Taylor had a gregarious and fun-loving side, he was usually "fairly quiet and businesslike."

In contrast, Captain Staley found the husky ex-sergeant to have the personality of an arrogant jock and did not think him a good fit in the unit. Lieutenants Lindsey and Mahoy agreed, as did a number of NCOs and EMs. To quote former dragoon Ron Decktor: "I never liked Lieutenant Taylor. He always had a smirk on his face, and he always had his smart remarks with the troops."

Regarding the other lieutenants, Lindsey was a seasoned pro by then, and Mahoy and Wheeler, though new, had their acts together. Ray Mahoy, already married and the father of two at age twenty-three, was a former national guardsman from small-town Indiana who'd served three years with the 101st Airborne before replacing his sergeant stripes with butter bars at OCS. The stocky, little ex-paratrooper "was a wild man," notes Richard Sears, "but still a nice guy and as it turned out, a good platoon leader." Gene Hotchkiss says Mahoy was "very aggressive—but he also gave a shit." Jim Hammerbeck took favorable stock of Mahoy when he saw the new platoon leader darting from vehicle to vehicle with a .45 in hand to check on his men during his first firefight. "I remember thinking, okay, now I know what kind of guy you are," says Hammerbeck. "Mahoy was for the troops," he adds, but was no pushover: "By God, he meant what he said, and if he said something, you did it."

Staff Sergeant Curtis J. Tinker, a laconic old country-boy platoon sergeant from Kentucky, provided the necessary counterweight to gung-ho Lieutenant Mahoy. Tinker stood about five-and-a-half feet tall; a chain-smoker, he was whippet thin, almost gaunt, and was "by nature, a very meek and quiet individual who didn't say much," notes Mahoy. "At the same time, he was a truly professional soldier, and a ball of fire if that was what the situation required." Tinker took care of his men. He did not raise his voice to exercise authority but treated all ranks with courtesy and respect. "He was dearly loved by us all, especially me," writes Mahoy. "We had a father-son relationship as far as I was concerned. Sergeant Tinker was my best friend, and taught me very patiently how to stay alive and keep my people alive."

November 9. There was no response to the pre-assault recon-by-fire, but the hope that the enemy had departed during the night evaporated when the grunts and cavalrymen started across the marshy rice paddy and a storm of fire abruptly commenced from the elevated edge of Thôn Hai 2.

Lieutenant Mahoy's platoon was in the lead, having just forded the stream by way of a narrow defile in the hilly terrain—the tanks, unable to pass, remained in an over watch position on the knoll—and broken into the open from the trees. Staff Sergeant Hammerbeck had no sooner opened up with his .50 in response to the enemy fire when his track, B-20, was stopped dead by a mortar round that scored a direct hit between the driver's hatch and the command cupola. Hammerbeck heard nothing, saw only a white flash. With no idea what had happened except that he was hit, he climbed from the cupola, shouting to his gunners to unass (as in, "get your ass off of") the track before the ammo inside began cooking off.

Taking cover, Hammerbeck saw that his gunners were wounded, too, and his driver missing. "Where's Nitz?" he asked. The answer: "Nitz is dead!"

Private First Class Robert F. Nitz had been killed instantly and sat dead in the driver's hatch of the track, which had begun to burn and smoke.

Lieutenant Mahoy, meanwhile, glanced to the side and was startled to see Staff Sergeant Hammerbeck standing beside his track, holding his bloody stomach—he had also been hit in the arms and face, and had a sucking chest wound, too—while staring at his platoon leader with the dull eyes of a whipped dog. Mahoy turned to his medic: "Get him medevacked!"

The next thing Hammerbeck knew, he was in the woods along the stream. According to an award recommendation for Lieutenant Taylor, the executive officer had sprinted across the paddies, hoisted Hammerbeck over his shoulders, and, unable to carry him all the way back, placed him behind a dike before racing rearward to get his track. Platoon Sergeant Donald L. Gilliam and Mike Esmond, who had moved forward with Taylor, attended to Hammerbeck until the executive officer returned with his track. Hammerbeck was loaded inside with one of his guys, and as he lay on the floor of the track, hot brass spilled down on him as Taylor manned the .50 and the gunners their M60s.

The track stopped, the back ramp came down. Hammerbeck was lifted onto a litter and, soon thereafter, into a Huey. The chopper lifted off, and the medic on board secured a pressure bandage over the hole in Hammerbeck's chest even as the sergeant moaned, "God, this burns like hell!"

"I know, Sarge," the medic shouted over the throb of the engine. "But you're gonna be okay—we're gonna get you outta here!"

Hammerbeck listened to the medic and, believing him, relaxed.

He was going to make it.

Lieutenant Lindsey moved past Lieutenant Mahoy's left flank to continue the assault, but as the lead track, B-11, reached the southeast edge of the raised hamlet, it was knocked out by a recoilless rifle. Moments later, Lindsey's command vehicle also took a direct hit. The remaining tracks maneuvered in all directions, firing madly, while Alpha Company pushed forward to take position along a wooded dike and begin pouring its own fire into the hamlet.

Colonel James O. McKenna, commander of the 3rd Brigade, 1st Air Cavalry Division, orbited the battlefield in his Huey; he later signed a witness statement supporting the award recommendation for Taylor:

> . . . the lead APC was hit at about 15 feet by a 75mm recoilless rifle . . . Suddenly[,] an individual, later identified as 1LT James A. Taylor, darted from the rear of the column and ran forward to the rear of the disabled vehicle and began pulling inert bodies from the vehicle . . . From my

vantage at about 300 feet above[,] it was a totally unreal nightmare with 1LT Taylor making his way back and forth at least twice to my own knowledge to the vehicle while mortar rounds, recoilless and [RPGs] peppered the area. Moments later[,] the vehicle exploded . . . I was convinced that anyone who went into that maelstrom would not survive. I have never seen such a splendid example of raw courage and concern for his fellow man as that displayed in those few minutes.

Though unmentioned, several others were also involved in the rescue, including Lieutenant Mahoy, who later wrote on the back of a photo of the incinerated B-11 track: "This is where I got my first silver star for pulling PFC [William R.] Beltran out of this one. It was burning and ammo was exploding at the time. He's alive today and in [a burn ward in] the states."

Lieutenant Lindsey was hurled inside the hull when a mortar round exploded behind his own burning track. Finally able to breathe again, Lindsey pushed the microphone button on his commo helmet—and saw blood running down his hand from a neck wound. He thought himself a dead man but came to his senses when he realized his throat had not been torn open. Patting himself down, he found no other injuries: his flak jacket had saved his life, blown off his back in the process. Lindsey clambered aboard a track as the entire line pulled back, the wounded having been rescued, and those tracks stuck in the mud hooked up to other ACAVs. "On their way out," recalls a former grunt, "I saw this one dude on the back of a track with his shirt off and his .45 out—firing at the wood line while his track was moving backwards."

Hastily organizing another assault, Captain Barovetto sent Lieutenants Mahoy and Wheeler straight into the enemy entrenchments at the northeast corner of the hamlet. "It was pure bedlam," writes Mahoy; everyone was talking on the radio at once, "and nobody was answering anyone. There were little personal battles going on everywhere: one NVA popped up no more than ten feet from my track and the gunner blew him away with the side M60."

At another point in the melee, Mahoy and crew realized that they were right on top of a 75mm recoilless-rifle position and in seconds filled the hole with a torrent of M16 and M60 fire from off the side of their track—the gunners escaped down a tunnel—then dismounted to throw the recoilless rifle atop the ACAV. The platoon later knocked out a second recoilless rifle. Meanwhile, Lieutenant Taylor was hit—superficially, as was his luck—when the enemy mortared his medevac point along the stream. First Lieutenant Dennis L. Robinson, the FO, was also wounded, apparently in the same barrage. The pilots from the 1-9 Cav were undeterred by the incoming fire: the choppers literally set down between explosions to kick out ammo and take aboard casualties.

Barovetto instructed Taylor to establish a new medevac point along a branch of the stream adjacent the northeast corner of Thôn Hai 2. En route, Taylor passed through an element from A/1-35th Infantry pinned down by an RPD. Taylor recalls personally taking the machine-gun position under .50 fire. The episode, and another, was described in a witness statement signed by Barovetto:

> [1LT Taylor] moved up the east flank and directed the fires of his track on the position. After assisting gunships in reducing the position, he moved to the [northeast corner of Thôn Hai 2] and discovered B-21 had been hit by a 75mm recoilless rifle round. Once again[,] 1LT Taylor dismounted and moved through heavy machine gun and small arms fire and began evacuating the wounded to the LZ.

Lieutenant Mahoy's witness statement differs somewhat from Barovetto's in describing the destruction of B-21:

> LT Taylor maneuvered his vehicle up on line with the [2nd and 3rd Platoons]. At 1300 hours, the B-21 track received a direct 75mm hit to the right front . . . wounding the entire crew. LT Taylor . . . moved his vehicle up beside the stricken B-21, which was burning and exploding . . . [LT Taylor] succeeded in removing the crew and getting them back to the LZ for the dust off.

Private First Class Hotchkiss was firing his M60 when "the two-one track gets hit, and the gunner on the right side rolls off the back of the thing, and he's laying in the mud, trying to crawl away, but his legs are just ripped to pieces." Hotchkiss and Pvt. 1st Class Jerry W. Gentry, the driver of B-21, dashed to the wounded gunner. "We got him to the back door hatch of my track, and the guys inside grabbed him and pulled him into the track."

Private First Class Robert D. "Sonny" Webster III, a track gunner, saw Gentry dragging a trooper who seemed to have been hit in the stomach and thighs. The injuries match those of the man rescued by Gentry and Hotchkiss. Perhaps it was the same man, and Webster and Hotchkiss simply no longer remember the other man being there, too. Perhaps not: Gentry was credited with making four trips through the crossfire to get the entire crew of B-21 to cover, and it is entirely possible that more than one of those crewmen had suffered leg injuries. No matter. Here is Webster's memory of that moment in the battle: "The wounded guy was laying there in shock. Gentry was holding his head and chest up and trying to drag him. He couldn't, so he yelled for help, and I ran over, and he and I dragged the wounded guy to another track and put him in there." At that point, the two dashed for the cover of Webster's track. Webster was in front, Gentry right at his heels. "The back door of the track was open. I dove in the track and rolled off the right, thinking Gentry would jump in right behind me—but he didn't. He'd gotten shot at the last second, and was crumpled up outside the door. I went back out, picked him up, and brought him in the track."

Jerry Gentry, unconscious, had a sucking chest wound.

Lieutenant Wheeler's track was hit twice by recoilless-rifle fire at the northeast corner of the hamlet. According to a written summary, Lieutenant Taylor "raced to the burning [B-36] vehicle and began removing the wounded crew[,] unmindful of the hail of intense automatic weapon and 75mm recoilless rifle fire being directed at him . . . Two more soldiers raced to assist him."

Mike Esmond was one of those soldiers, though bleeding from the nose and mouth from the blasts that had hurled him off the command track. "You're just getting in there, and getting your guys out," says Esmond. "You're not paying attention to the fire or anything else." The medic was hit again—mortar shrapnel—while loading the casualties into a track bound for the medevac point. "You were totally afraid," continues Esmond. "I mean, how many Hail Marys can you say in five minutes—but if somebody was in peril, you would do your damnedest to help them. I would say that ninety-five percent of the people in Bravo Troop would have given their life for the next guy."

Barovetto finally ordered Mahoy and Wheeler to break contact. Lindsey lost a track at that time, as described in Mahoy's witness statement:

> The troop was forced to draw back out of the objective and came on line in the rice paddy on the edge of the objective[,] preparing for another assault. Track 1-0 received a direct hit to the front by 75mm fire . . . causing the vehicle to burn and explode. Again[,] LT Taylor . . . ran forward while under heavy fire and began removing the wounded personnel from the track. The track was burning and exploding and shrapnel was flying all around. At this time[,] the element received another 75mm hit.

Staff Sergeant Tinker brought up the rear, having led a team of four volunteers who, working under fire, stripped the radios and machine guns from the disabled B-21 track; on the way out, Tinker shot and killed an NVA.

Lieutenant Wheeler went out on a medevac and then, shrugging off his injuries, returned on a resupply ship. Twenty-five dragoons were medevacked. Perhaps a dozen others were treated in the field, including Staff Sergeant Bouche and Sonny Webster, who both realized they'd been hit only after the unit pulled back to regroup. Webster's elbow was raw and bloody. Bouche dug fragments out of his legs with his fingernails. "I was very fortunate," he says, "because shrapnel's weird: it can tear you in half, or it can just pepper you."

Gene Hotchkiss and his best friends, Privates First Class Robert R. Iervolino and David J. Genus—a pseudonym—loaded Jerry Gentry into a Huey. The man was dead by then. Iervolino could have climbed on the medevac, such were his injuries, but he refused. The word was passed to get ready for a third assault, at which Genus "just tightened up," notes Hotchkiss. "He literally froze. It was like he was a stone statue." Genus was tagged for a medevac, as was a young trooper from the Dominican Republic, who also broke down. Hotchkiss and Iervolino lifted Genus inside the helicopter. Their comrade stared straight ahead, arms wrapped like cables around his knees. The helicopter departed. Hotchkiss and Iervolino lay against a dike, facing each other, too numb to speak as they wondered how they would survive the next attack.

Unexpectedly, a reprieve: the third attack had been called off.

One of Captain Chaplinski's platoon leaders knocked out a recoilless-rifle position with hand grenades. After calling in two sets of jet fighters, Chaplinski instructed the lieutenant to attempt a flanking maneuver that the enemy had anticipated and positioned a machine gun to deal with: the point man was killed, a staff sergeant mortally wounded. Thereafter, the grunts found themselves pinned down on the edge of the hamlet. Those who did not stay low enough fell victim to a hidden sniper who killed four grunts with head shots.

Now alone on the field after the cavalry's retreat, Captain Chaplinski made radio contact with Staff Sgt. David H. Wainscott, tank section leader of 1st Platoon, B Troop. The tanks fired main-gun rounds into the hamlet from the knoll across the stream. Wainscott moved forward to Chaplinski's position to discuss bringing the tanks across the blueline. They finally decided such a maneuver was impossible. Wainscott promised to provide all the fire support he could, made his way back to the streambed, and there was shot by the sniper as he raised up for a last look. "Wainscott was a well-liked leader, and one hell of a tanker," writes Ken Bouche. "He knew we were catching hell, and wanted to get his tanks in to us, and that is what cost him his life."

With night falling, Captain Chaplinski made the decision to leave his dead and crawl back to the stream along a paddy dike. The company commander led the way, followed by his radioman, who had the mike jammed inside his shirt to keep it out of the mud. The radioman occasionally raised up slightly to readjust the mike and, doing so once too often, was shot in the head—the final victim of the unseen sniper. "You talk about an incredible shot in the gloaming," notes a former grunt. "Many speculated the sniper had an infrared scope."

Keeping low, the first of the grunts reached the blueline. One moved downstream to secure the flank and was dumbfounded when a squad's worth of NVA emerged from positions along the streambed and disappeared down a trail leading southeast toward the hamlet. The wide-eyed grunt held his fire, not trusting that his mud-covered M16 would not explode in his hands if he pulled the trigger. The presence of enemy to the rear explained why some grunts had sworn they were taking fire from both directions during the battle. Other enemy soldiers appeared in the dusk half-light to climb aboard the disabled and abandoned B-36 track. "Somebody saw a couple gooks jump inside," recalls Hotchkiss; in moments, "there were thirty to forty machine guns firing in the back door of that thing. We sure as hell didn't want them using our M60s and the .50-caliber on us, so we smoked our own track. I don't know how many went in, but I guarantee you nobody came out of that vehicle."

Darkness closed upon the battlefield as Barovetto circled his tracks in the paddies on the west side of the blueline, and Chaplinski's grunts joined the tanks atop the knoll on the east side. Three dragoons had been killed, eight grunts. B-11, B-20, and B-36 were total losses, while B-10, B-16, and B-21, though damaged, would be recovered. The B-37 track had been hit in the fuel line but towed into the laager. Five other vehicles were down with mechanical problems, leaving B Troop with only a mortar track, six M48s, and eleven ACAVs.

There was much reconning-by-fire as Barovetto and Chaplinski advanced on the hamlet the next morning, November 10, but little return fire until Kimmel went in for a closer look: the command ship was disabled in a sudden fusillade, the pilot forced to make a crash-landing. The area was secured without further incident, and Chaplinski ordered some villagers to drag his dead from the paddy in front of the hamlet, in case the bodies had been booby-trapped. Actually, the enemy had not molested the dead, except to strip them of their dog tags. The vegetation scraped away by the gunships and air strikes revealed that a wagon-wheel trench system had been superimposed over the hamlet: from a bunker at the center hub, the enemy commander could send reinforcements down the different spokes to wherever they were needed on the outer circle. Demoralizingly, the enemy had meticulously policed the battlefield, taking even their brass, and overlooking only a single body. Enough shallow graves were subsequently found in the area, however, to claim forty-one slain VC and NVA.

The scene of battle shifted southeast of LZ Ross on November 13 when the commander of B/1-9 Cav was shot down while attempting to capture an enemy soldier placed as a lure between two hamlets. The aerorifle platoon—the Blues—was surrounded upon landing to secure the Huey, and almost every one of B Troop's twenty-six OH-13s and Hueys was shot down in an expert crossfire of AK-47s and .51-caliber machine guns. Chaplinski and A/1-35 landed in the dark to reinforce the Blues and were ordered by Kimmel come daylight to pursue a large group of NVA vacating the area. Chaplinski refused: he had to secure the Blues until they were extracted. After a heated exchange, Chaplinski finally agreed to get one platoon moving while waiting for the extraction helicopters. Tracers arched toward the command ship, meanwhile, from an antiaircraft position far to the southeast. "Sir, you are taking fire," Chaplinski told Kimmel, who seemed not to hear. "Sir, please be advised that you are taking fire." Kimmel finally acknowledged the fire: "We will attempt to rise above it."

The command ship was still at fifteen hundred feet when its rear rotor was shot off. The pilot struggled for a few seconds to control his ship, then the tail swung completely around, the nose dipped, and the Huey spiraled to the ground. Kimmel was killed, along with his operations officer, an artillery officer, an assistant operations officer, and the four-man helicopter crew. The Blues were finally extracted under heavy fire. The enemy subsequently recovered maps, radios, and machine guns from the field of wrecked helicopters.

Not a good operation, not a success.

Captain Staley was returned to active duty after many surgeries and months of recuperation, though his request to return to Việt Nam was denied. For his last battle, Staley was awarded a Distinguished Flying Cross that fit neatly between his two Silver Stars and three Purple Hearts. Captain Barovetto and Lieutenants Lindsey, Robinson, and Wheeler were awarded the Bronze Star, and Lieutenant Mahoy the Silver Star. Gilliam, Tinker, Esmond, and Webster received Bronze Stars, as did the next of kin of David Wainscott, Thomas Scott, Jerry Gentry, and Robert Nitz. Posthumous Purple Hearts and Bronze Stars with V were the usual consolation prizes for ending up in a body bag in Việt Nam.

Lieutenant Taylor, meanwhile, was recommended by Harrington and Lundquist for the Congressional Medal of Honor. To ensure that Taylor would survive to receive the nation's highest award for battlefield heroism, should the recommendation be approved up the chain of command, he was reassigned to command Headquarters Company, 123rd

Aviation Battalion, at Chu Lai. While in the rear, Taylor was pinned with a Distinguished Service Cross that proved to be an interim award: four months after completing his tour, newly promoted Captain Taylor was one of four heroes around whose necks President Johnson fastened the Medal of Honor during a televised ceremony in the White House.

"I was watching the news after coming home," notes Ron Decktor, "and there's Lyndon Johnson giving Taylor the CMH. I fell through the floor."

"Of all the goddamn guys," mutters Gene Hotchkiss.

Speaking for Staley, Lindsey, Mahoy, and many others, Sonny Webster comments: "Everybody choked on Taylor getting the Medal of Honor."

The general consensus was that Taylor deserved a Bronze or Silver Star like his fellow officers, not the nearly sacrosanct Medal of Honor. A number of former officers are under the impression that Major Lundquist was determined to secure a Medal of Honor for the glory of the First Regiment of Dragoons, and that Taylor's award recommendation was born of this desire more than the specifics of what had happened at Thôn Hai 2. Why was Taylor picked to play the lead role in Lundquist's quest? Because he was one of the few in the squadron with whom Lundquist was on good terms. By way of explanations, "that sounds pretty good to me," says Staley. Taylor is outraged by such speculation about how he came to be awarded the Medal of Honor. "Character assassination," he calls it, a slur upon both himself and Lundquist. Fairly or not, Taylor has been cold-shouldered by certain former comrades at reunions because he has shown no modesty over the years about his Medal of Honor.

Ray Mahoy offers perhaps the wisest counsel on Jim Taylor and his Medal of Honor: "I'd wager that medal is like a gigantic weight around his neck."

The View from Above

OCTOBER–DECEMBER 1967

LIEUTENANT COLONEL HARRINGTON WENT airborne during the big Cigar Island battle and, having exposed himself to mortal danger, was duly compensated with a Silver Star. Harrington was not actively involved in many other operations but spent most of his time with his sergeant major, with whom he shared a tent at Hawk Hill. "The sergeant major was an old guy," recalls Chief Dunn. "All he did was his laundry, and the colonel's, and take care of their mail and other personal needs." George Norton has the same memory of the colonel and sergeant major: "Nice enough fellas, but they didn't run the unit."

Major Saint ran the unit. The de facto squadron commander was intolerant of error but generally gave the troop commanders a loose rein. "Saint was cool," says Norton. "Boy, if you screwed up, you knew it, but his rule was the guy on the ground, he's the one with the problem and he's making the calls."

Admired by most, Saint had his detractors, to include Nate Boyd, who resented the major as an overly ambitious West Pointer who dreamed up overly aggressive operations for the sake of his resumé: "He was trying to make a name for himself, and it seemed like he never took into consideration the little guy down there on the ground who was trying to carry out his orders."

Whatever else might be said, Major Saint did not hesitant to take his helicopter into harm's way. "I did a lot of dumb things," says Saint to explain his Silver Star, Distinguished Flying Cross, and thirteen Air Medals. Saint carried an M16 with a shortened barrel and retractable butt stock known as a CAR15 Colt Commando, and when the tanks and tracks "flushed game," he would go after the fleeing individuals with his command ship. "We had very strict rules of engagement," notes Saint, who says that he only fired on military-age males with weapons. Did the major and his door gunners actually nail any Charlies? "I'm sure we did. Some guys would turn and fight. Other guys would jump in a hole, or go into the bushes, and we couldn't find them. The main objective was to stop 'em so that our ground units could catch up with 'em."

In one incident, Saint spotted an individual carrying a satchel. The man disappeared into the undergrowth. Thinking the satchel might contain valuable intelligence, an excited Saint had the pilot drop him off, "and then I went rummaging around, looking for the guy. It was the dumbest thing I ever did. I didn't even have a radio with me." Saint's helicopter took hits during a low-level chase of another fleeing figure, and the pilot broke off the pursuit and headed for the nearest firebase to inspect the damage. Saint recalls another day in which the tables were turned on the hunter: "There was one guy running along, and we were chasing him. I didn't see that he had a weapon, then all of a sudden, he turned around, and I remember the bluish-green flash as he shot us down. He got both pilots, one in the leg and one in the arm." The leg-shot pilot kept a grip on the cyclic stick, and the one with a bullet in his arm worked the foot pedals, while heading for Tam Kỳ. The shot-up chopper could no longer hover, "so we made a runway landing like a plane."

The Daily Grind

NOVEMBER–DECEMBER 1967

THE KILLS RACKED UP by the A-15 tank, commanded by Platoon Sgt. Charles Nathan Boyd, included a man in civilian clothes who sped along Highway 1 with several AK-47s hanging from his moped. The imprudent guerrilla—or militiaman, or civilian, or whatever—was spotted from an observation post some three thousand meters off the highway. "The guy was just driving down the road like it's Sunday afternoon," recalls Boyd. "I put an HE [high explosive] round on him. I'm watching the guy with my binoculars, and that damn ninety-millimeter round looked like it hit the front wheel on that bike. Parts of him went all over the place."

Boyd had two slogans painted on the turret of A-15, to include on one side the unofficial name of his tank, *Nathan's Killing Machine*, and on the other side:

Yea, though I walk through the valley of the shadow of death
I shall fear no evil, for I am the meanest motherfucker in the valley.

The bit about being the meanest motherfucker in the valley was a "worn-out soldier's boast," notes one ex-GI. "In Boyd's case, however, it was true."

In another incident, the enemy fired a mortar round at a convoy being escorted by A Troop. The round fell short. Boyd noticed a wisp of smoke curling above a distant hillock, and before the mortar crew could adjust its fire, he pulled to the side of the road and punched off three rounds. The scout track sent to inspect the damage reported three dead Việt Cộng.

The nice-guy lieutenant nominally in command of the platoon rode on his track in silence during operations. Boyd ran the show and, being the model of an old-army NCO, was almost as tough on his men as he was on Charlie. During overnight missions, Boyd slept in the bustle rack of his tank, his men on their vehicles. No stretchers, no air mattresses. "These guys, if you let 'em, they'll be out there throwing up pup tents and all that shit and going to sleep," explains Boyd. In addition, no one was to dismount for any reason during the night. That kept things simple: anything seen or heard on the ground was to be immediately taken under fire as the enemy. "To check the lines," notes Boyd, "I could sit there in my tank, and I could see every vehicle I had with my starlight scope. We were all within a hundred meters of each other." Should the man behind a .50 look to have nodded off, Boyd would get on the radio; if no one answered, "those guys would get a wake-up call. When you bounce an M79 round off the side of a track, it wakes 'em right up and they get the message."

Platoon Sergeant Boyd was not resented for his methods. On the contrary, "everybody respected him, and everybody appreciated him," says Jerry L. Anderson. "Boyd was rough, but he damn sure took care of his people: you mess with his people, you're messin' with the bull. Boyd was comical, too," continues Anderson. "He was a lot of fun to be around." The platoon was deployed one scorching hot day in a rice paddy in which nothing stirred except a lone water buffalo. Many hours having passed in dull conversation, Boyd broke the tedium by suddenly announcing that he'd always wanted to shoot a water buffalo right between the eyes with his .45. Everyone perked up as "Boyd walked up to that water buffalo," recounts Anderson, "and popped him with his pistol—and you could see the bullet bounce off the skull. All it did was piss off the water buffalo. Boyd come a haulin' ass back to his tank with the water buffalo in hot pursuit. Everybody's laughin' and cheerin.'"

Boyd was on excellent terms with 1st Sgt. William McPherson, better known as "The Bear." Lieutenant Norton, reassigned as troop exec, recalls both McPherson's droll wit and how the barrel-chested topkick would wake his "favorites" in the morning by flipping their cots over. McPherson actually loved his soldiers, though "he would break your hands if you let them know it," muses Norton. Boyd conspired with McPherson about securing replacement parts for his vehicles and anything useful and extra for the men. Thanks to McPherson, Boyd had two refrigerators in his bunker-bar at Hawk Hill that were always stocked with beer. Boyd's Bastards essentially ran on diesel and beer, and Boyd himself on quart bottles of Scotch. During one respite in the rear, Boyd and Jessie commandeered a Mechanical Mule, which was returned with concertina wire wrapped around the wheels: their alcohol-fueled misadventure had apparently included crashing through some perimeter fencing.

Nate Boyd had a little white mongrel named Bullshit. The platoon also acquired a pet pig after plowing through an ambush in a hamlet east of the highway. One of the village pigs, a sow, was caught in the crossfire, its belly torn open. When the intestines trailing behind the unfortunate animal caught on something, the pig fell over dead. One of Boyd's tank commanders scooped up an orphaned piglet squalling in the chaos, the intention being to fatten the thing up for a barbecue. Everyone fell in love with the piglet, however: it followed the troopers like a puppy and was as affectionate as one, too. As the weeks passed, the potbellied pig, covered with coarse black hair, grew no more than ten inches high, a fun little mascot that slept in the bunker-bar when not cavorting around the platoon area. "If you walked in the bar, he'd wake up and start snortin'," recalls Boyd. "If you were having a beer, you'd better give him one, too." The pig, in fact, was named after his favorite brand. "We got three mess kits," recounts Boyd, "and we put Budweiser in one, Miller in the other, and Schlitz in the last one. He drank all the Budweiser, so that's what we called him."

One driver attached a nightie to the radio mast of his track because, noted Tom Bursott in a letter home, "[he] claims that is what he is fight[ing] for."

"Boyd had a wild bunch, but they were good guys," says George Norton. "Boy, if you were in a fight, those were the guys you wanted."

Boyd's Bastards drank beer. Certain troopers in the other platoons were into weed, to include the 3rd Platoon track crew whose bunker featured a psychedelic sign on the door: The Mad Hatter's Tea Party. David Eady would never forget the night the door of his own bunker opened, and there stood Platoon Sergeant Jessie in the sunken entranceway, rain pouring down behind him; he took in the smoke-filled scene without expression, then said before turning to leave: "You guys better be bright-eyed and bushy-tailed when we move out in the morning."

They were. There developed a routine to the operations around Hill 29: an early morning mount-up in the motor pool, a day spent looking for trouble, a return to base camp at nightfall, and a hot meal courtesy of the troop mess section. Solid contact being infrequent, some of A Troop's sweeps turned into lackadaisical souvenir hunts: Boyd's Bastards returned from one patrol with a midget-sized statue of Buddha that was used to decorate the roof of their bunker-bar. "We had a little meeting about the pilfering," recalls Leon Palatas, then with the 2nd Platoon of Alpha Troop. "Some of us used to ask, 'What if someone was to come to our house like this [and take things]?'"

The disdain many had for the locals was obvious. It was about this time that some of the track drivers took to edging bicycles and mopeds off the roads and into ditches. There were other games to relieve the boredom: Boyd's Bastards were sitting atop a knoll, waiting to move out, when one of the troopers "got a wild hair," recalls Larry Gaydon, "and went down and strapped C-4 to this farmer's water buffalo, and blew the poor water buffalo into a million pieces."

Many thought such behavior not only amusing but also justified. "When I first got there, I felt so sorry for them people and the way they lived, I couldn't stand it," says Ronnie Fortner. "Your attitude changes in a hurry. They were all VC. They would bow and let you go by, and then shoot you in the back."

On the other hand, Spc. 5th Class Richard J. Hoover, a regular on his second tour and medic for Boyd's Bastards, conscientiously examined and treated the villagers as his comrades searched their hootches; on one memorable occasion, Hoover delivered a baby in a hut, assisted by a wide-eyed Tom Bursott. Wayne Byrd and Gerald Hardin, loader and gunner on A-29, would have as many as twenty kids crowded around the back of their tank as they tossed them packets of Kool-Aid sent from home in such abundance as to fill several ammo cans. They also tossed the bars of tropical chocolate that came with the C-rations; such chocolate would not melt, required a hammer to break off a piece, and was so unpopular with GIs that the tank crew might have fifty bars saved up in another ammo can. Byrd and Hardin would throw a bar in one direction, watch the kids scramble, then toss another in a different direction once the dust had settled. Byrd noticed something during these antics that made it impossible for him to hate the Vietnamese: "The kids didn't fight over the goodies. The rule seemed to be that the chocolate bar belonged to whoever got their hand on it first—and when we were done tossing everything out, those kids would sit on the ground and divide everything up so that everyone got the same amount."

Larry Graham described one of their nebulous little contacts in a letter to his wife: upon receiving automatic fire "from a cement house out in the hills," the platoon "immediately turned and fired towards the house. I shot M79 rounds and blew the front doors off[.]" Graham next lobbed a round straight inside the building. "[A]fter the shooting stopped[,] we went up to the house and found a mother (40–50) and 6 kids. It turned out she got shot in the left breast by scrapnel [sic] from my M79. But Sgt Boyd gave me a pat on the back cause one way or another she knew that the sniper was going to shoot at us. Our medic patched her up and we left. We never found the sniper."

The lieutenant of Boyd's Bastards was riding on Sergeant Fortner's track when a burst of fire brought the sweep to a halt. Fortner spotted a military-age male who flung aside his big white conical hat as he dashed into some bushes, the better to hide. The lieutenant drew his .45, and Fortner dismounted from his command cupola with his M16. Their quarry bolted at their approach, and Fortner fired three quick shots from the hip, not really aiming, but nevertheless dropping the man with a shot that ripped through his buttocks. While being questioned by the troop's ARVN interpreter, the unarmed, unidentified man—who had made himself fair game by running—bled to death where he lay.

Another day, another sweep, and A Troop pushed through a hedgerow atop an earthen berm, followed by ARVN soldiers. Their advisor got Doc Gaydon's attention—they were sitting together on the ambulance track—and pointed to a small hole in the berm. For an instant, a face appeared in the hole. The advisor ran over with Gaydon and another medic and then asked who had a grenade. Gaydon did, and the advisor told him to frag the hole. The medic tossed the grenade underhanded—and it hit the edge of the hole and popped straight into the air. Time stood still as the grenade fell back to earth and rolled into the hole only an instant before exploding. The man inside was killed. "Someone pulled the body out," notes Gaydon, "and we just moved on, you know."

Dick Taskey and Tom Bursott no longer recall how the prisoner came to be sitting with them on the back of the infantry track, but there he was: naked save for a pair of black shorts, a bandage wrapped around his right shoulder. His back was streaked with blood. There were inquires on the radio regarding the need for a medevac. The answer: negative. Bursott recalls saying that " 'no, no, we've got one that's still alive,' and the word came back over the radio: all prisoners have died. I don't know who made the decision, but we were given to believe that the prisoner on our track was not to be taken in." Why bother? What intelligence could this anonymous guerrilla really provide? As such, the wounded prisoner was tossed overboard. Taskey took a blurry photograph of the young man as he lay among the green shoots of a rice paddy, propped up on his elbows and looking back at the camera over his left shoulder. The man's mouth was half open, his expression blank. For all he knew, he was being released. Instead, Taskey shot the prisoner to death with his M16. The man's bandage also caught a round or two, and as the cotton floated back down, Taskey turned to Bursott and joked: "So that's what they're made of!"

Raised at Fort Hood, the 198th Light Infantry Brigade had landed at Chu Lai in October, allowing the 196th to move north and relieve the 1st Brigade, 101st Airborne Division in the Quế Sơn Valley. Soon thereafter, B and D/4-31st Infantry, reinforced by a platoon from the brigade cavalry troop, attacked Hill 63 and neighboring Hill X, held—according to intercepted radio transmissions—by elements of the 3rd Regiment, 2nd NVA Division. The battle that gloomy and overcast Thanksgiving Day, November 23, was ferocious, casualties heavy. A third rifle company, B/3-21st Infantry, was choppered in, only to be pinned down on its LZ, at which point tank support was requested from the 1-1 Cavalry.

To avoid mines, Platoon Sergeant Jessie struck out cross-country with the four tanks that had been sitting in A Troop's motor pool at Hill 29 when word came to immediately mount up and rush to the aid of a heavily engaged infantry unit in the Quế Sơn Valley. John Guzik thought Jessie the perfect man for the job, perhaps even more so than the renowned

Boyd. "Boyd was aggressive, perhaps too aggressive at times," writes Guzik. "Boyd always seemed to charge right in, where Jessie would sort of size things up before taking action. Jessie was an impressive figure. He had an air of confidence and an easy manner—but you always remembered that he was in charge."

Arriving at the scene of the battle, Jessie's ad-hoc tank section was joined by the platoon from the brigade cavalry troop and sent to the aid of pinned-down B/3-21st Infantry. The tanks and tracks worked their way across the wet paddies, maneuvering around boulders behind which grunts had taken shelter, then came on line and pushed into the hedgerows from which the enemy was firing. "I recall topping a sand berm, and in the vision block, seeing the faces of terrified NVA," writes Guzik. "They dropped everything and ran. I don't blame them." Tank commanders laid down a sheet of machine-gun fire, while gunners squeezed main-gun triggers as fast as their loaders could put the next round in the breach. "We mowed them down," exults Guzik, "and saved the infantry!" For doing so, Platoon Sergeant Jessie won a second Bronze Star and, peppered in the neck and hand with shrapnel, would also receive the Purple Heart. Guzik describes "a very calm, cool, and collected Jessie holding his map in his non-bloody hand as he had a conversation about the next action to be taken."

In the meantime, D/4-31st Infantry finally took Hill 63. Jessie's tankers celebrated Thanksgiving with the turkey units from their C-rations while bitching about missing the feast being laid on for the rest of the guys at Hawk Hill. As plans were made by radio, Jessie monitored the push of the company to which his tanks had been attached. "They had no idea we were listening," writes Guzik. "The company commander was telling a platoon leader not to take any chances [when the attack resumed the next day]. They had taken some tough hits, so 'Get those tanks *out front!* Let them take the fire.' Jessie seemed almost amused. I was shocked when he broke in on the conversation and berated the officers. He also assured them that we would do our part in a *coordinated* effort."

Hill X fell to C/4-31st on November 24. Afterward, D/4-31st, accompanied by the tanks and tracks, swept north toward the Sông Lý Lý, which ran the length of the valley. Two fresh companies assumed blocking positions along the river. The hammer never met the anvil because

D/4-31st came under heavy fire in the paddies between. Platoon Sergeant Jessie's tanks pummeled the enemy, as did howitzers and jet fighters. The NVA did not budge. Chinooks delivered fuel blivets. Guzik and Pvt. 1st Class David S. Kossowski, the driver, left the protection of their tank to refuel A-35. "I recall Jessie getting pissed at a sniper that was interfering with our refueling from one of the bladders," writes Guzik. "Dave and I were ducking. Jessie was shooting."

On November 25, Jessie's tankers again supported D/4-31st, whose commander called in more air strikes to level the hamlets in front of them before charging in to capture two small boys and a mamasan. The enemy had decamped during the night. John Guzik recalls that "there were many dead NVA strewn across the battlefield—shot up, blown up, and bloated." Dave Kossowski was upset by the scene, "so much so," notes Guzik, "that he snapped at me for making some of my usual [wise guy] comments about how the bodies looked like mannequins and didn't smell very good."

The infantry held onto Jessie's tanks another week. When Jessie complained about a lack of support, First Sergeant McPherson flew out with ammunition, fuel, and, for each tank, a case of orange soda, a mailbag full of ice, and a good, hot meal in a mermite can. "Afterwards, here come a bunch of infantrymen, and they wanted to know if there was enough for them, too," remembers Wayne Byrd. There was, but Jessie, feeling that his tankers had been ill-used, ordered them not to share anything with the infantry. Byrd felt terrible telling the grunts as much, for they had been living on a box or two of C-rations a day, while the tankers carried enough for three meals a day. On the other hand, when the company commander himself asked about getting some hot chow, Byrd relished being able to talk down to an officer, and from the height of his tank at that: "Sir, if we was to give you some, there'd have to be enough for all your men because you're supposed to eat last, and since there's not enough to go around, my orders are not to give you any." The tanks departed the next day. "McPherson personally took care of the problem," recalls Byrd, "and got us released."

Jessie's overworked tanks were sent to the squadron rear for a maintenance overhaul. With some free time on their hands, the tankers stashed their pistols under their cots before leaving for the evening movie at Fat City. Unexpectedly, a shot rang out. "I turned, expecting to see a hole in the floor or the top of the tent, and a big dumb smile on the face of whoever had accidentally fired the round," recounts Guzik. "To my horror, Dave Kossowski was laying on the floor with a severe head wound." Medics were summoned, and Guzik recalls that when he visited Kossowski in the hospital in Chu Lai, "he was in a coma, and had a head the size of a pumpkin." Kossowski never regained consciousness and died eight months later in a Stateside hospital. The incident was recorded in the squadron log as an accidental discharge. Questions were nonetheless raised when it was discovered that Kossowski had already tossed his pistol under his cot and that the .45 that went off in his hands actually belonged to another tanker. Why had Kossowski pulled someone else's pistol from its holster? Was it possible that the nineteen-year-old GI, noticeably moody and withdrawn after the Quế Sơn action, had attempted suicide? One of his fellow crewmen speculated as much to Guzik. Guzik did not agree: "To me, it was obviously an unfortunate accident. I would like to continue to believe that. I remember Dave as a good army buddy, and an excellent soldier. I was proud to serve with him, and glad we drank a few beers together at Fort Hood."

Platoon Sergeant Boyd would recall that by the time his own overworked tanks and tracks were pulled off road duty, "we couldn't even turn without breaking track." The platoon stood down to await replacement parts. As it happened, the ammunition supply point for the Blue Ghosts, who flew up every morning from Chu Lai, was adjacent to Boyd's bunker-bar, and, one thing leading to another, many of Boyd's Bastards, being otherwise idle, began joy-riding around as door gunners. Boyd, too. In fact, Boyd was blazing away with an M60 during the rescue of a gunship crew downed on Cigar Island when he was shot in the leg on December 6. The round caught Boyd in the left calf, apparently after ricocheting off the skid and losing some of its punch: he didn't know anything had happened until the other door gunner blurted that he was bleeding. The pilot landed at Baldy, where Boyd's trouser leg was cut open and a pressure bandage applied. Next stop: Qui Nhơn. The wound was debrided, then stitched, the bullet left where it was, deep in the muscle. "Nobody ever said a word about us flying as door gunners until I got shot—and then the shit hit the fan," remembers Boyd, who received a letter from McPherson while recuperating, warning that the chain of command was up in arms about the unauthorized flights. "They were going to court-martial me, but nothing ever happened."

The Pineapple Forest

NOVEMBER–DECEMBER 1967

HAVING MOVED INTO THE Pineapple Forest on Halloween, Captain Brown and C Troop, as well as the engineers tasked with flattening the area, operated from a base camp on the north edge of the woods. Rolls of concertina wire were staked around the circular patch of raw earth and more than a dozen tents erected inside: troop tents, mess tents, supply tents, a commo tent, and a tent for the command group, too. The engineers pushed up berms behind which the M48s and ACAVs faced outward at night while guarding the perimeter.

The Chinook that resupplied the base camp each morning delivered not only fuel and ammunition but enough foodstuffs to run a diner: doughnuts, eggs, and cartons of milk and orange juice for breakfast; sandwiches, apple pie, and Kool-Aid for lunch; and for dinner, beer, soda, and steaks cooked to order on field stoves. In addition, the troops plucked pineapples and wild bananas during patrols and went fishing with hand grenades. It was not a bad war in the Pineapple Forest, all things considered. Charlie Troop's platoons alternately protected the bulldozers as they felled trees—very boring—and, weather permitting, for the monsoon rains sometimes produced mud so thick and deep that armor could not pass, ran missions in those sections of the forest not yet scraped clean. The local-force VC did little more than snipe at the intruders destroying their sanctuary, armed as they were with old carbines and Thompson submachine guns, and obsolete bolt-action Mosin Nagant rifles from Russia.

Specialist Fourth Class Max Pryor sent home a Polaroid in his letter that described Charlie Troop's first contact in the Pineapple Forest. The photograph showed an ACAV parked in a sandy area. "[T]he two people in black [next to the track] are V.C.s we got today," explained Pryor. "One man[,] one woman[,] both dead. The woman was their medic . . . I didn't kill any of these. I did shoot at one this morning but doubt I got him as I couldn't get [my driver] calmed down enough to shoot good. He kept moving the track on me."

From Pryor's other Pineapple Forest letters:

[Staff Sergeant Coleman G.] Hillman got a V.C. while we were out. Shot him with [an] M16 at about 300 yards . . . I saw the V.C.[;] he had just one hole in his chest. He lived about an hour. This one had $90 on him [and was, according to papers on the body, a supply sergeant dispatched to buy provisions from a hamlet in the area].

This morning we left the bace [sic] camp at 7:00 A.M. Along about 8:30 or 9:00 A.M. got a call over the raido [sic] [that] some V.C. were spotted just South of us . . . So we cut out through the boon dock rice fields[,] and what to our su[r]prise[,] up jump 5 VC [armed with carbines, and] running like hell away from us towards the river. We all got on line and start shooting[,] and I do mean shooting[,] all six tracks[,] two guns per track[,] and[,] man[,] the lead was flying. Well[,] when the smoke of the battle lifted[,] one V.C. [was] dead[,] one [was] wounded[, and] one [hiding] in a hole had shed his black cloth[e]s for some fire engin[e] red under wear[,] and tossed his weapon into the hedge row . . . The wounded one [was] a medic woman[,] had her legs shot up bad. Sent her out on a dust off. Enclosed is a picture of the dead V.C. 35 yrs old[,] hard core . . . No G.I.s hurt. So far[,] so good[,] but it[']s hell on your nerves.

In a subsequent contact, C Troop and the crack ARVN rangers participating in the operation killed three guerrillas and captured two. Three dragoons were finally wounded the next day when a booby trap made from a dud 155mm artillery shell exploded under their track. In addition to the damaged vehicle, "[a] lot of the [other] tracks are getting in bad shape," noted Pryor. "Mostly sprockets. I don't know how some of them keep running." The troop maintenance section, which miraculously kept these overworked vehicles in action, posted a cocky sign in front of their shop: "We've done so much with so little for so long that now we can do damn near anything with nothing."

Though some of the hamlets in the forest were evacuated and razed at the start of the operation, the ARVN left alone those deemed loyal to the government. Charlie Troop did not make such distinctions: any hootches in the vicinity of a sniper incident were burned down; the fires were started by inserting a lit cigarette into a ball of C-4 and tossing the plastique atop a thatch roof. "We didn't ask. We just started doing it," recalls Pryor. "It wasn't an order. In fact, we were finally ordered to stop burning down the hootches."

Max Pryor's letters to his wife continued:

[W]e stop at a hutch [sic] an[d] look into the tunnel[,] and we've got our self [sic] a real live P.O.W. [Prisoner of War]. So I'm asking him a thing or two[,] but he don't understand me and I dam[n] sure don't understand him. So I hear [Sgt.] Durst say their [sic] they go across the rice [paddy,] and sure enough there goes six of them running like hell[,] to[o] far away to shoot. So we wrap [the] one we have up and start back in. Well about half way back to the bace [sic] camp[,] . . . Durst[']s track hits [an anti-personnel] mine[,] scares hell out of him . . .

Today we had a V.C. to give himself up . . . Seems as if things are getting to[o] damn hot for him since we started running around through his woods. I wish every dam[n] one of them would give up and then meby [sic] they would let me come home . . .

If the V.C. don't get me[,] this boy I got driving . . . is sure as hell going to get the job done by himself. I now have four stitches in the top of my middle fingure [sic] right hand. Just lucky it didn't break the dam[n] thing. Here's how it happened. We are about 2,000 meters out of bace [sic] camp. We are crossing a ditch when . . . Durst calls me and says I better cut a new trail or I may get stuck. So I have [the driver] go right out of the old tracks . . . Well[,] there is a tree on the other side leaning toward me[,] and this driver hits it like a fool and catches the .50 Cal barrel[,] which swings the gun and mashes my hand against the shield[,] cutting my fingure [*sic*] to the [bone]. I could have killed him for doing it. I'll wait until this evening when they get back and eat his ass out real good.

On November 17, Captain Brown was informed that three main-force VC companies had slipped into the Pineapple Forest to overrun C Troop's base camp. The information came from a VC captured by the ARVN. "This P.O.W. gave the places they were to mass [for the attack]," wrote Pryor; the areas were plastered during the night with artillery fire, after which an ARVN patrol reported "26 dead and blood trails running all over the dam[n] place. So guess they were real[l]y I [*sic*] after us, but got their minds changed."

On November 28, a mortar track was firing the nightly H&Is when one of the rounds landed within the perimeter, wounding Staff Sgt. Gabino Montoya and killing Platoon Sgt. Hillard E. Williams. As the story was later told, Williams only dropped to his hands and knees when the mortar men shouted a warning about the short round; for keeping his head up like an NCO while his troops ate dirt, Williams suffered a sucking chest wound. Pryor wrote home that Williams "sure was a good man[,] to[o,] and I real[l]y liked him."

Pryor noted that his original platoon leader, reassigned as troop exec, had been replaced by 2nd Lt. Ronald J. Wojtkiewicz, "fresh out of R.O.T.C.[,] green as grass. But he'll learn[,] I guess." During the lieutenant's first patrol, a man walked into the ambush set up by Hillman's infantry squad along a trail. Hillman leapt upon the man in mock fury, screaming like a madman and knocking him to the ground. Hillman put his knife to the man's throat: "Are you a VC?!" Not understanding it was all a joke, the new lieutenant pleaded with Hillman not to kill the man. "I just about got sick from laughing," wrote Pryor, noting that the "VC" turned out to have nothing on him except a wad of piasters: "Said he was going to Tam Kỳ to buy a cow[,] a likely story."

It appeared to the men of Charlie Troop that they had taken control of the Pineapple Forest. "When we first got here[, the villagers] were afraid of us [and] would hide," noted Pryor. "They [now] tell us where the V.C.

are[,] how many of them[,] and what kind of weapons they have." The village children beamed at the GIs, which "real[l]y makes you feel good," noted Pryor. Why had the villagers turned against the VC? "The V.C. come into there [sic] homes," explained Pryor, "and take there [sic] food[,] and we come in and give the[m] food [and] medical care and treat them nice." The enemy was demoralized: "The wives of the V.C. that live not more than 2,000 meters from this Bace [sic] Camp are trying to get them to quit fighting and give I [sic] up."

Actually, the main-force VC scattered by the artillery barrage were still in the area, preparing to complete their mission.

The moon did not rise over the base camp the night the troop exec was in command in the temporary absence of Captain Brown. No stars shone through the low clouds. The troopers on watch, one per vehicle, literally could not see their hands in front of their faces. They also could not see the company's worth of guerrillas stealing into attack positions north and northwest of the perimeter. Moving with cat-like stealth, the unseen guerrillas went unheard, too, as they wrapped tape around the strikers of trip-flares and snipped paths through the concertina with wire-cutters. The crews of a mortar and recoilless rifle readied their pieces: the instant they opened fire, the assault troops were to dart through the breached wire and overrun the base camp.

The shelling began fifty minutes after midnight on December 3. Specialist Fourth Class Gary L. Henspeter, manning the .50 on C-21, immediately began raking a sunken creek that ran into the base camp from the north, an obvious avenue of enemy approach. Henspeter was alone on his track, which was positioned behind a berm to the right of the creek. Max Pryor's track on the left side remained silent: the man on watch had just ambled into the platoon's troop tent, and his replacement had not yet ambled out to the C-20 track.

Startled awake, Pryor "could see flashes of light everywhere," he wrote, and rolled off his cot "towards the sand bags we have around the tent[,] and lay there for a few seconds[,] trying to figure out what in hell was going on." Realizing that the mortar fire was probably the prelude to a ground attack, he grabbed his helmet and rifle, then moved to the doorway of the tent. There was a pause in the barrage. "I break for good old 21 track[,] never run so fast in all my life. Opened the back door and get behind the .50-cal. Well[,] about that time[,] the dam[n] V.C. start laying it on our young asses again. I'm looking[,] but I can't see where the little bastards are at[,] can't see a thing[,] is blacker than hell out."

Private First Class Michael L. Colicchio was peppered in the buttocks with shrapnel when a mortar round blew down half of one of the tent's sandbag skirts. Unconcerned about the wound, Colicchio was very concerned that the bare light bulb dangling from the ceiling would attract the enemy like moths to a flame. Indeed, one of the guerrillas who had penetrated the perimeter under the barrage lobbed grenades at the glowing gap in the sandbags.

Colicchio screamed for someone to shoot out the light. Private First Class Michael D. "Duck" Newland, lying on his back, emptied his M16 at the light bulb but succeeded only in ventilating the roof of the tent. Colicchio pointed his .45 at the light bulb as he kept screaming for someone to shoot out the light and then, feeling like a fool, took aim himself and pulled the trigger. The tent went dark, and Colicchio, gathering his wits, counted to five, jumped through the hole in the wall, and sprinted to C 21. Amid the shouts, curses, and commotion in the shrapnel-ripped tent, meanwhile, Staff Sergeant Hillman, who'd caught a fragment in the back, died in the arms of a fellow GI.

Climbing aboard his track, Colicchio handed up four boxes of .50 ammo to Gary Henspeter, who had been wounded himself by then, then manned one of the M60s. By chance, Colicchio's first burst ignited three trip-flares, suddenly illuminating the perimeter, "and[,] by God[,] there is Charlie himself," wrote Pryor: the flares revealed a squad's worth of Việt Cộng in the creek bed between and directly to the front of C-20 and C-21. Caught in the sudden glare, the guerrillas tried to duck, but Henspeter, up high in his command cupola, immediately "had his 50 on them[,]" continued Pryor, "and is shooting there [sic] guts out[.]" Pryor dipped the barrel of his own machine gun toward the enemy, "and we both blaze a path on them. I look to my left and see some I [sic] there[,] so turn the gun on them and shoot the hell out of two of them."

Pryor continued firing to the front, unaware of the VC to the rear, one of whom trained an RPG on the back hatch of his track. The explosion blew the hatch in half. Regaining his senses, Pryor found himself sprawled inside his track, surrounded by smoke. He thought the vehicle was on fire and meant to evacuate the thing when "two more [mortar] rounds come in so close I think I better risk the fire on two on[e] than the lead out side." There was no fire, however: instead, shrapnel had ignited a smoke grenade. Pryor reached to turn on his radio, but there was no radio: it had been blown away. "Then it dawns on me that I got some thing running down the back of my legs. Yep[,] it[']s blood[,] but we are still having a hell of a battle. Well[,] we shoot two more and everything stops coming in. What a releaf [sic][,] I ain't kidding you one bit. My Mouth is so dray [sic] I can't spit nothing[.]" As the attack fizzled, Pryor hailed his buddy Newland, who'd been "helping the wounded boys in the tent and getting them out . . . Duck and I get to shooting some at nothing."

Tanks blasted the night with canister as the exec requested artillery, gunships, and a flareship. When the radio went dead, 1st Sgt. Richard F. Williams and two men pushed the troop commander's radio-jeep to the command track so that commo could be reestablished. Caught in his skivvies when the attack began, Williams wore only helmet, flak jacket, pistol belt, and jungle boots as he tightened up the defenses and directed that the wounded be moved to the helipad. However astonishing his appearance, the troops were reassured that Williams had taken control of the situation: their tough but fatherly topkick was a veteran of both Korea and a previous tour in Việt Nam.

In the silence that followed the enemy attack, the first round of supporting artillery could be heard rushing through the night air: shockingly, the 155mm shell exploded in the center of the base camp. The exec called for a check-fire. Gunships circled the base camp instead, machine guns blazing. Pryor told Newland, meanwhile, he thought he'd been hit in the ass. Newland struck a match to confirm the injury: it looked like Pryor had taken a blast of birdshot to his hindquarters and the back of his legs. Shaken, Pryor asked for a cigarette. Newland ripped open a carton of C-rations for the pack of Kents inside, then sent Pryor to the helipad. "I get there," wrote Pryor, "and[,] boy[,] it's a mess."

Specialist Fourth Class John A. Davis and Charles L. Motin, two of the medics patching up the wounded at the helipad, had themselves been wounded. Total casualties for Charlie Troop: two dead, thirty wounded. Max Pryor saw that the crotch of his driver's pants had been cut away and a big white field dressing secured around his genitals: half the head of the man's penis had been removed by a chunk of shrapnel. The medevacs landed by flare light. Pryor ended up on his stomach on a gurney in an evac hospital at Chu Lai as a doctor whose white tennis shoes had turned black with dried blood plucked the shrapnel from his buttocks and legs, flicking it to the floor. The casualties would have been worse had the attackers not been throwing the homemade potato-mashers known as Chicoms, modeled as they were after the grenades produced by the Chinese communists: twenty-five dud grenades were found by morning's light, along with four bangalore torpedoes, an RPG launcher, and five AK-47s.

The body count from the sweep of the perimeter: twelve.

The number of probable kills claimed by Charlie Troop: twenty.

Not one to take things lying down, First Sergeant Williams had words with a one-star general who helicoptered into the base camp at first light. The general allegedly pointed to the battle junk littered across the area and demanded to know why there had not yet been a police call. Another version of the tale has the general raising hell about a tank whose engine, or pack, had been pulled for repairs before the attack. The two-ton deck plate had not been replaced, as it should have been, and, as a result, an incoming mortar round had exploded inside the empty engine compartment, damaging the interior of the M48.

First Sergeant Williams was transferred out of the unit within days of his confrontation with the general. It happened that the dragoons had begun an infusion program at that time in which a certain number of troopers were sent to different units across Việt Nam. Those units, in return, sent the same number of their own GIs to the 1-1 Cavalry. Such a mixing of personnel, required of all units new to the war zone, ensured that an outfit was no longer made up entirely of men who would rotate home at the same time, to be substituted en masse by green replacements. The program was universally despised: no soldier wants to be torn from those men alongside whom he has trained and undergone his baptism of fire. Officers argued that the program was not only bad for morale but unnecessary: the normal replacement of casualties would have been enough to stagger rotation dates, especially for those units fighting in I Corps.

Williams might have fallen victim to the infusion program. The timing of his transfer, however, told the men of Charlie Troop that their beloved topkick was being punished for standing up to a general in their behalf.

As it happened, the reassignment was to have fatal results.

The executive officer received the Silver Star, as did Gary Henspeter, whose fire was credited with breaking up the attack. First Sergeant Williams, Mike Colicchio, and Max Pryor were awarded Bronze Stars, along with the medics and those dragoons who'd manned their vehicles despite wounds. To serve the needs of career officers, the number of kills recorded in the squadron log more than doubled in subsequent reports, and the quick, sharp firefight was transformed on paper into a four-hour battle in which C Troop fended off a battalion of VC and NVA marching on Tam Kỳ.

The troop lost one more man during the Pineapple Forest operation: Pvt. 1st Class Michael J. Saunders, driver of C-10, which ran over a mine while pursuing a group of unidentified Vietnamese. The explosion flipped the track over; an acetylene torch was used to cut a hole in the armor so Saunders' body could be recovered. "Losing a man to a mine, that makes you bitter," recalls a former Charlie Trooper. "That makes you want to encounter the enemy."

Max Pryor spent three weeks at the 67th Evac Hospital in Qui Nhơn, during which he underwent additional surgery to remove a piece of shrapnel in his heel. "I wish the people back home could see some of the boys that come in here," he wrote his wife. "Some are so dam[n] shot up you wouldn't believe it if I told you. And not a one of them I've seen ever complains. Last night they brought in two V.C. shot all to hell," he continued. "They get the same treatment that the rest of us get. I guess it['s] only [the] right thing to do[,] but still[,] you get to wondering about it." In another letter, Pryor commented on another badly wounded prisoner in the hospital: "Meby [sic] he'll die[,] I hope."

Though Pryor enjoyed trading war stories with Platoon Sergeant Boyd, also recuperating at Qui Nhơn, he was otherwise miserable—pricked with too many needles and wracked with fever and diarrhea, as well as homesick, unable to sleep, and anxious about returning to the field. Pryor kept his concerns from his wife, who was worried enough with both a husband and a kid brother in Việt Nam. Instead, he opened up to his own brother.

"I keep telling myself that you were over here and you made [it] okay," Pryor wrote to the ex-Seabee. "But[,] you know[,] there ain't a dam[n] thing a man can do about getting killed. I've seen several people over here get smoked and die. It don't look like there is anything to it. They just quit breathing for good. I keep thinking about all them good times I had back home and how much I'd like to get to do it again. What I real[l]y want you to know is that if I do get it over here[,] it was for nothing."

The war was futile, thought Pryor, because the politicians in Washington didn't have the guts to wage total war against Hà Nội: "I think any country that fights ought to either shit or get off the pot . . . [W]e are the best there is[,] I've no doubt about it. But your [sic] held back in dam[n] near everything you do."

Pryor cautioned his brother that "I'd just as soon you'd burn this up after you read it[,] no one needs to know how I feel. I just wanted you to."

The Best Defense Is a Strong Offense

DECEMBER 1967

ON DECEMBER 5, B Troop of the 1-9 Cav pounced on a party of NVA spotted atop a ridge two klicks north of LZ Ross. Supported by gunships, the aero-rifle platoon made quick work of the surprised enemy, killing seventeen. This was no ordinary group of NVA: many wore camouflage uniforms, leather pistol belts, and matching gold rings, and were equipped with compasses and binoculars of Chinese and Russian make. In addition, the victorious Blues picked up map cases and pouches stuffed with documents. Before being lifted out, some of the Blues peered through the captured binoculars and saw that the enemy's position had afforded them a panoramic view of LZ Ross.

The brigade intelligence officer established that nine of the enemy dead were officers, to include a regimental commander: the Blues had wiped out the command group of the 3rd Regiment, 2nd NVA Division. The captured maps and documents indicated that the enemy was planning a major offensive in the Quế Sơn Valley. No one played cute with the intelligence windfall: meetings were held in which all troops on the firebase were informed that the enemy was massing for a full-scale ground assault on Landing Zone Ross.

The briefings got everyone's attention, to say the least.

§

Captain Barovetto's troops encountered only the rare sniper as they churned across rice paddies and islands alternately lashed by monsoon rains and covered by mist. Smoke funneled skyward in the wake of the patrols: the airmobile brigade had been granted permission to destroy those hamlets identified in the captured documents as staging areas. Lieutenant Colonel Bob L. Gregory, new commander of the 2nd of the 12th Cav, was particularly zealous in putting hootches to the torch and, seeing the war in black-and-white terms, seemed unable to distinguish between the enemy and those who lived in enemy territory. During one patrol, he instructed that an elderly farmer be sent in for questioning. The company commander on the scene ignored Gregory: he had neither the heart to tear the pitiful old man from his half-demolished home nor to burn him out. In response, as the disgusted captain later informed his fellow officers, the battalion commander—who wore skin-tight black gloves and carried a CAR15—shot the old man from his command ship and reported the kill as VC.

Returning to the firebase, Captain Barovetto's tanks and tracks pulled into defilade positions excavated by bulldozer between the infantry bunkers. The crews used the guard shacks on the perimeter as sleeping positions. Tenting was draped over the doorway so that letters could be safely read by candlelight: when the howitzers fired, the concussion would snuff out the candles. With the temperature rising to no more than seventy-five degrees during the day, the troops were supplied long-sleeved, olive-drab, woolen undershirts to keep the chill off during patrol. At night, with the temperature falling to fifty-five, they curled up in the extra blankets they had also been issued.

The gregarious Captain Barovetto, conscientious about knowing his men as individuals, swung an entrenching tool alongside them as they reinforced their positions with sandbags. The crew of each vehicle also positioned to its front a 55-gallon drum filled with jellied gasoline—phougas—and rigged for detonation with a claymore mine. If conventional firepower did not stop the enemy, the phougas was to be set off as a last resort. "We were expecting a human-wave attack," notes Richard Sears. "It was very frightening to contemplate ten thousand NVA trying to charge across your little compound."

Trooping the line at night to keep those on guard jacked up, Captain Barovetto also cautioned that he'd better not find anyone asleep—or smoking pot. The stuff was readily available from the merchants who set up shop outside the main gate of Ross: in addition to doing laundry, cutting hair, and selling black-market beer and canned food, they also peddled little four-packs of marijuana cigarettes in plastic bags. Ron Decktor recalls that the crew of his platoon's mortar track "was having a party one night with these guys they were camped next to from the 2nd of the 12th Cav. They were drinking and smoking something," continues Decktor, when the mortar men came up with the brilliant idea "to fire a mortar round straight up to see if it would come straight down. I heard the pop, and all of a sudden these guys started running all over the place away from the track. The round landed just outside the wire."

To bolster the confidence of the troops, and intimidate the enemy, Mad Minutes were fired at random times during the hours of darkness: that is, every man behind an M16, M60, M79, or .50-caliber machine gun on the bunker line, as well as the crew of the base's M55 Quad-50, would commence firing on signal and continue blazing away for at least sixty seconds. The perimeter would literally light up from the muzzle flashes as thousands of red tracers dissected the black void or, hitting something, ricocheted away in dazzling arcs. The troops loved the Mad Minutes, though it had originally been disconcerting to hear the rounds snap-snap-snapping just overhead from the Quad-50, which fired from the high ground behind and above the bunker line. The tank and track crews quickly learned to bend their antennas and hook them down before a Mad Minute, lest they lose them to the Quad-50.

In addition, B-52 bombers conducted a nighttime "Arc Light" on suspected enemy positions in the Qué Sons. They flew the usual six to a formation, and too high to be seen or heard from the ground. Each of the six B-52s carried 108 bombs, and the mission total of 648 was enough to moonscape a strip of jungle about a kilometer wide and three kilometers long. The effect of the bombing was part earthquake, part lightening storm. "They started on the back side of the mountain, so all we could see at first were the flashes," notes Sears. The explosions walked to the top of the ridge, then "all the way down into the valley toward us. It was absolutely the most incredible thing to witness."

§

During December the 11th Light Infantry Brigade arrived from Schofield Barracks, Hawaii. As a result, the Americal had five major combat elements: the 11th, 196th, and 198th Light Infantry Brigades, the attached 1-1 Cavalry of the 1st Armored Division, and the attached 3rd Brigade, 4th Infantry Division.

The Turning of the Screw

DECEMBER 1967

CAPTAIN DAVID E. ROESLER, a twenty-six-year-old South Dakotan and graduate of West Point, Class of '64, took command of A Troop on December 15. Originally assigned as logistics officer, Roesler—who wore jump wings and a Ranger tab—had been vocal about getting a troop command. Finally in the job he wanted, Roesler led a two-platoon sweep across the sands east of Highway 1 the day after replacing Conrad. One of those platoons was Boyd's Bastards, which, absent its wounded namesake, was now under 2nd Lt. Daniel J. Guida, a replacement officer also on his first mission with Alpha Troop.

Lieutenant Guida had to call in a medevac when a trooper was nailed in a one-shot, hit-and-run incident and then again when probably the same sniper nailed a second trooper. One of them, Pvt. 1st Class James E. McGuinn, was standing beside his vehicle as a broken track was repaired when he was suddenly felled. As the general area was sprayed with return fire, Ron Fortner, the vehicle commander, rolled McGuinn into one of the tread marks behind their track. McGuinn had been shot in the stomach. It was McGuinn's second wound and, looking up at Fortner, he asked, "Sarge, is it bad enough for me to go home?" Fortner told him the happy truth: "I believe it is."

The sweep turned southwest, and perhaps an hour had passed and two kilometers been crossed when one of the supporting Blue Ghosts took a round while skimming past the village of Vĩnh An. The shot came from the outskirts of the village, which stretched along a stream for some thousand meters. The pilot went in for a closer look and, passing directly over the spider hole in which the VC was crouched with his AK-47, took a burst of fire that disabled the little Loach. The pilot crash-landed near A Troop. The helicopter burned on impact. Another Blue Ghost landed to take aboard the crew, one of whom had been shot in the leg. What happened next was in accordance with the principle of collective retribution: the sky filled with gunships and, as recorded in the squadron log and recounted by ex-medic Larry Gaydon, "they began flying in there one after another, groups of 'em, and just leveled that village. There was so much firepower going in there, it was unbelievable."

As the war rolled along, Captain Roesler, cool and confident, claimed a reputation as the most aggressive troop commander in the squadron. The troops respected him. The noncoms loved him. There was an arrogant undertone to Roesler's hairy-chested persona, however, that some lieutenants found off-putting; to quote one of them: "I think Roesler was trying to emulate George Patton—he was a tough sonofabitch, and don't you forget it."

Bottom line about Captain Roesler, according to one of his former platoon leaders: "He hated dinks, and loved making contact." The lieutenant was disturbed that the unit moved single file between wooded areas, making no attempt to screen the flanks, and finally questioned Roesler about his tactics. "I want them to ambush me," Roesler replied. "Then I can kill them."

During one of Roesler's early missions near Cigar Island, "I remember there were three men in a raft," says Dan Guida, "and Roesler taking an M79 grenade launcher and shooting at 'em, but he didn't hit 'em." The men in the raft immediately paddled out of sight. Were the Vietnamese in the boat military-age males who had broken curfew? Perhaps A Troop had just come under fire, and these might be snipers trying to slip away? No and no, says Guida: "It was just three guys in a raft, and he popped a round at them. I think he said something about, you know, that they were VC or something."

On December 21, Lieutenant Wallace's platoon, minus its tanks, started across the Trường Giang at the narrow midsection of Cigar Island. The command track and a scout track successfully swam the river, but the front of Sgt. 1st Class Thomas R. Kisner's infantry track dipped slightly about halfway across: filling instantly with water, the vehicle nose-dived out of sight, leaving three troopers bobbing in the river. The driver finally popped to the surface to join them. The waterlogged cavalrymen were rescued by a Blue Ghost, who dragged them to shore across the surface of the water as they hung onto the skids of the Loach.

Trapped in the command cupola, Kisner drowned, as did a black trooper just assigned to the track. Their bodies were brought up by navy skin-divers. Sergeant First Class Kisner was "really a great guy," wrote Larry Graham. "He [survived] Korea[,] and then he goes and drowns [in Vietnam], what a waste."

Separated from the rest of the unit, Lieutenant Wallace and the scout track accompanying his command track linked up with a platoon choppered in from the 196th Light Infantry Brigade, then pushed south in the light provided by a flareship to find a good defensive position. Contact was made along the way, a body count of three reported. Finding a sandy piece of high ground dotted with scrub pines, the grunts dug hasty foxholes around the two ACAVs.

When the flareship finally broke station, an artillery battery provided illume, but when each parachute flare hit the sand and winked out, there was a period of some minutes before the next one popped overhead. The enemy struck during those pitch-black interludes. "Lot of green tracers were coming over our heads, and there were a couple hits on the vehicles," recounts Michael F. Dolan, then the lieutenant's track commander. The enemy had at least one RPD. "They'd let off a burst and move," notes Dolan. "It got pretty intense on one part of the perimeter. I was on the .50, and just mowed all the fuckin' trees down. Infantry guys were coming back to us: we broke out a case of M16 ammo for 'em, and hand grenades. Man, it felt like Custer's Last Stand out there."

Lieutenant Wallace would be decorated for controlling the return fire, plus gunships and artillery. The enemy backed off before dawn, leaving fourteen bodies, according to the squadron log, after which Captain Roesler came across the river with the 2nd Platoon and the remainder of the 3rd. The next day, December 23, Alpha Troop followed the beach down the ever-narrowing island and found a tunnel while setting up a blocking position for the infantry. Private First Class William Preston went in with a .45, shot a VC who threw a grenade at him, then backed out, stung with shrapnel, ears ringing from the report of his own pistol. Preston donned a gas mask, went back in behind a CS grenade, and lobbed two of his own grenades at shadows at the end of the thirty-foot tunnel, killing four more VC—and winning the Silver Star.

The mission folded up then, a blazing success, though some tough stuff happened out there, according to Mike Dolan, which was not recorded in the squadron log. To begin with, not all those counted as dead were actually dead when found: when a VC sprang from a bunker with an AK-47 later determined to have only one round left in the magazine, "he got shot in the side of the head, then got finished off by somebody stampin' on his head." Two prisoners were added to the body count, says Dolan, when "they died of Excedrin .45"—shot in the head with a pistol wielded by a vengeful GI. Dolan was told that another prisoner was lashed to the front of a tank and driven through a row of thatch-and-brick hootches, an experience the man did not survive. The only official suggestion that body counts were valued more than prisoners might be found in A Troop's last report before recrossing the Trường Giang: a detainee just "picked up" was shot while "attempt[ing] to escape."

Finally, Dolan tells of seeing VC who had been decapitated: "The heads were impaled on a fence inside a village." Mike Dolan thought Charlie got what he deserved, and he speaks about these alleged incidents reluctantly, and somewhat angrily; as he says: "What happened in Vietnam should stay in Vietnam."

Platoon Sergeant Boyd circumvented the policy that patients whose convalescence at Qui Nhơn last more than twenty days would be evacuated to Japan by simply cutting out his own stitches with a pair of scissors when his departure date approached. The doctor making the morning rounds squinted at Boyd's leg, remarking that he had not removed the stitches. "You sure did, doc," replied Boyd. The doctor examined Boyd's chart: there was no such annotation. "Well, you had a good lookin' nurse with you," joked Boyd. "Maybe you were too distracted to write it down." The doctor, knowing he was being had, brusquely told Boyd to get up and walk down the ward and back, which the tough old soldier did, refusing to limp or otherwise acknowledge the pain shooting through his leg. Marked fit for duty, however grudgingly, Boyd flew up to Chu Lai, and then hopped a resupply bird to Hill 29 on or about Christmas Eve.

During Boyd's absence, a good ol' boy staff sergeant from Alabama who flew the stars-and-bars from the radio mast of his track had been infused into the 1st Platoon of A Troop. Tom Bursott recalls that the black troopers were galled to be riding under the battle flag of the Confederate States of America. Bursott also recalls that a female prisoner identified as a medic was placed on the staff sergeant's track for return to Hill 29. The platoon bogged down in a mud-slick rice paddy on the way home, however, and was forced to spend the night where the tracks had slithered to a halt. The next morning, the staff sergeant "popped his head up," says Bursott, "and said something to the effect that: 'That VC nurse was real good to me.' I had a buddy on that track, and later on he said, yeah, the sergeant had raped her inside the track. Rumors flew that she had been raped repeatedly: a couple other guys had decided to get in on it." Bursott's letters home make no mention of an alleged rape; he does note in a letter written during the holiday season that the staff sergeant was no longer in the unit and that: "The first shirt [McPherson] made us take [the rebel flag] down[.]"

Lieutenant Guida and the recently returned Platoon Sergeant Boyd would later disavow any knowledge of a female prisoner being violated in any way, shape, or form by Alpha Troop. Still, the staff sergeant's sudden disappearance implies that Boyd and First Sergeant McPherson—more savvy than the green lieutenant—had gotten wind of some type of troubling incident and palmed off the offender on another unit. More explicitly, Dick Taskey speaks of an alleged incident that dovetails with Bursott's account. Taskey does not recall Bursott's staff sergeant but says the troopers on a track taking a female prisoner to Hill 29 "made her give them blowjobs. She told her story to somebody outside of our outfit," presumably after being sent to the rear for interrogation, and with questions being asked from above, "Platoon Sergeant Boyd kind of held a meeting, and chewed everybody's ass about what happened." At that point, "it got hushed up," says Taskey. "It didn't go no farther than that." In other words, no court-martials, no dishonorable discharges, no ruined lives for the sake of a lousy VC.

Two things lend credence to this barbaric story: first, Tom Bursott, a proud veteran, would have no reason to invent a tale of rape.

Second, other veterans of Alpha Troop would speak of a repeat of the incident which took place in the coming months.

Having gotten away with it once . . .

Bursott and some of the black guys took the Confederate flag left by the staff sergeant from Alabama to the firing range at Hill 29. They used the flag to zero an M60, then took the tattered stars-and-bars back to their bunker, notes Bursott, "and any new guy that came in after that, we pointed it out to him and said, 'That's what happens to white crackers around here.'"

Combat operations continued through the holiday season, even as the dragoons were overwhelmed with presents and care packages from home. "It[']s Christmas Eve today, and don't believe what you hear about a Christmas truce," Larry Graham wrote his wife. "It[']s all a lot of bullshit."

Lieutenant Guida was sweeping along the Trường Giang on Christmas morning when his platoon took fire from a tree line, paused to return the fire, and then continued across the sand only to lose a track to a mine. Three men were wounded, including Sergeant Fortner. "The explosion blew me out with the turret," he recalls. "Bummed my knee up." Guida was instructed to laager up after the medevac and wait for the arrival of a helicopter with the call sign Reindeer. The chopper was decked out with holiday decorations, and when it landed, "Major Lundquist popped out in a Santa Claus suit," recalls an astonished Nate Boyd, who liked the usually hardnosed executive officer. "He came out to wish us Merry Christmas and all that good shit, and he brought our mail with him."

At some point during the holiday season, A Troop stopped near a hamlet east of the highway, and while the adults were being questioned about guerrilla activity in the area, recalls Tom Bursott, "I taught the kids a Christmas song: 'Jingle Bells,' or something like that. Then a buddy of mine came back in [from a patrol through the same hamlet], and said, 'Oh, that was the damnedest thing: we pulled into this village, and all these kids started singing "Jingle Bells"!' All I did was smile." The smile was soon wiped off Bursott's face. "We went back into that area a day or two later," he recounts, "and we had to medevac a Vietnamese that we'd talked with because the Việt Cộng apparently thought he'd been too friendly with the Americans—so they broke his arms and legs, and cracked his ribs—just for talking with us. We put the poor guy on a medevac."

The skies above Hill 29, and every other base, lit up on cue when the clock struck midnight on New Year's Eve: tracers, flares, illumination rounds, every kind of munitions available, and plenty of it. Beautiful. Even units in the field, and operations continued right through the latest truce, did their part to usher in the new year; to quote Larry Graham's latest letter: "I'll bet you can guess what I was doing at midnite last nite! We were roaring across a rice paddy in hot pursuit of Charlie. We did celebrate with 1 can of soda or beer per man—and we all fired some hand flares from our vehicles. It was so exciting!!"

PART TWO
1968

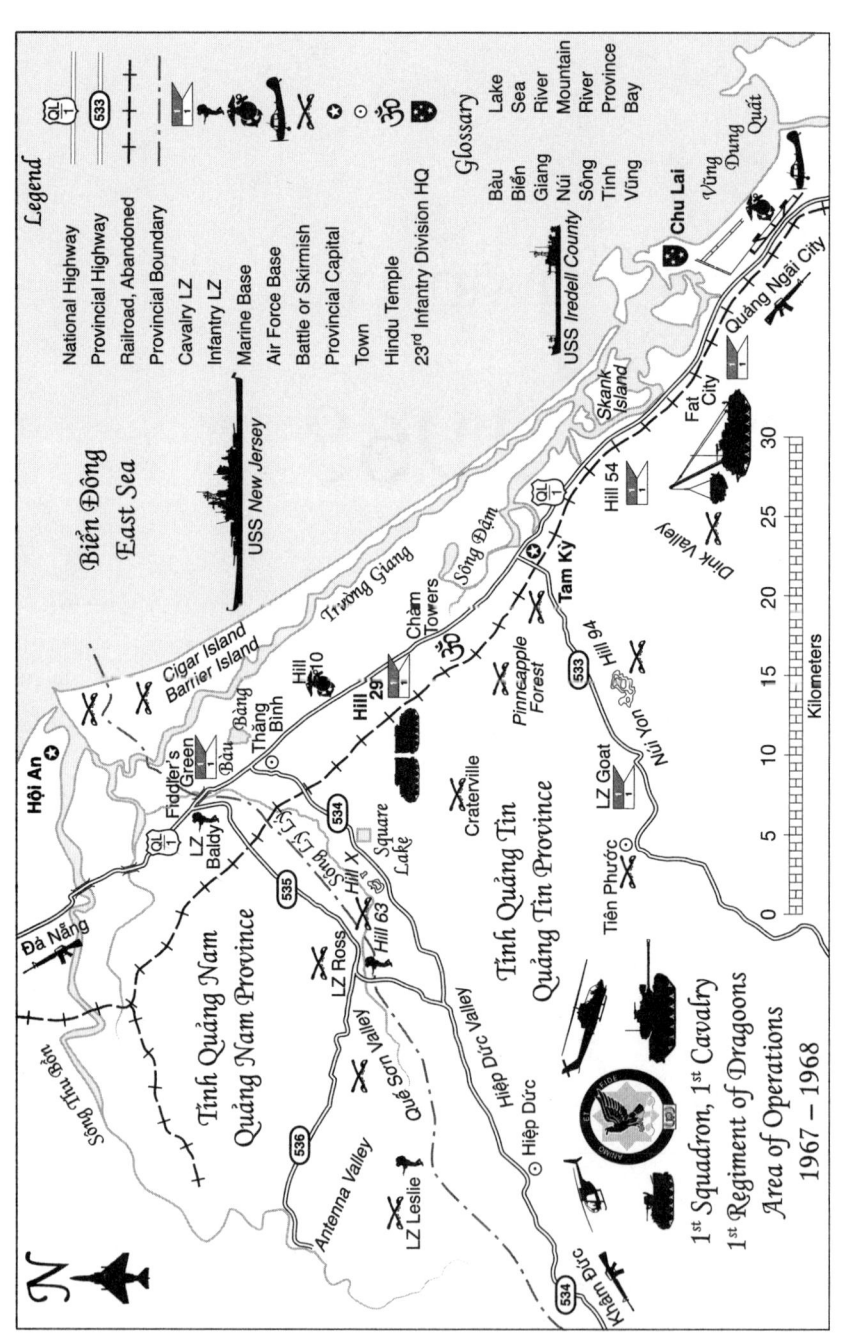

Changing of the Guard

JANUARY 2 AND 7, 1968

ON THE SECOND DAY of the new year, Lt. Col. Walter C. "Mike" Cousland assumed command of the squadron, and on the seventh, Butch Saint, reassigned to division, was replaced by Maj. Wade E. Medbery, Jr. Nothing unusual there: officers usually spent three to six months on the line and the balance of their tours in a staff position. The constant reshuffling might have wreaked havoc on unit cohesion, but it served the ambition of the regulars who needed combat duty, preferably in a command slot, to climb the next rung on the career ladder. There was a waiting list for such commands. The process was known as ticket punching, and that, transparently, was why Cousland, who was being groomed for general officer, had been recommended by the armor branch to command the 1-1 Cavalry in Việt Nam.

The selection seemed preordained. Mike Cousland was the son of a colonel and was second-generation West Point, Class of '53. As a new lieutenant, Cousland, fluent in Spanish, given his father's postings in Latin America—the son also spoke a bit of French and Italian—was detached to the U.S. military mission in El Salvador from his parent unit in Panamá. Cousland served as aide-de-camp to a division commander upon returning Stateside in 1956. Next: captain's bars, the armor advance school, and command of a tank company in Germany, 1959–1961.

Earning his masters and a promotion to major, Cousland served on the faculty of the English Department, U.S. Military Academy, from

1962–1966. Handsome, sophisticated, and poised—a very eligible bachelor—Cousland finally married a beautiful and vivacious divorcée with two young children in 1964. Their daughter was born in 1966. Pinning on silver oak leaves, Cousland attended the Command and General Staff College at Fort Leavenworth, Kansas, and, upon graduation, assumed duties in July 1967 at United States Army, Vietnam (USARV) headquarters at Long Bình, near Sài Gòn. Six months later, he got his command. Thus, Mike Cousland: an urbane gentleman of thirty-six who would have succeeded in the academic or business world but had no qualms clamping on a helmet and taking his turn in a hell-for-leather outfit like the First Regiment of Dragoons.

Major Medbery of Clinton, Oklahoma, had originally received a reserve commission through the ROTC program at his local state college in 1956. Following six months on active duty, he spent eight years in a variety of jobs, from accountant to service manager in a car dealership, before being recalled on the eve of the big buildup for Việt Nam. Built like a fireplug, Medbery sported aviator shades and a white-walled flattop, and had what he describes as the personality of a chainsaw in an icehouse. The major could certainly be overbearing, but he was a bulldog whose bark was usually worse than his bite.

Given the differences in background and temperament, the relationship between Cousland and Medbery was to prove chilly. Medbery was more in sync with Major Lundquist, who, all hard feelings aside, was doing a terrific job keeping replacement troops, parts, and vehicles, plus the beans, bullets, and bandages, moving forward from the squadron rear at Fat City.

In any event, a new command team for a new year.

Like Nothing that Had Come Before

JANUARY 3–16, 1968

*H*AVING HEARD WOLF CRIED *too many times, B Troop, and the 2nd of the 12th Cav, came to doubt the predictions of an attack on LZ Ross. If the capture of the enemy's battle plans had seen the attack called off, the daily patrols, around-the-clock artillery fire, air strikes, and earth-rumbling Arc Light had presumably forced the NVA to seek refuge deep in the Quế Sơn Mountains.*

Not so. Final preparations for the offensive having been completed during the deceptive lull, the 3rd and 21st Regiments, 2nd NVA Division, were poised to hit LZ Ross, as well as LZ Leslie, an outpost at the far end of the valley, just below the ridge that separates the Quế Sơn Valley from the Hiệp Đức Valley. The 1st Main Force VC Regiment was to simultaneously strike the 196th Light Infantry Brigade in the Hiệp Đức Valley. The enemy went on radio silence on New Year's Day—an indication that he was on the move—and on January 2, C/2-12 Cav made heavy contact along a ridge west of LZ Ross. Two GIs were killed against 39 NVA. In addition, Company C took two prisoners who informed the brigade intelligence officer that they were part of a thousand-man unit that had come forward with mortars, antiaircraft weapons, and six 122mm rocket launchers, a weapon not previously encountered in the Quế Sơn Valley.

§

Night fell, the hours passed. Ken Bouche ambled over to visit Ron Decktor, on guard in the TC hatch of the platoon leader's track, and the two were idly sipping beer and watching the wire when, astonishingly, a red glow came screaming from the darkness, aimed straight at them and trailing sparks. It took a dumbfounded instant to recognize the apparition as an incoming rocket: the two scrambled inside the command track as the thing passed overhead to burst behind them in a dazzling thunderclap. The time: 1:37 a.m. January 3.

Rocket followed upon rocket, and as enemy soldiers darted into the wire under their own barrage, each infantry bunker, and tank and track in defilade, hosed down its assigned field of fire. It was Mad Minute time, for real, and without pause. "We lit it up with everything we had," says Decktor, who was banging away behind his .50, while Bouche alternated between both M60s. Soon enough, a flareship was orbiting overhead, and a cargo-plane-turned-gunship of the type nicknamed "Puff the Magic Dragon" arrived with three miniguns that flashed at six thousand rounds per minute per gun: every fourth round was a tracer, and the effect was that of a red waterfall. In the clamor and din, Decktor's lieutenant, apparently unnerved by the rocket that narrowly missed his bunker—wounding the field mechanic whom Bouche had sent to fetch the green platoon leader—never climbed aboard the command track.

The incoming was so intense that even a veteran like Gene Hotchkiss hesitated before leaving cover and making a break for his own track. Climbing aboard, Hotchkiss lobbed several M79 shells toward a boulder shielding an enemy mortar crew and was preparing to fire again when suddenly shocked with a whip of pain: his left hand was on fire, as if stung by hornets.

The other machine gunner, who had set up a dismounted firing position, suddenly stood beside the vehicle, shouting at Hotchkiss: "Give me that M79! You keep missing—I wanna get them sonsabitches!"

"I think it blew up on me!"

"There's nothing wrong with that grenade launcher, you dumbshit: a mortar round hit right next to you!"

Hotchkiss handed over the grenade launcher and, with knuckles skinned raw by shrapnel, opened up with his M60. One of their mortar tracks, meanwhile, expertly dropped a white-phosphorous round on the enemy mortar men.

Richard Sears, acting tank commander, saw nothing in his sights as he methodically worked the tank's coaxial machine gun back and forth, and up and down, too, so to rain tracers on any enemy in the paddies below the firebase. Though not under ground attack, Sears was in jeopardy nonetheless: the back deck of his tank was stacked with 90mm rounds pulled from the ready rack that afternoon for a tank that was short of main-gun ammo. The other crew never picked up the rounds, however, and the enemy now bracketed Sears' tank with mortar fire, trying to touch off what would have been a catastrophic secondary explosion. As such, while Sears kept up his fire, another crewman had no choice but to exit the turret and, while fully exposed to the fire, pass the rounds up to the third member of the crew, who returned them to the ready rack.

Ron Decktor and Staff Sergeant Bouche exchanged fire with enemy soldiers tucked behind boulders in the creek bed directly to the front of their track. "Bullets were hitting the boulders," recounts Decktor. "Sparks were flying. We had illumination, and I could see 'em running around the boulders and stuff, and at some point I thought I could hear 'em yelling at us, too. When the flares burned out, the canister would just drop: it made a weird whistling noise on the way down. I was scared to death." The grunts dug in beside the vehicle held their M16s above their position, firing blindly. Decktor bellowed at them to get their heads up. No way: the track had the real firepower. Decktor was blown back against his gun tub when a mortar round hit the berm in front of his track. Ears ringing, he resumed firing, only to have "something hit to the right of us, and I got a dent in my helmet about two inches above my ear, and a little steel shard in my face. Bouche was really concerned, but it wasn't bad: we just pulled it out of my cheek, and I got back behind the .50 again."

The effect of the sustained fire of a cavalry troop and three rifle companies: not a single enemy soldier got through the wire at Landing Zone Ross.

Friendly casualties: one dead, a handful of wounded.

The night glowed at the far end of the valley where D/2-12 Cav was fighting for its life at LZ Leslie, the enemy having breached the bunker line behind a barrage of tear-gas shells. When the hilltop was finally taken back, the bodies of fifty-eight NVA were counted. U.S. casualties: fifteen KIA, at least fifty-five WIA.

Tasked with pursuit, Staff Sergeant Tinker led a dismounted patrol out of Ross on the drizzly morning of January 3. Tinker was questioning villagers in a nearby hamlet when a scout ship detected movement in a tree line. The spot marked with smoke, Tinker's patrol advanced across a furrowed peanut patch. Sergeant Webster had the lead, one man to his right rear, another to his left rear: a triangle-shaped point team. Webster recalls glancing back at Spc. 4th Class Barry J. Schmidt, the man to his left rear, "and I couldn't even believe it, but he had cradled his M16 to light a cigarette—and there was [the crack of] one AK-47 round [at that moment], and he went down."

The patrol was returning fire when Tinker—casually walking about while his men were at the prone—kicked Webster in the foot to get his attention and told him that he had to get up there and get Schmidt. Webster wormed his way to Schmidt with another dragoon and, dragging their gut-shot buddy from the furrow in which he had lain, enemy and friendly fire crisscrossing just overhead, saw him lifted out moments later on a Huey.

Captain Barovetto came forward with tanks, tracks, and infantry, and worked the next enemy-held tree line with artillery fire. Going in afterward with a small team, Tinker maneuvered behind an NVA guarding a mortar pit, knocked the man insensible with the butt of his .45, then flattened another NVA who sprang from a spider hole. The second enemy soldier begged to surrender. Tinker obliged him. Leaving several men with the prisoners, Tinker came upon a second mortar position where he captured a third NVA and another 82mm mortar, a feat that earned the laconic old soldier the Silver Star. Ten other enemy soldiers were slain in the woods, to include four blown away with a canister round. Barovetto exultantly announced that anyone who wanted to see what canister did at point-blank range should take a look. The terrified prisoners were placed inside a track. Webster was standing beside the lowered back ramp when a trooper sitting inside engaged one of the bound and helpless North Vietnamese in a menacing conversation about how he was probably the bastard who'd shot Barry Schmidt. "As soon as I heard that, I knew what was coming," says Webster, and when the trooper "grabbed his Bowie knife and lunged to slash the prisoner's throat, I grabbed him and got him out of there."

The enemy had left clutches of bodies around the firebase, some hanging in the wire. The dead were regulars with green uniforms, web gear, tennis shoes, AKs, RPGs, and Chicoms. How many were killed depends on the log or after-action report being consulted: 138, 143, 212, 242. In any event, more than the dragoons had ever seen. Tying ropes around the feet of the dead, the cavalrymen dragged them behind their tracks—more bodies were stacked on the back ramps—then rolled the bodies into burial pits, a jumble of arms and legs and lolling heads. Ron Decktor notes that "It was messy: flies and maggots and everything. I remember one of the guys throwing up. I mean, it was really nasty."

Lieutenant Colonel Gregory spent four days planning, reorganizing, resupplying, and waiting for good flying weather before kicking off the full-scale, post-attack sweep of the Quế Sơn Valley on the morning of January 7. Scout ships drifted over the paddies and tree lines, and Gregory went airborne, too, as A/2-12 Cav, followed by C/2-12 Cav, hiked down a slightly elevated dirt road that ran in a crooked line all the way from Ross to the end of the valley, a distance of eight kilometers. Captain Barovetto and B Troop followed with the firebase's bulldozer, which was to smooth out the steep banks of a stream that cut the road a klick and a half out to allow passage of the M48s and ACAVs.

Company A was a klick beyond the stream, and passing through Xuân Quế 5 when enemy soldiers draped with leafy branches were seen moving along a tree line to the south. Gregory excitedly ordered Company A into the attack. Sensing an ambush, the company commander left his weapons platoon on the road to provide fire support, and advancing with his rifle platoons, indeed walked into a trap, coming under blistering fire from three sides. Company C, moving forward, also found itself in a hornet's next of explosions and intersecting tracers. Overeager and fearless, Gregory swooped in low, using his command ship as bait so to pinpoint the enemy and destroy his positions with return fire. "Mayday, mayday!" Gregory suddenly shouted. "We're goin' down!"

§

The cavalrymen, watching the battle to their front, saw a helicopter plummet from the sky and disappear behind a tree line. Captain Barovetto's voice shortly crackled over the radio: the infantry colonel had been shot down, and Bravo Troop was to fight its way to the crash site. The lead tracks forded the stream by way of the freshly cut crossing site and then turned off the road in the vicinity of Xuân Quế 5 to move cross-country to the wreckage. Staff Sergeant Gary L. Boggs, commanding the lead tank, B-29, squared up before gently descending into the paddy, as did Spec Four Sears, acting commander on B-24. The next tank, B-34, went in at an angle, threw tread on the downhill side, and slid into a ditch. Sears was infuriated, convinced that the tank commander—a cocky, foul-tempered staff sergeant with a reputation for being all mouth—had deliberately immobilized his tank to avoid the battle awaiting them. Two tracks were left behind to secure B-34.

As for the tracks in the lead, under Lieutenant Mahoy, "we didn't know who the hell was where, or what was going on," recalls Gene Hotchkiss. "We pulled up on this little hill, and spread out. We started shooting up the area like they told us to, and all of a sudden, a guy stood up with a white t-shirt. I got on the intercom: 'Cease fire! I got an infantry guy in front of us, waving a t-shirt!'"

The man waving the t-shirt had exposed himself out of sheer desperation: because of a misunderstanding about who was where in this tangled-up melee, B Troop was firing into Alpha Company. The company commander later reported that their fellow Americans killed several of his wounded, lying helpless in the bomb crater where casualties were being collected.

Barovetto let out an anguished cry and, jumping to the ground, was running towards the infantryman with the white t-shirt when an NVA popped up from a spider hole and pole-axed the troop commander with a burst of AK-47 fire.

Several troopers braved the crossfire to drag their captain inside a track. The grim-faced driver headed rearward, desperate to get Barovetto to safety. He didn't make it. The troop commander was lying on the floor, a medic bent over him, when an RPG hit the side of the vehicle: the blast peppered the crew, badly injured the medic, and killed Capt. John L. Barovetto.

People frantically talked over each other on the radio as Lieutenant Wheeler took over B Troop—a wall of gunfire provided the background noise—and another lieutenant assumed command of Company C, whose commander had also been killed, along with thirteen infantrymen. There being no way to reach the command ship, "we were instead told to pick up the wounded," recounts Sears, "and fight our way back to LZ Ross. The whole thing was getting out of control. The whole thing was breaking down: hundreds of NVA had let us pass through, and now they were coming out of their holes to cut us off."

Staff Sergeant Boggs, commander of B-29, moved forward to provide fire support as the casualties were loaded into the lead tracks. Richard Sears followed in B-24. Next: Ron Decktor and B-16. "We were maybe fifty meters behind the tanks on kind of a trail, and taking fire from all directions," recalls Decktor. "It was really hairy. We couldn't see a lot, so we're just firing blindly off to the flanks." All at once, the track commander spotted "about ten NVA off to my right, trying to flank us, get behind us—they were running—I could see 'em through the trees maybe seventy-five feet to my right, down a little bit of an embankment. I swung the .50 around," continues Decktor. "You had to swivel the turret around, that little cupola, and our track was leaning a little bit to the right, so the gun swung around real easy from the weight, and me and the M60 gunner on that side opened up, and I think we took all of 'em out."

Decktor leaned forward to grab a fresh ammo can just as the platoon sergeant fired his M79 from the cargo hatch. The round flashed down Decktor's arm, ripping his sleeve and leaving a black skid mark. Decktor looked in astonishment at the platoon sergeant. Not knowing what else to do, they both burst out laughing, then instantly turned back to the task at hand: reload, keep firing. Their brand-new platoon leader, also standing in the cargo hatch, was frantically popping away with his M16. "The lieutenant was pretty shook up, but he was okay, he was functioning," says Decktor. "He was a good guy, it was just all new to him. It was a hell of an introduction. He'd only been with us a matter of days, and he'd seen nothing but all this craziness the whole time."

Staff Sergeant Boggs trained his main gun to the left front as his tank slowly advanced on the trail, Sears to the right front. Suddenly, a smoke-trailing rocket zipped from the bushes on the right to strike B-29. Moments later, another streamer of smoke, another hit. Ordering his driver to halt, Sears leveled the main gun on the rocket team and squeezed the override trigger.

Nothing. The tube did not bark: Sears forgot that he had cut the power when Barovetto gave the order not to fire the .50s or 90s after B Troop accidentally shot up the infantry. Power to the turret, main gun, and coaxial machine gun were controlled by three toggle switches at the gunner's fingertips. Absent a gunner—the tanks were running with driver, loader, and commander—Sears had dropped inside the turret to hit the switch that shut down the main gun.

Sears presently reactivated the main gun and squeezed the trigger. Popping back up into his command cupola, he took a quick look down the side of the tank, pistol in hand, to make sure no one had taken advantage of his absence to try to climb aboard. Eyes low, he did not see the NVA who rose with an RPG launcher over his shoulder, aimed directly at Sears. Ron Decktor did see the enemy soldier as he lined up his shot—saw, too, the assistant gunner crouched beside him—and frantically swiveled his gun tub from the right, where he'd been firing, to the right front to mow down the rocket team. The North Vietnamese triggered the RPG just as Decktor finished swinging the .50 about and, furious and sick at being a few seconds too slow, opened fire with a vengeance. "I put twenty or thirty rounds of .50-caliber right at 'em," says Decktor. "I think I saw the RPG launcher flying in the air, so I'm sure I got 'em."

Richard Sears didn't know what hit him: there was a terrific blast and a sledgehammer-like body blow—then he came back to reality inside the turret, unable to see, ears ringing, commo helmet missing.

Mercifully, he passed out, unaware of the extent of his injuries.

The second rocket to hit the lead tank had penetrated the turret, wounding Staff Sergeant Boggs in his legs and the driver, Spec Five Frank Moses, in the back of his shoulders. Though wounded, Moses fired his .45 from his hatch, when the lead tank reached a position to cover the recovery of the wounded, and Boggs his .50-caliber machine gun, pausing between bursts to lob grenades.

It was time to get out. B Troop allegedly fell apart during the retreat to LZ Ross: officers of the 2nd of the 12th Cav would speak of disorganization, panic, and tracks that refused to stop to take aboard casualties. There was undoubtedly some of that, but many dragoons were also decorated for their heroism: Lieutenant Mahoy, for example, for personally carrying casualties to his track amid the crossfire, and a wounded Staff Sergeant Tinker for delivering devastating .50 fire into the NVA. Private First Class James E. Nowicki was credited with crawling close enough to an enemy mortar to destroy the position with his M79, and Private First Class Jorge Gomez with using hand grenades to eliminate several enemy soldiers setting up a recoilless rifle.

Private First Class Hotchkiss was to be pinned with a medal for the relentless fire he laid down from B-22, starting with the left-side M60 whose gunner "was down inside the track, helping somebody or something," he recounts. "I fired his gun until something broke and it basically blew apart, then I pulled mine off the other mount and was shooting that off the left side till it just got so hot after awhile that it wouldn't fire anymore, either. We burned up pert near all the ammo we had that day." The grunts kept to the right side of the armored vehicles to avoid the fire from the left side of the road. "I remember one infantry guy trotting up close to my track, and a mortar round hit within ten feet of him. I watched him go down, but then he kind of got up, and was trying to crawl, and a couple guys went over and grabbed him and threw him in one of the ACAVs." The withdrawal, says Hotchkiss, "it was a hell of a mess."

Sears awoke as the loader secured a tourniquet around his arm. The tank commander passed out again, then jerked back to reality, his neck throbbing with pain: someone was pinching the hell out of his jugular vein.

"Man, that hurts!"

"I gotta stop the bleeding!"

The medic who'd climbed into the turret thumped Sears with a morphine syrette, which looks like a little needle-tipped tube of toothpaste. To administer: stick into muscle, squeeze the tube empty. Feeling no pain, Sears said that something was wrong with his eyes. The medic told him not to worry.

That was the medic mantra: "Hang on, you're doing great, we'll have you on medevac in no time." No reason to inform Sears that the muscle had been shorn from his right forearm, the ulna and radius fractured. Sears did not need to know, either, that his face looked like hamburger, or that his perforated eardrums were leaking fluid. His right eye had been injured and was squeezed shut. His left eye, popped from its socket, hung dead on his cheek.

Sears was conscious of the sound of the tank's hydraulics and the hammer strikes of rounds ricocheting off the armor. *I'm not going to make it.*

A sudden thought pierced him: *Oh God, my parents . . .*

Reaching the firebase, the driver of B-24 pulled up to the aid station. Sears moaned as he was lifted through a hatch: a piece of shrapnel had cracked one of his teeth into the gum, and, though numb everywhere else, whenever anything touched his jaw, the pain was dazzling. Of all the damn things!

Sears ended up on a stretcher in the aid station. The driver of B-24 barged into the tent, shouting, "Where's Dick?"

"He's right there," grunted Moses. "He's dead."

Sears stirred, grunted: "I'm not dead, yet."

A medevac landed despite mortar and automatic-weapons fire. Wind blasted through the cabin during the flight to Chu Lai. "I'm freezin'!" Sears wailed from his litter, going into shock. Moses couldn't take it: "Shut up, shut up!"

Lieutenant Colonel Richard S. Sweet, deputy brigade commander, flew in to take command of the 2nd of the 12th. The division's chief engineer, a lieutenant colonel, was briefing Sweet when he abruptly asked to borrow the new colonel's CAR15 and fired a burst into the grass just on the other side of the perimeter fence, killing an NVA who was preparing to throw a grenade.

Lieutenant Dickens, aide-de-camp to the assistant division commander, met B Troop at the main gate at LZ Ross. Designated the acting troop commander, Dickens had just disembarked from the general's helicopter—which hovered but did not land for the fire—and still wore clean, pressed fatigues and an army baseball cap with silver bar pinned to the front. As the lead elements slowed at the gate, the trail elements were forced to stop under fire. Needing to get everyone moving again, Dickens grabbed a platoon leader, but the young man was incoherent: surely, it must have been the brand-new lieutenant in 1st Platoon. Dickens sent the lieutenant to the aid station to get him away from the troops, then turned to the NCOs to get everyone inside the wire, deployed to their defilade positions, and resupplied with ammunition as quickly as possible. The shell-shocked lieutenant aside, had B Troop gone to pieces? "What I encountered was not a unit in panic," writes Dickens, "but one almost anesthetized by exhaustion and the intensity of the action they had just come through." Indeed, while checking positions, notes Dickens, "I recall seeing a rather long row of poncho-covered bodies, including Barovetto's, laid out near the battalion aid station."

Lieutenant Colonel Sweet, having called Lieutenant Dickens to the 2-12 TOC, informed him that the remnants of Company C, about forty men, were cut off, surrounded, and running out of ammo back in Xuân Quẽ 5. Sweet instructed Dickens to ride to the rescue. Dickens, stunned, asked if the colonel had considered the risks involved: not only were the troops exhausted and the enemy plentiful, but they had only two hours of daylight left. Replied Sweet: "Your unit is the only one with a chance to reach them quickly."

The acting troop commander told his noncoms that they would leave the tanks behind, pour on the artillery to clear the way, and move in column at max speed, laying down fire to the flanks. If all went well, they would reach the grunts "before it got too dark," recounts Dickens, "get them loaded up, and haul ass back to Ross. My NCOs thought it was nuts. So did I, but I never gave any hint to them. To their credit," continues Dickens, "and especially to the credit of the B Troopers, everything and everyone was loaded up and ready to go in short order. I put a vehicle in the lead whose commander said he knew exactly where the infantry was—and who volunteered to lead. My track was second in line."

Moving out, the last track had barely cleared the main gate when Dickens was contacted on the troop net: "Bravo 6, where the hell are you going?"

"This is Bravo 6. We're going for Hurricane Charlie 3-6."

"This is Champion [either the assistant division commander or General Koster himself]. The hell you are—get back inside the wire!"

The tracks reentered the base with mortar rounds walking in behind them. A rocket superficially wounded Dickens while checking positions that night, and another rocket ignited the helicopter refueling area. Grunts and cavalrymen smothered the blaze with fire extinguishers before the flames spread to the nearby ammunition supply point. "We knew we were going back out in the morning," notes Ron Decktor. "I couldn't sleep all night."

The grunts made their stand atop a hill. Two helicopters swooped in after dark, taking hits, to kick out desperately needed ammo, and the senior lieutenant called in a ring of fire from five howitzer batteries, dropping salvos on his own position as needed. The enemy pulled back, and a rescue was effected the next day as B-52s pounded the NVA escape routes up into the Quế Sơns. The madness was subsequently distilled into award citations. Captain Barovetto was posthumously awarded both the Silver and Bronze Star. Among those decorated with the Silver Star: Mahoy, Wheeler, Boggs, and Tinker. The Bronze Star: Gomez, Hotchkiss, Moses, and Nowicki. Richard Sears awoke from surgery with a tube down his throat, his head encased in bandages. The doctor abruptly informed Sears that though his shrapnel-pierced right eye still retained some vision, he had lost his left eye, and his shattered right arm had been amputated below the elbow. With that, the doctor moved on to the next casualty, and Sears—the high-school jock—quietly collapsed inside. The life he had known was over. He would never have it back. He would never be whole again. He was twenty years old, the maimed winner of a Silver Star and Purple Heart.

On the morning of January 8, Captain Reed joined B Troop at LZ Ross. Reed, a regular army officer, was commissioned from ROTC in 1962 and had served with cavalry units at Fort Benning and in Germany. He was an honor graduate of the Maintenance Officer course at Fort Knox. His education and experience as a squadron maintenance officer in Germany had marked him for assignment with the 1-1 Cavalry. This would be his third command.

The troop was ready to move out to rescue the C/2-12 Cavalry soldiers who had been left behind and surrounded by the NVA when Captain Reed arrived by chopper at first light on January 8. He reported to the acting 2-12 battalion commander, a new major who had been a company commander and who had just returned from R&R the day before. He had been assigned as the battalion S3 and had celebrated his promotion with his wife in Hawaii just 48 hours earlier.

B Troop accompanied the remnants of the 2-12 Cavalry to a hilltop overlooking the site of the surrounded soldiers. Not one sniper round or mortar round was fired at the task force. The soldiers, almost all wounded, were taken out of their defensive position by choppers. The lieutenant from the 2-12 Cavalry who spent the night on the ground with his surrounded soldiers received a Distinguished Service Cross for actions taken to organize and command the troops who had been left behind. He and one of the NCOs stayed awake all night calling and adjusting the artillery fires that probably saved their lives. Over four hundred rounds of artillery had been fired during the night to keep the NVA from over-running the hasty defensive position.

On January 8, a patrol from D/3-21 Infantry came under mortar fire upon crossing the stream that ran the length of the Hiệp Đức Valley. The grunts rushed across an open paddy to gain the cover of a tree line only forty meters ahead. Enemy soldiers were entrenched in the woods. They cut down most of the patrol in a sudden fusillade of automatic-weapons fire. The company commander was among those killed. The panic-stricken survivors took cover behind dikes, where they were pinned down, outflanked, and picked off one by one.

The company topkick, First Sergeant Williams—late of the dragoons—took shelter in a deep creek bed with a platoon sergeant and four grunts. Williams popped an M79 round at an advancing enemy soldier. The shell exploded behind the VC, who fell face-first into the mud. Hearing voices to the rear, Williams shouted to hurl grenades over the embankment. No more voices.

First Sergeant Williams, Platoon Sergeant Booker, and a radioman named Cannon started up the terraced rice paddy carved step-like on the hillside above the ditch. They were followed by a grunt named Coglin. Williams was hit in the right hand—the top was torn away, all bloody pulp and bone splinters—but nevertheless returned fire with his M79. Williams ordered Oliver, one of the last two men in the creek, to come on while the rest laid down cover fire. Oliver was nevertheless cut down. "I'm hit, I'm hit!" he screamed. "God, it hurts!"

"Take it easy," Williams called to Oliver. "I'm hit, too. I know it hurts, but we've got to keep calm. Don't scream. It will draw attention to us."

The grunt died screaming for his mother. "Okay, Harker," Williams shouted to the last man in the creek. "We're going to make it out. We'll get a gunship here in a matter of minutes. Don't panic—and don't use up all your ammo. I'll tell you when to fire on automatic. Otherwise, keep it on semi-automatic."

The enemy leapfrogged toward the creek, running forward one or two at a time, and then dropping. Unable to raise his head for all the fire, Williams fired his M79 like a mortar while Cannon shouted directions from a vantage point above. Except for a single jet fighter that came in under leaden clouds to drop its bombs, Williams' group was on its own: no artillery, no gunships, and no sign of the rest of Delta Company. Cannon was hit in the back by mortar shrapnel. Booker was killed. In addition, a grunt who'd escaped the massacre in the paddy crawled into the ditch, only to die there, bleeding from a leg wound he had shrugged off as he kept a vigil for approaching VC over the sights of his M16.

Harker heard voices and, looking over the embankment, saw a VC with an AK-47 leveled on First Sergeant Williams, who stood with his helmet off and his hands up. More guerrillas appeared: Harker and Cannon were also captured. Coglin either played dead or managed to slip away. One of the Việt Cộng stripped the wristwatch from the dead GI in the ditch, almost pulling his arm out of the socket. The guerrillas also recovered weapons and ammunition from the dead Americans lying about the area, then led their three prisoners toward the jungle as night fell and the light drizzle of the day turned to a downpour.

Williams and Cannon, temporarily separated from Harker, took cover with their guards when artillery fire thudded into the woods, then, moving on, they crossed paths with a number of female guerrillas: black pajamas rolled to their thighs, they carried mortar tubes and automatic weapons. Led down a trail, Williams and Cannon found themselves at a stucco house with a tile roof and brick patio. Lanterns lighted the scene, and the prisoners could hear field phones ringing: a command post. The pair were placed in a cooking shack behind the house and soon joined by Harker, who had been stabbed in the side by the VC he had wrestled with during an impulsive escape attempt. Ignoring their guard's admonishment to keep quiet, Williams whispered to Harker, "My hand is killing me, but they won't give me anything for it because I won't talk. I'm not going to tell those bastards anything."

Soon enough, a fourth prisoner was shoved into the kitchen, a rifleman named Strickland. The enemy used commo wire to tie the men together for the march to the mountains, Harker in front, then Williams, Cannon, and Strickland. The wire, wrapped around elbows and biceps, with elbows pulled back as far as they would go, was brutally tight. The group set out along a muddy trail in the rain, two guards in front and two to the rear. First Sergeant Williams encouraged the exhausted Harker to keep moving, and when Harker slipped down an incline, pulling the wire deep into Williams' arms, the rugged old soldier patiently got the group organized to walk in unison and negotiate subsequent hills by sitting and sliding down together.

At daybreak, the prisoners, still tied, were placed behind wooden bars in a cramped, underground cave. The guards finally loosened the wire, if only a little, and feeling returned to numb and swollen arms. The march resumed, led now by a teenage girl. Crossing a river by boat, the prisoners entered a hamlet where they were placed in a hootch and provided bowls of rice while curious villagers gathered at the doorway. The hamlet showed signs of having been bombed. The prisoners were told that the residents had suffered many casualties and hated Americans. That they allowed the prisoners to use their guesthouse, it was explained without irony, demonstrated "the generosity of the Front."

Delta Company lost fifteen killed, nineteen wounded, four missing. The next day, January 9, A/3-21 Infantry was ambushed in the same area, even while moving past Delta Company's dead in the paddy and along the terraced hillside. Another debacle, another shocking list of casualties: twenty dead, seventeen wounded, and four more men hauled off into captivity by the VC.

On January 10, the 1st Platoon of B Troop advanced on enemy-occupied Sơn Trà 1, only a klick southwest of Ross on Route 535. Losing a tank along the way to a mine, the cavalrymen established a blocking force on one of two low hills straddling the roadway while artillery pounded the objective in preparation for an attack by the 2nd of the 12th Cav. "We were sitting on the tracks, eating C-rations and just kicking back," recalls Ron Decktor, when an unwary NVA materialized in the paddies below. "He was just walking along the top of a dike, a pack on his back, and carrying an AK-47, with a dog trotting along behind him." The cavalrymen opened fire, only to come under heavy fire themselves from the tree line behind the lone NVA. Two tanks and the infantry track were knocked out by recoilless-rifle fire during an aborted assault on the tree line. Staff Sergeant Bouche, his face masked in blood from shrapnel wounds, ran back into the crossfire to retrieve the M60s from his wrecked ACAV. "Another guy volunteered to go with me," says Bouche, who won the Silver Star. "He grabbed one machine gun, I grabbed the other, and we threw as many ammo belts as we could carry around our necks and got the hell out of there." The tank retriever sent to recover the damaged vehicles was itself damaged by enemy fire. With dusk approaching, the decision was made to get out. As jets rolled in to napalm the abandoned vehicles, "the bad guys were standing up and shooting at 'em with AKs," notes Decktor. "They were brazen as hell."

Williams' hand stank from gangrene. So, too, the gaping, maggot-dripping wound in Cannon's back. On the third day of the march, a VC medic finally poured alcohol on their wounds. Bald and white-bearded, Williams leaned on a walking stick, his arm in a sling, as the hike continued through the rain and mist, the ascending terrain growing more rocky and primeval.

Lieutenant Colonel Gregory's helicopter was finally secured on January 16, and the colonel, pilot, and one of the door gunners unearthed from a shallow grave near the wreckage. Gregory had once remarked that he would either do well enough as a battalion commander to make general, or he'd get killed. As it happened, he won in his death the Distinguished Service Cross.

After the offensive, the units controlled by the 3rd Brigade of the 1st Air Cavalry Division reported 53 KIA and approximately 120 WIA.

The 196th Light Infantry Brigade, Americal Division, reported 65 KIA and approximately 150 WIA—plus 11 missing in action.

Pacific Stars & Stripes reported communist losses at 1,755: almost a fifteen-to-one kill ratio, if the body count is accepted at face value, and thus another resounding triumph. It was, in reality, another in a long line of ashen "victories" that secured not a hectare of land for Sài Gòn, nor affected Hà Nội's manpower pool a whit, but added only to the assembly line of flag-draped caskets wearing down the resolve of Washington and Middle America.

On the eighth day of the march, Williams' group—joined by a captured helicopter pilot, crew chief, and door gunner—started up a steep mountain by way of bamboo steps constructed under the jungle canopy. Montagnard porters going down with supplies passed the prisoners, going up. Up the mountain the prisoners went, down the other side, then up a hill atop which sat a cluster of hootches: a prison camp, occupied by another half-dozen Americans.

End of the line. An enemy officer barked at First Sergeant Williams to drop his walking stick and stand at attention. He warned the prisoners that if they did not obey the camp rules, they would be severely punished.

Next: disease, starvation, misery, death . . .

Sorry 'Bout That

JANUARY 1968

"WHILE GETTING SOME AMMO for the track[,] some snipers opened up on the choppers[,] so we just pulled up to the [perimeter] fence and cut loose at the general direction," wrote Max Pryor, recently promoted to sergeant and returned to C Troop, regarding an incident at Hill 29 on January 3. "Some how we killed an Arvin. I'm sure sorry[,] but can't help that now. Boy[,] the Capt. sure got riled up[,] to[o]. Ain't no telling how much papper [sic] work."

Like a lot of wounded men coming back for more, Pryor had a case of the shakes. Unable to sleep or eat, he went to the squadron surgeon. "He gave me some pills," the new sergeant wrote home. "[T]hey don't help that I can tell."

Captain Brown and C Troop twice established overnight positions in Tam Kỳ during the first week of January in anticipation of ground attacks. "Park[ed] the tracks in dark cornors [sic] and weighted [sic]," wrote Pryor. Nothing happened the first night in town. Mortar shells whistled in the second time around.

Sergeant Pryor caught a chopper to Fat City on January 13 on the way to Chu Lai to attend the Americal Division Leadership Course. Startled awake by a shot during the night, Pryor grabbed his M16 and cautiously stepped outside to find a dazed and prone GI who'd been shot across the top of his skull. There was no enemy on the scene. Rather, a fellow GI had shot the man for unknown reasons. "Come to find out he'd knocked on the raido [sic] room hootch," reported Pryor. "[N]o one answered so—opens the door and this kid [inside] shoots him. C[h]rist[,] what a place. I hope they Court Marshel [sic] the son of a Bitch. But most likely they won't do a dam[n] thing to him."

The course lasted ten days. As a graduation exercise, Pryor and a staff sergeant took out an "ambush patrol with 17 new recruits," he wrote. "Some of them are so dam[n] scared I wouldn't be su[r]prised if they don't faint before we get started." The staff sergeant, just as new and equally shaky, "kept getting up and walking around talking to people which is the wrong thing to do. Called in a report of 5 V.C. 500 meters away which was a dam[n] lie because you couldn't see that far. I just kept my mouth shut and didn't say a dam[n] thing. I'm glad we didn't [really] see anything[,] he'd have gotten half of his patrol killed before it was over."

Third in the class, Pryor came back with three stripes and a rocker—the troop commander and first sergeant cautioned him to walk softly among the Regular Army staff sergeants—and was reassigned as a scout-section leader, "[w]hich means I am no longer on good old 21[,] I'm now on 22 and I'm over 23 track[,] to[o]."

No sweat: nerves steadied, Pryor was back in the game.

On January 10, 1968, the men of the 1-1 Cavalry were ordered by Maj. Gen. Samuel W. Koster, commanding officer of the 23rd Infantry Division, to wear the Southern Cross patch on their left shoulders. This was despite the fact that the 1-1 Cavalry remained at all times in Việt Nam an integral part of the 1st Armored Division back in Texas. Major generals outrank lieutenant colonels, however, and the order was obeyed. Thereafter, the original dragoons from Fort Hood and those who joined the squadron before January 10 wore the patch of both units; later replacements wore only that of the 23rd Infantry Division.

Good Hunting

JANUARY 1968

CAPTAIN ROESLER GOT PLENTY more of the action he craved at the beginning of the New Year. Larry Graham, grenadier on the infantry track in Boyd's Bastards, enthusiastically wrote his wife about two of A Troop's missions:

> We just came back in after a rousing time with "Charlie." Official results were 12 captured V.C., 17 killed (V.C.), and 1 wounded V.C ... I gotta go now[,] honey, we're gonna [mount up and] roll over "Charlies" ass [again]. Oh[,] by the way, of those 17 kills[,] our track got 5 and one was mine ...
>
> ... we just came back from [Cigar Island] and we captured 32 and killed 7 more. I brought [another] one down!! ... Anyway[,] I love to go there on a mission ... the hunting (VC type) is great!

During one of these missions, Lieutenant Guida's tanks and tracks turned upon a hamlet from which the platoon had taken fire. Amid the furious exchange of fire, Tom Bursott saw a flash of white—someone dressed in white, running—and swung his M60 on the apparition. Everyone in range seemed to do the same, realizing only belatedly that the target was a terrified old grandfather. Bursott, who usually hit what he shot at, no longer cares to recall if the papasan succeed in dashing from between the VC and the Americans.

Afterward, as dismounted cavalrymen fanned out to search the hamlet, Lieutenant Guida was confronted by a last VC who sprang from nowhere with an AK-47. Guida instinctively threw his arm out and pulled the trigger of his .45. "He was coming at us, so I don't have any regrets about shooting him," says Guida. Still, a decent, middle-class Catholic boy from Long Island could not dismiss the man he killed as just another gook. "I call him Nguyen, you know. He was probably around thirty-five, an older fellow. He comes and visits me every now and then. It's just a bad memory from Vietnam."

The dead were left where they had been killed, to be buried by the villagers, while the military-age males in the hamlet were loaded aboard the tracks with sandbags over their heads, hands tied behind their backs.

Guida recalls taking out his little Instamatic: "I've got pictures of somebody passing by a hootch, and the hootch catching on fire."

Captain Roesler returned to Cigar Island on January 18, and eleven more confirmed and suspected guerrillas—the former were armed, the latter empty-handed but reported as evading—were racked up by hard-charging Alpha Troop. "It was a free-fire zone," explains Mike Dolan. "If it moved, you killed it. It was really starting to get crazy out there: when in doubt, empty the magazine."

The next day, Roesler accompanied a sweep north of base camp and east of the highway. Finding nothing in the gray drizzle, Guida's platoon finally led the way back home over the dunes, complacently taking the same route, in reverse, used on the way in that morning: a fundamental, if common, error where rough terrain limited the routes available to armor. Two tanks were up front, per routine: better a tank hit a mine than the tracks that followed. Along the way, Boyd told Sergeant Fortner, commander of the lead track, to fall out, with a second track providing security, and blow in place a dud bomb half-buried in the sand near a little hamlet belonging to the village of Hương Mỹ.

Specialist Fourth Class Leslie D. Matchett, commander of the mortar track, took Fortner's place as lead track behind the tanks. Dismounting, Fortner discovered that the dud bomb, a five-hundred-pounder, had been opened up and the explosives inside removed. Hurrying to rejoin the column, Fortner radioed Matchett: "Drop back, and I'll get back in my place."

"Ah, you've been eating this damn smoke all day," replied Matchett, referring to the diesel fumes of the lead tanks. "I'll eat it awhile."

Less than a hundred meters later, the lead track hit a mine. The explosion was enormous—presumably, a five-hundred-pound bomb's worth of nitro starch—and "I haven't figured out why all of 'em wasn't killed 'cause it blew that track up in the air, and it was turning flips," says Ron Fortner. "I was in shock."

Sergeant Fortner ran to his buddy Matchett, who was sprawled unconscious some two hundred feet from where his mangled track had landed. The command cupola lay in the sand nearby, and the engine block, also ripped from the vehicle, was off in another direction. Doc Hoover appeared within seconds. "The medic we had was great," recalls Fortner, but even as the two did what they could for Matchett, the track commander stopped breathing. Matchett must have died of internal injuries, notes Fortner: "He wasn't torn up. His upper lip was busted, but that was the only mark I could see on him."

Captain Roesler got on the horn to instruct Guida to "take care of that village," which the lead platoon gladly did with torrents of M60 and .50-caliber fire. Nate Boyd, glad to have had a commander like Roesler who understood that villagers who did not warn of mines were as guilty as the VC, recalls with satisfaction that "a lot of the hootches caught on fire from the tracers."

Larry Graham, riding on the back of the mortar track—the infantry track was down for repairs that day—landed face first after being blown overboard. Coming to his senses, he realized through the roar in his ears that the platoon was blasting away. Unsure what was going on, he instinctively reached for his grenade launcher. The weapon was gone. Graham rolled onto his back to get at the .45 in his shoulder holster, "but by now, our medic had arrived," he writes, "and told me I wouldn't need it as they had everything under control."

Doc Hoover assured a shaken Graham that he had a million-dollar wound in the form of a broken leg. Graham wasn't so sure: able to take only short, shallow breaths, he lied when asked if he was in pain for fear that if given morphine, he'd pass out and suffocate. Private First Class John

A. Rogers, meanwhile, was pulled from the driver's hatch of the mortar track, suffering from head injuries. Rogers was a replacement whose name was barely known to the men who loaded him aboard the medevac that soon landed.

Private First Class Richard H. Brummett saw the body of a young man when his 3rd Platoon tank moved up near the smoldering hamlet: word was that the boy, standing off to the side when the column approached, had been seen running after the mine exploded and was accordingly cut down by Boyd's Bastards. The only other villager in sight was a papasan who pathetically held out the dead boy's government identification card, meaning to show that he was a loyal citizen. Brummett says that Platoon Sergeant Boyd—who had just lost his first man killed and was boiling—struck the old man, heaved him into the crater left by the mine, and destroyed the identification card.

A volunteer and true believer, Brummett had spent the previous six months down south with the 1st of the 4th Cavalry, 1st Infantry Division, before being infused into the First Regiment of Dragoons. "It was quite a shock to see my new unit in action, because I knew how it was supposed to be done," says Brummett, who previously "could not understand all the anti-war protests back home as we were genuinely trying to win hearts and minds." Brummett's original troop commander, Capt. Thomas N. Sherburne, a two-tour West Pointer, strictly enforced the rules of engagement. The unit could only fire if fired upon, and only at identified targets. If a sniper's hiding place could not be pinpointed, Sherburne instructed his men to merely wave in the guerrilla's direction or give him the finger, lest civilians be injured by indiscriminate return fire. "If you hit a tree and it fell into a rice paddy," adds Brummett, "Captain Sherburne had you get out of the tank, pull the tree out, and apologize to the farmer for damaging his crop. The attitudes of the enlisted men were identical in both units," he continues. "There was some grumbling in my first unit that we weren't being tough enough on the locals, but leadership made all the difference as to whether guys actually felt free to take out their anger on the civilians."

Brummett's bottom line: "Captain Sherburne was winning the war in III Corps while Captain Roesler was thrashing about in I Corps manufacturing Viet Cong."

Few dragoons would have agreed with Brummett's take on the situation. Having watched Matchett die in the sand, Ron Fortner recalls that "really, at that time, I'd have called napalm in on that village if I could have."

John Rogers succumbed to his injuries upon being medevacked.

Captain Roesler called Guida into his hootch a day or two after the loss of the mortar track. "Roesler said he was transferring me," recalls Guida, who was exiled all the way back to Chu Lai. "That was it. There was no discussion. I think the fact that I wasn't a career officer was part of the animosity between us. I wasn't Regular Army. I was U.S. I was drafted. I was there, putting my time in. I guess maybe he didn't like the idea that I had a short-timer's calendar."

Larry Graham was still recuperating from his injuries—facial burns, ruptured eardrums, broken leg, broken back—when a letter arrived for him at Brooke General Hospital in San Antonio, Texas. It was from one of his buddies. "[E]nclosed is a picture I've dedicated to all of you that were on Matchett's track," his buddy wrote. The photograph showed the black GI kneeling near a tangled-up pile of VC bodies. The letter continued: "This will never get even for what happened to you but maybe looking at it will ease the pain now and then."

Skirmishes

JANUARY 1968

ELEMENTS OF C TROOP were providing security when Tam Kỳ was hit by mortar and automatic-weapons fire on the night of January 26–27. Routine patrols commenced at daylight. "I got you a V.C.," Max Pryor wrote his wife. "[O]ne shot in the back. I gave the [guerrilla's] rifle to a chop[p]er pilot who was helping us. All in all . . . us and the chop[p]ers got 6 dead [and] 1 wounded[, but] on the way back to hwy one the lead tank hit a mine."

That same day, the 3rd Platoon of A Troop, now commanded by a stocky ex-sergeant with OCS bars—the troops were unimpressed by the man's pugnacious bluster—made contact west of Tam Kỳ during a joint operation with the ARVN. One of the track commanders, a staff sergeant, was injured when his .50 misfired and exploded in his face. "We really got into the shit that day," recalls David Eady. "The sergeant got blown out of the hatch, and hit the floor, and that was it for him—we had to get him out of there." The TC had sometimes mused how Eady, nicknamed Baby Eady because of his youthful appearance and innocent outlook, would react in a tight situation. As it happened, Eady took the TC's place despite shrapnel in his arm and guided the buttoned-up driver back to the medevac LZ, for which he won a Bronze Star. Warned by villagers of a waiting ambush, Captain Roesler called in arty (artillery) and air strikes as night fell. The Blue Ghosts reported killing fifteen VC. The enemy was nowhere to be seen the next day, save a single military-age male who was spotted running and taken down by Alpha Troop.

Lieutenant Colonel Cousland won the Silver Star. "For nearly 10 hours on two successive days," the citation reads, transforming a skirmish into something far more impressive on a future general's resume, Cousland "remained aloft in his helicopter and directed the joint forces to a stunning victory over the Viet Cong force. . . . Frequently directing his helicopter to levels as low as 25 feet to locate and mark targets, he personally directed fire against enemy bunkers. . . . [Cousland also] land[ed] in the face of intense sniper fire, in order to physically point out these enemy locations to the ground commanders. . . . Cousland's unquestionable valor and avid devotion to duty are in keeping with the highest traditions of the military service."

"It was discussed," recalls Wayne Byrd. "An officer would get a medal and it was over nothing, the least little thing."

Tết

JANUARY–FEBRUARY 1968

*T*HE WAR USUALLY SHUT *down during Tết, a holiday of great religious and familial significance that ushers in the Lunar New Year. In this instance, General Westmoreland canceled the holiday cease-fire in I Corps on January 29, concerned as he was about the encirclement of the marines at Khe Sanh in the northwest corner of the country: the view at MACV was that the communists, pushed to the hinterlands and on the verge of defeat, were planning in their desperation a spectacular recreation of the siege of Diện Biên Phu.*

Unbeknownst to Westmoreland, the communists hoped not only to take Khe Sanh—presuming that the siege was not simply a ruse—but had been planning since the summer of '67 to use the 1968 Tết cease-fire as cover for an unprecedented wave of attacks designed to topple the regime in Sài Gòn. The onslaught would be known to a shocked world as the Tết Offensive.

Emerging from the jungle, the enemy planned to strike for the first time the urban centers of the country and win the war in a single decisive moment: surely, the ARVN would shatter under the blow of a hundred sledgehammers striking a hundred towns and cities, the urban masses would rally to the revolution, the government would fall, and the United States would be left with no option but to negotiate a withdrawal from South Việt Nam.

> Jumping the gun, certain enemy units attacked five cities in the northern part of the country shortly after midnight on January 30, the first day of Tết, and a full twenty-four hours before the offensive was scheduled to begin. Other, smaller flare-ups included a brief attack on Thăng Bình ten kilometers northwest of Hill 29 on Highway 1. Government troops drove off the VC even before a reaction force arrived from C Troop of the 1-1 Cavalry. Elsewhere, the festivities began on schedule with feasts and firecrackers. At the time, half of Sài Gòn's army was home on leave.

Now commanded by Capt. Walter Reed, B Troop started down the highway from Hill 29 the first morning of Tết, then rolled into a firefight after turning east on the dirt road to Vân An: a government soldier ran down the road toward the lead platoon, urgently shouting, "VC, VC, VC!" Figures streamed from the north side of the village, heading to a wood line along the dikes of a waterlogged paddy. "We opened up on 'em from the road," notes Ron Decktor, "then we did a left face and started off across the paddies after these guys."

Exultant at catching the enemy in the open, Staff Sergeant Bouche would describe sitting behind his .50 and laughing as he "blew this one person away. I was just taking pieces at a time. He kept getting up—but it wasn't a him—it was really a *her*. I didn't know till I went past the body." Captain Reed sent one platoon to block the enemy's retreat, even as the Blue Ghosts went to work around Vân An. The results: eighteen detainees and a thirty-six body count. Only one weapon was captured, however, and almost all the prisoners soon released as "innocent civilians." The whole thing had been a mistake, says Decktor: "We killed a bunch of 'em, but it ended up that they were mostly civilians [trying to flee the enemy attack on Vân An]. There was nothing we could do at that point, so we went back to the road, and found an ARVN who had been shot through the stomach. I tried to call in a medevac, but they said they wouldn't send a chopper out for an ARVN—so he just laid there and died."

Ken Bouche makes no mention of dead civilians when describing the incident at Vân An to an outsider. The incident was nonetheless something of a tipping point for him. Having been wounded twice, and with two valor awards pending for his actions in previous firefights, he was reassigned off the line soon afterward. "I sat down, and I bawled like a baby," recalls Bouche, "because I realized how sick I had become: when you can shoot another person and laugh while you're doing it, you're sick. You're not human when you're in combat. Human life means nothing to you anymore—but if you didn't have that attitude, you wouldn't have made it back home."

Westmoreland canceled the cease-fire altogether on January 30 in recognition of the fighting in I and II Corps, and issued a "maximum alert" to all U.S. units, a relatively routine step taken in anticipation of an enemy show of strength for propaganda purposes, not an all-out, win-the-war offensive. "[T]he Viet Cong surprised us," Brig. Gen. John Chaisson of the MACV staff candidly informed the press during Tết. "I've got to give 'em credit for having engineered and planned a very successful offensive, [at least] in its initial phases. It was surprisingly well-coordinated, it was surprisingly intensive."

Though the incident does not appear in the logs, Wayne Byrd describes how an enemy unit, marching on Tam Kỳ, attempted to bypass the bridge on which three tanks were outposted from the 2nd Platoon of A Troop. "We could hear them calling cadence, and sloshing through the paddies," says Byrd, who wondered if the VC were pumped up on narcotics, oblivious as they were to the tanks silhouetted against the night sky. Speaking in a whisper, the senior NCO said that on the count of three, each tank was to start its engine, flip on its searchlight to blind the bad guys, and open fire. "The range was about a hundred meters," notes Byrd. "My tank fired three canister rounds. The others fired four apiece. We broke 'em up. We got a body count up in the fifties."

In anticipation of a possible attack, the 1st Platoon of C Troop secured the rectangle-shaped refueling point and supply depot that faced Highway 1 on the northwest edge of Tam Kỳ. Two tanks and five tracks sat at various points along the perimeter fence between bunkers occupied by crewmen from the self-propelled howitzers on site and the Seabees building a new provincial hospital. Two tracks and the platoon's third tank had been detached to the highway bridges, otherwise outposted by militia troops, northwest of Tam Kỳ. When the attack did indeed materialize, at approximately 4 a.m. on January 31, sappers—part commando, part demolitions expert—blew up two of the bridges to impede the reaction force presumably to be dispatched from Hill 29.

Lieutenant Colonels Huáng Đình Thơ and Philip L. Bolté—province chief and his senior advisor—coordinated the city's defense from a bunker as incoming mortar shells exploded, outgoing artillery fire thudded into the paddies across which the enemy moved toward town, and tracers were exchanged along narrow streets between the invading VC and a troop from the 4th ARVN Cavalry. "[T]he Viet Cong actually entered the province capital complex," notes Bolté. "We even killed a couple of them in the province chief's office."

The scene lit by flares, the dragoons swept the rice paddy on the northwest side of the supply depot with fire, pinning down an attack force that attempted to close on the perimeter by way of a creek bed. The cavalrymen, artillerymen, and sailors shot those guerrillas who exposed themselves. In return, Sgt. Jack R. Lockridge was killed when a recoilless-rifle round slammed into his tank. The action continued after sunrise, and a jeep with a Seabee at the wheel dodged sniper fire to deliver ammunition to the M48s and ACAVs.

Failing to gain a foothold, the enemy pulled back when gunships and jet fighters began rolling in by the dawn's early light. Even as one battle fizzled, another flared as the bridge outpost confronted a second wave of guerrillas. Staff Sergeant Durst, newly assigned as platoon sergeant for 1st Platoon, C Troop, fired canister into the enemy until Captain Brown arrived with the 3rd Platoon from Hill 29. It is unclear if the reaction force forded the streams that cut the highway or if marine engineers had hastily repaired the damaged bridges, but after linking up with Durst, Brown—to win the Silver Star—threw the firepower of ten more tanks and tracks into the enemy. One track commander, Sgt. Edgar L. Bolding, was killed by recoilless-rifle fire, but when the melee ended, Charlie Troop and the Blue Ghosts claimed a body count of thirty VC.

The 1st Platoon reported an additional fifty-seven kills and, as noted in the division log, "took map off NVA officer with plans of attack on Tam

Ky[.] 1-1 Cav to determine if any routes of progress, assembly area[s], etc on it." Cousland landed with Captain Donaldson, now the squadron intelligence officer, who culled through documents found on the dead and determined that they were from the 1st Main Force VC Regiment, 2nd NVA Division.

The 2nd Platoon of A Troop, sent to cut the enemy's line of retreat, made contact below the mountains west of Tam Kỳ. Two tracks were hit by RPGs.

Gunships were diverted, medevacs requested.

The enemy was everywhere. A squad of sappers attacked the U.S. Embassy even as guerrilla battalions clashed with MPs and ARVN in the streets of Sài Gòn. Supposedly inviolate rear-echelon bases in the capital area had also come under ground attack: Long Bình, Biên Hòa Air Base, and Tân Sơn Nhất Airbase. The sedate market towns of the Mekong Delta swarmed with VC. Incoming rockets damaged and destroyed marine jet fighters at Chu Lai and ignited a spectacular explosion in one of the bomb dumps. Đà Nẵng was under attack by at least a regiment. Huế had fallen to a division . . .

There was a brief attack on Tam Kỳ after midnight on February 1. Part of A Troop, moving toward town, ran into an ambush in the dark: two tracks were damaged by RPGs, and five cavalrymen were wounded.

The enemy mortared Tam Kỳ during the night of February 1–2. On February 2, A Troop was ambushed again but, turning the tables by charging, racked up five kills, including a female VC. The action resulted some weeks later in the presentation of numerous Bronze Stars. In addition, Platoon Sergeant Boyd won a Silver Star for killing five enemy soldiers as he led his platoon through the ambush. Never happened, says Boyd, who was on the back of the command track that day with a .45 that remained in its holster—"If everybody's doing what they're supposed to be doing, a unit leader doesn't need a weapon"—and credits the medal to an awards clerk "who read a lot of comic books."

Though the officers got the big medals, and more of them, all ranks in the U.S. Army were well decorated in Việt Nam. How fair was the system? Platoon Sergeant Boyd had killed his share of communists, though not on the day and under the circumstances described in the citation to his Silver

Star. Did it matter that the citation was incorrect in details if true in spirit? And what of the medals pinned to Doc Gaydon and two other medics for treating several troopers peppered with shrapnel: in other words, says Gaydon, for simply doing their jobs? Shouldn't citizen-soldiers be rewarded for keeping their heads up and doing what had to be done under fire? Wasn't it good for morale? Not according to the soldiers themselves. "The citations were filled with so much exaggeration and hyperbole, it was ridiculous," says Max Pryor. "Ninety percent of us were draftees anyway. Who gave a shit about medals?"

The enemy attacked Thăng Bình before dawn on February 3. The action was visible to those elements of C Troop laagered nearby. "Watched a town burn," wrote Max Pryor. "The V.C. hit it around 3:30 A.M. this morning. Just like watching the movies back home. Then in came the Artilaly [sic] and shot the hell out [of] the outer edge of the village. I don't know how many V.C. they got but I'm sure they got quite a few. I shot one last night with a M79 gernard [sic] launcher, but couldn't find him when it got daylight. Boy, he was sure moaning and groaning last night. I guess one of his buddys [sic] drug him off."

The enemy attacked the refugee center in Tam Kỳ before dawn on February 4. The place went up in flames, either deliberately put to the torch by the guerrillas or as a side effect of the flares, tracers, and incoming mortar shells and rocket-propelled grenades. The results were hideous in either case: seventy-one buildings destroyed, nineteen civilians wounded, twenty-five killed. Three Ruff Puffs were wounded, and, officially, nineteen bodies were left behind by the VC.

Captain Donaldson arrived shortly after the attack to speak with Lieutenant Colonel Bolté: the latest intelligence indicated a thousand enemy soldiers were poised to hit Tam Kỳ again that night. From his jeep, Donaldson noticed a middle-aged American in civilian clothes moving among the dead VC. He was presumably an advisor from the CIA station house in Tam Kỳ, which ran the local Provincial Reconnaissance Unit, wholly removed from Bolté's control. The PRUs had a fearsome reputation: they were alternately said to be prison scum or firebrands who'd lost relatives to communist terrorism during this savage civil war. The PRUs gathered intelligence from villagers and carried out eye-for-an-eye counterterrorism against the Việt Cộng. According to legend, they were paid by the number of left ears they collected.

Which was exactly what the American in civilian clothes was doing: collecting ears. "I remember thinking, oh my gosh, look at this," says Captain Donaldson. "I mean, this is all the myths you've heard about."

The night passed uneasily but without incident.

Intelligence warnings aside, the battle for Tam Kỳ was over.

The communists having been repelled everywhere they attacked, Max Pryor wrote home that the war was as good as won: "I kinda look to see this thing come to an end in meby [sic] two mo[nths] from now . . . Time will tell. I know one thing for sure[,] the best they got can't whip us. We are just to[o] well supplied and have to[o] much determination to ever let it happen."

The Tết Counteroffensive

FEBRUARY-APRIL 1968

TẾT WAS A MILITARY disaster for Hà Nội. The urban population did not rise in revolt, and the ARVN did not disintegrate. Their backs against the wall, the government troops—stiffened by their advisors, who took command in some cases—hung on long enough for Westmoreland's army to ride to the rescue. The enemy was driven from most towns and cities within a matter of hours or days, except in Huế, where U.S. marines were pitted for nearly four weeks in a grinding, house-to-house battle against well entrenched VC and NVA.

Between January 30 and February 24, when the communist flag flying over the citadel of Huế was finally hauled down, 2,200 Americans were killed in Việt Nam. The ARVN lost about twice as many. Enemy casualties cannot be measured with certitude, but tens of thousands of VC and NVA undoubtedly perished in the Tết Offensive.

The civilians also suffered terribly. To minimize military casualties, U.S. units used firepower as lavishly in the cities as in the countryside and, in so doing, flattened block upon block of residential neighborhoods, inadvertently killing thousands of pro-government citizens. The communists, meanwhile, murdered hundreds of so-called "enemies of the revolution"—for example, the families of ARVN officers—and as many as three thousand during the occupation of Huế. The killings were exceptionally brutal: some of the victims in Huế were bound and buried alive. Elements of the 1st Air Cav and 101st

Airborne Divisions, tasked with cutting the enemy supply lines leading to Huế, found thirty civilians who had been shot in the head in one hamlet, fifteen more in a ditch in another hamlet, including children whose skulls had been crushed with rifle butts. No wonder the marines and GIs were sometimes treated as liberators during the battle for Huế, a response not often observed during the Việt Nam War.

General Westmoreland pursued the enemy in a series of highly successful operations known collectively as the Tết Counteroffensive: as the guerrillas fell back, mauled, from the towns and cities to regroup and make a stand in outlying villages, they were dug out in heavy fighting that continued through March. There followed a lull across most of the country as the communists, bled white, finally melted away into their deepest enclaves. To cap the victory, the 1st Air Cav Division broke the siege at Khe Sanh on April 8 and then invaded the A Shau Valley, a previously inviolate enemy bastion in the mountains west of Huế.

Higher command had seen in the enemy's decision to fight in massed units a golden opportunity to finally exterminate the VC and NVA. Accordingly, the machine had been turned loose during the counteroffensive to stack up bodies like cordwood as a landscape of craters and wrecked villages metastasized across South Việt Nam. One could either marvel at the efficiency of the machine—take pride, that is, in a hard job, professionally done—or comment as one officer did upon coming home at the end of 1968: "I am sickened by the number of people we have killed . . . This is not my concept of a soldier's career, just killing, killing, killing."

Actually, the dragoons had no other mission.

The rural villagers had offered no warning during the months the guerrillas had prepared for the onslaught on the towns and cities. The meaning of this silence was clear, and combat units acted accordingly. To quote a former dragoon platoon leader: "Everything was fair game after Tết. Every village that wasn't under definite government control was considered hostile—and they were."

Two of Staff Sergeant Pryor's letters to his wife attest to the indiscriminate destruction unleashed during the counteroffensive:

We went out today[,] didn't see much[.] I burned three houses just because and that was about it . . .

... I wish you could have seen us today[,] we real[l]y messed up a big village. Burned and ran over every dam[n] house they had ... Tomorrow we go out to cigar island and we'll burn and destroy every dam[n] thing we can ... Meby [sic] we'll even get to shoot some V.C.

Private First Class Thomas M. Andersen participated in a number of field missions with A Troop but served mostly as a radioman on Hill 29; his letters home during the counteroffensive were brutally frank:

Occasionally, our troop brings in a prisoner or two. It troubles me that the prisoners are treated so badly ...
More prisoners brought in, badly beaten ...
I don't support the war, and think we are only hurting innocent people by being here. Does it help the poor farmer when we run over his rice paddy with our tanks and armored personnel carriers? I don't think so. Anyone wearing black pajamas and running is considered VC and shot. As a result, many innocent people are killed.

According to the squadron log, rarely did a day pass but any number of military-age males, attempting to evade, were engaged and, in their deaths, counted as VC. Never mind the absence of captured weapons. One day, Pryor watched as a Loach hovered over a teenage boy, who huddled under the rotor wash. The pilot asked if Charlie Troop wanted a prisoner. Negative. With that, the door gunner fired the kid up with his M60. Nobody blinked. "You go crazy," muses Pryor. "You get to like killing. Why shoot somebody once? Put twenty rounds into him. Make damn sure he's dead—then take his picture."

In an environment that condoned atrocity, each unit developed its own code of conduct. Every platoon burned hamlets and cut down those who tried to hide—those were the rules—but most did not interrogate prisoners with their fists or otherwise act the part of vandals and murderers. Platoon Sergeant Jessie of the 3rd Platoon, Alpha Troop, had a particularly good reputation in that regard. "Jessie didn't trust the locals," says John Guzik, "but he was never overly brutal, and generally speaking, his demeanor was carried by the whole platoon."

Richard Brummett reflects with pride that Jessie had an almost English attitude about fighting a clean and proper war. When a landing zone had to be cleared at the edge of a hamlet, a frustrated Brummett finally leveled an M79 at several villagers who were ignoring his shouts to move out of the way. Platoon Sergeant Jessie immediately told him to cease and desist: "Brummett, don't you point your weapon at no civilians! What's the matter with you?"

The worst thing Guzik ever did was use a magic marker to draw a smiley face on the sandbag he'd secured over the head of a detainee, and then twist the corners into little ears. Guzik thought the comical sight might soften the treatment awaiting the prisoners at Hill 29. Less amusingly, the tedium of another search of yet another sun-baked hamlet was broken one day by taking snapshots of two middle-aged Vietnamese being forced to do regulation army push-ups: while one trooper demonstrated the proper technique, another provided incentive to the man alongside whom he squatted by holding a bayonet under his belly.

There exists another photograph that shows the pugnacious new 3rd Platoon leader, 2nd Lt. Ronald L. Snyder, squatting at the edge of a ditch while training his .45 on the detainee sitting opposite him, arms bound at his sides, his back against the road wheels of a track. Two troopers hold the man's head up by the hair so he cannot avoid the pistol in his face. Another GI grins at the scene. The troop's interpreter, Sergeant Phụ, gently touched the lieutenant on the shoulder and explained to Thiếu Úy Snyder that he was interrogating the village idiot. The lieutenant holstered his pistol.

If Jessie was not the one bringing prisoners back to Hill 29 black, blue, and bloody, then who? The collective answer: Boyd's Bastards. Richard Brummett says he saw a medic in Boyd's Bastards beating villagers over the head with a mattock handle. Likewise, David Eady recalls 1st Platoon troopers smacking, shoving, and cracking villagers in the back of their heads with the butts of M16s during the search of a hamlet. "Boyd's people were more aggressive than you needed to be," says Eady. Rumor had it that Boyd's Bastards killed as many prisoners as they brought back. Indeed, a veteran who joined Boyd's Bastards at the time of Tết recalls a staff sergeant tank commander in the platoon who had a reputation for being vicious with his knife: "I saw him beat a suspect, then drag him into a hootch. Only the sergeant came out again. There was a lot of muttering by other troops, and I got the hell away from there. Kind of cowardly on my part. Maybe prudent: the whole atmosphere felt wrong, dangerous."

First Lieutenant Christopher Noble, medical platoon leader, was out with A Troop when contact was made, several suspects rounded up, and a team of military-intelligence types choppered in to assist in the interrogation. Later, Noble ended up guarding an individual described as a hardcore VC who had a sandbag over his head and wrists bound so tightly that the man's hands were purple balloons. Noble took off the sandbag when he noticed the blood oozing through the mesh, "and there was a little old man," he recalls, "scared to death, with a caved-in, broken-up face." Noble cut the cord around the old man's wrists, then gave him a drink, laid him on a litter, and medevacked him to Chu Lai—where he promptly died. When questions were asked by division, Noble says that Roesler tried to pass the buck: "He accosted me in the aid station: 'What did your medics do to that guy?' I turned around, and said, 'We *received* that patient in that condition from you and *your* boys.' We were not friends after that. We were never friends. The guy would have been a great Nazi."

Regarding the rumors of summarily executed prisoners, a former Charlie Trooper says, "Well, that's a fact. Of course that happened sometimes. Guys got tired of getting shot at every day," he explains, "and then when you went into these little villages, you'd get a couple military-age males, and you knew damn well that they were the ones who'd been poppin' at you. They had to go. They're not going to tell you anything. They're gonna lie through their teeth, so if we had one we *knew* was VC, or if one gave us a problem, or tried to get away—*whatever*—he probably had a bad day."

The enemy began walking mortar rounds toward Staff Sergeant Pryor's bridge outpost at 9:30 p.m. on February 11. To escape the incoming, Pryor's two scout tracks and a third commanded by Staff Sgt. Marvin W. Barnard raced to the next bridge down the highway. The shelling ceased after twenty-five or thirty rounds, and the tracks backed up to their original position. The mortaring immediately began again, and the tracks again took off. Fifteen explosions later, the tracks returned, but despite the artillery fire brought down on a tube flash, the shelling began for a third time. At that point, wrote Pryor, "we said the hell with it and stayed put after we moved."

As noted in the letter, Pryor was on guard some hours later, about two in the morning on February 12, when "some son of a bitch shot at me twice." Pryor shouldered an M14 rifle mounted with a starlight scope to find the sniper: "I looked to the N.E. and great gobs of goose grease[,] there in the middle of the rice field about 250 to 300 meters from me was 50 V.C." Pryor passed the rifle to one of his guys who, as instructed, dropped the first and last man in line, whereupon Pryor "cut loose" on the middle of the column with his .50 "and didn't stop shooting for about 5 minutes." Barnard and the other TC also placed a sheet of machine-gun fire across the paddies—barrels were glowing red—then slacked off. For the next twenty minutes, Pryor noted, "we just shot short bursts."

The guerrillas scattered. With illume bursting overhead, some were seen taking shelter in a nearby hamlet. One of the cavalrymen lobbed M79 rounds in their direction: two hootches began burning. The area was swept at first light, and six slain guerrillas counted. Pryor stripped the bodies, looking for souvenirs and anything of intelligence value. Four rocket-propelled grenades were found in a slim wicker basket that had a bullet hole in one corner. In addition, a carbine and grenades were policed up, as well as the base plate for a 60mm mortar. To mark the success, Staff Sergeant Barnard, senior man by date of rank and time in service, was pinned several weeks later with a Silver Star.

Pryor had taken a wad of piasters from one of the dead VC. He had no intention of turning the money over to the squadron intelligence officer with the other captured material. Instead, his troopers spent the money at a little, ramshackle whorehouse on the way back to base camp. "Why not?" muses Pryor. "They're young boys. They could get killed tomorrow."

The platoon was deployed in a blocking position at the wooded edge of the ville when one of the track commanders reported hearing a lot of noise in the hootch to his front. Platoon Sergeant Boyd, the acting platoon leader, gave the sergeant permission to investigate. There was, moments later, a burst of automatic-weapons fire and urgent shouts that a man was down: the trooper checking out the hootch had simply opened the door, only to be shot at point-blank range by the Việt Cộng hiding inside with an AK-47.

The date: February 15. The place: Thôn Hai 3, located astride the old French railway halfway between Hill 29 and Tam Kỳ. The situation until then: another turkey shoot of armed and unarmed VC. The scouts and maneuver platoons had finally run out of targets, and five hours had since passed without incident. Now, Boyd barked at his .50 gunner to open fire and furiously added to the barrage with one of the M60s, shooting up the hootch in front of which the casualty lay. Pulling forward, Boyd and another dragoon quickly lifted the man onto the back ramp of the track, and the driver backed up to their medic.

Trying to maneuver forward, Arvin Schoep found his path blocked by the medic and several others who were kneeling over somebody. Schoep stopped. The keyed-up track commander shouted: "Get the fuck up there!"

In turn, Schoep stood in his hatch and, thinking the man on the ground was a wounded prisoner, screamed at the medic: "Move 'im the fuck out of there!" Schoep couldn't hear the medic over all the gunfire, but he could read the man's lips as he looked up and shouted back: "It's *Davis!*"

Schoep felt sick: Spc. 4th Class Herbert C. Davis of Blairsville, Georgia, was a nice guy of twenty who just wanted to do his time and get back home. Everyone had met his parents at the squadron picnic at Fort Hood, as well as his wife, who was frantic with worry about her draftee husband being shipped to Việt Nam. There was nothing the medic could do for Davis: shot a dozen times, he was probably already dead when he hit the ground. Platoon Sergeant Boyd, furious, presently overheard a scout pilot talking on the radio about VC running down a trench on the other side of the railway berm and shouted to his driver, "Haul ass—these sonsuvbitches ain't gettin' away!"

Reaching the area into which the scout ship was firing, Platoon Sergeant Boyd spotted a guerrilla, or at least the top of his head, as the man dashed down the trench, trying to escape the Loach. Boyd told his gunners "to cover my ass, and not leave the track," he recounts, "and I just jumped off the vehicle. I wanted these guys bad. It's payback. I had a .45 and some grenades with me, and I run up there and straddled the trench, and that guy's runnin' towards me, not knowin' I was there. That's as far as he got. I think he saw me at the last second, but he didn't have a chance to bring his weapon up before I killed him."

Unable to jump into the narrow, enemy-sized trench, Boyd jogged along the edge and right into another VC. "He's standing there with a grenade in his hand, trying to get the pin out," recounts Boyd. "I shot him in the chest, but every time I shot him—and I shot the sonofabitch five times, you could see the dust flying—he kept coming back up, wanting to pull that grenade pin." Down to his last round, Boyd finally "shot him between the eyes—and it wasn't one guy there, there was two—and the round went right through both their heads."

Boyd realized that he'd actually been shooting the guerrilla in front of the one with the grenade, who had been unable to get the pin out because his comrade kept bouncing into him. Boyd was joined then by his tank driver, who'd grabbed his M16 and come running. There were other enemy further down the trench. Luckily, Schoep's track pulled up nearby. The track commander dismounted to help Boyd, "so I got out of my hatch, and jumped behind the .50-caliber," recalls Schoep, "and just started laying down rounds across the top edge of that trench." The enemy held their weapons up to fire back without exposing themselves, and "as grenades would get thrown into the trench," notes Schoep, "they'd get thrown back at us. I kept firing until I about melted the barrel, while the guys on the ground worked up closer and closer, and finally put enough fire into the trench that we knew there wasn't anybody coming out."

Eight guerrillas were killed. The bodies were dragged into the open and searched, whereupon Boyd discovered why the guerrilla he'd shot five times in the chest had not been killed outright: the three-inch-thick pay book tucked inside his shirt had absorbed the slugs. The pay book listed the names of numerous local VC. "S2 was glad to get that," notes Boyd, who was to be decorated for charging headlong into the Việt Cộng. "They seemed to think that was quite heroic. I didn't do it because it was heroic. I done it because I was *pissed*. You don't think right when you've lost a man. You let emotions rule, and you shouldn't do that, especially if you're a unit leader: you've got to keep a cool head. I didn't, and they chose to give me a medal for going after the people who killed Davis instead of commanding my platoon."

The medal in question: the Distinguished Service Cross.

Three of the enemy dead were decapitated. Jerry Anderson, arriving on the scene after the deed was done, took photographs of the carnage from his driver's hatch. One photo shows six bodies. Most have been stripped to black shorts. One is naked. The three heads sit together on the ground. In the next photo, one head is off by itself, and a grinning trooper in steel pot and flak jacket holds up another by its hair. "There were some guys there, hauling the heads around, showing everybody," recalls Anderson, who says that in the heat of the moment it seemed absolutely justified to so avenge themselves upon the VC.

Lieutenant Norton, the troop exec, was informed that Boyd had decapitated the slain guerrillas with an ax and had to be restrained. Anderson heard talk along the same lines, as did Max Pryor, who comments: "Boyd went kill crazy. You get crazy if you drink vodka by the quart." There was talk that the decision was made, after a psychiatric review by the squadron surgeon, to remove Boyd from the field. The ex-surgeon, Philip H. Davis, M.D., recalls a young trooper confiding that he had seen the illegal killing of a civilian but has no memory of being informed of anything as lurid as beheadings. Nevertheless, Lieutenant Noble, the medical platoon leader, would later avow that, yes, the rumor was true: "Sergeant Boyd was having fun decapitating dead VC. His own men turned him in. The aid station was open: anybody could come in, and what was said was confidential. [Davis] gave Boyd a choice to either accept a medical unfitness report, and be discharged, or agree to go back to the United States and receive psychiatric treatment, never to return to Vietnam."

Boyd remained in command of his platoon while the recommendation for his receiving the nation's second-highest award for combat heroism and, according to Noble, his reassignment for psychiatric reasons were processed at division. The decapitations continued. Dick Taskey says he saw one of his buddies try to remove a head with a bayonet: "Dead flesh don't cut very good with an old bayonet, so he finally used the carpenter's saw we had in the track."

The 1st and 3rd Platoons were operating together on March 17 when a scout chopper flushed and fired upon a military-age male. It was Richard Brummett's impression that the individual was wounded, not killed. Whatever the case, a track from Boyd's Bastards was the first to reach the area. Brummett claims that a certain sergeant—he uses the man's name—jumped from the track, beheaded the VC with a single powerful chop of a machete, "then stood on the top deck of his track and posed for photographs uncannily like the Benvenuto Cellini sculpture *Perseus with the Head of Medusa*."

Brummett was a little bug-eyed at the scene, and a field mechanic riding on his tank teased him: "Don't get sick now, Brummett."

A note about Pvt. 1st Class Richard H. Brummett: there was probably no more idealistic and introspective a young man in the squadron. An only child, his mother was a devout Catholic, his father a hardnosed, overbearing military man who had originally dropped out of high school to join the marines during World War II. Brummett's father married his mother after fighting on Okinawa and serving in China. Brummett was born nine months and twenty days later, in March of '47. Brummett's mother refused to leave her New York neighborhood to live on military bases, so he grew up in a row house in Flushing; fortunately, his father's last two assignments before retiring as a gunnery sergeant in 1963 had been at the Brooklyn Navy Yard and the local recruiting station. Camping trips with his father had involved rigging shelter halves and lessons in tactics and supporting arms, including how to call in 105mm artillery with the aid of a topographical map. Marksmanship was taught with an old rifle. Brummett was absolutely enthralled.

Nuns in grammar school, and Marist monks in his all-boy, tie-and-blazer Catholic high school, educated Brummett. Upon graduation in 1965, he was tall, skinny, and bespectacled—a self-described "wimp." That fall he entered the Marist Novitiate in Esopus, New York. His religious convictions could not beat his patriotism and thirst for adventure, however, and, wanting both to prove himself and do his part in the war blazing on the evening news, he quit the monastery to join the U.S. Army in March 1966.

A city kid who rode the subways to high school, Brummett did not know how to drive—anything. The first motor vehicle he ever drove was an M48 tank at Fort Knox, Kentucky. Volunteering for Việt Nam, he was shipped to Germany. His first day on post in Büdingen he again filled out the papers to transfer to Việt Nam. He finally got his wish in July of '67. Brummett originally served, quite proudly, with the Big Red One near Sài Gòn. In the Fourth Cavalry he was a dangerously inept tank driver, and when a number of troopers in his unit were selected for infusion into the First Regiment of Dragoons, he found himself heading up to I Corps in January of '68.

Platoon Sergeant Jessie put Brummett in the driver's hatch of his tank. Bad move. Jessie might as well have been sitting on a bucking bronco with Brummett driving, so he made him the loader instead. "Brummett blossomed into an excellent loader," recalls ex-gunner John Guzik. The two became good friends. David Eady also recalls Brummett as a good buddy, though he jokes that the guys would chide the earnest and erudite Brummett because he had not only enlisted but had actually volunteered for Việt Nam: "We told him he was nuts!"

Richard Brummett's idealism was relentlessly stripped away while serving with Alpha Troop of the 1-1 Cavalry, Americal Division. "When I first arrived," he recalls, "Guzik told me they had Genghis Khan and Attila the Hun in the troop: Roesler and Boyd." Guzik was quite open about this since he had it written on his helmet cover: "Attila the Hun is alive and well in the 1st Platoon." If Brummett's first troop commander had believed in winning hearts and minds, Roesler operated under the countervailing theory: grab 'em by the balls, and their hearts and minds will follow. Brummett says he saw the captain walk up to an animal pen in a hamlet, coolly shoot two cows in the head with his CAR15, then walk off. The destruction seemed a matter of whim. Brummett points to a photo of Eady leaning from a track to catch the thatch roof of a hootch on fire with his lighter. "Why were we burning this village?" he asks with a shrug. "I have no idea, except that it was there. Burn a village, kill cattle, what the hell: just another day."

Apparently bored with burning villages, Captain Roesler sometimes destroyed them with a bridge tank nicknamed the Swatter. As Brummett put down on paper shortly after the end of his tour, the bridge tank "hydraulically extends a 60 foot bridge over a river or ravine. At rest[,] the bridge is folded in half like scissors upon the tank. As it is extended[,] it is first straightened completely out at an angle of about 30 degrees to the horizontal, and then lowered to the ground. Excellent, decided our captain. He would line up the bridge tank with a row of huts and have [the bridge] lowered repeatedly onto them, pressing the huts into the ground as if swatting mosquitoes."

On the way back to base after the first mission with a newly attached flame-thrower track, Captain Roesler stopped outside a hamlet and had the residents rousted out of their hootches. "Placing the flame-thrower [track], or 'Zippo' as it was called, in position, the troop commander ordered its crew to destroy the ville," wrote Brummett; however, the flame-thrower "failed to ignite. Was this a hardcore Viet Cong village that had to be destroyed? No, it was a test target for a new weapon, because as soon as it became apparent that the Zippo was a dud [,] we simply went on our way, harming not a soul nor destroying a single hootch, and leaving the open-mouthed Vietnamese wondering what had spared them."

These incidents could all be chalked up as acts of military necessity, for in addition to aggressively seeking out and killing the enemy, was it not policy to deny the guerrillas shelter and provisions by destroying hamlets in areas outside government control? Military necessity, however, did not cover rape. Both Guzik and Brummett recall hearing talk of village girls being taken advantage of when the opportunity arose during patrols. Guzik says he actually saw a troubling incident that "involved members of our own 3rd Platoon who were having their way with what seemed like an unwilling subject. I do recall some of the faces. However, they shall remain nameless. I could not understand why this would happen when prostitutes were readily available just outside the wire. I felt ashamed, but didn't even consider reporting what was happening."

Spec Five Guzik was placed in acting command on those occasions that Boyd was down a tank, and Jessie, his platoon being otherwise idle, lent him A-35. During one such mission, east of the highway, Brummett drove the tank over a sand berm and into a garden that had been excavated to just above the water table. The tank sank up to the hull on one side, hopelessly stuck. While waiting for help with the tank's engine off, Guzik and Brummett thought they heard voices, though no one was in sight. They traced the sound to the smashed berm. Digging, they discovered a sand-covered man in a collapsed bunker. They hauled the man out, only to find a woman underneath him, both dressed in black pajamas. The two were dazed but otherwise unharmed: the sand had cushioned them from the full effect of being run over by a fifty-two-ton tank. Something about the pair just smelled VC, and since they lacked identification cards, Guzik bound their arms behind their backs and requested a helicopter. Boyd's Bastards arrived before the chopper, stole the prisoners, threw them aboard a track, and roared off "like Hell's Angels," to quote Brummett. Upon returning to Hill 29 after being towed out of the wet sand, Brummett says he saw the two suspects being unloaded from a track behind the troop headquarters: "The man appeared battered, and the woman could hardly walk. It was said that the whole platoon raped the woman, but I don't believe it. Some, likely, but surely not all."

Rumors aside, Guzik says he saw a gang rape during another mission during which his tank was attached to Boyd's Bastards: "We were sweeping a village. I was on the ground, snooping around for enemy stuff, when I noticed some 'excited' activity in a hootch. As I approached, an acquaintance from the 1st Platoon was walking out, shaking his head in disapproval. I could clearly see what was going on behind him. He looked up at me, and stated something to the effect, 'You don't want to go in there, Guzik.'"

Guzik could not but respect Boyd for his courage but thought the platoon sergeant "had gone beyond the realm of how to conduct oneself in combat. Boyd got out of hand, and there was no one there to reel him in. His platoon loved him, however, embraced his tactics, and he got results."

Indeed, given leaders of ferocious martial prowess like Roesler and Boyd, why worry about how they treated the enemy and those who helped the enemy?

Brummett complained once to his buddies that they were all complicit in the crimes being perpetuated. Replied another trooper: "Get off it, Brummett."

One veteran of Boyd's Bastards, prodded with intrusive questions, speaks to the time "some of the guys were chopping heads off of dead gooks, and setting them on the edge of a well in a village. I think we had heard that if you chopped off the heads, they wouldn't go to the happy hunting grounds or something like that." The veteran pauses, then remarks that he has said too much, and asks that his name not be used when discussing the mutilation of enemy dead. "Chopping off heads, that's just such a foul thing that I wish I hadn't mentioned it. For the most part, we were pretty good guys, but war is so ugly."

Arlen Kolstad, a scout in the 3rd Platoon of A Troop, was the very image of the educated, humane, thoughtful Norske farmer from Minnesota. When his cousin, a grunt down south, went KIA, the army assigned him to accompany the body home.

Kolstad returned with disquieting news: His family and neighbors, the stolid farmers of the upper Midwest, had turned against the war. His aunt and uncle desperately wanted to believe their son had died for a noble cause. They tried but they could not believe.

This unwelcome information nibbled away a bit more ground from under Brummett's faith in the war.

Kolstad was the man who pondered the symbolism of having Capt. Joseph Conrad along on a journey into the heart of darkness.

"At least we have Katz and not Kurtz in the 3rd Platoon," Brummett offered.

"Right," replied Kolstad, "Kurtz is in the 1st Platoon. In fact, he owns it."

"There it is."

Arvin Schoep, another unassuming farm boy from Minnesota, saw his share of ugly with Boyd's Bastards. "We were just out there, and kind of beyond the edge sometimes," he says. "I know rapes happened. One time in particular, couple guys grabbed one of the girls in a ville we were searching, took her in a hootch, and took turns at her." The brutality seemed sanctioned from the top. "You can't say it was an order, but they didn't want us to take prisoners," notes Schoep, "so what do you do with 'em, you know?" As a result, "some guys got to the point where they just wanted to kill. Any chance they had, they killed." Schoep was a track commander when "a couple of my guys had this old man and woman down on their knees, and they kept asking for permission to kill 'em." Negative, said Schoep, but when the word came to saddle up, one of the troopers ordered the detainees into a tunnel, then pitched a grenade in with them before climbing back aboard the track. "Oh God, I had nightmares about that. Part of me was so tempted to report him, and yet I didn't. Back home, that GI with the grenade would have been your typical All-American Kid."

They shot villagers for running and fragged them for hiding. "Most of the hootches would be empty," says Dick Taskey, "so you knew they were probably in their family bunkers, so you'd pitch in a grenade or two and get rid of whoever was in there. It was murder: these people we were killing had no weapons."

Murder didn't matter. Neither did rape, says Taskey: "I've seen stuff that happened: you just kept going, forget about it, you didn't care. They weren't nobody to us by then. They just weren't human, I guess. After awhile, you harden into it," Taskey, continues, "and then you kind of liked it, and it became like squirrel hunting: you wanted to get your limit every day. Something happens to your brain in combat. Something takes over, and you're capable of anything. My thinking, it wasn't right. I kept thinking, well, half a million of us here: if we all kill ten people, we can go home pretty soon."

Dick Taskey—crazed from booze and death—says that he once entered a hootch to find a number of people attending a woman giving birth. Their frightened wails infuriated him: they weren't innocents; they had probably been out the night before planting mines. "I was so mad that I remember rippin' the baby out of her," Taskey claims, "and throwin' her down on the dirt floor, and killin' everybody. I don't even remember who I killed, seems like maybe half-a-dozen grown-ups and a couple kids, I can't say. We knew they were all against us, so you just kill 'em. Get rid of 'em all. That was the thought: kill 'em in the worst way that you could, it just made you feel better."

Good ol' Dick Taskey, the savage killer of a family? Was it really possible, or is the tale a self-flagellating invention: punishment for his sins?

Whatever the morality of burning and bombing hamlets, and disregarding civilian casualties in pursuit of the enemy, blatant atrocities really were "isolated incidents," to borrow the phrase the military adopted to cushion and put into perspective the issue of war crimes committed by U.S. forces in Việt Nam.

Such incidents were most frequent up north, where appalling casualty lists wore grunts to a vengeance-minded frazzle, and unit commanders tended to take off the gloves in the face of a deeply entrenched VC infrastructure supported by waves of NVA. One result of the special pressures of I Corps: the outrages of the Tiger Force. Another: these bits of writing from a marine corporal in the Quế Sơns in 1967: ". . . we went through a ville. The guys killed two men—murdered them—and two water buffalo calves, all just for kicks. They also made a girl undress and stood there laughing at her standing there nude . . . We make more VC than we kill by the way these people are treated . . . [S]ome of the things that take place would make you ashamed of good old America."

The stage having been set, the situation spun out of control in some units during the intense combat of Tết and the counteroffensive. On February 8, in the midst of a three-day battle, Company B of the 1-35 Infantry, 4th Infantry Division (opcon to the Americal), slaughtered under orders the livestock of a hamlet controlled by the NVA. Next, nineteen women and children were rounded up—one of the women was raped—then mowed down by a gung-ho lieutenant and a pair of grunts. The company commander turned a blind eye. One of the medics did not, and because he reported the incident, an investigation was carried out that confirmed the murders. The investigation was then buried.

Throughout the counteroffensive, a certain Company C, 1-20 Infantry, 11th Light Infantry Brigade, Americal Division, routinely brutalized villagers during its operations in Quảng Ngãi Province. When a sergeant was killed by a booby-trapped artillery shell and another man hideously wounded— blinded, a leg blown off—survivors of the patrol shot a woman working in a rice paddy, then "kicked her to death and emptied their magazines in her head," a GI wrote his father. "They [also] slugged every little kid they came across. Why in God's name does this have to happen? These are all seemingly normal guys; some were friends of mine. For a while they were like wild . . . This isn't the first time, Dad. I've seen it many times before . . . My faith in my fellow man is shot all to hell. I just want the time to pass and I just want to come home."

On February 22, Sgt. Robert B. Selby of B Troop, a thirty-year-old regular, was shot and killed by a sniper out on the sand flats between LZ Baldy and Cigar Island. "I was directly behind him when one shot rang out. It went in one side of his helmet and out the other. He never knew what hit him and we never saw the person who fired the shot. Our policy was that if we took any incoming fire, we went to the nearest village and leveled it," notes former platoon leader Ray Mahoy. "We destroyed all the rice we could find, killed the water buffaloes with .50-caliber machine guns, and burned down the hootches with Zippos."

On February 24, the enemy mortared Hill 29 for the first time. The shelling began at two in the morning and lasted thirty minutes. Twenty rounds or so fell short of the wire; an equal number impacted around the squadron TOC. In response, the tube flash spotted from a guard tower was taken under tank fire from the bunker line. Staff Sergeant Pryor passed a bottle of Jack Daniel's with his guys as they watched the fireworks, which included artillery fire. When the platoon sergeant chewed him out for not manning his machine gun, he responded, "Fuck 'em, they're shootin' at the colonel!"

On February 27, the 1st Platoon of A Troop, with a new lieutenant on the command track, carried the PRUs to a certain hamlet west of Tam Kỳ. Intelligence indicated that the villagers were hiding several wounded communist officers, and indeed the PRUs found a VC major, as well as a female medic. Meanwhile, a scout pilot reported seeing black-clad figures scurrying into a trench in another hamlet several klicks north in the Pineapple Forest.

Platoon Sergeant Boyd, smelling blood, hastened toward the second hamlet. Reaching its southern outskirts, Boyd faced a berm and a wall of bamboo, over and through which his platoon crashed on line. Expecting the worst, Jerry Anderson, driver of the command track, gripped a .45 in his free hand, arm extended from his hatch. The enemy was unprepared for a fight, however: figures scattered in the face of the attack, and Anderson, for one, winged one VC who aimed a rifle at him and another who threw his weapon down and tried to run. As for Boyd, he saw upon dropping down on the other side of the berm that his tank was straddling a trench from which twenty or thirty terrified faces looked up at the fifty-two-ton monster. Boyd trained his main gun down the length of the trench and let fly a canister round. At least one of the Việt Cộng kept his wits about him: an RPG struck the infantry track, whose commander cried to Boyd, "1-5, somebody just shot a damn torpedo at me!"

"Well, goddamnit," replied Boyd, "shoot one back!"

The explosion merely gouged silver divots in the olive-drab armor; several infantrymen, including Dick Taskey, received flesh wounds.

Tom Bursott, one of the machine gunners on the infantry track, cut down the brush from which the rocket had flashed, trailing smoke. No more RPGs: the gunner and his assistant, Bursott later found, were stitched across the midsection by the fire he'd blindly laid down with his M60. Bursott grabbed an M16 when the machine gun malfunctioned and, twisting around to check the rear, saw a VC rise from a spider hole with a Chicom. The man managed to fling the fuming grenade—it fell short—even as Bursott shot him in the chest.

Drivers and vehicle commanders stayed with the tracks while the rest dismounted to secure the area. Sergeant Gary R. Bakewell yanked two startled guerrillas from their spider holes. One was unarmed and taken prisoner. The other hung onto his AK-47, and Bakewell's partner blasted him with his M16. Having knocked out one or two positions, Taskey approached a bunker with an ARVN interpreter, who shouted at those inside to surrender: "Chiêu hôi!" There was a defiant reply, at which Taskey pitched in several grenades, then flagged down a tank that flattened the earthen mound beneath its treads.

Left behind while a thrown tread was repaired, Staff Sgt. Bobby R. Butler, an excellent tank commander infused from the Big Red One, finally rushed to the battle. Butler confronted a large hootch from which a young woman sprang, firing an AK-47. She was cut down. Next, Butler used his tank like a battering ram against the hootch. The walls of hard-packed earth were thicker than expected, and when they collapsed Butler saw that the hootch had concealed a maze-like bunker filled with people. "It was like an ant bed," he says, an aid station, really. The terrified nurses and patients were not spared because those among them who were armed "started coming out and firing," recounts Butler. "I had the .50 working, and the gunner engaged some targets independently with the coax. I think we fired the main gun, too. It was chaotic, to say the least. There was a pile of dead people when everything was said and done."

The sky was aswarm with helicopters, to include Cousland's command ship, and so many Blue Ghosts that every terrified VC trying to escape through the woods seemed to have a scout or gunship in hot pursuit. The enemy was already in complete disarray when Captain Roesler arrived with the rest of the Alpha Troop at the forty-five-minute mark and, deploying the 2nd and 3rd Platoons on a north–south line, rolled west through the hamlet. Taking fire from diehards in the hedgerows to the front and rear, Roesler had a gunship make strafing runs within a few meters of his buttoned-up tanks and tracks. As the action finally petered out, Staff Sergeant Butler watched and listened to the directions being given on the radio, as several troopers carefully maneuvered toward a lone VC who rose at intervals from behind a paddy dike to fire his AK-47. The cavalrymen wanted a prisoner. The enemy soldier had other ideas. Presumably out of ammunition, he stopped firing and curled around a grenade. "All of a sudden, there was a muffled explosion," remembers Butler, "and his body flew up in the air. He killed himself rather than be captured."

Jerry Anderson climbed from his hatch when the firing stopped to take a look around, "and a guy in black pajamas jumped out of a hole," he recalls, "and started running away from the village. I was still shaking so bad that I emptied a full clip on him from my .45 and missed every round. One of the other drivers tossed me an M16. I fired one shot and the man dropped." Anderson walked over and "rolled the body over, and, hell, he looked like somebody's grandpa."

When several troopers returned to the infantry track, Anderson showed them a tunnel that had been overlooked. Since he was one of the smallest guys in the platoon, the others volunteered Anderson to check the tunnel out, and, stripping off his flak jacket, he wiggled in with flashlight and .45. Inching along, he rounded a curve and found himself face-to-face with a VC. The man did not have his weapon at the ready. Anderson shot him and then, ears ringing, backed out of the tunnel and suggested they smoke the rest of the enemy out. The smoke grenades did the trick: a half-dozen Việt Cộng, the fight completely knocked out of them, emerged from the tunnel before they suffocated.

While Roesler's boys mopped up, Captain Brown and Charlie Troop, having rushed to the scene from base camp, established a line in the rice paddy west of the hamlet. The tanks and tracks had barely gotten into position to block the enemy's retreat when "hell[,] there are V.C. running all over the dam[n] place," wrote Max Pryor, "so we start shooting and killing . . . I saw 5 run into a bunker[,] I put a White phosphorous [sic] gernard [sic] in it with them[,] kill all 5. Had 4 in a ditch and put a hand gernard [sic] on top of them[,] killed one and real[l]y screwed up the rest of them good . . . The tanks real[l]y brought smoke."

Some few enemy fired back, and plumes of paddy water shot up around the tanks and tracks. The guerrillas, hitting nothing, could themselves be seen cartwheeling as .50 slugs connected with them in midstride as they ran along the paddy dikes. "Like shooting ducks in a barrel," said Captain

Brown. Pryor was positioned between two tanks, the one to his right commanded by Staff Sergeant Durst. When several figures ducked into a bunker, Pryor pulled alongside Durst so he could jump aboard the tank and physically point out the enemy's hiding place. Pryor pulled forward to pinpoint the position exactly with tracers and was just starting back when both tanks fired, turning the bunker inside out. Pryor was caught in front and between the two gun tubes: the concussion and roar blew his commo helmet from his head and busted his eardrums. The action continued sporadically. Those enemy who succeeded in slipping through or around Charlie Troop's line were fired upon at a distance as they disappeared into the woods to the west. Those who did not lay as bloody rags in the mud and water. Describing the carnage, Pryor wrote to his wife that: "I'm sure this isn't the kind of letter you'd like to read but I aim to get them before they get me."

The killing had been easy and plentiful, and the young troopers had loved it, says Boyd: "You know what their thing was, don'tcha? *Payback.*"

The position secured, Boyd requested a dust-off for the major who had been captured in the first hamlet and eventually transported to the second. The major lay incapacitated on a stretcher. His nurse, however, was uninjured, and glared with such hate-filled intensity that Boyd sized her up as the kind of fanatic who would blow herself up with a hidden grenade in an attempt to kill an American. "Them people, they're somethin' else," he muses. Amazingly, no one had tied the nurse, "so I pulled my .45 out," adds Boyd, "and she got a full-body search, I tell ya, and then I secured her hands with plastic cuffs [zip-ties]."

Boyd was enjoying a cold beer atop his tank when the medevac arrived. The pilot wanted to know whether or not the landing zone was under fire.

"The LZ is cold," answered Boyd. "Bring 'er in."

The cavalrymen were in the process of opening the demolished bunkers with entrenching tools and pulling dust-covered bodies into view. "Damn," the pilot exclaimed. "Looks like you guys had a good day!"

They had indeed: at the cost of a half-dozen wounded dragoons, the body count was a true and honest 148. There were a dozen NVA in khaki uniforms among the dead VC. Another 20 of the enemy had been captured, along with enough weapons to fill two ACAVs. The haul included two mortars.

The dead were searched, and the prisoners, bound and hooded, crammed behind the trim vanes of several tracks. "We had 'em stacked in there any way we could," notes Jerry Anderson, who recalls one of the prisoners tumbling from one of the tracks. "We were running so close together that the next vehicle in line ran over him. I ran over him, too. Everybody ran over that guy."

The battlefield was swept the next day by two platoons led by scout ships. The bodies of many of those killed the day before had already disappeared. Scattered contact was made with more outgunned and disorganized VC: a wounded guerrilla was captured and enough kills tabulated to boost the final box score to 182. The reward: dozens of decorations, to include Silver Stars for Cousland, Brown, Roesler, and his platoon leaders, plus Boyd, Butler, and Taskey, as well as Bronze Stars for Durst, Bakewell, Jerry Anderson, and others. Echoing the attitude of the troops themselves, the squadron newsletter declared that the lopsided victory had once again "shown how the Cav with its fire power and mobility and spirit is the best unit in Vietnam[.]"

Tom Bursott tells this story about Alpha Troop: "We were out somewhere, and the new FO was going to do some spotting rounds, and I remember diving under a track because he accidentally called the artillery in on us. He got his legs blown off, and we kind of said, you know, he deserved it."

The dragoons cut new lieutenants no slack, especially the latest one assigned to Boyd's Bastards. One can sympathize with a green lieutenant trying to take the reins of such a wild, proud, and independent platoon. "I'll tell ya, that was my platoon," says Boyd. "Lieutenants come and go." Unfortunately, the new lieutenant arrogantly eschewed advice, even from Boyd, no doubt feeling his authority was challenged by the brusque old warhorse. More than once he sank an overloaded track in a stream, or sent his scouts down narrow and deep creek beds despite being warned that he was inviting an ambush. Having made all the wrong moves in an already tricky situation, the lieutenant became a marked man. "Nobody said anything directly," recalls Jerry Anderson, who drove the lieutenant's track, "but you could tell that if he really pissed someone off, it was going to happen: he was going to go out one day and not come back."

The lieutenant almost didn't come back from a village search east of the highway on March 3. The GIs were using iron stakes to "probe in the gardens, because they'd hide weapons and stuff right underneath the plants," says Boyd, "and you know the Vietnamese, they started hollerin' about it, and my guys would just point an M16 at 'em and tell 'em to get the hell out of the way."

Boyd recalls that the new lieutenant upbraided him for the troops' treatment of the villagers: "That's no way for an American soldier to act."

"Lieutenant," replied Boyd, "this ain't the Second World War. Every damn one of these sumbitches out here is enemy unless he proves he isn't."

"Well, that's not the way I do business."

The lieutenant "called a goddamn meeting right there in the middle of the village, and really raised hell," says Boyd. "I just turned around and walked back to my tank. I wasn't going to listen to that shit, and I didn't want to face him down in front of the men." Boyd knew Roesler would straighten the lieutenant out when they got back to base camp, "so I let him have his way."

The platoon was rolling across the sands again when a command-detonated mine exploded under the lieutenant's track, marked as a command vehicle by its two radio masts. The others had only one. The blast punched a hole through the bottom of the track with such force as to blow off three road wheels, send the cupola flying—along with track commander, lieutenant, medic, and gunners—and tip the vehicle on its side. The VC who'd detonated the mine took off like a jackrabbit, but Boyd vaporized him with a canister round: all that remained was a Hồ Chí Minh sandal sitting on the ground. The other sandal had been blown sky-high. It seemed to hover for a moment, notes Bursott, "and then just dropped next to the first one. The guy had literally been blown out of his shoes."

Jerry Anderson hadn't heard the explosion that ruptured his eardrums, didn't know the track had been bowled over, but he knew something was wrong and, disoriented, stood to exit the driver's hatch. He fell face-first into the sand, the world having turned sideways. Anderson tried to stand, but Bill McKinney, his best friend, appeared and told him to lie down: "You're hurt!" Anderson: "I am not!" McKinney: "Feel your back!" Doing so, Anderson was shocked to find his arm smeared with blood.

Doc Hoover pricked him with a morphine syrette. The medic's thumb had been jammed back against his wrist, but he ignored the flopping digit as he treated the casualties, to include the gunners, who had each broken a leg on impact. McKinney and Bursott helped Hoover tie off bandages and keep everyone calm. While assisting the medic, Bursott called to the new platoon leader: "Lieutenant, we need to get these guys dusted off!"

The lieutenant was ringy from the blast, however: instead of coordinating the medevac, the lieutenant posed for photographs in front of his tipped-over track. Disgusted, Bursott turned and shouted to one of the track commanders to make sure a dust-off was on the way. At that, the lieutenant told Bursott that it was his job to handle casualty evacuation. Whoever made the call, the medevac soon approached. "Lieutenant, we need to get these guys on stretchers," said Bursott. The half-dazed lieutenant said to wait a minute, he wanted another photo. Bursott exploded: "Sir, if I get a chance, *I'm gonna shoot you.*"

Cooling down after the mission, Bursott thought better of actually pulling a trigger on the platoon leader. Someone in authority had apparently decided it was better to be safe than sorry, however: back at base camp, Bursott discovered that a captured rifle in his possession—an untraceable murder weapon—had officially been authorized as a war souvenir in his name and tacked on the wall of the platoon bunker so it couldn't be quietly taken along on patrol.

Waking up from surgery, Jerry Anderson was informed that of the many pieces of shrapnel and debris he'd absorbed, the worst offender was the corner of a metal ammo can wrapped around a bullet. The other stuff had been plucked from the muscles of his back with relative ease. The triangle-shaped chunk, however, having ripped through his side to lodge in his inner thigh, required major surgery to remove and five months of recuperation in Việt Nam, Okinawa, and William Beaumont Army Hospital in El Paso, Texas.

Doc Hoover, having completed the six months on the line expected of medics at the time of his injury, was pulled back to the aid station on Hill 29.

The new lieutenant stayed with the platoon. On another patrol, "some mamasan came up," recounts Bursott, "and here was this child in her arms, no more than two or three years old, that the Viet Cong had literally cut open because they thought the parents were loyal to Saigon. The lieutenant said that medevacs were only for American troops. We butted heads over that, and he finally did bring in a dust-off. I have no idea if the child survived."

The beer ration failed to arrive. Dick Taskey was also out of homemade hooch. The results were dramatic. Taskey went temporarily insane, and his buddies had to pin him down, wrest the M16 from his hands before he killed the lieutenant (as he raved he would), and lash him to a stretcher.

Few acts of rebellion were so extreme. Mostly, the troops, no longer intimidated by rules, regulations, and rank, operated with the passive-aggressive, don't-tread-on-me attitude of the seasoned combat soldier. Staff Sergeant Pryor, instructed by the platoon sergeant to police the trash-filled ditch behind his track's position on the bunker line, palmed the job off on his driver, only to be surprised shortly thereafter by a thunderous explosion, followed by a gentle rain of metallic particles: the driver had used about twenty pounds of C-4 to vaporize the litter of beer cans and empty C-rations. The platoon sergeant was furious, but Pryor just cracked a grin: "Well, he got rid of the trash, didn't he?"

Pryor was sitting at one end of the five-hole latrine at base camp when a lieutenant appeared at the doorway to rail at the guys passing a joint at the other end: "I can smell that shit!" The mellowed troopers shrugged and offered the new draftee catchphrase: "What are ya gonna do, send me to Vietnam?"

Richard Brummett recalls a tank commander of exceptionally limited intellect who was still only a buck sergeant, though in his late thirties, because of repeated reductions for excessive drinking. The over-age, dull-witted sergeant was "panicky and dangerous in action," notes Brummett, "but a hard ass in base camp. He was very unpopular with his crew and would do things like hold back mail until certain assigned tasks were finished." One night while some 3rd Platoon soldiers were drinking, Brummett continues, a fed-up crewman "announced he was going to frag the bastard. Another trooper very smoothly slipped the frag out of his hand and replaced it with a smoke grenade. He did not give any indication that he noticed and set off for his crew's bunker, where the sergeant was sleeping alone. He locked the door and dropped the smoke in the firing port." Afterward, the sergeant "was not seen for several days. When he finally returned, he was quite subdued."

There were other incidents of dragoon-on-dragoon violence. Staff Sergeant Pryor had infused into his scout section a black GI whom he quickly sized up as an unreliable doper. Pryor woke his people up one morning to pull maintenance or put on new track. The GI did not move. Pryor gave the guy's cot another kick: "C'mon, let's go, get your ass up." The GI accused Pryor of picking on him because he was prejudiced. Pryor's fuse was dangerously short after half a year in combat, and, infuriated at such back talk, he recalls that he "grabbed a pick handle and began beating the guy. I probably would have beaten him to death if the other guys hadn't dragged me off of him."

When originally put up for sergeant, Sonny Webster of B Troop had gone back to base camp with another hopeful from his platoon to take the final verbal exam. The names of those who passed were read by the colonel in a troop tent. Returning to his seat after shaking hands with the colonel and being handed his promotion orders, Webster saw that his erstwhile buddy had left, obviously ticked at not having made the cut. Webster sought him out to offer some no-hard-feelings comments, but the kid replied with a menacing leer: "Well, if you get killed, I'll get those stripes—so you better watch your back."

Webster walked away in shock. Disbelief soon turned to fury, however, and he found the kid and got in his face: "You try anything, and I'll fucking kill you." The spec four was from the mean streets of New York, and if his story was to be believed, he was in uniform because a judge had given him the choice of the army or prison after he pulled off an armed robbery with his brother. The kid's pride had been stung when not promoted, but Webster was convinced that he was mostly concerned with the extra pay that came with the stripes. The kid made a point to tell Webster to forget about it the day after they exchanged threats. "In big cities, it's all about reputations," explains Webster. "If you challenge somebody and they don't challenge you back, then they're a punk. If they challenge you back harder than you did them, then they're cool. I guess he believed I'd kill him because after that, he couldn't do enough for me; it was like, 'I'll do this, and I'll do that, and what about this, sarge?'"

Unwilling to take such obsequiousness at face value, Webster recalls well the look-over-your-shoulder paranoia that came with serving with such an unbalanced trooper. Webster was uneasy, too, about having to depend for his life on nice guys who weren't made for war: "I saw guys crying because they got a Dear John letter, and I'd think, dude, you're probably not even going to be alive by noon, what the fuck do you care about your girlfriend?!" There were also the new guys to worry about. "The replacements didn't have a clue what they were doing," notes Webster, and as they filled more and more slots "there wasn't the same camaraderie anymore." Bottom line: each man really soldiered through his tour alone, a constant ball of fear in his gut. In response, Webster was one of those who mellowed out between missions with beer, pot, whiskey, and Darvons. "I did all that stuff," he says, if only to stay sane. "You're under so much stress, you're using alcohol and drugs to get to a normal place. That stress and fear was the underlying cause of the drug and alcohol abuse in Vietnam: you knew you were never safe, anywhere, at any time."

Charlie Troop was working with a straight-leg unit when Staff Sergeant Pryor leveled his M16 on two grunts raping a girl in a hootch and warned them, he recalls, "that if I ever caught them pulling that kind of shit again, I'd blow 'em away. They sheepishly picked up their shit and got out of there."

Lieutenant Colonel Cousland caught a small fragment in the arm during a hundred-round bombardment of Hill 29 that began after midnight on March 4. On the scene at first light, the Blue Ghosts destroyed a mortar position atop Hill 34, five klicks west of Hill 29 at the mouth of the Quế Sơn Valley.

In response, Cousland called in air strikes from his command ship and then ordered C Troop up Hill 34 under the command of Capt. Michael B. Prothero, a highly professional West Pointer. The tracks and tanks, followed by A/3-21 Infantry, had rolled almost atop the expertly camouflaged enemy before the NVA opened fire with AK-47s and RPGs. One of the bushes near Max Pryor came alive, running, and the startled track commander swung his .50 about and cut down the leaf-covered North Vietnamese. "The firefight was ferocious," recalls Pryor, a point-blank exchange in which "you could see their eyes as you squeezed the butterflies on 'em. They fought to the death in their bunkers. We were laying down so much fire, I had to pour oil over the barrel of my machine gun."

Cousland ordered Prothero to pull back. Pryor was tagged for evacuation because of a piece of shrapnel in the web of his left hand between thumb and forefinger, and eyes turned to red slits from gunpowder and flying bits of debris. The landing zone was hot, the medevac overloaded, the two medics on board frantic as they tried to attend to everyone. The trooper beside Pryor gasped for air. Remembering their training about sucking chest wounds, Pryor ripped the plastic wrappers from two packs of cigarettes and slapped one over the hole in his buddy's chest, the other over the exit wound in his back. The trick worked.

Captain Prothero's cavalrymen, and A/3-21 Infantry, went up Hill 34 from a different angle on March 5. The result: a knocked-out tank, a mortally wounded crewman, another withdrawal, and more medevacs. Another assault was made on March 6, this time over a rocky hill and across a rice paddy. The enemy commenced firing while the tanks and tracks, piled with grunts, were still in the open. One of the M48s was disabled by recoilless-rifle fire that killed the commander and driver. The line pulled back. The disabled tank, left behind, was destroyed with main-gun fire from the other tanks. "Charlie Troop [has] uncovered an enemy fortress," a dragoon wrote home. "Air strikes seem to have little effect. Charlie Troop found bunkers with walls eight feet thick."

Having held onto the fortress for three days, the enemy gave it away for free on the fourth morning of the battle. That is to say, those still alive among the defenders slipped away under cover of darkness to rally with other enemy units and occupy other positions in the patchwork of hummocks, rice paddies, and tree lines around Hill 34. The battle continued.

The B Troop XO, 1st Lt. Donald Mattaro, was commanding B Troop (Captain Reed was on R&R) with A/3-21 Infantry attached. On March 8, the task force made heavy contact. That evening the force set up night defensive positions in a small hamlet at the insistence of the infantry captain. All B Troop personnel knew that armored vehicles needed to be positioned in the rice paddies with clear fields of fire for several hundred meters. The captain of the A/3-21 Infantry, who obviously out-ranked a first lieutenant, pulled rank and selected the combined force defensive positions in a hamlet filled with trees and brush. He then posted listening posts forward of the positions without informing the B Troopers. The NVA pounded the laager after dark with forty rounds of mortar fire, wounding ten grunts and twenty-three cavalrymen. Three more grunts were wounded and one killed by Bravo Troop's return fire: tragically unaware that infantry listening posts had been placed forward of the M48s and ACAVs.

Captain Reed returned to Hill 29 on the morning of March 9 and was immediately told that B Troop had inflicted friendly casualties and was ordered to fly immediately to the defensive site. When he confronted Lieutenant Mattaro and the infantry captain, it was clear that the two had argued over the defensive positions the night before. A/3-21 Infantry was detached from B Troop that morning.

Following air strikes, B Troop was advancing on its objective on March 9 when heavy fire was received from a wooded hillside. Sergeant Webster sat cross-legged on the board placed across the hatch inside his gun tub, methodically firing his .50 into the trees. When his right foot fell asleep, he dropped it down to get the blood circulating—just as an RPG hit the side of the track, blowing open the aluminum skin and stinging his dangling foot with shrapnel. The troop gained the crest of a small, bald hill and formed a protective circle, only to be mortared. "We were sitting ducks," says Webster. "Here's the beautiful part: all the guys taking care of me took off. I'm laying on a stretcher. I've got my foot bandaged up, and the morphine's hitting, but I got up and started running." A medevac landed after artillery fire quieted the mortars—tracks and tanks were blasting away, too—and "they threw us on board," notes Webster. "The chopper got hit three or four times from small-arms fire, but we got out of there."

The battle petered out. Two Charlie Troopers were killed, however, when their track hit a mine during the mop-up phase of shooting stragglers and unearthing dead NVA from trenches, bunkers, and hasty graves.

The final body count was put at 375.

Sergeant Webster spent a month aboard a hospital ship and, upon discharge, was reassigned to the squadron rear in Fat City in recognition of his two Purple Hearts. Webster had a good case of short-timer's fever by then and recalls being put in charge of a detail "that did whatever it did, which I can't tell you a lot about because I wasn't concerned and didn't show up most of the time."

Staff Sergeant Pryor was reassigned all the way back to a guard tower at division headquarters as part of the Chu Lai Defense Command. The transfer was the result of a dragoon, who, poring over the army manual like a convict studying the law, had discovered a life-saving wrinkle: any GI wounded three times qualified for immediate reassignment to the rear. "Word spread like wildfire," recalls Pryor, "and people demanded to be pulled off the line."

Pryor was one of them, thanking his lucky stars that his hand and eye injuries from Hill 34 had been recorded as separate wounds: he thus received two more Purple Hearts to go with the one from the Pineapple Forest. Befriending another thrice-wounded staff sergeant, a proud black man from Mississippi, Pryor and his buddy decompressed in the rear with Jack Daniel's. "I was drunk for thirty straight days," he says. "I didn't slow down until I looked in the mirror, and my face was bloated like I had elephantiasis. I realized I was killing myself."

On March 14, Captain Reed and B Troop killed four military-age males in coordination with the Blue Ghosts and captured two others. Sergeant Decktor snapped a photo as his right-hand gunner tormented one of the bound and blindfolded detainees with a switchblade. "He was teasing the guy, poking him with the switchblade," says Decktor. "Nobody got hurt. He was just playin' with him—fuckin' with him—that's the way we were. The guy was scared to death."

Some hours later, while the column passed through a cemetery, the vehicle behind Decktor's, B-28, suddenly went straight up from a command-detonated mine; flipping over before it crashed back to earth. Decktor ran to one of the men thrown from the mortar track, saw that he was dead, then, realizing that they were under fire, clambered back behind his .50 to join those returning fire. The enemy quickly withdrew. The upside-down mortar track was in full flame by then, the ammo inside cooking off. Captain Reed and the 2nd Platoon leader helped pull two badly wounded troopers to safety. The driver was still trapped inside, and, frantic at the thought that he was burning to death, the lieutenant and several of his men attempted to hook up tow cables from a tank to right the track. The heat was too much. Convinced that the driver was already dead, Reed ordered everyone back before someone else got killed.

When the fire finally died, the track was turned over, and what was left of the driver was recovered. "I was one of the guys that carried the body out in a poncho, and it was a mess," remembers Decktor, who prayed that the driver had been killed instantly when the track landed on him. The driver, Pvt. 1st Class David F. Cosby, had told his buddies at Fort Hood that he would die in Việt Nam. However nervous his demeanor, and however many times he requested a job in the rear, Cosby nonetheless did his job. He never let anyone down. "Cosby was a black kid from Philly," says Decktor, "and a really nice guy."

The occasional taunting of a prisoner aside, Ron Decktor tried to fight the fair fight in an unfair war, as did the rest of Bravo Troop. The pressures were intense, however, and Decktor recalls the day he almost lost it and came within a hair's breadth of doing something he would have regretted for the rest of his life. A truck passing a marine outpost on Highway 1 had detonated a mine; a marine had been killed, his chest blown open, heart literally ripped out. Sickened and infuriated, Decktor swung his .50 on the hootches a stone's throw from the scene of the crime. "I said, shit, these people knew about the mine, let's take out the village," he recalls. "I said, let's just level this place—fuck 'em—screw 'em—kill 'em all—that way there's less people to worry about."

No one fired, not even Decktor. All had wanted to, however. Try telling a soldier whose friends have been maimed, dismembered, and burnt to a crisp by mines that the villagers were victims, too. If they said nothing of the mines, they risked an "incident" with the Americans. If they pointed out the mines to those who passed through during the day, those who ruled the night might very well leave them on the side of the road with a bullet in the brain, a warning to others. "They had nothing," Decktor says of the villagers. "They were just poor, primitive people caught in the middle, but you don't see it that way in the heat of the moment: you're frustrated, you're pissed, you want revenge."

The grunts took no greater revenge during the war than that executed on the sixteenth of March 1968 by Task Force Barker, a provisional battalion of the 11th Light Infantry Brigade, in Quảng Ngãi Province. The grunts were braced for battle as they leapt from the Hueys that morning. The company on the ocean side of the objective area, B/4-3 Infantry, tripped two booby traps; a platoon leader was killed, seven men wounded. Company B swept the nearest hamlet and was starting into another, Mỹ Khê 4, when the point platoon opened fire and didn't stop shooting until ninety villagers were sprawled across the sand.

In the meantime, C/1-20 Infantry landed on the west side of Mỹ Lại 4. Again, no guerrillas were found, only villagers. These, the officers and men of Charlie Company slaughtered as they razed the hamlet, along with neighboring Bình Tây. When the shooting, raping, and burning fizzled out after four mad hours, another 347 villagers lay dead, according to a subsequent army investigation. The Vietnamese themselves list the names of 504 victims of what became known collectively as the Mỹ Lại Massacre.

There were infantrymen who refused to fire and a scout pilot who landed near a ditch piled with bodies to rescue a pitiful few survivors. The pilot, CWO Hugh Thompson, was one of those who reported the outrage to his superiors. Almost certainly, the task-force commander already knew what had happened. Indeed, it has been alleged that the lieutenant colonel had tacitly encouraged the destruction of everyone and everything in the troublesome hamlet of Mỹ Lại 4. The brigade commander, and General Koster, saw the columns of smoke from their helicopters and knots of bodies scattered about the area, but they assumed the villagers had been killed impersonally by artillery. When informed of a possible massacre by the ground troops, Koster allowed the incident to be covered up with a falsified body count of 128 VC. The victory was trumpeted in the division newspaper and received a mention in the Pacific Stars & Stripes. The truth would eventually be revealed with devastating results.

When the 1st and 3rd Platoons of A Troop turned into a hamlet west of the highway called Mậu Hoà on March 18, two young men were seen scrambling into a bunker. Platoon Sergeant Boyd fragged the bunker and then began questioning an old man squatting in front of a nearby hootch. Instead of responding with the usual deference, the old man—bone thin and wearing a wispy goatee—wagged his finger and scolded Boyd in high-pitched Vietnamese. Boyd says that he knocked the defiant old man to the ground and fired a shot next to his head to encourage him to answer the troop interpreter. The old man was then turned loose.

Boyd's description notwithstanding, it seems clear that the old man ended up as another of the "VC" kills reported to squadron that day by

Alpha Troop. Staff Sergeant Davis Bennett, a veteran of the 3rd Platoon, in a sworn statement said: "I saw the [old] man being thrown down [a] well, and heard a hand grenade go off inside the well, and also heard some shots being fired, but I was too far away to see who was involved. I do know that it was Boyd's platoon that was around the well."

David Eady recalls talk that it was Boyd who disposed of the old man. John Guzik says that he indeed witnessed Boyd kill the old man from the vantage point of his tank turret. Richard Brummett's account of the incident is the most explicit: the old man "was fighting to get away from Boyd" as the platoon sergeant hauled him to the well; after dropping the old man, Boyd "then threw a fragmentation grenade down the well. . . . Boyd was bitching to himself that the grenade did not kill the man, so he took out his .45 pistol and fired two or three rounds into the well . . . [T]hen he turned and began giving orders . . . [H]e said, 'Okay, let's go check this place out.'" Brummett says that he is ashamed that he stood frozen while murder was committed before his eyes: "I should have tried to stop him, but I was afraid of Boyd, and I was afraid of his men."

Boyd led the way across the sands the next morning, moving east on an unpaved road, as Captain Roesler controlled the two-platoon operation from a helicopter. Staff Sergeant Elwood L. Houston followed Boyd in A-34. Spec Five John Guzik, acting commander of A-35, followed Houston and was trailed, in turn, by the tracks of the 1st and 2nd Platoons. Upon crossing an intersecting north–south footpath, Boyd, misinterpreting Roesler's directions, turned left off the unpaved road in the direction of a parallel earthen berm. Roesler immediately barked over the radio: "No, no, no, you're going the wrong way!"

Boyd radioed Houston, who had continued forward, to stop—"I belong in front"—and was coming up from behind when a huge explosion suddenly shook the column. Richard Brummett—sandblasted across the back of his neck as he sat atop Houston's tank—dropped inside the turret to man his battle station, unsure if someone had hit a mine or if one of the other tanks had accidentally fired its main gun past their ears. Brummett gradually became aware of a horrible mechanical screaming and stuck his head up. He couldn't see anything: the blast had enveloped them in a surrealistic fog of fine white sand.

When the haze cleared, the cavalrymen saw that Boyd's tank, hurled through the air by a five-hundred-pound bomb converted into a mine, was straddling the earthen berm, facing away from the rest of the column. The road wheels were missing, the entire left track was in the mine crater, the right track flopped off to the side, the main gun bent. The engine was stuck at full throttle, the rear sprockets spinning madly. Brummett—the first to reach the wreck, and so pumped-up that he almost ran into one of the screaming sprockets—dashed to the front of the tank to find the driver coated in black soot and bleeding from ears, nose, and mouth. The man was still lucid, however, and frantically trying to shut down the engine. The engine shut-off toggle would not respond, and the sprockets continued whirring at a speed dangerously beyond their design limits.

Platoon Sergeant Boyd was slumped in his hatch, still semiconscious after having his face bashed into the back end of the .50-caliber machine gun. "I never heard nothin' or felt nothin'," he recalls; one second, he was talking on the radio, "and the next thing I knew, I was laying on a stretcher. I remember raising up, and I tried to say, shut that goddamn tank off—but nothing came out."

Boyd's jaw was broken, and part of his shredded lower lip hung wetly against his chin. Doc Gaydon threw a dressing around Boyd's head and hit him with morphine. The runaway engine was howling all the while. One of the noncoms on the scene thought to silence the engine with a 90mm HEAT round. Guzik objected. "I prevailed, knowing, or hoping, that it would be less dangerous to get inside the turret, open the access panel, and crimp the fuel line," recalls Guzik. "The rounds in the ready rack had spilled over but looked safe enough." Brummett got the job, and, after he reemerged, the engine consumed the last of the diesel in the disconnected fuel line and finally shut down. The medevac landed then while gunships blasted the surrounding area. "I remember thinking," writes Guzik, "that it was a good thing Boyd was going to the sidelines."

Houston and Guzik were left to guard the remains of Boyd's tank until it could be evacuated, while the rest of the unit roared off for the nearest hamlet on their maps, Phước Âm 3. Firing soon erupted, and smoke rose over the trees in the distance. There was chatter on the radio about killing all the animals in the ville and burning down the hootches. The squadron log records that A Troop killed one military-age male in the general vicinity, and the Blue Ghosts three more.

The situation had calmed when a half-dozen women and girls appeared on a footpath that intersected the unpaved road: chogi poles on shoulders, a basket at either end, heading north, they were apparently returning from market. For no apparent reason, a crewman on Guzik's tank named Herman Schneider stood up, waving his arms and screaming madly at the girls to get away. The women and girls, not looking up, stepped a little more quickly and were already past the tanks and increasing the distance with every step when "Schneider picked up an M79," says Brummett, "and fired one perfect round into the group, dropping two of the girls into the sand. The survivors shed their burdens and ran off."

Drafted at age twenty-six, and acting middle aged, Schneider was unimpressed with the rambunctious young troopers among whom he'd been thrown and, adopting an abrasive persona, was intent on doing his job, keeping his head down, and returning to his good job and productive life in St. Louis. He was uninterested in killing guerrillas, let alone civilians. "Every man has his breaking point, however," notes Brummett; perhaps seeing the tank ahead of his blown sky-high "was the last straw for Schneider. The next Vietnamese he saw, he killed." Brummett was shaken by Schneider's outburst: "If a mature, level-headed man of twenty-six could commit this needless crime, then anyone could do anything."

Perseus and Medusa; The Old Man in the Well; The Two Girls in the Sand. March 17, 18, and 19, 1968, stand out as three hammer-blow days of horror and moral failure in A Troop.

Captain Roesler and A Troop, followed by C Troop, crossed the Trường Giang on March 20 to kick off a major operation on Cigar Island, since renamed Barrier Island. A Troop soon reported taking fire from guerrillas attempting to flee in fishing boats and, in response, sinking thirteen sampans and killing twenty-two VC. That is not how Dick Taskey recalls the incident. "We were just moving down the beach, and somebody got the idea to test-fire their weapons," says Taskey, noting that once one crew opened fire, the rest spontaneously followed suit. "We aimed at all these gooks out there fishing in their little sampans. We were shootin' ducks in a pond, you know—just target practice."

After securing landing zones for their infantry support, A and C Troops swept north, making scattered contact. Between the grunts, cavalry, and gunships, twenty VC were reported killed, and four weapons captured. Pushing on to the wide end of the island, A Troop and D/1-20 Infantry ran into an entrenched force that knocked out two tracks with recoilless-rifle fire. By the end of the hour-long firefight, thirty grunts and cavalrymen had been wounded, and a sixty-four body count was reported, along with five more weapons. Platoon Sergeant Jessie, cited for wiping out a squad of guerrillas with his .50, won a Silver Star.

The operation, big as it was, has mostly faded from memory. No wonder. Firefights were so frequent during the counteroffensive as to bleed together. "We got more of them than they got of us, but they still kept comin'," notes Bursott. The platoon was returning from one patrol when Bursott, sitting in the rear-guard position on the back of a track, glanced to his right, "and here was this guy walking along a little hill there, fully loaded—pith helmet, green uniform, web gear, and AK-47. I started to turn to alert everybody, and I looked back and he was gone, and I just kept my mouth shut because we were going back to a hot meal and showers. I didn't see any sense in wasting time looking for the guy."

Having already denied a request for more troops, President Johnson went further during a televised address on March 31, announcing a partial bombing halt of North Việt Nam that he hoped would lead to negotiations with Hà Nội. Johnson, physically and spiritually exhausted, concluded his address by declaring that in order to devote his attention to ending the war, he would neither seek nor accept the nomination of his party for another term as president.

The professional officer corps was outraged. In the view of military men, the president was snatching defeat from the jaws of victory. The enemy had never before been so bedraggled than at the end of the counteroffensive: the VC were crippled by losses, the NVA pushed back into the hinterlands. The time had come to invade North Việt Nam, not enter into peace talks in Paris.

Military men blamed political cowardice, and demoralizing, overly pessimistic news accounts, for denying them the victory they thought they could have won in Việt Nam. Such a view was born of a passion to justify their terrible sacrifices, and those of their soldiers and marines. The kind of victory described by the officer corps, however, was not possible. Yes, the enemy had been beaten to the ground, but the Vietnamese would undoubtedly rise from the ashes, as they had done when defeated in the past by the Chinese and French. The enemy possessed the manpower and the will to fight for decades. No corresponding will existed in Sài Gòn, Washington, or the heartland of America.

At that point in the war, almost twenty-five thousand Americans had been killed in Việt Nam. Such losses, and the lack of progress they implied, had more effect on public opinion than any anti-war protests on college campuses. The mothers and fathers of Middle America could not support further escalation of the war after Tết revealed the delusions that were the light-at-the-end-of-the-tunnel promises of Johnson and Westmoreland. Sensing the public mood, Richard M. Nixon campaigned for the presidency in 1968 on the assurance that he would bring peace with honor to Việt Nam.

Their tank being down and away for repairs, Guzik and Brummett trotted to the maintenance track instead when the 122mm rockets began to fall on Hill 29. The motor sergeant and crew were buttoned up inside, no fools they. Concerned that the Motor Bear's poorly maintained machine gun might blow up in his face, Guzik beat on the side of the track, demanding a head-space-and-timing gauge. The driver's hatch opened all of three inches, just wide enough for a hand to offer the gauge to Guzik. The hatch immediately closed again.

Ignoring the incoming rockets, Guzik and Brummett unscrewed and correctly adjusted the machine-gun barrel's head space and set the timing. "Of course, the mechanics had not greased the gun-mount ring in months," adds Brummett, "and the .50 was partly frozen in place: up and down movement, but no side to side." As such, Brummett, standing fully exposed on the deck, pushed the cupola back and forth to Guzik's commands "while Guzik, also exposed, squatted on the closed commander's hatch and water-hosed tracers at the launching flashes of the rockets. It was great fun. More so knowing that a pack of mechanics was cowering in the track beneath us." Brummett saves the best part of the story for last: "Did I mention we were completely stoned?"

The war had finally reached that point for Brummett. Deeply troubled by the brutal conduct of their operations, he says that he spoke with a visiting Catholic chaplain, who said only that: "These things happen in war." Disgusted, Brummett stopped going to Mass, and took solace in beer and weed, at least at night. "Guzik was fond of saying, 'We laugh and we joke, but we don't play around,'" recalls Brummett. "By that he meant that we could smoke dope and tell jokes in the evening, but on patrol we were all business. Guzik was good: he could put a 90mm round through a water buffalo at three thousand meters."

The war had wrought other changes in Richard Brummett. For one, he was becoming quick on the trigger. Brummett was on guard atop A-35 when he spotted a light out in the distance. Given the standing order to shoot at any "light in the night," Brummett requested and received permission to open fire and had already lined up the main gun when a new guy, Spc. 4th Class Brandt S. Neubacher, brought him to his senses: "That's probably just a farmer in a hut, Brummett: don't you dare shoot at him!"

Neubacher was from Berkeley, California, and he was embarrassed by his hometown's national reputation. He believed in America, and to make amends he joined the army and volunteered for Việt Nam from a safe posting in Germany.

Another day, and Brummett, instructed to burn down a village, shouted at the hysterical peasant women pulling at his arm to back off. "They did not understand my English," recounts Brummett, "but I think they understood the flat side of my .45 laid vigorously across their slant-eyed, sloping foreheads."

Brummett was dismounted and providing security for his tank when a man approached, whining in the singsong language of the Vietnamese. "He pawed at my sleeve," notes Brummett. "'Go away,' I said. 'Beat it.' No effect. 'Di-di-fuckin'-mau!' [Get out of here!] I pushed him down the trail. He returned at once. I kicked him in the butt. He returned again, like a dog who crawls to you and whimpers at your feet." The man's behavior was inexplicable and infuriating. Brummett would later wonder if the man had been trying to divert his attention from something he wasn't supposed to find. In any event, Richard Brummett, former novitiate, was possessed of an urge to bash the annoying man's brains out with the butt of his M79. The mood has never really passed: "There are days even now when I somewhat regret not having killed that particular gook."

It is good that he did not kill that day, for Brummett felt he already had enough blood on his hands. In the event of sniper fire, the platoon sergeant would train the main gun on the area from which the shots had come, and Guzik and Brummett would open fire. If the target was close, they'd blast the bushes with canister. Otherwise, they used HE. "One or two times, we flushed people out," recalls Brummett. "They panicked and ran. At least, *somebody* ran: snipers, farmers, who the hell knows?" The dragoons fired at anybody who ran at their approach. The act of running was proof of guilt. "You run, you die," explains Brummett. "I never saw any of these people, as I was the loader, but Guzik was looking through the sights and pulling the trigger, and he'd say 'Got one' or 'Got two.' I kept a tally of our kills. We killed thirteen runners. Guzik thought it was morbid to keep count. In his mind, it was just a job."

Guzik had the right attitude; it did a combat soldier no good to think deeply about what he was doing. It was not the way to keep one's sanity.

Brummett almost lost it the day Captain Roesler gave the order to fire on two hamlets visible from the top of Hill 34 on which Alpha Troop had stopped for lunch. One ville, Đông Mỹ 1, sat at the foot of the hill and was to be hosed down with the .50-cal machine guns of the scout tracks; the other ville, Châu Chanh, about two klicks north across a valley, was to be blasted by the 90mm cannon of the tanks. Roesler might have seen enemy troops in his binoculars, though Brummett doubted it: "Maybe he'll say he saw an NVA regiment out there. Well, he didn't. Nothing had happened. No sniper fire, no provocation, no land mines—nothing—just for dessert we're going to shoot up two villages."

Staff Sergeant Houston gave the command to fire, and the gunner pulled the trigger on the round already in the breech. Brummett instantly replaced it with one from the ready rack, then gave the word that indicated the breech block was closed, and he was safely out of the way of the recoil: "Up!"

Before firing, the gunner said, "On the way!" The cycle was repeated several times: "Up ... Fire ... On the way ... Up ... Fire ... On the way!"

Houston said to switch from HE to Willy Pete: white phosphorus. When the first WP round exploded in the distant ville, Brummett says that Captain Roesler offered his congratulations: "You got arms and legs with that one, 3-5."

The overly excited gunner—not Guzik that day—pulled the trigger at that moment, failing to wait for his loader's all clear. The recoil of the main gun barely missed Brummett. Pissed that he'd almost had his right arm shattered, sickened by the captain's enthusiastic pronouncement, Brummett used the manual lock to shut down the main gun and climbed out of the turret. Ignoring Houston's shouts, Brummett sat on the turret and cradled a grease gun—an obsolete submachine gun issued to tankers—and stared at Roesler, who watched the action through his binoculars, talking all the while on the radio. "I considered going over there and killing Captain Roesler," says Brummett. "This is difficult for me to talk about, but hearing Roesler say that you had just murdered people on his behalf, at his orders." The captain was a butcher, thought Brummett. He needed to pay. "I went through the options in my mind. I knew I couldn't hit him with that damn grease gun from where I was sitting. I would have to walk over to his track and say, excuse me, captain, I need to kill you now—and shoot him." An appealing thought, but in the end, "I felt badly about the Vietnamese but not badly enough to spend the rest of my life in Leavenworth—so I just sat there." A second moral failure for Brummett.

Brummett says Roesler finally ordered a cease-fire then, no longer interested in the two hamlets, gave the word to continue the patrol. No approach was made to either ville to assess casualties inflicted.

David Eady's memory of their tactics mirrors Brummett's. "It was very confusing," says Eady. The unit was in a free-fire zone, "and you'd do it"—that is, fire at anything in black pajamas—"but sometimes you felt like, wow, you didn't know, you didn't know if they were VC; you just saw these people down there in the rice paddies, and you take 'em out. Captain Roesler would order us to do whatever: we'd just come up on a hill and look down there, and there'd be people out in the rice paddies, and 'Open fire!'"

The Road to Tiên Phước

APRIL 1968

THE CINNAMON-GROWING VILLAGE OF Tiên Phước sat at the end of a thin, crooked valley, eleven kilometers long, which cut through the mountains west of Tam Kỳ. Province capital and village were connected by an overgrown track, Provincial Route 533, the bridges along which had been destroyed during the war between the French and Việt Minh, leaving the U.S. Special Forces team at Tiên Phước dependent on helicopter resupply. Guerrilla activity in the area having increased dramatically as of late, apparently in preparation for an attack, General Koster tasked the 198th Light Infantry Brigade with opening the road to Tiên Phước under the codename Operation Burlington Trail. Cousland, having harbored doubts about the reserve officer serving as his S3, finally tested Major Medbery by having him put together the plan for the squadron's role in the operation. "That's the first time I did anything without Cousland's guidance, and the first time I was to be allowed to go out into the field," recalls Medbery. "I briefed Cousland on the plan when finished, he made a couple changes, and away we went."

The operation kicked off on April 9. With Major Medbery overhead, as he would be throughout, A Troop moved down Route 533 to rendezvous with the engineers who were to construct a new bridge alongside the long-ruined one in the village at the mouth of the valley. An attached platoon from C Troop, moving into the hills north of the road, made contact and reported a big body count. As the bridge building continued on April 10, the command track of the attached platoon, trying to climb a steep bank after crossing a stream, slid backward onto a mine. The track commander was blown from his hatch and badly injured. The driver was mortally wounded. The other four men on board were killed instantly, to include Lieutenant Wojtkiewicz and Spc. 4th Class Kimmey D. Hobbs, a gentle, well-liked medic who had always worked just as hard to save the lives of wounded prisoners as his fellow dragoons.

The bridge finished, A Troop and an infantry company moved across on April 11. The column, hemmed in by bouldered and forested hillsides, passed an abandoned, bullet-pocked church and an old French steamroller draped with vines. "The terrain we cross is hazardous enough to give a [vehicle] commander a few gray hairs," wrote radioman Tom Andersen, who, granted his wish to go to the field, had been made acting TC for Lieutenant Norton. "We maneuver along a narrow valley no wider than a footpath, while fording rice paddies and streams. It is very difficult for armored vehicles to traverse because of the dense vegetation and mud-holes. This is excellent ambush territory."

Reaching another downed bridge, Lieutenant Norton checked the stream for a good spot to place their bridge tank. "We started moving the AVLB forward," he recalls, "and the whole hillside suddenly erupted." Norton realized that the enemy, watching unseen from the high ground, could have nailed him at the stream but instead held their fire until more targets appeared. Because the tanks and tracks could not climb the hill, an ARVN infantry unit moved forward. "Those guys were good," says Norton. "We kept the main-gun and .50-caliber fire about fifty meters ahead of the ARVN as they worked their way up the hill. It was crazy, but the coordination was perfect: the ARVN cleared the hill, and we dropped the AVLB and continued down the valley."

As dusk approached, the bulldozers that had been widening the road flattened the brush at the edge of a small hamlet to provide fields of fire as cavalrymen and grunts set up for the night. Specialist Fourth Class Robert E. Johnston, the medic attached to the 3rd Platoon of Alpha Troop, was on watch after midnight on April 12. Sitting atop the command track, he scanned the rice paddy to his front with a starlight scope. Nothing moved in the paddy, nor in the tree line on the other side. The only things of note were half a dozen lumps, or spots, that appeared darkly against a landscape painted fluorescent green in the scope. Maybe twenty minutes later, Johnston turned the scope back on. He couldn't be sure, but it appeared that the spots, while retaining their pattern in relation to one another, had edged a bit closer to the night laager. Getting uptight, Johnston dismounted to spread the word that "I think I got something out there."

The guys on the tank next door could see the spots in their own starlight scope but could discern no movement. They prudently trained their main gun on the area, however, as Johnston continued to spread the alarm. He was not taken seriously. Johnston was a skinny, blond kid from Minnesota, very bright, but also hyper and nervous, a replacement not yet trusted by the veterans. "I was trippin' and stumblin' in the dark, making quite a bit of noise," he recalls. "I had half the troop awake, and people were pissed at me." Johnston returned to his track, put the starlight scope to his eye again, "and a figure stood up, looking straight at me, and waved." Terrified, Johnston jumped behind an M60 and cut loose, sparking everyone on that side of the laager to open up, too: "They turned that whole rice paddy upside down and inside out."

There was a pause, a moment of silence, then the thump of mortar rounds hitting the bottom of a tube in the tree line across the paddy and a swarm of AK-47 tracers. Learning more about enemy tactics, Johnston would later wonder if the VC who waved had been trying to draw fire so the cavalrymen would reveal their exact positions. If that had been the plan, says Johnston, it almost worked because "the enemy mortar team put a round between five vehicles in a row. Had they been over just a couple feet, they would have hit all five."

One infantryman was killed, and Johnston treated several cavalrymen superficially wounded when an RPG hit their track, but the return fire, including artillery, was intense. "I play 'Audie Murphy' and open fire with the .50-caliber machine gun," noted Andersen. "Once the FO cranked up the arty, the bad guys kind of boogied out of there." The outgoing fire "continued for most of the night. I grabbed a grenade launcher. I had always wanted to shoot one of those, so I plunked a few rounds out into the trees."

The official body count was ten.

The movement down the forbidding valley continued on April 12. The tanks and tracks circled up on a hilltop before dusk and were hit through the night by automatic-weapons and mortar fire. The dragoons poured return fire into jungled ridgelines lit by flares. "The amount of firepower an armored cavalry troop had was incredible," recalls Andersen. "You couldn't imagine how anybody in front of us could survive. It was like the Fourth of July."

Whatever punishment was meted out to the enemy, Lieutenant Norton was informed that the cavalrymen also killed several ARVN during one of the night attacks on Alpha Troop. The government soldiers, out on a listening post, had been pulling back when cut down. "We felt terrible," says Norton, "but their commander said, nope, they didn't do what they were told to do: they had been instructed to stay in place in case of attack because if you try to come back in the middle of the night you've got a chance of being shot up by your own guys."

First Sergeant McPherson, riding on the ambulance track when contact was made on April 13, provided cover fire with the .50 while several wounded grunts were loaded aboard. The topkick himself was superficially injured, either during the original melee or later when a tank ran over a mine. Alpha Troop rolled into Tiên Phước on April 14. The townspeople greeted the cavalrymen with cheers and banners, and carabao having been slaughtered for the occasion; a feast was laid out for the conquering heroes. After the celebration, which was interrupted by sniper fire, A Troop handed the mission off to B Troop and was on its way back home when ambushed at the mouth of the valley. "We counterattack and . . . score a few kills," wrote Andersen. "When we arrive at base camp, my adventure is over, and I return to radio watch."

Major Medbery was awarded the Bronze Star, as was Capt. Robert Kaczor, the new squadron S2. Kaczor had come under fire but didn't feel he had done anything special by riding to Tiên Phước and back with A Troop, and he asked Major Lundquist why he had written him up for a medal. Lundquist told Kaczor that as S2 he didn't have to go to the field, and he should be recognized for such initiative. Likewise, Lieutenant Norton and First Sergeant McPherson, whose duties usually kept them in the rear, received Silver Stars.

The dragoons were made responsible for keeping Route 533 open, and before the end of the month, Charlie Troop ran over another mine while escorting a supply convoy to Tiên Phước. Two troopers were killed.

One of the New Guys

APRIL–MAY 1968

ON APRIL 22, PLATOON Sergeant Jessie, to be reassigned off the line in a matter of days, ran over a mine on the road between Ross and Baldy. The tank was being towed back to Baldy when it hit a second mine. Between the two blasts, Jessie and the four troopers on the tank were all injured, to include Guzik and Neubacher. "My wound was not very dramatic," writes John Guzik. "I wasn't even aware I was hit until I felt some wetness on the back of my shirt. It was blood. The doc stated that I needed some stitches, so I was dusted off, stitched up, and sent back to the field in time to pull my shift on guard that night."

Brummett had previously taken over as driver—having finally learned how to drive—but with his hand in a cast from a maintenance accident, he had not been at the wheel when the rest of the crew was wounded. Instead, one of the new guys, Pvt. 1st Class Patrick J. Scognamilio, had been driving A-35. Scognamilio had been trained as an eleven-delta, but because the unit needed tankers more than armored reconnaissance scouts, 1st Sgt. McPherson had turned the new guy over to Brummett: "You teach this kid how to be a tank driver."

Scognamilio was the only man for whom Brummett was ever responsible during his army career, and he took the assignment seriously. Brummett taught Scognamilio—an outgoing Italian kid from Brooklyn, with whom he got along wonderfully—about driving, engine maintenance, and the hundreds of nuts and bolts that continually worked themselves loose from the tracks. The most important lessons were about mines. The dragoons did not fear firefights; they feared mines. Brummett warned Scognamilio to beware of "stream crossings and all roads away from the main highway. They were not paved, and without a mine-detection team, it was asking for grief to ride on such a road. Finally, I told him to watch the civilians. If they were running and hiding, it meant trouble."

Scognamilio was a draftee like most, but he'd watched the Tết Offensive on television before shipping out, and his attitude reflected the growing disaffection with the war. "Scognamilio was the first soldier I heard say that he did not want to die in Vietnam," notes Brummett. "I assured him that if he stayed with me, and that big ugly tank, he would survive his year in Vietnam."

Dmitri Gudanov mentioned after a patrol that a certain member of the unit, known to be an obnoxious jerk, had assaulted a village girl. Much to Brummett's disappointment, Gudanov, a quiet, inoffensive young man, blithely said that he went next. Scognamilio happened to be there. Brummett didn't want the new guy to think such brutality was acceptable in this alien world into which he'd been thrown, so he drew his .45, and, holding it vertical, said to his buddy: "Gudanov, if I catch you raping another woman, I'll blow your head off."

"Brummett," said Gudanov, "I believe you will."

First Lieutenant David L. Miller, recently infused into the dragoons, took over the platoon on May 7 and immediately moved out to escort a convoy. The column was nearing Ross when "the track in front of me exploded," writes Miller, "and did a lazy spin, ending right-side-up in a shallow stream under the road." The vehicle landed atop the track commander, who'd been hurled from his hatch: the body was half underwater, pinched between the hull and a drive sprocket. It was a bad scene, "and people just seemed to vegetate and space out on me," recalls Miller. "Someone said we were going to have to cut him in half to recover the body." Miller disagreed and recalls the troop exec "saying he knew I'd make it with the cav when he flew in to check on the new platoon leader and found me underwater with a wrench, taking off the sprocket so I wouldn't have to send a young trooper's body home in two pieces."

The troops considered the businesslike Lieutenant Miller a marked improvement on the faux-tough lifer who'd been in nominal command from Tết to Tiên Phước. "Miller gave the impression of being a tolerant and decent guy," writes Brummett, "who just happened to be an officer."

The son of a workingman, Dave Miller had grown up hunting, fishing, and trapping with his three brothers in upstate New York. All were athletes and all-around go-getters in high school. One was to command a marine engineer company in Việt Nam. Dave Miller's own path to the war zone began when he was drafted upon taking a semester off after two years as a music major at New York State University. He was selected for OCS and, finding that he very much liked the military life, set his sights on a career in the U.S. Army.

Lieutenant Miller had seen his share of action—two wounds, six personal kills—while in Quảng Ngãi with the armored cavalry troop of the 11th Light Infantry Brigade. Nonetheless, upon joining the 1st of the 1st Cav, "I could tell from the stories and captured weapons laying around that they had seen a lot more than I had." That everything at Hill 29 was underground because of mortar and rocket attacks was also something new. Miller had previously spent most of his time guarding bridges. The dragoons, however, had their own area of operations, had their own helicopter support, and hunted daily. The squadron exuded confidence. "The officers were gallant, carefree, blood-and-guts leaders," writes Miller. The noncoms were sharp, and, as for the troops, "they knew what to do, and they did it. They were independent, seasoned, and bloodthirsty: I don't ever remember taking a prisoner during my time with A Troop."

Lieutenant Miller had been with the platoon a week when they were ambushed. In response, Johnston snapped photos. Miller whacked the medic on his helmet and told him to start shooting. "I'm a non-combatant," protested Johnston. Miller barked at him, "Shoot—or get off my fuckin' vehicle!" Johnston begrudged the lieutenant a few rounds, but the ambush had no sooner been suppressed than he was taking pictures again. Miller could only laugh. Everybody loved Doc Johnston: he might have been a nervous wreck on arrival but had seasoned out after Tiên Phước. Miller saw Johnston run through crossfires to reach their wounded and crawl into a bunker with a .45 and a flashlight, but he recalls mostly the medic's sense of humanity: "Doc is one of the kindest guys you'll ever meet. He considered everyone in the platoon his personal responsibility. He'd also take time to treat a local kid, or old man or woman, while the rest of us were just trying to catch a break."

On patrol, "we went where we were told, and did what we were told," writes Miller. "Tactics were pretty much mapped out. When you got hit, you returned fire. If the contact was substantial, you got arty and air going. You made sure everyone was on the same page, moving, shooting, and communicating. I tell people that combat was like being in a play. I knew what my lines were, and I delivered them on cue. We had the firepower to suppress just about anything, and most engagements were over rather quickly." Between contacts, "you had to continually fight boredom and apathy. You took care of your people," concludes Miller, "and tried to send them all home."

Lieutenant Miller believed in his army, his country, and the war, but nonetheless he questioned why the 1st of the 1st Cav seemed to torch everything in its AO. "It seemed rather pointless: the villagers rebuilt within a week. The civilians were absolutely dirt poor. Everything they had was in that straw hut. It wasn't much, and we burned it. It made no sense to burn their life's possessions, and then try to make friends by giving them a box of C-rations."

Doc Johnston offers this take on the destruction: "That's why you don't start a war lightly. The repercussions go all the way down the line to the simplest peasant just trying to survive on his little plot of land. We'd never fought a guerrilla war before. We didn't know how to behave, quite honestly."

A view of the U.S. Marine air base Chu Lai from the air looking south. Also the home of the Americal Division, Chu Lai was about 160 miles southeast of the Demilitarized Zone. *U.S. Army photo*

Cavalry troopers on the USS *Iredell County*, a World War II–era tank landing ship, en route from Đà Nẵng to Chu Lai, August 1967. *Jim Dickens*

USS *Iredell County* unloading troops on the beach at Chu Lai, August 1967. Facing the camera with his hand on his canteen is B Troop commander Captain John Barovetto. *Jim Dickens*

Left: Captain David H. Staley, commander of B Troop, at a Fort Hood formal ball before leaving for Việt Nam. *Jim Dickens*
Right: Major Donald Lundquist and 1st Lt. James Dickens (a platoon leader in Bravo Troop, 1-1 Cav) on the USNS *General Walker*, August 1967. *Jim Dickens*

Dismounting infantry follow tank-infantry strategies learned in World War II and Korea. *Author's collection*

An M60A1 armored vehicle–launched bridge (AVLB) deploys over a creek in Quảng Tin Province. *Peter Dovi*

A dead armored cavalry assault vehicle (ACAV) lying on its side—a view of the top deck. *Noel Rytter*

Alpha Troop, 1-1 Cav, on the beach at Cigar Island. Although it had the white sand of a tropical paradise, the island was sown with booby traps and honeycombed with tunnels and bunkers. *Bob Johnston, Medic, A Troop, 1968*

A mortar track by some fishing boats on Cigar Island. Many of the inhabitants of the fishing villages dotting the shoreline of the island were loyal to the VC. *Tom Bursott*

Left: First Platoon Sergeant Charles Nathan Boyd of A Troop with a captured AK-47. "I told these kids . . . if you're smart enough to listen to me, most of you are going to come back alive." *Charles Nathan Boyd*
Right: Specialist Fourth Class Dick L. Taskey served with Boyd. "Something happens to your brain in combat. Something takes over, and you're capable of anything." *Author's collection*

An unidentified 1st Platoon, A Troop, tank crew. *Tom Bursott*

Left: Captain John Barovetto, commander of B Troop from November 1967 until he was killed in action on January 7, 1968, and (in background) Sgt. 1st Class Curtis Tinker, also of B Troop, in late 1967. *Maj. Raymond H. Mahoy (Ret.)*
Right: Charles Nathan Boyd at the entrance to 1st Platoon's bunker club on Hill 29, 1-1 Cav's base camp beginning in October 1967. *Charles Nathan Boyd*

Private First Class Tom Bursott, A Troop, with battle damage to his track. "We worked hard and played hard. If we did good out in the field, we partied when we got back. . . . We were Boyd's Bastards." *Tom Bursott*

Specialist Fourth Class David Eady of 3rd Platoon, A Troop, burns a hootch in Quảng Tin Province after Tết. "Captain Roesler would order us to do whatever: we'd just come up on a hill and look down there, and there'd be people out in the rice paddies, and 'Open fire!'" *Peter Dovi*

After Tết, 2nd Lt. Ronald L. Snyder of 3rd Platoon, A Troop, confronts a Việt Cộng suspect in Quảng Tin Province who turns out to be a mentally disabled civilian. *Peter Dovi*

Việt prisoners, hands tied, sit behind the splash board of an ACAV. *Tom Bursott*

Middle-aged Việts are forced to do regulation army push-ups: a trooper demonstrates the proper technique, while another trooper provides "incentive" by holding a bayonet under one man's belly. *Peter Dovi*

Platoon Sergeant Boyd's badly damaged tank, A-15, being loaded onto a Dragon Wagon by two M-88s, March 1968. *John Guzik*

After hitting a land mine on Highway 1, a Shell Oil truck is engulfed in flames. *Tom Bursott*

Specialist Fourth Class Robert E. Johnston, the medic of 3rd Platoon, A Troop, bringing in a dust-off. He joined the platoon in the spring of 1968. *John Guzik*

Doc Johnston. "We'd never fought a guerrilla war before. We didn't know how to behave, quite honestly." *Bob Johnston, Medic, A Troop, 1968*

First Lieutenant David Miller became platoon leader of 3rd Platoon, A Troop, on May 7, 1968. "You took care of your people and tried to send them all home." *Bob Johnston, Medic, A Troop, 1968*

Major Frederic Filbert, who took over as 1-1 Cav executive officer in May 1968, hands out goodies to orphans in Tam Kỳ. *Frederic Filbert*

Crewmen from A-30 and A-35 enjoy the morning sun atop A-35 east of LZ Goat. Background, left to right: Spc. 4th Class Peter Dovi, commander of A-30; Spc. 4th Class David Eady, left gunner on A-30; Pvt. 1st Class Patrick Scognamilio, loader of A-35; and Spc. 4th Class Sendre James, driver of A-30. Foreground: Spc. 4th Class Richard Brummett, driver A-35. All were on board A-35 when it hit a land mine on Highway 533 east of LZ Goat just minutes after this photo was taken, June 23, 1968. *John Guzik*

The aftermath. Staff Sgt. Elwood Houston and Bob Schlagel examine mine damage to A-35, including a blown-off right tread and a warped hull. *Tom Bursott*

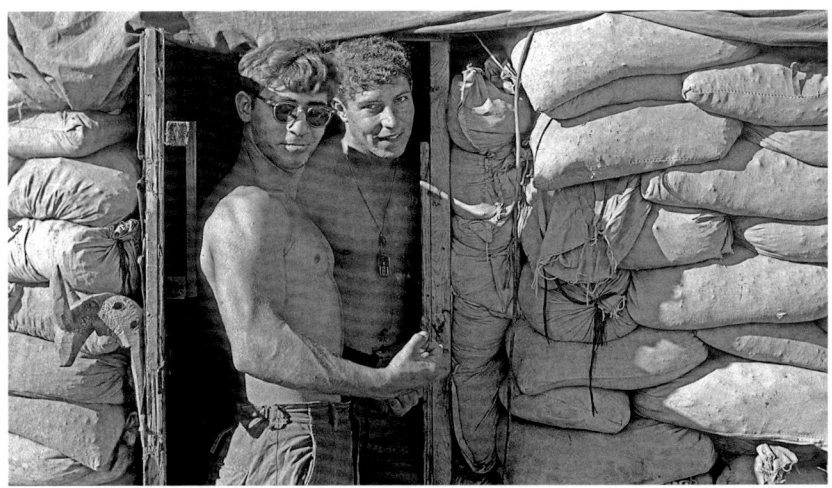

Private First Class Patrick J. Scognamilio and Spc. 4th Class Brandt S. Neubacher at the A-35 bunker on Hill 29. Both new arrivals in the spring of 1968, they were killed on July 6, 1968, when the tank Scognamilio was driving hit a land mine, also killing Staff Sgt. Elwood L. Houston, Spc. 5th Class John L. Hasford, and Spc. 4th Class John L. Roberts. *John Guzik*

Major Don Lundquist (left), Capt. Dave Roessler (middle), and an unidentified trooper examine captured weapons at Hill 29 in 1968. *Charles Nathan Boyd*

Sergeant Steve Blossom and Spc. 4th Class Mike Hoban with an ARVN interpreter and Việt children. Blossom and Hoban were killed in action by a land mine, August 5, 1968. *Bob Johnston, Medic, A Troop, 1968*

Lieutenant Colonel Richard Lawrence (right), commander of 1st Squadron, 1st Cavalry, and Gen. Creighton Abrams standing outside the operations bunker at Hill 29 in the fall of 1968. Abrams toured the base after 1-1 Cav fought a major battle near Tam Kỳ in late August. *Richard Lawrence*

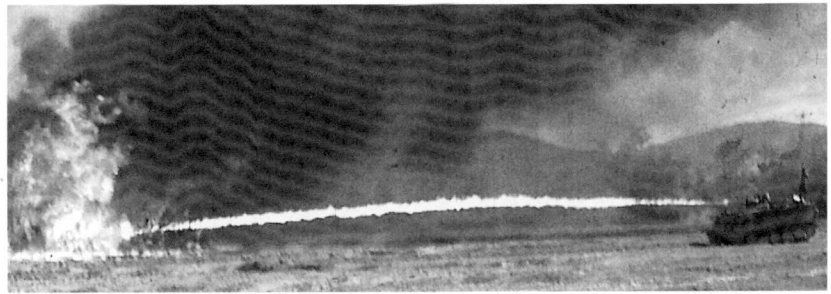

An M132A2 twelve-ton flame-thrower track, commonly called a "Zippo," burns a hooch. This was often done in reprisal for attacks unrelated to the villagers who lived there. *Bob Johnston, Medic, A Troop, 1968*

Bob Johnston, Medic, A Troop, 1968

Driving a track required a surprising degree of finesse: there were lots of ways to get stuck, from the common problem of getting bogged down in the mud (above, east of Highway 1) to the unusual mishap of breaking through the surface crust and burrowing into the dry sand beneath (below).

Author's collection

Cavalry with dismounts on the beach on Barrier Island during Operation Daring Endeavor, November 1968. Marines and dragoons worked together on this cordon-and-search operation. *Author's collection*

After its last day in the field in March 1972, 1-1 Cav heads up Highway 1 to Đà Nẵng. Along the way, a Huey of the Việt Nam Air Force would repeatedly buzz the armored column. *Richard Brummett*

The Mayor of Fat City

MAY 1968

MAJOR LUNDQUIST, THE WAR having served his career exactly as planned, departed some nine months into his tour to attend an advance course at Fort Lee, Virginia. He wore at the time the Silver Star, three Bronze Stars, ten Air Medals, and three Purple Hearts, and he would soon be further rewarded with silver oak leaves and command of a tank battalion in his native Germany.

Medbery thought Lundquist's laurels well earned. "Lundquist was one of the finest officers I've ever worked for," says Medbery. "He was a hard sonofabitch. He didn't take shit off anybody, whether they be a private first class or a general officer, and he got the job done." Lundquist went out with the line units whenever possible, and to ensure that the morning supply convoy from Fat City to Hawk Hill delivered exactly what was needed, he helicoptered up to the TOC each evening to discuss the squadron's logistical needs over a cup of coffee with Cousland and Medbery. One ex–platoon sergeant notes appreciatively that "when we called for resupply, we got what we asked for. Major Lundquist's attitude was, 'No bullshit, just send it out.'"

The squadron rear was Lundquist's private fiefdom, and he lived the good life there. In fact, he posted a sign decorated with the regimental crest, a martini glass, and a four-aces spread of cards that spelled out the situation:

WELCOME TO "FAT CITY"
MAJ DONALD C. LUNDQUIST • MAYOR

- Air Conditioned Club and Guest Rooms
- Gambling Casino
- Swimming Pool
- Nightly Floor Show
- Excellent Dining
- Air Shows
- Shooting Gallery
- Blackhawk Support

Major Lundquist took his poker as seriously as his drinking and raked in a lot of cash, mostly from junior officers who usually had to fold as the better-paid exec kept upping the ante. "I got trapped into one of his poker games, and lost a hundred dollars to him," recalls a former lieutenant. "The guy was a prick, but you socialized with him because there would be more grief if you didn't. It was kind of like, 'We're having a poker game—show up.'"

The floor shows involved rock bands, usually with a blue-eyed, blond-haired lead singer, and little Filipino strippers who kept their white go-go boots but lost the matching vest and miniskirt to reveal a tasseled black bikini. To let the boys know what they were fighting for, the bands and strippers sometimes helicoptered to Hill 29, where they did their act atop a bridge tank while whooping GIs crowded close with cameras. "You've got to give those girls credit," recalls a former captain. "They're out there performing in front of several hundred animals!" Regarding the opposite sex, it was rumored that Lundquist, though married, had his own personal whore; indeed, avows Chief Dunn, "Lundquist would send his driver to pick her up from her village in the evening, deliver her to his tent, and then take her back in the morning. I saw her many mornings sitting at his desk, waiting for her ride home. I questioned this practice, but was told to forget it as it was none of my business."

Lundquist's impressive rack of ribbons also raised some eyebrows. For the record, the major—who personally handled all award recommendations—won his first Air Medal during the Dink Valley operation, credited with flying eight times into the hot LZ to unload supplies, then silencing with artillery the enemy position that downed the medevac. Lundquist's next medal, a Bronze Star, was awarded for an attack on Fat City on October 2, 1967. The attack, as described in the squadron log: "Hotel 6 [a guard post, reports] 1 round ... at 2252hrs ... [and] 2 rounds ... at 2245hrs. Distance between 800–1100 meters."

The attack, as described in Lundquist's citation:

> Hearing the initial burst of fire, Major Lundquist ran from his quarters to the scene of the action, armed with his M16 rifle. Major Lundquist detected a 6 to 10 man enemy force attempting to breach the barbed wire fences and immediately opened fire with his personal weapon. Disregarding the enemy automatic weapons fire and a painful wound in the neck and shoulder area, Major Lundquist moved among the friendly positions and directed their fire at known and suspected enemy locations. Major Lundquist's heroic actions were responsible for the defeat of the enemy forces and the protection of the Squadron's logistical base.

According to squadron lore, Lundquist squeezed off a few shots at the sniper and was burned on the neck when some brass from his M16 stuck in the collar of his flak jacket, picking up a cheap Purple Heart. Lundquist's second Air Medal with V was for manning an M60 and nailing three VC from a Loach during A Troop's operation west of Tam Kỳ on the eve of Tết. Lundquist was credited with killing eleven more VC from above when A and C Troops demolished the base camp in the Pineapple Forest and for this received the Silver Star.

Major Lundquist's second and third Purple Hearts were also collected during the counteroffensive. Captain Davis, the squadron surgeon, and Lieutenant Noble, the medical platoon leader, were convinced that both wounds were fakes. Noble tells a story of Lundquist showing him a thin scab on the back of his hand, claiming to have taken fire in his helicopter, and presenting a field medical card for his signature. "I already filled it out," Noble quotes the major as saying, "and you *will* sign it, lieutenant." Noble did. Davis has a similar story. Following a bombardment of the base camp, Davis writes that Lundquist "came into the aid station with what was supposedly an injury from the shelling. From what I saw, the injury was no more than a cigarette burn." Davis nonetheless signed off on the Purple Heart. "I did not stand up for what I knew to be the truth. I have regretted that episode to this very day, but how could I accuse a superior officer of lying when I was not present at the time he claimed he was injured?"

On April 17, 1969, Lieutenant Colonel Lundquist hit all the targets in front of his tank as his battalion qualified on the gunnery range at Grafenwöhr, Germany. Upon returning to headquarters to celebrate, Lundquist dropped dead from a heart attack. He was only thirty-eight years old, and, though in seemingly top physical condition, his hard-drinking, hard-charging life had caught up with him. There were former dragoon officers almost tempted to smile at the news.

Lieutenant Norton met the new squadron exec while overseeing the repair of a tank with broken torsion bars. Torsion bars were a tank's suspension system, backed up by its six massive shock absorbers. One splined end fit into a torsion bar anchor, the other the housing of a road-wheel arm. If a torsion bar broke flush to its anchor point, the repair work involved in removing the stub and putting a new bar in place could take all day. A combat unit didn't have that kind of time, "so some bright, energetic young trooper," recalls Norton, "discovered that if you measured where the anchor point was, you could cut a hole in the armor with a cutting torch, and stuff a little C-4 up in there to shake the broken piece loose."

The new executive officer went exploring when he heard the muffled explosions, and, finding Norton's work party, asked, "What's going on?"

"Sir," said Norton, "we're blowin' torsion bars."

Norton explained the procedure to the crew-cut major, who then commented, "Well, of course, you've downloaded all the ammunition and fuel?"

"No, sir. We don't have the time. We need to turn this tank around and get it back out in the field in two hours."

"What?! Who's in charge here?"

"I am, sir," said Norton, who would later joke that he was obviously the officer in the group since he was the one with the t-shirt while everyone else was stripped to the waist in the scorching heat.

The major said that they didn't repair combat-loaded tanks with plastic explosives at Fort Knox and that he would have to report Norton to Cousland. As it happened, Cousland told the major not to worry.

Such awkward introductions aside, Maj. Frederic J. Filbert, the new exec, was to prove as adept as Lundquist at meeting the squadron's administrative and logistical needs, and was otherwise a breath of fresh air: he loved soldiers and soldiering, treated all ranks with respect, and was well-regarded in turn. Like his predecessor, Filbert got out with the line units as much as possible and survived the crash of a Blue Ghost gunship riddled with .51-cal fire. Unlike Lundquist, however, Filbert received only a single valor award and, out of respect for the young officers and troopers who he says were the real heroes in a great unit, declines to discuss the circumstances of his Distinguished Flying Cross.

Major Filbert was much involved on the civil-affairs front, delivering extra supplies and donated goods to the two orphanages adopted by the dragoons. Filbert's compassion was genuine. Once, having landed with the command group behind a troop in heavy contact, he walked to the top of a rise for a better view and saw a man laboriously plowing his small rice paddy behind a slow-moving water buffalo. Nearby, tanks, tracks, and jet fighters made noisy, smoke-billowing war. The farmer paid no attention. He had survived the Japanese occupation and the war against the French. Now, the Americans were here. None of it mattered to the peasants, Filbert realized. They didn't care if they were ruled by Sài Gòn or Hà Nội, they just wanted the bloodshed to end.

The communists, undeterred by their losses during Tết, unleashed a second wave of attacks on the eve of the opening of the Paris Peace Talks. Devoid of realistic military goals, the so-called Mini-Tết Offensive of May 1968 was a suicidal show of strength designed to discredit Sài Gòn's claims of success and otherwise exacerbate the war-weariness gripping Washington. The two weeks of Mini-Tết—the costliest of the war in terms of U.S. casualties, and sandwiched between the national traumas of the Martin Luther King and Bobby Kennedy assassinations—included the shelling of a hundred towns, cities, and military installations, street fighting in Sài Gòn, meat-grinder battles along the DMZ, and the spectacular destruction by the 2nd NVA Division of the Special Forces camps at Ngok Ta Vak and Khâm Đức in the Americal Division AO.

The enemy, inevitably butchered but having made the intended point, withdrew to the jungle after Mini-Tết. There, during what the newspapers called the summer lull, the communists regrouped and resupplied in preparation for a Third General Offensive to be launched across South Việt Nam.

LZ Goat

MAY–JUNE 1968

CAPTAIN KACZOR, PROTÉGÉ AND former aide-de-camp to the assistant division commander, assumed command of A Troop on May 26. From a well-to-do family, Bob Kaczor, age twenty-seven, was married to a schoolteacher, held a degree in philosophy, and was an ROTC Distinguished Military Graduate from Seattle University. More to the point, he was a smooth and competitive young man—part intellectual, part athlete—presently considering a military career but bound to go far down any path he finally decided upon. As a troop commander, Kaczor was to win three Silver Stars. Reassigned to squadron after his fourth Purple Heart, he would use his free time to learn about helicopters and thereafter fly as an unofficial gunship pilot with the Blue Ghosts.

Though approachable, Captain Kaczor remained insulated, even from his lieutenants, so as not to involve emotions in the decision-making process. "Life was very fragile," he notes, "and I wouldn't allow myself to get close to anybody for fear of them being blown away." Kaczor "ran a pretty tight ship," recalls a former platoon leader. "He stayed on top of everything. He didn't care how hot it was, you wore your flak vest, you wore your steel helmet—a lot of units didn't do that—and it paid off in terms of fewer casualties." Kaczor was "also a stickler for maintenance," adds the former platoon leader. "Before we would go out in the morning, he'd take his head-space-and-timing gauge, and get up on every tank and track, and check the .50s," the upshot being that the lieutenants had already checked, knowing Kaczor would be watching over their shoulders. "Kaczor was a pain in the ass, but when we got in a fight, other people's .50-calibers would fire two rounds and jam, while ours always worked."

Everything tightened up a little under Captain Kaczor, to include the manner in which the locals were treated. It happened that division issued a directive at the time Kaczor took command forbidding the burning of hamlets. Similar edicts had been handed down from time to time in the past, but under Roesler, villes continued to go up in flames, or be crushed under tank treads when Cousland was overhead and would have seen the smoke. Kaczor did not shrug off such orders. At that point, and it was as if a page had been turned, no more hootches were torched, no more prisoners beaten, and no more enemy dead beheaded by hard-charging Alpha Troop. Kaczor recalls operating with infantry units "that were a little on the strange side," which is to say that he saw grunts wearing lanyards from which hung enemy ears. "I didn't say anything because they weren't my troops, I had no command function over them—but if anything like that would have happened in my unit, if the platoon leader or platoon sergeant didn't straighten that person out, the first sergeant would have, and there would have been serious consequences. We didn't operate like that."

However outstanding a reputation Captain Kaczor was to earn, the new troop commander's first mission, launched on his second day in command, went all wrong. Making contact and claiming a body count, A Troop ran out of daylight before reaching, as instructed, a newly established firebase on a small, steep hill at the mouth of the valley leading to Tiên Phước. Kaczor pushed on but, progress being slow, finally abandoned his cross-country route and gambled that he could take the road without hitting any mines. The enemy won the bet when the troop ambulance track—Alpha Bandaid—suddenly exploded. The cavalrymen, thinking they were being ambushed, sprayed the darkness for five or ten minutes before the situation was sorted out. The driver of the demolished, upside-down track was found in the paddy, missing both arms and both legs. "I didn't know what I was going to do," recalls Doc Johnston, "but there really wasn't anything that I could do. He was pretty much gone."

Having picked the wrong vehicle on which to ride, an ARVN interpreter and a Kit Carson Scout—defectors who served as interpreters and experts on enemy tactics—were also killed. "We sat there all night with no attempt to deploy," recalls Brummett. "No listening posts, either." One track with a dead starter had to leave its motor running, "so it was impossible to hear anyone who might be sneaking up on us," adds Brummett. The illumination rounds that burst all night over the banana trees on the left side of the road cast evil shadows as the flares swayed at the ends of their parachutes. The black void on the right—a rice paddy—was equally frightful. Brummett half expected to be overrun, "but the enemy was not everywhere, and we lived till the dawn."

Mine sweeps were deployed in the morning and immediately found one a few feet in front of the lead tank. Spec 4 Peter Dovi, the TC of A-30, was a steady Italian kid from New Jersey who was known for his specialty of digging up land mines. He let Brummett help as they uncovered a crude mine consisting of a plastic bag filled with what appeared to be C-3. The detonating mechanism was an AA battery with wiring routed through a short section of one-inch bamboo containing the contacts and then to a blasting cap. Those contacts came together when a tank drove over the mine and crushed the bamboo. Tracks in the dirt from the night before showed where A-35 had run over this mine both going forward and then again as the troop pulled back together after Alpha Bandaid blew up. This mine was too small to kill a tank, but a dead, wet battery saved A-35 from a broken track and possibly some blown eardrums.

Spec 4 Dovi could be a rascal, and here he bled off a little tension by throwing an ounce of the unstable C-3 against the flat side of the platoon leader's track. Unconfined, the plastique made a harmless mini explosion, but it was fun to see an officer jump.

The firebase was a short distance farther down the road, and A Troop arrived safely that morning after digging up that other mine. The cavalrymen nicknamed the place LZ Goat.

Lieutenant Noble, medical platoon leader, mistook the little splashes as minnows before realizing that enemy fire was splattering the paddy across which C Troop was deployed, facing an enemy-occupied hamlet. The hamlet had just been strafed by jet fighters. Obviously, the enemy was still in position. As the fire was returned, the M60 manned by the left-gunner on the ambulance track jammed. Concerned about some nearby heavy brush, Noble—manning the right machine gun—turned to shout at the gunner to clear his weapon. Something exploded at that moment, and Noble sank in slow motion to the bottom of the track, the other gunner landing atop him. Noble listened, detached, as the senior medic shouted on the radio: "This is Bandaid: we're hit, we're hit!"

Coming back to reality, Noble realized that his neck was stinging and that the left-gunner's own neck was bright red. Captain Prothero pulled up in his command track and called to Noble: "Are you all right, Chris?"

When Noble indicated that he was fine, one of Prothero's machine gunners said, "Hey, why don't you look at your fuckin' helmet, sir?"

The backside of the camouflage cover on his helmet had been shredded. As best could be determined, the super-heated exhaust of a rocket-propelled grenade had singed Noble and the left-gunner as it shrieked past, and when the RPG self-destructed, the lieutenant's helmet caught some of the shrapnel. Noble would always wonder if he would have been killed or blinded had he not happened to turn and shout at the other gunner just as the RPG was fired. Thus did the medical platoon leader win a Purple Heart on June 5 during a joint U.S.–ARVN push into a troublesome valley in the mountains northwest of Tam Kỳ.

Lieutenant Colonels Cousland and Thơ orbited the action in one helicopter, Major Medbery in another. When the dragoons made contact, Thơ ordered the ARVN to withdraw, then had Cousland return him to Tam Kỳ. Medbery—to win a Silver Star—recalls landing himself at Tam Kỳ, where he "demanded that the province chief turn his troops back around and send them back into the valley with our guys. He acted like he didn't know me." Returning to the battle, Medbery went in low to appraise the situation and, in so doing, came under high-caliber fire from the high ground to either side: a large bullet hole appeared in one of the main rotors. Informed that a gunship had been shot down, Medbery's pilot wanted to go back for the crew. Did Medbery agree? "You bet your ass," answered Medbery. "We were drawing fire from two different directions as we landed, and I told the door gunners where to shoot to suppress the fire," recounts Medbery, who disembarked as the gunship crew ran toward his helicopter, "and helped load those four guys aboard."

§

Though not camouflaged well enough to avoid detection, the mortar pit discovered by Lieutenant Miller on June 7 was otherwise textbook perfect, six feet deep, with ammunition shelves carved into the earthen walls. Looking at the firebase from the pit, Miller could see his platoon sector, some two thousand meters distant. Miller contacted Staff Sergeant Houston, whose tank sat at the highest part of the firebase, and had Guzik make a range card so he could hit the position blindfolded in the dark with the 90mm. Miller also had the FO riding on his track register the pit as a high-priority artillery target. Before moving on, the cavalrymen carefully replaced the bushes meant to conceal the position.

Back at the firebase that evening, Lieutenant Miller was drinking a beer atop Houston's tank when he realized that the mortar pit was blinking in the dark: a mortar team had moved into the position and was dropping rounds down the tube. Miller shouted at Houston and the artillery FO to commence firing, then took off for his command track, which sat in hull defilade at the bottom of an earthen ramp. Miller was coming down the ramp when he was suddenly picked up by an explosion to his immediate rear and hurled into the back of his track. Miller, regaining his senses—but unaware that the collision had skinned raw his forehead, nose, and chin—saw the back door slam shut in his face. He pounded and yelled amid the incoming but, getting no response, finally climbed topside and jumped down through the cargo hatch. Adrenaline pumping, Miller shouted: "Who in the hell locked me out?!"

"Gee, lieutenant," mumbled a GI, "we thought you were dead."

Specialist Fourth Class Robert W. Schlagel, the track commander, fired on the mortar pit with his .50, but because the target was just beyond tracer burnout range, he basically just lobbed the bursts toward the enemy, hoping he was hitting something. Unlike Miller, Schlagel does not recall preregistered fires. Instead, as he was the only one returning fire, he recalls Captain Kaczor getting him on the horn to request the enemy's coordinates and then having him adjust artillery fire onto the mortar pit. "The one-five-fives on the hill fired the place up for about five, ten minutes," recalls Schlagel, "and that was it: no more enemy fire."

The enemy had lobbed three-dozen rounds. The twenty dragoons with minor injuries included Tom Bursott, who picked up a little sliver of steel in his back. Bob Schlagel had also been injured, though not by the enemy. "I didn't have a shirt on," he explains, "and standing behind that .50-caliber, the expended brass comes out the bottom of the weapon, so I had these perfect burn circles on my stomach." Schlagel had also cut his hand on a cotter key while reloading and cocking the weapon. The medic treated Miller's skinned face and provided salve for Schlagel's burns and a Band-Aid for his hand. "The medic filled out casualty cards," notes Schlagel, "and the next thing I know, I got a Purple Heart, and the lieutenant got a Purple Heart."

The ARVN unit on the hill "had not dug in yet," notes Miller, "and had a lot of casualties: about thirty dead and wounded, if I remember right."

One other minor casualty of the evening was the hootch that Guzik and Baby Eady had built to escape the trailing-off rains of the dying monsoon. The azimuth for hitting that mortar pit put the flash suppressor of the 90mm right over the hootch. So, when Guzik blasted the mortar crew, he also destroyed his own abode with the muzzle blast.

Despite frequent mortar attacks, the cavalrymen enjoyed a not unpleasant sojourn on LZ Goat. Contact was light, and helicopters delivered beer and ice each evening, plus mermite cans of fried chicken and mashed potatoes. The Mad Minutes "were great fun, and even more so with a little weed," notes Richard Brummett. The dragoons mostly battled the ARVN, who stole everything in sight, including John Guzik's Peter, Paul, and Mary tapes, which they unspooled and used to decorate one of their new bunkers. Incensed, Guzik had Brummett back their tank up to the bunker and pump diesel exhaust through the firing port. The situation made Brummett jumpy: suppose the ARVN retaliated by lobbing a few grenades their way in the dark of night? Not likely, but Brummett had short-timer's fever, and many whose tours were almost complete became paranoid indeed. "One day, I just could not stand it one more moment, and blew every one of my claymores at once," he recalls; in response to "an anguished call from Captain Kaczor, Lieutenant Miller calmly got on the horn, and made up some utter bullshit to cover for me. Another time, I just had to get to the rear for some real or imagined errand. Miller made believe he bought my story, and let me go off on the next chopper to Hill 29."

Alpha Troop finally departed LZ Goat on June 23. Shortly after passing the ambulance track demolished on the way in, Staff Sergeant Houston's tank, though led by two teams of mine sweepers, hit a mine that blew off the right tread and warped the hull. The driver's hatch, the lock of which had broken that very morning, swung into Brummett's commo helmet, giving him a concussion. Brummett recalls crawling unsteadily to the side of the road and finding a "Chiêu Hôì" leaflet inviting him to surrender to the VC attached to a nearby bush, presumably by the same guerrillas who had planted the mine: "That was rubbing the salt in, the little fuckers!"

Brummett also recalls that one of the engineers came back "with a real shit-eating grin" and said, "Oh, I guess I missed one, huh?" David Eady—riding on the tank because his track was down for repairs—had been hurled through the air to land on a helmet, his own, as it happened. Eady was in enough pain, and Brummett sufficiently dazed, that Doc Johnston filled out casualty cards for both. "One whole year, and I never got a scratch," muses Brummett, "and then with seventeen days left on my year I end up with a Purple Heart on my last scheduled day in the field because of a broken hatch lock and seventy-five pounds of nitro starch."

Another Patton

JULY–AUGUST 1968

ON JULY 1, MAJ. Gen. Charles M. Gettys, the new division commander, passed the squadron guidon from Cousland to Lt. Col. Richard D. Lawrence. Cousland was going out on a high note, having won the chestful of medals, including five valor awards, required for his career, and being further lauded for his squadron's forty-to-one kill ratio, the highest in the division. The change-of-command ceremony was a real show that "includ[ed] 3 generals," noted one of the attendees, plus a "helicopter formation & acrobatic jets."

The incoming squadron commander, Dick Lawrence, hailed from west Texas, where his father, a celebrated trial lawyer, was paid for his services during the Depression with bacon and eggs, chickens and sides of beef, horses and saddles, and even pure-bred hunting dogs. The family moved to Houston when Lawrence was thirteen, and as a high-school ROTC cadet, he became enamored with the idea of a military career while following the campaigns of World War II. Graduating in 1947, he spent two years at the Virginia Military Institute before receiving an appointment to West Point with the Class of '53.

Lieutenant Colonel Lawrence received his orders for Việt Nam upon receiving his doctorate in industrial engineering from Ohio State University. He was thirty-seven years old, married, and the father of two, a brilliant officer on the proverbial fast track who, like Cousland before him, needed the proper combat credentials to ensure his seemingly inevitable rise to general officer. "I wanted a squadron command in a cavalry unit but knew that if I left it to chance, odds were not good," notes Lawrence. As such, he wrote to a colonel who, ten years before, had commanded the squadron in which Lawrence had served as a troop commander. The colonel was presently commanding a brigade in the Americal Division. As Lawrence would be arriving just as Cousland was leaving, the colonel "went personally to the division commander," notes Lawrence, "and supported my assignment as the new commander of the division cavalry squadron. The assignment was waiting for me when I arrived in Vietnam."

Turning to former subordinates of the assertive, hands-on type, Lawrence brought in James A. Logan, a captain on the promotion list to major, as his S3, and Max B. Ogas—the scowling bulldog was a Mexican-American from Texas—as squadron sergeant major. The genial Major Filbert, an unknown holdover from Cousland, impressed Lawrence enough to retain him as the squadron executive officer throughout his command of the 1-1 Cav. "Filbert and Lawrence played good-cop-bad-cop," jokes a former platoon leader. "Lawrence was the firebrand, and Filbert was kind of the voice of reason in the background."

Lieutenant Colonel Lawrence, a firebrand indeed, "reminded me of George Patton," recalls Filbert. "He was extremely knowledgeable and aggressive, and not afraid to call a spade a spade." The new squadron commander quickly developed an excellent rapport with his troop commanders and impressed all ranks for his personal courage and tactical smarts. No cool voice on the radio, the intense, hyperkinetic Lawrence also became known for the colorful and pointed language he used as he directed his units. "Lawrence was one of a kind," says Bob Kaczor. "He was very decisive, the absolute epitome of a combat commander: he *commanded*. The guy just exuded leadership."

When medevacs couldn't land because of heavy fire, Lawrence used his command ship to get his wounded off the battlefield. The squadron commander was also a visible presence on the ground, whether riding on the back of a track or leading, as he once did, a prisoner-snatch mission that involved two infantry squads, the PRUs, and the Blue Ghost Blues. Intelligence indicated "that a high VC official would be in his home village, which was in our area of operations," notes Lawrence. "We made a helicopter assault landing and found the official, a security chief, in a bunker where we had word he might be. We wounded another VC and had him evacuated. We had word on a VC secretary in the area but did not find him and were finally lifted out with our catch."

Given Lawrence's reputation, and that of his squadron, many senior officers visited Hill 29. The guest list included Gen. Creighton C. Abrams himself; the new theater commander was presented a certificate making him an honorary member of the 1st Cavalry Regiment. Soon after, a colonel-turned-brigadier-general "was invited up for a promotion party," recalls Lawrence. "We downed a good bit of drink in his honor, which was a good respite for our officers, who had been under lots of stress. We all had a good time. As was custom," continues Lawrence, "I took out my trench knife and cut the new star off his collar, and the aide's insignia off his aide-de-camp's collar, and pinned them both on the wall at our small officers club. The general, an old tanker, thought it was great. I was glad of that because I hadn't known how he would react."

"Lawrence was a truly superior commander," says one former dragoon, speaking for all. "We would have gone through hell for him."

First Lieutenant Thomas H. Jackson, a year out of the military academy, and only a week in the field, called a halt when a dud bomb was spotted to the side of the trail being followed by the 3rd Platoon of A Troop. The bomb was a thousand-pounder, and the scouts sent to investigate reported that the explosives inside had already been melted out through a large hole cut in the metal casing. The ground where the guerrillas had squatted was littered with peanut shells.

When the scouts returned, Jackson gave the word: "Move out."

"Roger," replied Staff Sergeant Houston, whose tank was leading the way two klicks southwest of Square Lake that sixth day of July.

Patrick Scognamilio was crouched on the trail at that time, having either seen something that didn't look right or wanting to more closely examine what was a foreboding situation. Not only was it likely that there was a big new mine in the area, but the platoon was halted just short of an intersection with an unpaved road, and Scognamilio's mentor, Brummett—who'd just left for "The World" the day before—had warned him of the VC's penchant for planting mines at road crossings. Scognamilio and Houston exchanged words, after which Scognamilio, following orders, returned to his driver's seat, started forward—and immediately detonated a mine that lifted the fifty-two-ton tank thirty feet in the air in a fireball of fuel and ammo.

Lieutenant Jackson, on the third vehicle in line, saw the grenadier on the second vehicle, a scout track, do a back flip onto the trail. The trooper suffered only a hairline fracture, saved by his helmet, the top of which was creased by whatever chunk of debris had hit the steel pot. In case the explosion was part of an ambush, Jackson, as trained, gave the word, and the platoon herringboned and laid down suppressive fire. When the firing petered out, and the smoke and dust cleared, the cavalrymen saw that Houston's tank had been blown into five pieces—hull, turret, cupola, back deck, and engine block—that lay at different points around a huge crater. The hull had landed upside down, missing all its road wheels, a gash torn in the underbelly. There were no survivors: all aboard A-35 had been killed instantly by a mine so powerful that one of the road wheels would be found a thousand meters away.

Captain Kaczor soon arrived with the rest of Alpha Troop, and Lieutenant Colonel Lawrence had the squadron chaplain dropped off by helicopter to console shaken, numb, and enraged troopers as they policed up their dead buddies. Staff Sergeant Houston and crew—Scognamilio and Neubacher, plus the gunner, Spec. 5th Class John L. Hasford—had been blown to pieces. Only the body of the platoon mechanic, Spc. 4th Class John L. Roberts, who'd been sitting atop the turret, was still intact, though the blast had reduced his internal organs to jelly. The cavalrymen recovered little things—eyeglasses, an ear, someone's left hand, a finger still wearing a ring—as well as Houston's headless, one-armed torso, identifiable by the tattoo on his left shoulder. The fate of Patrick Scognamilio was the most troubling: as the driver, he was probably still inside the tank, but there was no way to recover his incinerated remains, for the hull glowed cherry red, untouchable, as the ammunition inside continued cooking off.

In addition to the body parts, which were wrapped in ponchos, the cavalrymen also discovered a wire that led to a vacant hiding place: the bastards who'd detonated the mine had slipped away, unseen and unscathed.

Galled, nerves raw, Alpha Troop backed out of the area, unwilling to continue forward lest more men be lost to more mines.

Richard Brummett had not been in the field since hitting the mine on the way back from LZ Goat, and not because of the concussion he suffered, which was mild enough, but because the clock ran out on his tour by the time his tank was ready to go out on another mission. It had taken a week to determine that the tank, its hull warped, would have to be sent to Japan for a complete rebuild. Several more days were spent getting a replacement tank ready for combat. By then it was the Fourth of July, and Brummett and the guys sat atop their bunker that night, firing all their hand flares and watching high-caliber illumination rounds burst over Hill 29 and every other firebase in sight, from the coast to the mountains, an overwhelming, dazzling display.

The unit prepared to move out the next morning. "I wanted to go on one more patrol, but that was foolish, as everyone told me," notes Brummett, who was to be leaving on a plane five days hence and needed that time to process out of the squadron and find transport to the air base at Cam Ranh Bay.

There had been much back-slapping in the motor pool as Brummett said good-bye to Neubacher, Scognamilio, and Hasford, who was taking turns going out on missions with fellow short-timer John Guzik. The order came to mount up. Brummett ran up as his tank started to roll and shook one last hand.

Brummett was sitting in an office in Chu Lai the next day with the cheerful clerk who was typing up his paperwork when a message was received that an entire tank crew had been lost to a mine. "Impossible," said Brummett. Mines might kill everyone on a track, but not a fifty-two-ton M48. The clerk sadly re-read the message. There was no doubt: A-35 had been destroyed, and, according to the code numbers translated by the clerk, Staff Sgt. Elwood Houston, John Hasford, Brandt Neubacher, Patrick Scognamilio, and John Roberts were all dead.

The clerk said that Hasford, with only thirty-four days remaining on his year in Nam, did not know that he was actually even shorter than that. It seems his mother was gravely ill and the Red Cross had arranged a compassionate early out for him. Two more days of paperwork and he would have been told to pack it up and get home to Detroit pronto.

Distraught, Brummett returned to Hill 29 aboard a supply truck. Brummett and Guzik, whose life had also been spared by a matter of timing, lay on cots atop their bunker that night under a beautiful canopy of stars. "We talked of those who had died," writes Brummett. "We talked of the universe, life, fate, or some such bullshit. We had a perfect meeting of minds. The next morning, neither of us could remember a damn thing we had said." Three days later, Brummett, numb, empty, was standing in line to board his Freedom Bird out of the Republic of Việt Nam.

Home on leave, Brummett called Scognamilio's mother in Brooklyn. He started to express his condolences when the mother—who had a telegram from the army declaring her son missing in action—interrupted to ask if he knew where Patrick was. Had he been found? "The mental picture the family seemed to have constructed," notes Brummett, "was of a tank found alone in the jungle, its engine running, and the crew having wandered off. I knew he was dead, so I mumbled something neutral and ended the call."

Wanting to do right by his friend's family, Brummett visited the Pentagon, where he was directed to the office of a major who had Scognamilio's file open on his desk. Brummett shared what he knew about Scognamilio's death, and the major, in turn, explained the difficulties in properly identifying what remains had been recovered. The major said that all they could be sure they had of Scognamilio were his eyeglasses and left hand. The image chilled Brummett, for he knew that Scognamilio had lost his left hand by copying him. "I used to drive with my left hand laying casually on the front slope of the tank," he notes. "Feigning an air of relaxed unconcern on those mined roads was a comfort to me. Roads where sudden death was not a sports metaphor."

To keep the family in the dark was a cruel matter of creating false hope, and Brummett was respectful but firm with the major in that regard: "Sir, we have to notify the family that he's really, truly dead. If the Army won't, I will."

"Okay," replied the major, sympathetically. "We can do that."

On the day of the funeral, all the apartments on the street on which Scognamilio had lived had flags out in his honor. At the funeral home—and the wake was a heart-breakingly emotional affair, very Italian—Brummett met his friend's parents, grandmother, uncle, and girlfriend. The casket was closed. Only Brummett knew what very little of Patrick Scognamilio had actually come home.

The casket was buried in a cemetery on Long Island.

Brummett returned to the army to finish his time.

Lieutenant Colonel Lawrence was at the scene of another mine incident—two dead, a track destroyed—on July 23 when a platoon from A Troop made contact seven klicks southwest of Hill 29. Going aloft, Lawrence was informed en route that the platoon was taking heavy fire from a hill just below the mountains. According to the map, the hill was home to Đức An 1, but the dragoons knew the place as Craterville, for the hamlet was no more, much of the area having been moonscaped over the course of many previous battles.

The platoon was on line and firing uphill as Lawrence called the Blue Ghosts—recently outfitted with the new, shark-bodied AH-1G Cobra gunship and redesignated as F Troop of the 8th Cav, 23rd Infantry Division—to screen the flanks, even while adjusting artillery fire on possible escape routes to the rear. Captain Kaczor and the rest of Alpha Troop, rushing from Hill 29, joined the firing line while Lawrence marked targets with smoke grenades, after which two jet fighters rocked the hilltop with bombs and automatic cannons.

The enemy having been boxed in, Captain Kaczor and Alpha Troop rolled over the position, all weapons blazing—"a beautiful, textbook attack," writes Lawrence—whereupon the scouts and infantry dismounted to eliminate the remaining NVA with hand grenades. Lieutenant Jackson fragged a bunker, killing two. The gung-ho West Pointer, who carried an old M3 grease gun, was also credited with mowing down two more North Vietnamese in a trench from his track, for which he would be awarded the Silver Star.

The enemy soldiers were not prepared for a fight. They had only fired on the first platoon that had unknowingly approached their position, it was later surmised, to deter the platoon's advance and allow time for a withdrawal. Most, in fact, were able to bug out before being overrun, only to be spotted on the next wooded hill to the south. Pinned down by gunships, encircled by tanks and tracks, few escaped this time as Kaczor's scouts and infantry again dismounted and went to work, aided by the Blue Ghost Blues. "My men moved from bunker to bunker, and spider hole to spider hole, and mopped them up," Kaczor—also to be awarded a Silver Star—was quoted in the division newspaper. "We killed several with grenades thrown in the holes, and several by simply going in after them."

Captain Kaczor was sitting on the back of his track as it pushed through some heavy brush when an NVA popped up to the rear, presumably from a spider hole over which the track had rolled, and cut loose with his AK-47. One round nipped the shoulder of Kaczor's flak jacket, and the troop commander, frightfully startled, twisted around and frantically emptied his CAR15 into the North Vietnamese. Checking the body, Kaczor saw that the soldier he had killed could not have been more than fourteen, one of the shockingly young replacements Hà Nội was feeding down the Hồ Chí Minh Trail to keep the war going after Tết. Lawrence's command ship, and an accompanying gunship, took hits from a .51 during a low-level pass over the action. Both sputtered to Hill 29, where Lawrence—another Silver Star winner—grabbed two boxes of grenades for Kaczor and departed aboard another Huey. Captain Richard K. Albers, M.D., the new squadron surgeon, attended the wounded Cobra pilots, as recorded in his journal: "one with hand ripped off[,] ... other [with] 2 GSW [gunshot wound] left leg and BB [both bones] fracture—he was in shock—had to work right on the helipad—got them squared away and dusted off [to Chu Lai]."

Kaczor reported eleven captured weapons and a body count of sixty-eight. "We couldn't get a prisoner," notes Lawrence. "They weren't giving up."

Making the tried and true error of reusing routes known to be passable to armor in otherwise rough terrain, Lieutenant Jackson, returning from patrol, used his bridge tank to recross a stream at the same point used on the way out that morning of August 5. The third vehicle in line—usually the platoon leader's, but in this case the mortar track—was flipped over by a command-detonated mine upon rumbling over the AVLB. The enemy's misjudgment spared Jackson but killed both the commander of the mortar track, Sgt. Steve Blossom, and the driver, Spec 4 Mike Hoban, whose comrades would wince when they saw his body dangling from his hatch like a rag doll when the vehicle was righted after the area had been hosed down and secured. Scratch two more good men. For nothing.

Having arrived in-country by troopship, as a unit, the dragoons departed like everyone else: as individuals, on a civilian airliner. The first to leave, and this handful included Dolan, Fortner, Palatas, and Rensi, had been sent to the war zone with only six months remaining of their time in the army. Their half-tours came to an end during Tết. The bulk of the Fort Hood originals—minus the thirty-three who died and the dozens too badly wounded to finish their tours—flew home no later than August 10, 1968, one year to the day the General Walker *steamed from San Francisco, bound for Việt Nam.*

The career men went on to new assignments, while the young lieutenants, sergeants, and troopers—Lindsey and Guida, Bouche and Pryor, Guzik and Eady, Bursott and Schoep and Taskey, Byrd, Esmond, Gaydon, Webster, Hotchkiss, Decktor, and all the rest—packed away their medals and uniforms, and wasted no time in getting back to work or heading off to college. They did not dwell on the war. They had lives to lead, things to do. They were proud to have served, however, and out of loyalty to those who'd died, most would have counted themselves as hawks, and never mind their hatred of the Vietnamese.

Lieutenant Jim Dickens, formerly of B Troop of the 1-1 Cav, was not just a hawk but, in a time of seething campuses and burning cities, a vocal champion of George Wallace for president. As it happened, the first person to welcome Dickens home from Việt Nam appeared to be a supporter of Abbie Hoffman. At the time of their encounter, Dickens had just spent two or three frazzling days in the out processing center at Cam Ranh Bay and a mostly sleepless flight across the Pacific, leaving him in a not altogether pleasant frame of mind when he finally landed at McChord Air Force Base near Seattle, Washington. Buses took the returning GIs to the Seattle-Tacoma Airport, where they would catch their flights home. Heading straight for the men's room, Dickens shaved and cleaned up a bit in the sink, then donned a fresh set of khakis and joined the line at the ticket counter. There, Dickens was approached by a bearded young man who, placing two fingers on Dickens' ribbons, archly asked, "How many babies you have to burn to get those?" The man was instantly punched out for his rudeness. "I decked him," recalls Dickens. "I mean, I didn't say a word, I didn't think about what I was doing.

I just decked him. He went down like a sack of sand." Two police officers appeared to haul the dazed peacenik to his feet, one under each arm, and take him away. "The cops never asked me my name, never even came over to me. I just stayed right in line, and there were probably a hundred people standing around, and they all applauded. It was like a standing ovation."

Captain Logan addressed the political situation in a letter written to his wife on the eve of the tumultuous Democratic convention in Chicago. Making reference to Richard Nixon, Eugene McCarthy, and Hubert Humphrey, the new squadron operations officer wrote that *"I have no idea who will be elected, but whomever he may be, he is going to sell me out and about ½ million other people over here."* By selling out, Logan meant that the politicians would not allow them to win the war by cutting the Hồ Chí Minh Trail and invading North Việt Nam. Why not? Because they were beholden to *"a bunch of people who can see no further than tomorrow and whose world ends at their back fences."* Unwilling to see the job through, the feckless American voter was condemning future generations to fighting a wider war as communism spread across Southeast Asia. *"If I sound bitter I am not,"* Logan continued. *"I don't believe in this war any more than the next guy. What I do believe in is containment of a threat to my country and to my family . . . [A]s long as the fighting is outside the [United States of America] then that is what is important to me."*

In preparation for a big push north of Barrier Island, Lieutenant Colonel Lawrence told Lieutenant Miller, now serving as the squadron maintenance officer, to get as many tanks up and running as possible. Having gone to the field to recover four dead tanks, Miller's recovery team did not make it back to Hill 29 until after dark on August 22. The tanks were towed to the C Troop motor pool. Given the urgency of the situation, Miller decided to set up lights, despite the base's strict blackout policy, so that the tanks could be worked on all night. It was after midnight, and Miller and a trooper were standing on the back of a tank, adjusting the transmission linkage under the lights, when the sound of mortar rounds leaving a tube suddenly echoed through the night.

Not thinking to jump inside the tank, Lieutenant Miller was still a couple of steps from the nearest bunker when something—actually, someone—slammed into his back, propelling him through the doorway to land in a heap in the dark. Miller shouted at whoever had crashed atop him to get the hell off and, getting no response, pushed the individual aside. Not until the barrage ended, and a light was switched on, did Miller see that he'd been flattened by Staff Sgt. Edward S. Stewart, the new C Troop motor sergeant. The thirty-one-year-old regular was dead. "His body was like jello," notes Miller, still haunted by the fact that Stewart had shielded him from receiving even a scratch from the mortar shell that landed just feet behind them. Captain Albers, meanwhile, awakened by "the sickening wail of sirens and crunch of incoming mortar rounds," as he wrote in his journal, went to work on the twelve casualties delivered to the squadron aid station. "Sgt who had been in country 11 days was DOA [dead on arrival]," Albers noted; he medevacked the three most serious casualties, including a young trooper who died en route to Chu Lai. "I spent the rest of the morning digging, sewing & cutting on the other 8 [casualties]—most are in good condition . . . I was not afraid for myself[,] but whether I did enough for the troops—I will never know about the boy who died—I will just have to live with a few nagging doubts. My medics did very well—I'm proud of them."

The enemy launched ground attacks on four of the division's firebases before dawn that same morning and mortared most of the others. In response, numerous air strikes were conducted on August 23, and it was while checking the results of one such strike that a helicopter took .51-cal fire in the vicinity of the Pineapple Forest. The Blue Ghost Blues overran the gun position, killing four NVA and capturing the .51, complete with tripod. Though province headquarters requested the dragoons provide a platoon the next day to support an ARVN sweep of the area, no particular urgency attached itself to the situation. "[T]he brazen manner in which [the enemy] engaged our gunships . . . should have been a tip-off that something was up," Jim Logan subsequently wrote to an army historian; since no alarm bells actually went off, the former operations officer chalked up the capture of the antiaircraft weapon as "the clue that wasn't."

In fact, the communists' Third General Offensive, long anticipated by intelligence officers studying captured documents was finally in progress— combat officers like Lawrence and Logan were not in the loop, which explains why they might have been unreceptive to certain clues. Even as battles flared throughout the country, approximately 1,300 troops from the 2nd NVA Division occupied positions on the western edge of the Pineapple Forest. The enemy was well equipped with mortars, recoilless rifles, and rocket-propelled grenades, and his bunkers, concealed within the vegetation that covered the island-like hummocks in the rice paddies, were mutually supporting and covered all likely approaches. The antiaircraft positions, and there were many, were doughnut-shaped, a pillar of earth left standing in the center around which a gunner could move to place fire on helicopters approaching from east, west, north, or south. It remains unclear if the enemy intended to draw his foe into a well-prepared killing zone, or if the bunker complex was a staging area for an attack on Tam Kỳ. Whatever the enemy's plans, he was met in place by the dragoons, and the Battle of Tam Kỳ, as the engagement became known, would prove to be the 1-1 Cavalry's biggest in Việt Nam.

The Battle of Tam Kỳ: Day One

AUGUST 24, 1968

THE TRACKS CAME UNDER a sudden barrage of fire from their front as Captain Logan and Sergeant Major Ogas watched from on high, the squadron command ship having arrived only minutes before the shooting started. One of the tracks soon began burning in the rice paddy. The rest of the unit, a troop from the 4th ARVN Cavalry, halted on line, facing west, to return fire on the wooded island held by the enemy at the southwest corner of the Pineapple Forest. First Lieutenant Thomas M. Ginz of the 2nd Platoon, A Troop, tasked with supporting the South Vietnamese, was not firing, having fallen slightly behind as a result of some of his tracks getting stuck at a stream crossing. Logan radioed Ginz to "get up on line with the ARVN, and get with the program!"

Ginz did just that. Logan returned to Hill 29 at that point to find Lieutenant Colonel Lawrence having a goodbye chat with the outgoing division chief of staff. Logan recalls being "not very polite" as he pulled Lawrence away from his conversation to brief him on the action. With the command ship refueled, Lawrence, Logan, and Ogas were soon aloft over the battlefield. Lawrence brought in two air strikes, whereupon the ARVN "launched an old-fashioned charge," notes Logan. "It was a wonderful sight to see their ACAVs, guns blazing, as they crossed the paddies, headed for the wool."

Caught off guard by the charge, Lawrence hastily sent Ginz across the paddy to protect the ARVN's right flank. Both elements made it into the wool, but when the ARVN lost a track to an RPG, the aggressive troop commander, bound by orders to avoid heavy losses, pulled back. Intending to pile on with additional forces, Lawrence had Ginz maintain his foothold. Ginz's platoon, though under intense fire—an RPG hit one tank—captured one recoilless rifle, knocked out another, and eliminated numerous NVA. The Blue Ghosts strafed directly between the tanks and tracks, such was the proximity of the enemy. Two gunships were shot up in the process. When another set of jet fighters arrived, Lawrence told Ginz to button up, then had napalm dropped within fifty meters of his position. The command ship darted in low so Lawrence could mark targets and the door gunners could lend some additional fire support. Lawrence recalls that when the machine guns jammed up, "we still flew passes, and all used our M16s on automatic to engage the NVA. It was absolutely wild."

Captain Jerry D. Frost, commander of C Troop, departed Hill 29 with two platoons. First Lieutenant Gary D. Williams, executive officer and acting commander of A Troop, followed with two more. Frost, in the lead, had a tank and AVLB hit by RPGs only halfway to the Pineapple Forest. Frost's cavalrymen suppressed the fire—blood trails led away from an abandoned trench—continued into the woods, and, pushing through more fire while fording a stream, finally assumed positions on Ginz's right flank. Williams approached the firing line from the rear after swinging around the east side of the Pineapple Forest, then moved into position on Ginz's left flank, at which point Lawrence sent both troops directly into the NVA positions, hoping to destroy them piecemeal. That did not happen because as "C Troop moved in and started to work the area over," Lawrence was quoted afterward, "we discovered that this was a major position in great depth." No matter which direction Frost maneuvered to outflank the enemy, he ran into still more bunkers. "In just about every area we moved into," continued Lawrence, "we were surrounded by NVA, so we just had to fight in three-hundred-and-sixty degrees. Most of our contact was at twenty-five yards. Tank guns were firing at [targets] less than fifty yards [away]!"

§

Pushing into the wool, Lieutenant Williams realized that Alpha Troop had broken through the opposing lines, so he, like Frost, ordered his cavalrymen to circle the wagons and open fire. Lieutenant Jackson, glancing over his shoulder as his platoon blazed away to the front, was startled to see an NVA with pack and AK-47 being chased across the center of the circle by Alpha Bandaid. "Doc Johnston was trying to depress the .50 to shoot this guy," recounts Jackson, "but he was so close, Johnston couldn't get the weapon low enough, so someone else on the track shot him, and then they ran him over and kept going."

Having dismounted the scouts and infantry to clean up any other enemy hiding in spider holes inside the circle, Lieutenant Jackson manned the left-hand machine gun on his track. Three NVA came into view about a hundred meters away. Seeing that one was carrying an RPG launcher, "I got a little excited and opened up with the M60," recounts Jackson, who was so excited, in fact, that "as I traversed across the group—and I have no idea if I hit them, or they bugged out—I managed to shoot one of my own radio antennas in half. It would have been funny and embarrassing had not a piece of the fiberglass antenna wounded one of my scouts in the neck." Though not terribly serious, the injury was painful enough and bled badly, and the scout "was pissed at me. He had every right to be mad and was bitching that 'My own platoon leader shot my ass up!'"

As the dragoons probed the island from different angles, Lawrence marked the various points of resistance on his map. In addition to bunkers and spider holes, "there were antiaircraft positions all over the place, at least six by my count," notes Lawrence, who put his command ship at great risk as he coordinated air strikes and gunship runs. Lawrence's pilot, a fearless young warrant officer named Dennis M. DeWine, who "went where I said, no questions asked, even if he thought I was crazy," would later describe the battle as "darting here and there at low level . . . flying on fumes to give the CO as much time on station as possible between refuelings . . . listening to commands being given over the radio . . . dropping smoke on the bad guys who you could see moving all over below us, and watching the F-4 Phantoms come in low and slow . . . It seemed like all the hostile activity in Việt Nam was right below us."

DeWine was repeatedly advised that he was taking fire, and, finally, as big green .51-caliber tracers crossed the nose of the aircraft from the right, something struck the windscreen in front of the co-pilot in the righthand seat of the Huey. DeWine thought the co-pilot had been wounded but saw that the Plexiglas had only been nicked. The next burst punctured aluminum. "A master caution light came on," notes DeWine. "I turned the aircraft away from the fire, ready for an emergency landing, but nothing else happened. We were still flying, all on board were okay, and no other warning lights came on." Not until DeWine landed at Hill 29 to refuel did his crew chief discover a bullet hole just below the fuel cap. DeWine recalls that most of "the bullet—presumably not a tracer, as I'm still here—went right through the fuel cell and out the other side, leaving another nice hole. I found the tip of another round sticking in the skin of an interior bulkhead when I opened an inspection panel. I still have that copper tip."

No other damage being visible, DeWine cranked back up and was overhead when one of Lieutenant Williams' tanks took an RPG. One trooper had part of his back blown away. Another, his hand mangled, "was in shock, white as a sheet and trembling," recalls former medical platoon leader Chris Noble, who was riding as a gunner on Alpha Bandaid and otherwise assisting the medics. Instead of waiting for the medevac that was frantically requested, Lawrence told DeWine to drop down and pick up the wounded. DeWine descended in a fast, tight spiral, pulled up to avoid another chopper that almost collided with the command ship, then "lowered the nose," he recounts, "and dove again for the LZ, which was between and to the rear of two tracks." The command ship settled on its skids, and the medics pushed six casualties into the cargo bay, bringing the number on board to thirteen, a lot for a Huey. "I attempted to bring the aircraft to a hover," notes DeWine, "but the RPM started bleeding off, an indication that we were overloaded and needed a take-off run to get out of the LZ."

The enemy was dug in directly to the front. There being no other way out, DeWine, needing as much of a running start as possible, recalls that with the crew chief and door gunner keeping an eye on the nearest trees, he "backed the tail boom into the tall, thick brush behind us as far as we could go, then announced to all that we were coming out: the aircraft fairly lumbered forward, oh so slowly, right between the two tracks and right over the top of the bad guys. I was looking straight ahead, but I heard a lot of shooting by all on board in the back. That we made it was just luck, and some bad shooting by the NVA."

DeWine delivered the wounded to Chu Lai, then shut down at Hill 29 to refuel, whereupon an eight-inch gash was discovered in the leading edge of one of the main rotor blades: a .51-caliber round had clipped the rotor about four feet from the end, another reason for the low RPM. "I often think about the load that was put on the damaged blade with thirteen people on board and max power being applied on the way to Chu Lai," notes DeWine. "It's a wonder we didn't lose the blade. Four feet off one blade is a guaranteed disaster."

Lawrence jumped aboard a replacement aircraft while DeWine and crew "smoothed out the rough edges on the blade," he recalls, "and talked to our maintenance people to determine if we could get back to Chu Lai. All decided that we could, and we did, but not without developing a slight vertical vibration on the way: the blade was starting to separate and flapping up and down. After we landed and maintenance saw the blade, they told me they wouldn't have flown it after all. Clearly, it wasn't our turn to die that day."

One of Lieutenant Jackson's tracks was hit in the side by an RPG that penetrated the armor, hit the radio inside the hull, and deflected straight up through the deck, directly in front of the gun shield behind which one of the side gunners was manning his M60. "The gun shield was pockmarked with shrapnel," recalls Jackson, "but the gunner didn't get a scratch. Weird."

At another point, an enemy soldier jumped up to empty his AK-47 at the side gunner on another of Lieutenant Jackson's tracks, apparently thinking his fire would penetrate the aluminum armor. "It didn't, and the machine gunner cut the NVA in half," notes Jackson. "When the fight was over, we got out and looked, and there were fifteen slugs in about a four-inch circle buried in the side of the track. You could just see the backs of the slugs sticking out of the armor."

Informed that infantry was on the way, Lawrence selected as a landing zone a clearing within a wooded area some thousand meters southeast of the battlefield. Lawrence sent Frost to secure the area. Specialist Fourth Class Wallace M. Colligan, a track commander with Charlie Troop and son of a patriotic, hard-working, Irish family from Terryville, Connecticut, would later describe "knocking down trees and trying to stay on line when you can hardly even see the tracks to either side of you, it was that thick in the wool." Unexpectedly, the woods turned out to be full of NVA. "It was absolutely nuts," says Colligan. "You didn't know where the hell they were going to come from. We kept on pushing through the trees, firing straight ahead and keeping in communication to make sure that we didn't fire at each other." Colligan's track passed over an unseen spider hole. The camouflage cover popped open, and the grenadier perched on the back of the track saw the face of an enemy soldier rising up to fire. The grenadier fired first with his M79, and Colligan recalls jerking around, "and all I seen was like part of the gook's head. I was in shock, but the grenadier just looked back at the gunners and myself and smiled. He did his job that day."

Breaking into the clearing, which was ringed with trenches, Charlie Troop circled up in the face of the most relentless barrage of fire yet encountered. One platoon leader had his arm removed by a rocket-propelled grenade while directing return fire from a tank. The entire crew was wounded, leaving the .50 to be manned by a brave Kit Carson Scout, who quickly became a casualty himself. Dismounted scouts and infantrymen "just went over to the trenches with bullets flying everywhere, and started shooting down into them," recounts Colligan. "Some of the guys actually jumped into the trenches." His machine-gun ammo expended, Colligan, a .45 on his hip, discarded his commo helmet, grabbed an M16, and dismounted, too. "I can remember running around like a nut, trying to get the gooks who were underneath the tracks in spider holes. I don't think anybody knew what was going on. It was like putting your foot on an anthill. They hit us so hard and fast, guys were just reacting spontaneously to get these ants off our feet: we had to take control of the fight."

As the enemy casualties piled up and his fire diminished, Captain Frost decided to risk a medevac, and Colligan helped his one-armed platoon leader to the LZ. "The lieutenant was a big, tall, lanky, crazy guy," recalls Colligan. "He took care of his men, and he was very aggressive: he would stand up there and shoot, he wouldn't hide down inside his track." The lieutenant, coolly smoking a cigar on his litter, said he wanted a beer;

someone produced a warm Ballantine. Colligan recalls that upon sliding the lieutenant's litter into the medevac that landed, the lieutenant "said he wasn't going anywhere without his arm, so back to the tank we go with bullets hitting between our legs, climb inside, find the arm, and run back to the chopper. We put the arm on his chest, and he gave us the thumbs-up and shouted 'Good luck!'—and off they went."

The 1st Platoon of C Troop, on patrol when the battle began and belatedly ordered to join Captain Frost as dusk approached, encountered a mine upon reaching the north edge of the Pineapple Forest. The blast turned over a track, wounding three troopers, and killing two. Amazingly, no other dragoons lost their lives during that mad day of close combat. "Fighting has been hard," Captain Albers, the squadron surgeon, noted in his journal. "[W]e've taken 30 casualties so far; 2 KIA . . . NVA body count over 100 at end of day. Worked steady all day [in the aid station on Hawk Hill] . . . 3 medics wounded . . . Lt Noble in field [with] A [T]roop—getting in a world of shit! Hope he's ok. [The colonel] has distinguished himself today—should be highly decorated."

Running out of daylight, Lawrence ordered Frost and Williams to break contact and rendezvous on a bare hill, good fields of fire all around, that sat astride a likely enemy approach route to Tam Kỳ. The ARVN cavalry troop, meanwhile, had already retired to the province capital itself, thus terminating all ARVN involvement in a battle in what was actually an ARVN AO. Instead of returning to headquarters for the night, Lawrence joined his cavalrymen on the hill, where he had his arm—gashed during all the commotion in the command ship—bandaged at the C Troop ambulance track. Lawrence next went around to talk to some of the Charlie Troopers. "Their morale was higher than a kite, and they were pumped to fight," notes Lawrence. "It was inspiring to me. If I had said we were marching on Hanoi that night, those troopers would have been in their vehicles, engines racing and weapons cocked."

General Gettys, the division commander, landed on the bare hill, easily within range of the enemy. Lawrence briefed Gettys from his map. The squadron commander's plan for the next day's assault was classic hammer-and-anvil: while A Troop attacked the island where the battle had begun from the east, and C Troop, pushing in from the northeast, hit the NVA dug in above the island, B Troop would establish a blocking position to the west. Since bringing B Troop into the action would leave Hill 29 uncovered, an infantry company was needed to secure the squadron headquarters. Lawrence requested two more infantry companies to accompany his two assault troops. "I also told Gettys that we needed more direct-support artillery, and as much TAC air as we could lay on," recalls Lawrence. "It was an intense time, but Gettys coolly asked a couple of questions, then said, 'You will have it [the infantry, artillery, and tactical air support], and anything else you want to clean them out.'"

The Battle of Tam Kỳ: Day Two

AUGUST 25, 1968

RESUPPLY WAS CARRIED OUT through the early morning, Chinooks delivering sling loads of water, ammunition, and fuel. Gunships rolled in on the wool, meanwhile, and sets of jet fighters further softened up the objective, even as Hueys landed with the promised reinforcements: B/2-1 Infantry of the 196th Light Infantry Brigade, and B/4-21 Infantry of the 11th Light Infantry Brigade.

The second day of battle began when Capt. Wayne J. Lewis and B Troop, moving overland from Hawk Hill, came under fire even before reaching their blocking position west of the Pineapple Forest. Lewis left one platoon to deal with the problem but encountered even more resistance as he continued south with the other two. Lawrence—realizing that the bunker complex was larger than first suspected—recalls that he "directed Lewis to run the gauntlet, and get in position to the enemy rear as we launched the main attack from the east."

With gunships strafing to either flank, Lewis reached the blocking position, only to find the area crawling with enemy soldiers: it was later determined that Bravo Troop had driven right into the middle of the regimental headquarters controlling the battle. Once again, a cavalry troop was forced to circle up and blast away at all points on the compass. The enemy, firing from trenches, RPG'd a track and then shot down the medevac that landed for the wounded. Another helicopter took aboard the wounded, and the crew of the first medevac, but caught an RPG in the tail boom on the way out. The pilot made a crash landing to the east, and the Blue Ghosts soon rescued all hands. Rejoined by its 3rd Platoon, Bravo Troop sat atop the enemy headquarters, notes Logan, "and raised hell for most of the afternoon." The dragoons ripped up commo wire, captured a recoilless rifle, and mowed down NVA just in front of their tanks and tracks. The enemy commanders "went ballistic," recounts Lawrence, explaining that "their radio net was being monitored by division intelligence, and we were getting the feedback. They were in a terrible panic."

Lieutenant Williams and A Troop were heavily engaged—the acting troop commander, in fact, had suffered a flesh wound—when Captain Kaczor disembarked from the assistant division commander's helicopter, fresh from R&R. "I climbed back on my track," recalls Kaczor, "and Gary Williams flew out on the general's chopper." Kaczor picked up a flesh wound himself as the battle for the enemy-occupied island continued. "It was one of the few times I got the platoons on line and led a charge," notes Kaczor. "I remember chasing the enemy around, trying to maneuver in the rice paddies and through the wool. I had two radio channels, troop and squadron, and I had Lawrence in one ear and the platoon leaders in the other. Lawrence would say to move Ginz over here and Jackson over there because he was up above, where he could see what was going on, and I would just relay that information to the platoons."

The battle took place in fits and starts as a tank and three tracks were hit over the course of the afternoon by recoilless-rifle fire and rocket-propelled grenades. Casualties were evacuated, and new angles of attack were decided upon while gunships and tac air worked over the NVA. Captain Kaczor was quoted afterward in the division magazine: "I had a lot of good men wounded—not seriously—but they refused to be dusted off, and remained to fight throughout the day."

The enemy held his ground despite bombs, napalm, and the point-blank fire of both Kaczor's cavalrymen and the grunts of B/2-1. An infantry sergeant was killed, as was Spec Four Jeffrey T. Cramer of the 1st Platoon of Alpha Troop: the twenty-one-year-old draftee, only weeks from going home, was firing his M60 when an RPG struck the gun shield. "My platoon never did manage to get into [the island] all day," Lieutenant Ginz of the 2nd Platoon was quoted. "Every time we got too near to it, the fire became so intense we had to go back."

Lieutenant Jackson and the 3rd Platoon were facing a trench at a distance of fifty meters when a jet fighter screamed low to unleash a burst of 20mm cannon fire into the NVA. The empty casings bounced off helmets and armor, "and about scared us to death," recalls Jackson. "We thought we were getting hit." At some other point, the platoon halted in the face of another enemy position: as the Blue Ghosts rolled in, "[w]e pulled up on a hilltop, waiting for the choppers to finish," Jackson also notes. "Then we went forward, but we advanced so far that we swept past the enemy's front line. We were getting hit from both sides and the rear. We had to fight our way out—but we really gave it to them."

As happened the day before, numerous machine guns burned out as ammo boxes were emptied one after the other in continuous bursts: instead of zipping straight and true, tracers flew down range in wild spirals from barrels glowing a translucent red. Some .50s got so hot that bolts welded to barrels. The numerous enemy cut down in the wild firestorm included five caught while trying to put up a radio antenna, plus the crews of a recoilless rifle and antiaircraft gun that were captured. Enemy casualties were such that two NVA emerged from their spider holes, stripped to their underwear, hands raised in surrender. "Oh, it was hot, it was really hot. We had green tracers coming at us, and we were just shooting everything up in return," says Robert Schlagel. More jet fighters screamed past, dropping cluster bombs, shredding hedgerows and trees, "and I can remember Captain Kaczor on the radio," notes Doc Johnston, "bitching up a storm about how they were supposed to let us know when they were going to use that stuff. We were lucky we didn't take any casualties."

Private First Class Stanley C. Goff of B/2-1 could hear bullets pinging off the tank shielding his squad during one of the assaults on the island. When the tanks and tracks pulled off to the flanks, "we all hit the dirt, out in the middle of the rice paddy, and started inching our way toward the dike [to our front]," Goff later told the author of a book about black soldiers in Việt Nam. Reaching cover, the grunts opened fire, none more ferociously than Goff, who ran to wherever his buddies pointed out targets and hosed down the positions with his M60. "I was firing like hell. I probably went through two thousand rounds." Goff's overheated machine gun finally malfunctioned about the same time the enemy fell back. "[W]ith the area completely quieted, a few of the other squads started to run into the wood line, crouched, searching, looking, weapons at the ready." They counted forty-one bodies, thirty of which were credited to Goff. Leaving the area atop a tank, an exhausted Goff "saw all these bodies, or parts of bodies—hands, arms—so much so that it was making me sick[.]" There were bodies "with backpacks on, t-shirts, parts of uniforms. Obviously, the NVA had tried to strip the bodies . . . [Y]ou knew they had dragged away as many bodies as they could. There were blood marks in the dirt."

Lieutenant Jackson spotted movement about two hundred meters away and, shouldering the M14 sniper rifle he kept inside his track, looked through the scope to see an enemy soldier in khaki fatigues and green pith helmet sprinting between two patches of woods. Lining up his target in the crosshairs, Jackson squeezed the trigger: the NVA dropped as if pole-axed. The body was later searched, and medical supplies were found. "It looked like he was a medic," notes Jackson. "He may have been trying to get to somebody when I nailed him."

The casualties included Lieutenant Jackson's platoon sergeant, injured when a rocket-propelled grenade hit his tank. "My medic was loading some wounded on a dust-off," recounts Jackson, "and at the last second, he jumped on the chopper, and left with the casualties." The medic had "been a pretty aggressive kid up till then," notes Jackson, but had been on the mortar track blown up by a mine three weeks earlier, "and I think that just broke his spirit." Such human weakness elicited little sympathy in a unit like the dragoons. "We could have had somebody die because we didn't have our medic," explains Jackson. "The medic refused to return after the battle. I don't know what his final disposition was in regard to a court-martial, but we never saw him again, which was good because if we had seen him, I think we'd have killed him."

Lieutenant Colonel Lawrence, needing to refuel, rendezvoused before departing with Doc Johnston's ambulance track on a brushy hillock behind the firing line. The back ramp was dropped, and five or six heat casualties were hastily loaded aboard the command ship. "As the last patient was being shoved into the cargo bay, the chopper lifted off with the man's legs still hanging out the doorway," recalls Noble. Those evacuated included the driver of Alpha Bandaid. "He was a real bullshit artist," says Johnston, suspicious that the driver declared himself a heat casualty upon reaching the landing zone. Lieutenant Noble climbed into the driver's hatch, which seemed kind of funny—an officer driving a track—and Alpha Bandaid roared back down the hillock. A grunt for whom there had been no room on the command ship manned one of the M60s. The return trip was gut twisting, since the enemy seemed to be everywhere, "and here we were, two medics and this sick grunt, out by ourselves," recalls Johnston. "There was contact all around us." The grunt was only semicoherent, his brain boiling, and "he kept pulling the trigger on the M60," notes Johnston, "and spraying these long bursts at nothing in particular. I wound up burning myself when I grabbed the barrel of the M60, trying to get it away from him."

To make matters worse, Noble recalls that he was skirting around the base of another hillock, trying to remain inconspicuous against the wool, when the ambulance track "suddenly listed off to the right at a steep angle" and slid sideways into a gully hidden within the vegetation. "Johnston screamed into the radio for help. It seemed like an eternity but was probably no more than ten minutes before two tracks approached and hooked lines on Bandaid."

Given all the vehicle losses, Doc Johnston's ambulance track was commandeered after rejoining A Troop to fight as a line track in Lieutenant Jackson's platoon. Soon thereafter, the battlefield was lashed by a sudden summer storm that cleared the sky of helicopters. "When it rained, everything stopped," recalls Johnston. "Everybody buttoned up, and I swear to God, I was the only person keeping watch from my vehicle, sitting there wrapped in a poncho." Johnston's vigilance was most fortuitous because a lone figure, camouflaged as a walking bush, casually appeared at the crest of the gentle rise to the front of Alpha Bandaid. The individual was so brazen—he made no attempt to take cover—Johnston wondered if the man was an ARVN, at least until a second figure walked up behind the first with an RPG. On second glance, the first figure could be seen holding an

RPG launcher. The second figure was obviously the man's partner, moving up to load the launcher. "That's when I realized I was looking at an NVA," recounts Johnston, who figured the RPG team was after the tank parked beside his track, "so I dumped a whole hundred rounds of .50 on this guy. I fired the whole goddamned hundred rounds. I was absolutely nonplused. I couldn't believe that this guy walked up solo right in the open. I know I got the first one. I think the second one got away. The tank crew later recovered a pistol belt off the body. I've still got it in a bag somewhere."

Except when grounded by the storm, Lawrence was airborne over what were essentially three distinct firefights as Troops A, B, and C attacked from three different directions. As each troop met resistance, "we backed off and called in air strikes," writes Lawrence. "Our FACs were extraordinary, going right in on the deck to mark targets for the jet fighters." There was .51-caliber fire "all over the air space, but not as intense as the first day because we had knocked out a number of the antiaircraft positions that first day. Nevertheless, all helicopters took heavy fire and were getting hit regularly." The commander of the Blue Ghosts finally accumulated enough holes in his Huey as to render the ship unflyable. So, too, Lawrence's own Huey. The crew chief discovered a large bullet hole in the fuel tank while refueling at Hill 29. The pilot immediately "shut the engine down," notes Jim Logan, whereupon "the crew chief discovered a hole in the main rotor, too. We were all very lucky. Although the helicopter was [shot up twice in two days], none of us [on board] was ever hit."

Taking sniper fire along the way, Captain Frost advanced on his objective—a wooded hillock just west of the Pineapple Forest and north of Kaczor's engagement—with the attached grunts riding atop the tanks and tracks. Frost approached from the east. The rolling terrain was crisscrossed with hedgerows that divided the rice paddies of the local villagers into individual plots. The hillock itself sat some two hundred meters behind a tree line in front of which C Troop halted so that B/4-21 Infantry could dismount and move into the thick vegetation to flush out any NVA lying in wait for the armor with RPGs.

The platoon in the center of the line came under fire from a hedgerow. Staff Sergeant Nicky D. Bacon, veteran of a previous combat tour, shouted at his squad to stay down as he charged the nearest machine-gun bunker and lobbed a grenade inside, killing the two NVA manning the RPD and a third with an RPG launcher. The leader of the squad on the right, as well as one of his grunts, and the platoon leader were badly wounded—the lieutenant was shot through the throat—while trying to outflank the enemy. Bacon and his men crawled to the pinned-down squad, knocking out two more bunkers along the way, then rescued the lieutenant and the wounded squad leader. Bacon was unable to reach the most forward of the casualties through the crossfire.

Captain Frost's cavalrymen couldn't fire with infantry to their front, but a track did move forward to evacuate the wounded. Sergeant William A. Swoveland and Spc. 4th Class Steve O. Nussbaumer—regular-army scout-section leader and draftee medic, respectively—dashed twice through the fire to carry the lieutenant and the wounded squad leader to their track for evacuation to a medevac landing zone that saved both their lives. Several grunts tried to restrain Nussbaumer when he started toward the third casualty—it was suicide, the man was actually on the far side of several enemy positions—but the medic broke free and took off, followed by Swoveland. Swoveland was cut down first, Nussbaumer just as he reached the crumpled-up grunt, across whom he sprawled, trying to shield the man with his own body.

Staff Sergeant Bacon tried to reach the three men now lying to the front but was again forced back by the interlocking enemy fire. The lieutenant from the left-flank platoon crawled to Bacon with one of his squads and, after coordinating cover fire, maneuvered against a machine-gun bunker only fifty meters to the front. The lieutenant's group had no sooner knocked out the position than another machine gunner opened fire, and the platoon leader was shot in the head. One of his grunts was also hit, bringing to five the number of casualties sprawled in front of the enemy bunkers.

Having already assumed command of his own platoon and the dead lieutenant's, Bacon took over the right-flank platoon, too, when the same gunner who had nailed the other lieutenant mortally wounded that lieutenant, as well. The gunner was in one of the doughnut-shaped bunkers with an earthen pillar in the middle. Bacon could see the man through the peep sight of his M16. "He would fire from the front, you'd throw a grenade, and he'd run back around behind the pillar—then he'd come right back around and start firing again," Bacon was later quoted. "He was a brave little son of a bitch. I must have killed [his assistant gunner] because his was the only helmet I could still see in the foxhole . . . I could see him moving, and every time you'd get to where you were close enough to get at him, [other enemy positions] would start wasting your ass from the flanks. I bounced rounds off his freaking helmet for an hour." Bacon finally jumped into the first enemy bunker he had grenaded and from there "was able to crawl down the hedgerow, and get close enough that I could blow [the diehard gunner's] ass off. I got him with two grenades." Soon thereafter, "the stupid sonsabitches tried to charge us," Bacon's account continued. "I was [still] down in one of their positions, so I shot the shit out of them. I had somebody else's M16. Mine had been shot up."

The rain was coming down as Bacon took the handset from a wounded radioman and asked for volunteers to come forward on a tank. Sergeant Roy Ames, tank commander, answered the call. Bacon recognized the man in the driver's hatch: a hometown buddy named John E. Ahrenberg, who, seeing Bacon, was equally amazed that two sons of Surprise, Arizona, could end up in the same rice paddy in Việt Nam. Caring not what a conspicuous target he made of himself, Bacon climbed aboard the tank to point out enemy positions to Ames and tell Ames he needed him to advance right into the NVA to take some of the heat off his rescue party: "Fire your shotgun round, and keep your .50 plastered on them—then back out while you're firing!"

Sergeant Ames advanced and withdrew three times at Bacon's direction, drawing torrents of AK-47 fire and numerous RPGs. "There were so many [NVA,] you didn't know where to fire, so you fired everywhere," Ahrenberg wrote for a history compiled by veterans of Charlie Troop. "This one NVA regular laid in a hedgerow so close I could see his eyes [when he] fired his RPG. The round hit our front slope and ricochet[ed] into the dirt . . . [In return, we] were firing as fast as we could load the main gun[.]" Ahrenberg saw a recoilless rifle "pointed right at us," but Ames "fired a canister round and took it out."

With the tank drawing most of the enemy's wrath, Staff Sergeant Bacon blazed away with his borrowed M16 and heaved grenades as his rescue party crawled to the five casualties—the lieutenant, two grunts, and two cavalrymen—in the kill zone. They tugged them a few feet before being forced back to the ditch where other infantrymen provided cover fire. Each time the tank withdrew, Bacon scrambled atop the turret to point out the next targets he wanted engaged while his men went back out for the casualties. "This is all happening in seconds," Bacon recounted. "The tank is taking rounds, shit is bouncing off [the armor]. [The tank commander] is taking hits on purpose."

Captain Frost and the commander of B/4-21 Infantry coordinated infantry-cavalry attacks on the flanks but got nowhere in the face of continuous fire from bunkers so well-constructed as to be all but impervious to M16s, M60s, M79s, .50-cals, LAWs, and even point-blank 90mm fire. The enemy put another recoilless rifle into action that scored two hits on one of the tanks, forcing it back. Frustrated, enraged, Staff Sergeant Bacon charged right into the hedgerow, firing from the hip, and caught the crew of the recoilless rifle as they were physically lugging the tripod-mounted weapon to a new position. Bacon killed the entire crew on the spot. That Bacon survived such moments was miraculous: after the battle, he discovered that bullets had not only cracked the grip of his first rifle but thumped into his rucksack, drilled holes through his canteens, nipped the heels of his jungle boots, and creased his helmet. In the heat of the moment, Bacon had only known that ordnance of unknown type was bursting around him, as he told a reporter: "I was knocked on my back by concussions. Those explosions sound pretty loud when they are about a foot away."

Bacon's rescue party finally got the casualties to a position near the ditch, then formed a human chain to pull them the last few feet to cover.

By then, all five of the casualties were already dead.

The casualties recovered, cavalry and infantry pulled back far enough to allow artillery fire on the enemy bunker complex, followed when the weather cleared by air strikes. The second day of battle nevertheless ended like the first, with the dragoons breaking contact—"the enemy dispositions were expansive enough that we could not get our arms around them," explains Lawrence—and pulling back to a good hilltop laager, this time south of the Pineapple Forest. Two more of Kaczor's tracks were hit on the way out, one of which had to be destroyed in place. Resupply was carried out, and the day's results tabulated: eight grunts and cavalrymen had been killed, plus a Kit Carson Scout attached to the dragoons, and another three dozen wounded. The reported enemy body count: 259.

That night, Captain Albers, the squadron surgeon at Hill 29, wrote in his journal, "it's been another 20 hr day without rest—constant flow of casualties." Albers noted that he'd spent the day running between aid station and medic bunker, where minor injuries were attended, and the helipad, where the seriously wounded were treated immediately inside blood-slick cargo bays before the Hueys took off again, headed for Chu Lai. Albers also helped carry the dead—zipped up in body bags—to the truck pit being used as a temporary morgue. In the midst of this activity, "Charlie hit us with another mortar attack tonight," Albers wrote. "My [aid station] medics, S5 [civil affairs personnel]—commo [personnel]—VHF [personnel] all helping [with the casualties]—all ready to drop . . . I'm ready to drop over too—God give me strength & skill!"

Sergeant Schlagel, scout-section leader, had spent the day behind his .50—he was credited with several kills—and realizing that evening "that I was the only NCO left in the [3rd] platoon [of A Troop]," he later noted, "I made sure everybody got their ammo and a hot meal, and I got the mail passed out." In the process, Schlagel came upon two kids, replacements, who "were about as exhausted as I was, and they were shakin'—cryin'—this was probably the first contact they'd been in and they were shook up. I was just a young guy myself, I wasn't twenty-one yet, and I wasn't afraid to tell 'em that I was just as scared as they were—but everybody had a job to do. I said, you've been through training, you know what your jobs are—*just do your jobs*—that's *all* you gotta do. They listened."

New guys weren't the only ones who had to regroup emotionally. "We'd get into a firefight, and I'd do all this silly stuff," notes Schlagel, speaking for many seasoned troopers who responded to battle instinctively, "and when it was over, I'd sit and think, damn, I could've gotten killed—why'd you do all that stupid stuff?! And you'd start shaking, and you'd grab a cigarette, and shake and smoke for an hour." Wrung out physically and emotionally, Schlagel couldn't help but lie down for a moment among the ammo crates in the laager to get just a moment of rest. The next thing he knew, someone was shaking him awake: "It was just before dawn, and I said, damn, I guess I went to sleep!"

The Battle of Tam Kỳ: Days Three, Four, and Five

AUGUST 26–28, 1968

LAWRENCE AND LOGAN HAD decided during the night, as the latter writes, "that after two days of head-on slugging it out, we ought to try something different on the third day." Instead of hitting the enemy from different directions, the infantry and cavalry formed a solid line, facing north from the laager. Next, an intense, twenty-minute preparatory barrage was fired by the 155mm howitzer battery on Hill 29. "It was magnificent!" exults Logan. "We were airborne just south of the barrage. I thought the explosions would knock us right out of the sky. As soon as the fires lifted[,] we began a general advance into the NVA positions. It was a grand plan, but the bad guys had left during the night."

There was actually some scattered contact, but with gunship and tac-air support, the enemy's rearguard elements were quickly "reduced," as noted in an after-action report—a body count of thirty-six was reported—and "[t]he rest of the day was given over to searching out the area and policing up the battlefield."

The report noted that B Troop detained two military-age males, presumably enemy stragglers or deserters who'd shed their uniforms and "who stated that 400 NVA had moved from the area the previous night heading north west."

Lawrence writes that the sweep of the bunker complex turned up "discarded equipment, impedimenta left behind in the haste to withdraw, lots of bloody clothing, but very few weapons, and no wounded. The enemy had dragged off all they could during the night, and silently enough that we heard no noises at our security outposts to indicate disengagement." The command ship skimmed low over the silent battlefield, passing above a thin stream that curled around the north and west edges of the Pineapple Forest. "The stream was flowing very slowly, almost still, and it was blood red from dead and wounded being pulled through the water," continues Lawrence. "Muddy ruts could be seen where the enemy had entered and departed the stream. The trail out of the area was pretty clear: they were making for the mountains and jungle growth to the west."

"We wanted 'em bad," recalls Wally Colligan. "Everytime we lost one of our boys, we wanted to go out and get a hundred of 'em in return." Ultimately, the war was a grudge match. Playing cards on which the unit name had been written were left on the bodies counted so far, adds Colligan, "or we'd put a little mark on their chest with a knife, or something like that. Crazy stuff. It happens. I mean, we were trying to break their stones every chance we could get. We were taunting the enemy, letting them know we weren't afraid to take them on again. We weren't afraid of a fight."

While checking the banks of the stream the next morning, a minesweep team from B Troop touched off a mine the enemy had left for their pursuers: one dragoon was killed, four grunts and cavalrymen wounded. Anxious to catch up with their foe before they reached the safety of the mountains, the dragoons were "frustrated" at such a bad start, notes Logan: "We lost a lot of time [medevacking casualties, then] clearing the area so the following elements could pass through."

Finally across the stream, Lawrence sent A Troop, a platoon from B/4-21 riding along, northwest the five klicks to Craterville where the Blue Ghosts were engaging a hilltop antiaircraft position. Lieutenant Ginz's platoon led Alpha Troop up the hill as a scout ship at the top rotated on its axis, tail boom almost vertical, making so tight a circle around the antiaircraft position that the gunner inside could not elevate the weapon high enough to hit the Loach. Conversely, the door gunner couldn't get the proper angle, either, as he blazed away with his M60. Roaring onto the scene, Ginz's people killed one of the NVA in the position, wounded the other, and seized the .51-caliber machine gun.

Fifteen packs were found in a trench, and most of their owners accounted for as the grunts and cavalrymen scoured the hilltop: ten NVA were killed and three captured, along with several AK-47s and a second .51-caliber machine gun. The enemy, well-equipped but completely unorganized, fired not a shot as they were hunted down in their spider holes. "The Kit Carsons lit the bushes on fire to rout these guys out," notes Johnston, "and there was a lot of shooting and grenading and all that stuff." One of those captured emerged from his hiding place with burnt hands and feet. Doc Johnston spoke encouragingly to the miserable-looking soul as he treated his injuries and recalls that "our interpreter was all pissed at me: 'Why you feel sorry for him—he's NVA!'"

Lawrence personally evacuated the prisoners to Hill 29, anxious for whatever intelligence they might provide. Lawrence and Albers, otherwise on excellent terms, disagreed on how that intelligence should be gathered, as the squadron surgeon recorded in his journal: "3 NVA prisoners brought in today—Col[onel] wanted me to bargain—if they talked, I would treat them. I refused—told him I was [a] Dr—I would treat them regardless— they were badly shot up & burned—had to dust off 2 [to Chu Lai] but they were alive."

When interrogated, the prisoners revealed that their antiaircraft platoon, on the march for several days to join the battle, had dug in atop the hill the previous night to get some rest before continuing on, unaware that those they meant to reinforce were already pulling back to the mountains at that point. The prisoners indicated that their exhausted platoon was still asleep when detected by the Blue Ghosts and, worse, that the RPG gunner whose first shot at the approaching tanks and tracks was to be the signal to open fire experienced a misfire. No rocket, no fusillade of fire. Instead: confusion, panic, and the loss of the entire platoon. The hilltop action was a most satisfying end of the battle for Alpha Troop, which rolled straight from Craterville to Hill 29.

Captain Lewis and B Troop became embroiled with an enemy delaying force upon reaching the end of a narrow valley that cut southwest into the foothills west of the Pineapple Forest: one tank took an RPG that penetrated the turret and ignited the ammunition inside. "The tank erupted in flames, but we extracted all the crew, burned severely," notes Lawrence, who was on the ground with Bravo Troop. First Lieutenant Bruce W. Brown, platoon leader, "breathed in the flames," adds Lawrence, "and seared his throat and lungs," leading to his death two agonizing weeks later after evacuation to the United States.

Captain Frost and C Troop joined the battle from a second valley they had been following into the foothills and fired to the front while the infantry attempted to outflank the NVA. Two grunts from B/2-1 Infantry were killed, and their bodies left behind as nightfall necessitated a withdrawal to a good defensive position in the paddies below the mountains. "I rolled up in a blanket and slept for a couple of hours," recalls Lawrence, spending another night out in the field with his men. The last of the wounded were medevacked to Hill 29 after dark, and Captain Albers wrote in his journal of "Running up to the helipad at 2000 hrs to treat patients between dust offs by flashlight [with] sniper rounds flying, [uniform] full of blood, tired, dirty[,] but somehow content[.]"

While pulling back, the flame-track attached to Bravo Troop became stuck and had to be left behind. Now, some hours after midnight, "an NVA got in the [abandoned] track and started it," as recorded in the squadron log, whereupon the dragoons called in artillery, and the track began burning in the night: "Unk[nown] if NVA set track on fire or if arty hit track."

Captain Lewis called in artillery on a platoon or two of bad guys spotted on the high ground that morning, but enemy casualties were unknown, and the day's events otherwise frustrating: neither the cavalrymen in the valley nor the infantrymen moving up the jungled slopes could come to grips with the retreating NVA, even as a track from Bravo Troop took an RPG, wounding five, and a track from Charlie Troop ran over a pressure-detonated mine, wounding seven hitchhiking grunts and five dragoons, one of them mortally. Another dragoon was killed instantly in the blast. Both of those who lost their lives at the end of the battle were replacements, less than a month in Việt Nam.

The enemy having vacated the field, Lawrence directed B and C Troops to join A Troop at Hill 29. "Action has calmed down," Captain Albers noted in his journal. "[A]ll troops back in—dirty, sore, tough."

That toughness especially impressed Captain Logan, who had only recently joined the dragoons from division headquarters. Having previously bemoaned political betrayal on the home front, and skeptical of the irreverent draftee troops, Logan sounded much more positive when he wrote home again after the Tam Kỳ action: "For a person who had such a gloomy outlook of America[,] I must admit I have made a surprising recovery. The real reason is that instead of being on the sidelines observing this mess [at division], I have finally gotten mixed up in the middle of it and I have had many chances to see how the pepsi generation holds up. They are unbelievable."

Major Filbert himself wrote that however much a "despair" the young cavalryman was to old soldiers like himself, "when the chips are down and the bullets ricochet off your track, he's your pride and joy, your fair-haired boy; a slashing, hard-charging bundle of nerve and sheer guts." Logan could not have agreed more. "As soldiers and fighters," Logan's letter continued, "ours are the best." Most impressive was the stoicism of these "kids" when hit—"[a]nd I have seen enough of them hurt in the past week to last me a lifetime"—and the risks troopers would take to rescue the wounded, whether buddies or strangers. "We had two infantry companies with us in our big fight and although we had never seen them before and [would] probably never see them again, while they were with us[,] they were part of us. I don't know if it is all based on survival being the common goal or if battle actually brings out the best as well as the worst in men. All I know is that I am impressed with the young men I have seen in the past few days and I am not worried about what lies ahead as I was before."

Lieutenant Colonel Lawrence was credited with defeating at least an enemy regiment and saving the province capital from destruction. Friend and foe had been equally matched in terms of numbers and determination. The enemy's advantage had been the strength and size of his bunker complexes; Lawrence's the weight of the firepower available to his squadron. The saving grace had been the relatively low cost with which Lawrence had been able to grind up the enemy, thanks to his up-front leadership and deft handling of a brigade-sized ground force, plus artillery, air cavalry, and tactical air support. "The victory was a great morale boost for the people and leaders of Tam Kỳ," writes Lawrence; in fact, Lieutenant Colonel Thơ—whom the squadron commander privately found to be "inept," his troops lackluster—visited Hill 29 with "an august body of 'founding fathers' in traditional garb to present two beautiful plaques inlaid with mother of pearl as a token of their appreciation."

President Nguyễn Văn Thiệu sent his congratulations from Sài Gòn, and in the same spirit of good fellowship among allies, the ARVN corps commander presented Lawrence, Filbert, and Logan, as well as the troop commanders and several dragoons of lesser rank, with his nation's Cross of Gallantry. The troop commanders also won Silver Stars, many others—Jackson, Noble, Schlagel, Johnston, Colligan, etc.—the Bronze Star or Army Commendation Medal.

In addition to 81 wounded, 9 dragoons and 7 infantrymen, plus a Kit Carson Scout, lost their lives during the Battle of Tam Kỳ. Officially, 548 NVA were killed. The number cannot be taken at face value. "I have no doubt that the body counts reported by the six elements engaged were in some cases duplicated and in others exaggerated," Logan wrote to an army historian. Logan noted, however, that the division's radio-research unit intercepted a message "from the 2nd NVA [Division] to its parent headquarters to the effect that the Division had taken over 700 casualties [both dead and wounded] during the battle and was moving into the hills to refit." Whatever the exact number of enemy casualties, "One fact remains clear and irrevocable," Logan concluded: the dragoons had "slugged it out toe to toe with the bulk of a North Vietnamese Division for three days[,] and then chased the remnants back into the hills."

The measuring and rating of battlefield heroism is a tricky thing, arbitrary in its results. Lieutenant Colonel Lawrence, for example, received an almost requisite Silver Star, his second, for Tam Kỳ, instead of the DSC recommended by Filbert and Logan. Private First Class Goff of B/2-1 did win a Distinguished Service Cross, and Staff Sergeant Bacon of B/4-21 the Medal of Honor. The dragoons, usually contemptuous of mere grunts, had nothing but praise for B/2-1 and B/4-21—in them, wrote Logan, "we had the best"—but were disappointed that their own Doc Nussbaumer did not also receive the Medal of Honor recommended by Lawrence. Instead,

Nussbaumer and Sergeant Swoveland were both posthumously awarded the Distinguished Service Cross. Disappointment was tinged with bitterness, a sense that Nussbaumer—always to be remembered as one of the squadron's great heroes—had been cheated out of the ultimate recognition he deserved because Major Lundquist had previously played so fast and loose with the awards system as to taint recommendations for the most prestigious medals from the First Regiment of Dragoons.

On the other hand, that Swoveland and Nussbaumer had acted as a team mitigated against either being singled out for the Medal of Honor.

Steve Nussbaumer, who turned twenty-one on the first day of the battle, was the medic who'd bandaged Lawrence's arm that night in Charlie Bandaid. As commanders do, Lawrence had asked the trooper about himself. "He told me he intended to go to college," recalls Lawrence. "He wanted to be a doctor because of his service as a medic. He was a bright young man with much enthusiasm and optimism for the future. What a fine young man, and what great potential."

Seeing the Elephant

SUMMER AND FALL 1968

DICK ALBERS, AGE THIRTY-TWO—doctor, husband, and father of four—was inspecting damage on the roof of the family's new home, an old Victorian fix-'er-upper, when his wife appeared, waving a letter: "You've been drafted!"

However much Dr. Albers had hoped to pass under the radar for another three years, at which point he would no longer be eligible for the draft, he gave no thought to trying to wiggle out of serving. "That's not the way I was raised," he says, referencing a youth in Blandensville, Illinois, where his father ran the railroad depot, his mother taught in a one-room schoolhouse, and his formative years were intertwined with the Depression and World War II.

Working his way through school, the phlegmatic, no-nonsense Albers, who wanted to be a country doctor like those back home—selfless men who led respected lives—graduated from college in 1954 and medical school in 1958. In between, he married his vivacious sweetheart Dolly. In 1966, when the selective service belatedly turned their lives upside down, Albers was practicing medicine at a suburban hospital outside Chicago. However disappointing the draft notice, and however emotionally uninvolved Albers might have been in the Việt Nam War, he accepted his fate philosophically: he was, after all, a political conservative who took seriously President Johnson's argument that the U.S. must honor its commitment to the Southeast Asia Treaty Organization.

Commissioned a captain, Albers learned the basics of soldiering, and practiced battlefield surgery on hapless goats shot in the service of their country, at the Medical Field Service School at Fort Sam Houston, Texas. Accompanied by wife and children, Albers was next assigned as a battalion surgeon in occupied Berlin. Instead of serving his entire military commitment with the Berlin Brigade, as he could have—and the duty was something of an adventure, with family trips to London, Paris, and Rome—Albers volunteered for Việt Nam after a year and a half of spit 'n' polish garrison duty. "When you're in the Berlin Brigade, you're talkin' the talk," he explains. "In Vietnam, you're walkin' the walk." It mattered to Albers that he also walk the walk because "once you get in the service, you develop this camaraderie, this esprit de corps. You want to be part of a unit that is effective, purposeful, and has a good reputation"—which ultimately meant a combat outfit. "I really felt this need to participate. I wanted to see the elephant"—a Civil War metaphor for seeing battle.

Home on leave, Albers moved Dolly and the kids into her mother's apartment in California to wait out his year in the war zone. Albers' younger brother, vehemently opposed to the war, was upset that he had volunteered. Likewise, Dolly's brothers, one a veteran of World War II—the good war, the big one, the one that mattered—angrily informed Albers that he was imposing an undue hardship on his family by going to Việt Nam. Albers agreed. "The sacrifice in Vietnam was not mine," he reflects, "it was Dolly's, but she said, 'Okay, I understand that this is something you have to do.'"

Captain Richard K. Albers, Medical Corps, U.S. Army, climbed aboard a Huey with several other replacements on June 25, 1968. For safety's sake, the pilot flew out over the ocean from Fat City, headed north along the coast, then turned west for Hill 29, ascending as he did so to avoid enemy ground fire. Reaching the base camp, the pilot descended from on high in a rapid and unnerving corkscrew, door gunners alert behind their M60s. Escorted from helipad to underground aid station, Albers shook hands with Captain Davis, the outgoing squadron surgeon, and also met Lieutenant Noble and the aid-station medics, all of whom would help him get oriented. The aid station's floor was plywood, its roof made of runway matting and sandbags. Supplies were stored in footlockers, casualties treated on litters laid across sawhorses. "Facilities primitive," Albers noted in his journal. "[N]o lab or microscope." The base camp, permeated by the smell of diesel fuel and burning human waste, was obviously at the end of the line: "The whole command lives in bunkers . . . no shade, dusty & constant [outgoing] artillery-mortar fire, [plus] rats in the bunkers."

The line troops returned at dusk, whereupon Albers was introduced to Lieutenant Colonel Cousland in the officers club, as well as the squadron's lieutenants and captains, who presently regaled themselves with war stories over cold beers. Albers knew they were in enemy territory but was shocked nonetheless to hear young American officers speak so casually of wasting anything in black pajamas without regard to age, sex, or status as civilian or combatant. "I sat for 2 hrs & listened to these men talk of killing & atrocity," the newcomer wrote that night, "and I felt sick & ashamed of the human race."

No turning back now. "I asked for it, I got it," as Albers had written at the replacement center at Long Bình. "Must roll with the punch!" he added at the end of his second day on miserable Hill 29. On the third day, "[we] loaded on the 'pig,'" Albers wrote, referring to the aid-station track, "and went to a nearby hamlet to hold my first 'medcap [medical-civic-action patrol].'" Albers was appalled at his first glimpse of rural Việt Nam. "Thatched roof huts—dirt floors, absolute filth & poverty," he wrote. The poverty was such that even such a small hamlet had several whorehouses of which the troopers from the line platoon providing security availed themselves. "The cows, water buffalo, hogs & chickens run all over the place," Albers continued. "The rice paddies surround the hamlet & are planted at staggered times so the farmer always has a crop to harvest. The [family] graveyards are indiscriminate[ly located] & all graves are surrounded by a little [circular] earthen wall to prevent flooding . . .

Some of the graves are shams—used by the VC to hide weapons or ammo."

The villagers "are very sensitive, inoffensive & modest," Albers wrote; their children were "beautiful," and "their smiles are a miracle among squalor."

Captain Albers and his medics handed out candy and bars of soap cut in half to prevent resale on the black market, while treating three hundred villagers:

> [M]y heart was filled to overflowing [with] compassion . . . Cataracts are rampant, parasitosis (peperazine), anemia, [and] malnutrition. Today I saw children [with] massive furunculosis & ulcers, burns, pneumonia, mastoditis, cleft lips & palates, traumatic enucleations of eyes, old polio, avitaminosis, phimosis, [plus] adults [with] enamel [erosion] & betel nut stained teeth, pregnancy, CA [cancer] of lip, lymphogranuloma[,] and one suspected plague. We accomplished some good today[,] but so much needs to be done to relieve this misery.

Back at base camp, Albers wrote that "I am again enthused, I feel like a doctor again . . . I am no longer afraid of dying in this forsaken place."

First Lieutenant David Venn, the squadron's exceptionally motivated and conscientious civil-affairs officer, ensured that if the dragoons took with one hand—burning, killing, contaminating rice with diesel fuel—they gave with the other. A week after his first medcap, Albers recorded in his journal that Venn organized another medcap at the Catholic school and orphanage in Tam Kỳ:

> Saw over 200 people today—again the lame, halt and blind. Again[,] the contribution was probably meager but managed to help a few [including six-year-old girl with] anemia or malaria [and] marked splenomegaly; [and] pathetic achondroplastic dwarf [for whom] opened abscesses, pulled teeth . . . I need a microscope—may have to steal one! After medcap finished invited to eat at the pastor's table. I swallowed hard and managed

to proceed—dirty bowls & glasses—chop sticks, flies—food was rice egg roll, rice noodles mixed [with] pepper & shrimp & peanuts, chicken gizzards, tea. All covered with raw sugar—the supreme complement to a guest. Surrounded by 15–20 people watching you eat.

When Lawrence replaced Cousland, Albers requested that the new squadron commander—whom he would come to greatly admire as a personable yet hard-driving leader of unquestioned authority—allow him to go out with the line troops, something normally not done by M.D.s. "I didn't want to be hiding back at base camp," explains Albers. "I wanted to see what the medics were doing in the field, so that I could better help them—and I wanted the medics to see that I was willing to be out there with them. I didn't want them to think that I would ask them to do something that I wasn't willing to do myself."

Lawrence flew Albers out to A Troop on July 10. Captain Kaczor handed him a beer—dismounted dragoons were presently fragging tunnels along a trail—then Albers climbed aboard Alpha Bandaid, which was carrying a refugee family in the trim vane: parents, kids, and two pups in a wicker basket. Kaczor's tanks "H&I'd the area," wrote Albers, and then away they went, on the hunt:

> moved out across the rice paddies and up into the hills in areas you wouldn't believe a vehicle could do. The area was thick with undergrowth—finally spotted some V.C. [with binoculars]— tanks opened up [with] 90s & 50s & W.P. & HE mortars. Area of strike was out of AO[,] so couldn't confirm [possible body count]—no return fire.

Alpha Troop rumbled on "[a]cross the interminable rice paddies," wrote Albers, and "thru villages deserted except for cows, old women & children."

Suddenly, more contact:

> all vehicles on line—all weapons firing—village on fire from tracers & W.P. Helicopters came in to confirm. Moved on home

[after the second contact] thru hamlet where V.C. killed the village chief recently. Hundreds of children lining the road[,] waiting to be thrown Cs . . . I only spent 5 hrs in the field but it's misery—heat, dust, sunburn, thirst in a country littered [with] ravaged hamlets, spent cartridges & litter of troops, fields destroyed by the heavy tracked vehicles. From the air it looks beautiful & serene—from the ground[,] a churned mess.

Captain Albers had no choice but to go out on missions, for "until you earned your spurs in that unit," he notes, "you were nothing, you were a non-entity. You had to show that you belonged." The dragoons were "very tough, very tight. The squadron was a totally closed society, like the Mafia." On birthdays and such, "everybody got shit-faced in the officers club," recalls Albers, "and the guest of honor got soaked in beer and had the fly of his trousers cut out with a combat knife." The dragoons did the same for visitors, and if someone refused such treatment "then they were a candy-ass. If you came to visit the hill, and didn't stay overnight, you were an even worse candy-ass." In other words, "to be part of the 1st Cav, you had to be a hard-ass, and the way you got to be a hard-ass was by doing hard-ass stuff." For a squadron surgeon, that meant "taking your turn on perimeter guard, and taking the Pig into action, manning your own .50-caliber. It meant resuscitating wounded troopers on the helipad, and putting the dead in body bags. It basically meant doing everything everyone else did, and resisting reassignment when the time came to a safe job in Chu Lai."

The squadron was so aggressive that "if we were rolling through your town, you damn well better not be on the road," intones Albers, "because we weren't stopping, and we weren't turning if somebody got in front of us." The rationale was simple: slowing down made it easier for an enemy soldier with an RPG launcher to line up his shot. The result was that the unwary, or the overeager among those hoping for a handout from the passing GIs, sometimes ended up with serious injuries. "We used to run over people, or at least clip them and knock them out of the way," says Albers; the casualties would be loaded in a jeep, "and when we came to a stop wherever we were going, they would get me to see what I could do for them. Usually, we'd have to call in a dust-off."

The dragoons were indeed hell on wheels. When different troops approached each other on the highway, the cavalrymen, being full of bravado, would toss smoke grenades into the path of their oncoming counterparts and then pop CS on the last track in the opposite row before both units disappeared into the purple haze. On bad days, the cavalrymen lobbed smoke and tear-gas canisters into towns along the highway, too. On good days, they tossed C-rations to the Vietnamese, though the guys on one mortar track added a twist: they'd punch a hole in one can, insert and light a small plug of plastique, and, using an asbestos glove, toss the superheated can into the squabbling crowd. The results were hilarious, at least to uneducated young soldiers, as the trick can went from one scorched pair of snatching hands to the next. Served the greedy bastards right, thought one of the mortar men, who saw adults pummel little children for the sake of a lousy can of ham and lima beans. "They'd fight like dogs," says the former mortar man. "They seemed like animals to us."

Captain Albers treated numerous civilians who got in the way:

Day began with a bang—3 Vietnamese casualties from [U.S.] artillery fire—ten y.o. [girl] dead [with] abdominal wound and evisceration; 15 yo [girl with] large wound in R flank—her mother struck in eye & chest . . .

Got the little girl with the deformed jaw from [U.S.] artillery sent down to Chu Lai for some surgery . . .

[Treated] 10 y.o. Vietnamese boy [with] multiple frag wounds of legs & hands. He was very brave & didn't cry once as we picked out the pieces . . .

[G]ot information that a Viet woman . . . in the village [adjacent Hawk Hill] . . . had been hit by [U.S.] artillery fire. Jumped in the jeep and went down for look-see. She was being transported in a hammock slung on a bamboo pole[,] covered by a woven bark blanket. When I lifted the cover[,] I thought she was dead—her right arm & foot covered by dressings. BP [blood pressure] good—gave her M.S. & transferred to litter.

Back to aid station—in shock—started I.V. Right hand almost completely blown off—she will lose it . . . She may be V.C. who was setting booby trap & had it go off. Dusted her off [with] her husband.

"It wasn't a problem," says Albers in reference to the collateral damage—civilian casualties—of the squadron's operations: "If it happened, it happened." The indifferent attitude was a direct result of division's appetite for body counts. "You learned to play the game," he adds, meaning that it was more important to kill communists than win hearts and minds, and that dead farmers ended up being tabulated as dead VC. "Ultimately, it didn't matter whose body was being counted. Every night, the squadron was supposed to report that day's body count to division, and the bigger the number, the better."

In addition to accidental civilian casualties, there is to be found in Captain Albers' journal a depressing catalogue of blatant abuse and war crimes:

2 prisoners brought in today—thrown off chopper, dragged around by hair. One beaten and brought into aid station . . .

Ate lunch [with] 2 helicopter pilots—discussed throwing prisoners out of [helicopters] while in air—sometimes necessary [when prisoner berserk and endangering the safety of the crew]—sometimes deliberate [to induce other prisoners to talk, or because it was inconvenient to detour to the prisoner-of-war compound in Chu Lai] . . .

[H]elicopter buzzed Hwy 1 this AM—hit & killed 2 Arvn Sgts . . . one decapitated—no reason—just horsing around . . .

V.C. prisoner brought in today who had been badly beaten & garroted—fortunes of war . . .

MP's [from detachment on Hawk Hill] damn near beat a V.C. woman to death today—she's still alive—I'm keeping her here [in aid station] to save her—they're afraid I'll dust her off & get them in [a] bunch of trouble [with the] Red Cross [in Chu Lai]—if they get her back[,] they'll kill her . . .

One of the troops murdered a V.N. girl (10 y.o.) today . . .

Medcap canceled today because of shooting of [another] child by one of our troops—big stink . . .

Much problems [with] rape, looting, destruction of innocent villages . . .

8 prisoners brought in tonight beaten & cut & broken. Took about 2 hrs to get them all fixed up. Possible VC[,] but 2 were blind & some of the others were just old fishermen . . .

Couple poor old farmers shot and beaten up today . . . [One said during treatment in aid station that] the GI's had [also] shot all his cows.

Captain Albers once saw an American, young enough to be a sergeant or lieutenant but without rank or unit insignia, who rode into base on the back of a militiaman's moped, some exotic, nonregulation submachine gun slung over his shoulder, a string of ears around his neck. It was Albers' impression that the ear-collector was assigned to the squadron—he regularly showed up to draw supplies and hover around the operations center—but actually "lived out in the villages with the PFs. They'd ride around on their little motorbikes, and make night raids on enemy-controlled villages, and assassinate people they *said* were VC. The guy scared me. We had some outlaws like him who I think were psychotic. They got off on the war. They enjoyed having a license to kill."

Those who collected communist ears in the dark of night would have argued that ruthless measures were required against a ruthless enemy, and many indeed were the depredations of the National Liberation Front. While the outlying hamlets belonged to the guerrillas, those nearest Hill 29 were ostensibly under government control. They were defended by militiamen, however, not dragoons, and, as such, were attacked with impunity so to punish farmers who paid their taxes to the wrong side and entrepreneurs who catered to the detested foreigners. "Whatever we won in the daytime, we lost at night," reflects Albers. On August 30, Albers wrote in his journal that his aid station "started receiving burn & frag casualties from 3 Hamlets outside our perimeter last night—VC hit again—burned out 70 families[.]" Six weeks later, as the monsoon season began, the enemy mortared Hawk Hill amid a brief ground attack on both the base camp and the adjacent shantytown. "For a while there[,] the sky was lit up and all the weapons on [the hill] were blazing," jotted Albers. "We prepared for casualties wearing our .45s in case Charlie got inside the wire and wanted to visit the aid station." No sappers penetrated the wire, and "troop casualties were [only] a few bruises & sprained ankles." Three villagers were killed, however. In addition, recorded an outraged Albers, "one pregnant woman shot thru chest & little boy shot thru arm. War on women & children!"

One of the guerrillas in the aid station had gunshot wounds in the hip and back. The other, a sixteen-year-old, was missing his left foot. His bullet-riddled right leg was shattered, and he had also been shot in the stomach. "Got him stabilized," wrote Captain Albers, noting that even as the Americans saved his life, the fanatical young VC "kept spitting at us—finally I got mad—slapped him & stuffed his mouth full of gauze—I wasn't proud of myself—just got mad."

Captain Albers was highly respected for his devotion to duty and willingness to take his risks in the field, and he was something of a father figure to his medics. The doctor could be a gruff father. Albers frequently chewed out the vocal and opinionated Lieutenant Noble "to let him know who was boss," adding elsewhere in his journal that "I'm not sympathetic to the problems of the medics—I have decided everybody can just do their job and shut up . . . My boys think I'm a hard ass which is all right with me!" Intolerant of malingering at morning sick call, the squadron surgeon was stone-faced even when treating combat casualties: "Survivors from mine explosion in a daze, frightened, discouraged, incoherent. I feel much empathy but cannot be sympathetic—tomorrow they will ride the tracks again and it may be their turn to die."

The medics and their stocky, crew-cut captain, who eventually sported a mustache that complemented his pugnacious demeanor, played horseshoes, volleyball, and football at the end of the day, stripped to cutoffs and jungle boots. They had cookouts, too, in their little picnic-table area, and sang along while Doc Johnston banged out "House of the Rising Sun" on the guitar until his fingertips blistered. "[H]e's really quite good," Albers noted in his journal. The hot dogs, beer, watermelons, letters from home, chess matches, stag movies, and steak-and-lobster dinners at the mess hall—yes, the U.S. Army was so rich as to ship steak and lobsters to lonely, little Hill 29—were not always enough to distract, however, especially during periods of inaction. "Time is seeming to drag a bit and I'm still depressed and grouchy," Albers wrote. "Got to snap out of it or I will go mad [with] loneliness and self pity." The surgeon ticked off in his journal a succession of "routine day[s] in this war of fantasy and half truths" that dulled minds and deadened spirits: "A miserable, wretched day. Everybody has been melancholy . . . Today has been a bitch—hot, boring, tempers short . . . Everybody dopey and mopey . . . Slow day again—rained all night and rained all day—mud, mud, mud, mud. No dust offs today—everybody hibernating in their bunkers. . . . Time for Charlie to end my misery with a well placed rocket!"

To signal their disaffection, the medics mounted atop the aid station a stuffed surgical glove, middle finger erect. As for Captain Albers, "I'm drinking too much," he confided to his journal. He promised to stop taking solace in a nightly visit to the officer's club, only to later admit: "Bought another case of champagne tonight—what the hell, it's only money & it makes me feel good." Albers was not alone. While the army busied itself sending potheads to the stockade, many of its regulars survived the war on the legal vices of alcohol, coffee, and cigarettes. In fact, Albers dusted off a regular army NCO who'd stopped drinking as his rotation date approached so to go home clean and sober, only to go mad at three in the morning with the DTs. Strapped to a litter in the aid station, the sergeant raved that monkeys were wrapping commo wire around his ankles while bugs crawled on him and crabs ate holes in the ceiling. "He was crazy, panicking," recalls Albers, who thought the sergeant would have opened fire on the hallucinations could he have gotten his hands on a weapon. Albers administered sterile alcohol by IV. "I just wanted to bring him to a reasonable mental state," he says, "and get him off the hill, and the quickest way to do that was to give him his medicine. We shipped him off to Chu Lai at first light: they could deal with his next seizure."

The rats that burrowed into the sandbag bunker walls attracted pit vipers, and at night, pitiful little death squeaks could sometimes be heard as predator met prey. The medics baited live-catch cages with peanut butter and Tootsie Rolls, and Captain Albers would inject the captured rats with thorazine so they would be mercifully unconscious when drowned. In the category of the unusual duties of a combat doctor, Albers was also tasked with ensuring that the prostitutes in the adjacent shantytown did not impede the mission by infecting dragoons with venereal disease. Having finally secured a microscope—the surgeon provided one of his medics cash to buy one during a Hong Kong R&R—Albers required a blood draw from each prostitute and treated those who tested positive for syphilis or gonorrhea with penicillin. The prostitutes did not appreciate Albers' needles. "Another whorehouse refused to cooperate today," he recorded in his journal; after much discussion with Lawrence and their counterparts in the ARVN unit that had jurisdiction over the shantytown, the brothel owner was made to understand that if the infected girl on the premises was not produced, the good doctor "was going to run over the damn [place] with a track—she came in [instead] and got [her] shot amidst much wailing & screeching."

To attend the needs of the shantytown residents, Captain Albers trained two enthusiastic local fourteen-year-olds as junior medics. Starting with the basics—simple hygiene, how to read a thermometer—the boys proved quick studies. "[T]hey're lancing boils," Albers wrote, "doing suturing, [and] giving shots all very well now." The boys also came along on medcaps. Amid the depression, frustration, and violence, the medcaps were a salve for the soul, a brief interlude when hard-bitten cavalrymen could be human again. "I had troopers begging to go on medcaps," recalls Albers, "because the people were *grateful* for what we were doing. The little kids would smile at you. They didn't hate you."

Official platitudes about civic action aside, Albers contends that division headquarters provided the barest support to the squadron's medcaps or its support of the nuns who ran the Catholic orphanage in Tam Kỳ and the headmaster of its Lutheran counterpart north of Hawk Hill. The officials of the Sài Gòn government were even worse. The provincial hospital in Tam Kỳ, for example, was understaffed, overcrowded, and administered by doctors who Albers describes as arrogant and indifferent. There was a huge cultural divide between the rulers and the ruled, he adds, and absolutely no sympathy for the underdogs. The peasants themselves were fatalistic and, as far as Albers could tell, seemed not to blame anyone for the miserable condition of their lives: the war and the attendant evils visited upon them by the soldiers of both sides were simply part of the never-ending, never-changing tragedy that was life.

And so it was that when Captain Albers and his medics arrived with boxes of toys and soap and clothes, Kool-Aid and cans of food—such days were festivals at the orphanages—the goods came not from division or provincial headquarters but from the parishioners of the surgeon's church back home in Illinois. "The children were precious and the gifts roundly appreciated," Albers jotted in his journal after one such visit to Tam Kỳ. The squadron's generosity attracted the attention of a television reporter who asked to accompany a medcap with his camera crew. "We said no," recalls Albers, "and that 'If you insist on coming, we cannot guarantee your safety.' In fact, we told him, 'If you take pictures, we'll hurt you.'" Albers and his medics did not want to be part of a feel-good report about happy little kids and the wonderful American GIs who played the part of their big brothers. "That was not reality," says Albers. The reality was that those wonderful American GIs were part of a merciless, well-oiled machine that had produced most of those orphans to begin with—in addition to killing countless children outright—in its relentless pursuit of body counts. "We felt like the reporter was invading our turf, and trying to take something away from us," says Albers. "Now, we would have had no problem with any reporter accompanying a combat operation because now you're putting yourself in harm's way. You want to experience the terror of combat, be my guest. Spend a few weeks with us. See what's really going on out there. But don't drop in for a day and try to put a happy spin on our war: 'We don't want it, so don't try it.'"

Whether the medcaps were publicized or not, Albers will never forget those orphanages as "little islands of joy in the midst of so much misery."

Nor would Albers ever forget Spc. 5th Class Patrick Stenger, a bespectacled draftee who'd originally joined the aid-station crew with such a sullen, chip-on-his-shoulder attitude that the squadron surgeon did not think he would be able to fit in. Albers told Stenger as much, but the kid quickly matured into one of the squadron's most outstanding young medics. "Pat came from a dysfunctional family," recalls Albers. "He had a bad relationship with his father, who told him he was no good so much he believed it. We all have the ability to change and improve ourselves, however, and when Pat saw the work the medics were doing, particularly with the civilians—when he saw that he could make a difference—the chip on his shoulder disappeared. He found his niche."

Stenger was the medic who got the microscope on R&R. In addition, "we'd go back to Chu Lai," recalls Albers, "and go around the various hospitals and aid stations in the rear, and steal the other equipment we needed. We put it all together, so we had a working lab out on Hawk Hill." Albers eventually had young Stenger promoted to staff sergeant—the kid was so good he could run the medcaps on those occasions when Albers was otherwise occupied. "I taught Pat and the other guys in the aid station all the stuff about the microscope and the lab," notes Albers, "and doing spinal taps, sewing up lacerations, debriding wounds, setting fractures, and all the rest. I mean, those guys could have practiced medicine in rural America without a license, and done just fine."

For Pat Stenger, the war was his epiphany, his realization that he could do something important with his life. In fact, with Albers' encouragement, he used the GI Bill to put himself through college and medical school after the army. "When I left the unit, I gave Pat the microscope from our lab so he would have his own scope when he went home and went to school," recalls Albers. Stenger actually interned with Albers after medical school and then joined the public health department. Along with his wife, a fellow physician, he "dedicated his life to the Indian population in a small town called Gallup, New Mexico."

Stenger and Albers stayed in contact until the ex-medic died of throat cancer almost thirty-five years after finding his purpose in life in Việt Nam.

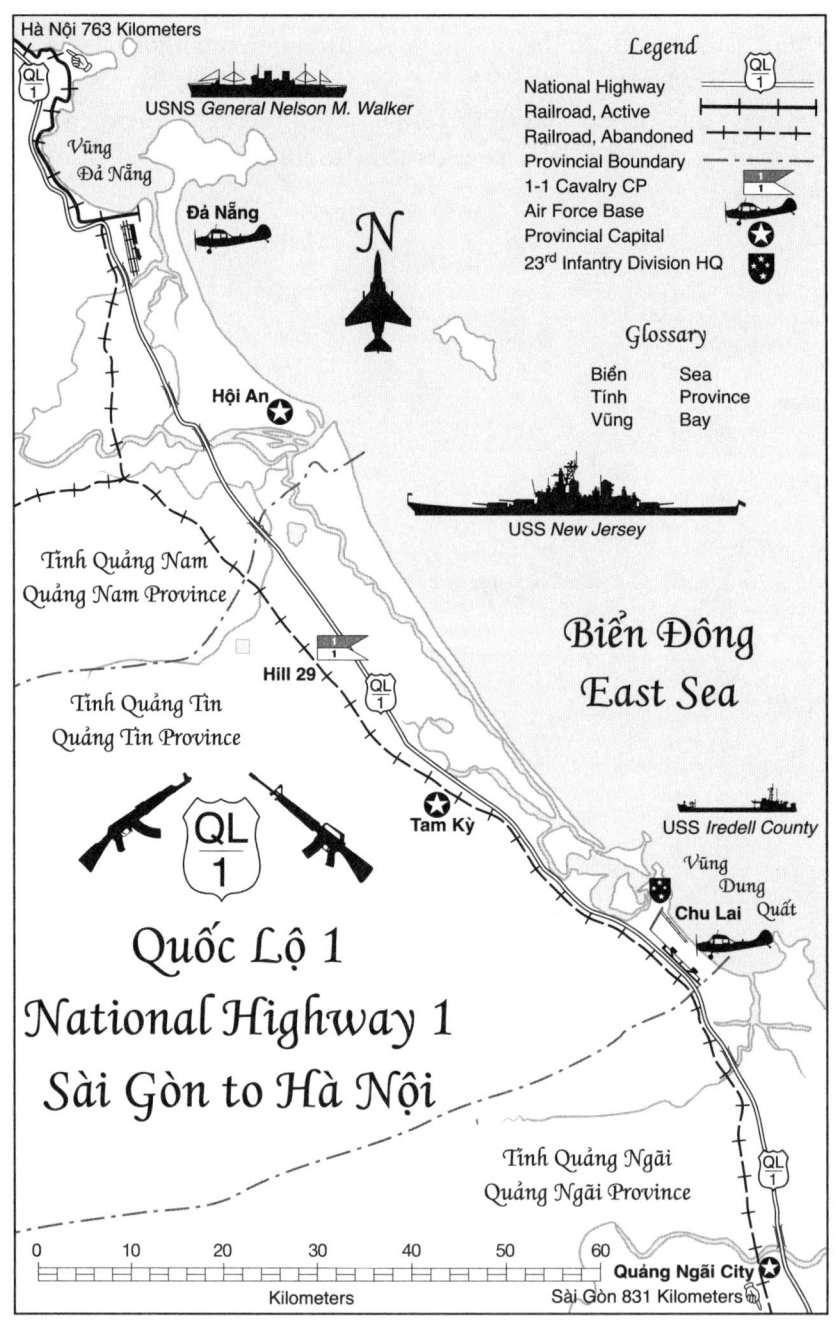

Finale to the Third General Offensive

SEPTEMBER 1968

DURING THE LULL THAT followed the Battle of Tam Kỳ, "we felt the NVA were licking their wounds back in the mountains," writes Lawrence, "and resupplying to continue the Third Offensive when they were ready."

In the meantime, on September 2, the dragoons launched the operation north of Barrier Island postponed by the Tam Kỳ action. The operation centered on a long-inviolate enemy stronghold near Hội An, along the coast in Quảng Nam Province. With the dragoons in blocking positions, a marine battalion landing team was to storm ashore, "and methodically sweep through in detailed, deliberate fashion, looking under every rock, so to speak," writes Lawrence. Afterward, provincial troops were to establish a long-term pacification program to bring the area under government control. Unfortunately, when the operation finally commenced, the marines could no longer spare one of their hard-charging landing teams, and the rain-lashed sweep was instead undertaken by Americal grunts. "The infantry battalion conducted a perfunctory sweep, moving way too fast," notes Lawrence. "There were caves and bunkers all over the place, and the VC simply went to ground and waited out the sweep. I was frustrated, and the operation mercifully ended in a few days."

Actually, the dragoons would return in time.

§

From Captain Albers' journal notes of September 9: "Charlie Troop in contact today—5 dusted off—Blue Ghost grenaded [with white phosphorus] some of our own men [in Alpha Troop]—one killed & several wounded."

Lawrence was alerted by division to be prepared to move on short notice to Quảng Ngãi City, capital of Quảng Ngãi Province and obvious prize of the enemy units massing in the hills to the west as part of the Third General Offensive. The city sat astride Highway 1 seventy-five kilometers south of Hill 29—well outside the squadron's stomping grounds—and was defended by elements of the 2nd ARVN Division and the 11th Light Infantry Brigade of the Americal Division. "General Gettys, it seemed, had made a decision to use the 1-1 Cav as the division fire brigade," notes Lawrence, "to march to a crisis anywhere we could operate with armor, make contact, and not let go until the threat had been destroyed. We would be ready. That's what cavalry is all about."

Gettys personally flew to Hill 29 on September 12 to give Lawrence the word to saddle up: having slipped around the task force that was supposed to stop the enemy in the foothills, the 95th Regiment, 3rd NVA Division, was poised to strike Quảng Ngãi City. "We were moving within the hour," recalls Lawrence. Led by Major Filbert, the squadron rumbled down Highway 1 as the sun sank, and through a lashing monsoon storm, ahead of which Lawrence and Logan flew to coordinate with the province chief and other U.S. and ARVN officers in Quảng Ngãi City. Next, Lawrence and Logan established a command post in the ruins of a Buddhist cemetery three and a half kilometers west of town. The lead elements of the squadron rolled in around midnight. The tail end of the column did not arrive until three in the morning, at which point Lawrence informed Kaczor, Lewis, and Frost that all three line troops—plus two attached infantry companies—would proceed west at dawn to find the enemy regiment threatening Quảng Ngãi City. "Our battle plan was straightforward," recounts Logan. "Make contact and kick their butts."

Moving generally abreast, the line troops, minus their overweight tanks, advanced from one likely enemy position to the next—mostly, the elevated islands in the sodden paddies—hoping to draw fire. Four kilometers into the sweep, Lieutenant Jackson's platoon, to which had been attached all the scouts in the troop, made first contact at 2:45 p.m. on September 13. Jackson was in an overwatch position on a small, bare hill at the time: one of his scout sections was moving around the flank of a suspicious island when NVA opened fire from the next island to the right. The rocket-propelled grenade that struck an M60 shield killed the gunner, and the driver—the only crewman uninjured by the blast—withdrew to Jackson's position, where a medevac soon landed. An RPG in its engine disabled the other track in the section, and the infantrymen who'd dismounted from the vehicle were pinned down. Jackson moved to the scene with three more tracks and spent two hours exchanging fire with the entrenched enemy while waiting for the rest of Alpha Troop.

In addition to bringing Kaczor forward on Jackson's right flank, Lawrence ordered Frost up on the left flank. Lawrence and Logan were pitching smoke grenades from the command ship when two parallel streams of tracers suddenly snapped past the open doorway. Spotting the twin-barreled .51 pumping out the tracers, the crew chief opened fire with his M60 from the other side of the Huey while the pilot "began violent evasive maneuvers," writes Logan. "Lawrence and I could only watch as the tracers continued to pass in front of our faces, so close I thought I could reach out and catch them, if I hadn't been so scared. The crew chief let out a whoop and the tracers ceased." Notwithstanding the near miss, Lawrence recalls the battle unfolding like a war game. "We used the air cav troop to secure the flanks, and air strikes to soften them up," he writes; afterward, C Troop advanced behind a wall of fire and "rode right over the enemy lines to the hedgerows behind. Then the infantry went to work." With grunts and cavalrymen pitching grenades into bunkers, "the NVA were running everywhere in a panic," continues Lawrence. "They did not stand and fight as well as they had at Tam Ky. Guess they never expected to see us so far south, and when we were committed, it was too much for them. We fought for several hours, trying to mop up the area. They hid where they could, and fought when cornered." C Troop reported a body count of forty-two VC and NVA.

The enemy facing Lieutenant Jackson's platoon did not panic. Doc Johnston, in fact, would be awarded the Silver Star for ignoring both a flesh wound and heavy fire—"the air crackled constantly with AK rounds," he recalls—to treat the wounded. The platoon's return fire was itself so intense that by the time Kaczor linked up with Jackson, the trees hiding the enemy's bunkers had been reduced to splintered stumps, nothing higher than two feet. Kaczor sent Jackson around the right flank of the enemy positions with his three remaining scouts. The lead track had closed to within forty meters of the island when it bogged down in the wet paddy. "I moved the second track up, and the troopers cross-cabled to the back of the first track to pull it out," recounts Jackson. "They started to pull back, the cables went taut—then the second track bogged down, too. I pulled forward with my command track, cross-cabled to the back of the second track, and ended up just as stuck. The fourth track pulled in behind mine, and got stuck, too—so there we were, four tracks, bogged down and cabled together in column—and that's when the bad guys started shooting at us again."

Unable to advance or retreat, and too close to the enemy to call in artillery or air strikes, Lieutenant Jackson's cavalrymen returned fire without pause, frantic to keep the enemy from drawing a bead on their immobilized tracks. Barrels burned out, and tracers flew like corkscrews. "We'd pour oil on the barrels to cool them down," recalls Jackson, "but they were so hot, the oil would catch fire." Amid the roar of M60s and .50-cals, Jackson used up all his M16 ammo, plus two thousand extra rounds for his pistol and grease gun. "The FO's radioman was down at the bottom of the track," notes Jackson, "and when I emptied my .45, I'd hit the magazine release and drop the empty magazine on the radioman's head, and he'd hand me a fresh magazine and reload the empty one."

The storm of fire did the job. Lieutenant Jackson was in radio contact with a Cobra pilot who reported between strafing runs that the four bogged-down tracks faced about forty NVA in a trench line. That was a lot of NVA, but the enemy soldiers—cowed by the torrents of lead—were covering their heads with one hand and blindly shoving their AK-47s and RPG launchers over the lip of the trench with the other, firing without aiming, and mostly firing too high. "They fired over forty RPGs at us, but didn't hit a single track," notes Jackson, who was nevertheless so unnerved by the warheads hissing just overhead that "to this day, I still jump when I hear the whoosh of a rocket on the Fourth of July."

The battle continued as the sun sank, and for several hours thereafter. "I'm not sure when the enemy finally bugged out," recalls Jackson, to be awarded his second Bronze Star. "It might have been around eight or nine, but it wasn't until two o'clock in the morning that the maintenance section got up there with the big recovery vehicles that could pull us out of the mud. By then, I don't think I had ten rounds left in the platoon." The enemy decamped under cover of darkness in such disorder as to neglect to recover all of their equipment and dead. To cover the retreat, the enemy mortared the squadron command post in the crumbling cemetery. Captain Albers, who'd already dusted off five of his medics—one with a concussion, two with combat exhaustion, two more with gunshot wounds—noted in his journal that he "had patients in [the] aid station when [the] mortars hit—all patients de-de-mawed [ran for cover] with thermometers. After the mortars came the mosquitoes. I slept very fitfully."

On September 14, Albers recorded that the "action picked up again. Choppers all over the place, some contact—casualties light—few frag wounds and a Vietnamese boy shot in face—bullet through cheek—enucleated an eye and lodged in the brain." The operation continued through September 15—another dragoon was killed—as infantry and cavalry "chased the enemy all the way back into the hills," writes Lawrence, "killing more than a hundred altogether." The squadron assembled that last day in a soccer field within the village of Sơn Long, along the highway just north of Quảng Ngãi City. Along the way, Lawrence's command group passed through the province capital, which turned out to be just another "hovel of shacks," Albers noted. "[S]uch misery I do not understand."

The line troops rejoined their tanks at the new laager and were joined, in turn, by fuel and ammunition carriers from Fat City. As the sun sank, mermite cans of hot food, plus cases of beer and soda, were divided up, even as troopers "spray[ed] the mud puddles [with] diesel to kill the mosquito[e]s," Albers wrote. "[S]lept fitfully [again]—rained [during the night]—tracks pulling in & out till 2 AM—patients [began arriving at aid-station track] at 5 AM—I'm tired and dirty."

The province capital had been spared destruction and, according to prisoner statements, an enemy battalion demolished instead. Much praise was forthcoming from division, which seemed amazed at the dragoons' ability to move so far on such short notice and then advance without pause to meet and destroy the enemy. "Just in a day's work for the cav," writes Lawrence. The squadron was in a cocky mood. Logan recalls that division had issued new radio call signs at the time of the road march to Quảng Ngãi City. "Those given to the cav were awful," he notes: overly complicated, ostensibly to confuse the enemy, and without sufficient martial ring. As such, Lawrence opted out of the division scheme, choosing instead to go by Hawk 6, and telling his captains to come up with their own names, too. Such independence of action "suited the troop commanders right down to the ground," writes Logan, "and we conducted the operation using made-up call signs." Afterward, Logan "received a nasty message from division requiring a 'reply by endorsement' for several hundred security violations [involving the made-up call signs]. I discussed this with Lawrence, and it was decided that the best way to handle the situation was a short note back to division headquarters, the gist of which was that we had killed a hundred NVA and saved Quang Ngai City, and that they could forget about any other response from us. We heard nothing further on these violations."

Even as the squadron had originally begun the road march south to meet the enemy, Lawrence was informed that a certain sergeant, a young regular with much combat experience, had allegedly raped a Vietnamese girl during a routine patrol the day before near Tam Kỳ. "I indicated that we would prepare charges on our return," notes Lawrence, "but not to put the individual under confinement at that time as we needed every individual we could muster." As it happened, the sergeant died a hero's death at Quảng Ngãi—killed while manning his .50—leaving Lawrence to write that "no charges were actually drawn up since the offender was KIA. I seem to remember commenting that any reason to charge the sergeant had been wiped out by a good NVA shot."

No sooner had one ugly incident been put to rest but another arose: the squadron was saddling up the morning after the battle when the village chief reported to Captain Lewis that several GIs had rampaged through Sơn Long during the night, stealing, beating up people, and, worse, sexually assaulting two girls after breaking into their home and evicting their parents at gunpoint. Lewis informed Lawrence, who recalls that "war is tough enough on the hearts and minds of soldiers. As leaders, we cannot let them sink to animal levels. We have to do all we can to maintain our humanity in combat. As such, I was very hard on those offenders brought to my attention." Lawrence had Lewis' troops fall out beside their vehicles while their platoon leaders searched inside for a decorative straw mat, transistor radio, gold bracelet, and gold necklace that had been reported stolen. Lawrence also had the village chief walk the ranks with two boys who had been beaten—both sported black eyes—and the family whose home had been invaded, hoping they could identify their attackers. They could not. Nor were the stolen items found. Frustrated, Lawrence "called B Troop to form up around me, said that I felt at least one or two of the men knew who was responsible, and implored them not to dishonor the squadron and those of their comrades who had been wounded and killed by withholding information to protect the guilty. I asked them to report what they knew after they had had time to reflect on the nature of the crimes that had been committed."

As the meeting broke up, Spec Four Peter F. Wilson—one of three troopers, it would become known, who had gone to the aid of the young sisters—walked past one of the men he'd caught in the act of violating the girls and intoned, "Maybe the colonel doesn't know who did it, but we sure do."

Wilson was not addressing a fellow trooper, but 1st Lt. Lynn A. Maxfield, the 2nd Platoon leader of B Troop. Upon returning to Hill 29, a young trooper reported Maxfield's participation in the assault. Shocked that an officer was involved, Lawrence recalls that he "questioned" the young trooper, "believed his account, and thus began the paperwork for a 32b Investigation for a General Court-Martial."

Testimony gathered during the investigation detailed the crimes committed by Lieutenant Maxfield, Staff Sergeant Czinege, Sergeant Eskowski, Spec Five Townsend, Spec Four Castro, and Private First Class Kerr—no reason to use first names—in the village of Sơn Long during the night of September 15–16, 1968. Castro was a tank driver in C Troop and friends with Czinege, who, with Eskowski, manned the AVLB attached to A Troop from the 26th Engineer Battalion, Americal Division. Kerr and Townsend manned the AVLB attached to B Troop. Maxfield recounted that when the laager was first established, he got a beer from a jeep-trailer filled with ice, soda, and beer, "and talked to the people standing around the trailer." Next, the platoon leader "made an inspection of my tracks to see that the people were pulling maintenance," then "went back to the trailer and got [another] beer and was drinking it when one of the local village boys was caught trying to steal some C-rations off a tank that was parked about fifteen feet away. The boy was spanked and then released. A couple more kids came up to the trailer, and tried to take some soda, but were chased away when some of my people, including myself, threw empty cans at them."

Shortly after nightfall, Maxfield, Townsend, and Kerr approached Czinege, Eskowski, and Castro, and asked if they wanted to go to the ville with them. They did. All had been drinking, and things got ugly when the group ambled into a hootch occupied by a father, mother, baby, and two boys. According to Eskowski, the "mamasan started raising some hell, and Lieutenant Maxfield hit her. The two young boys tried to stop him, and Townsend laid into them. He gave them a pretty good working over, as was evident the next morning [when they appeared with black eyes in the company of the village chief]." Townsend pushed the boys onto a bed. The mamasan ended up "sitting on the floor[,] holding a crying baby in her arms," stated Kerr, adding that Maxfield and Czinege "were both fondling her breasts as she sat on the floor." Castro mockingly asked the boys sitting on the bed if they wanted "chop-chop"—food—before pouring a large pan of rice over their heads. Continuing down the road, Castro, "who was pretty drunk," noted Eskowski, "started pounding on the hootches and kicking down the doors." Glancing into one hootch, Eskowski saw Castro "standing with a radio in his hands . . . I asked [him] where he had gotten the radio from. He said that it was lying on the table, and that he was going to take it. Later that night, I saw it on his tank, [but] where it went from there, I don't know."

Lieutenant Maxfield, Spec Five Townsend, and Private Kerr barged into another hootch to find Tặng Kỳ Sơn, age thirty-nine, standing with his wife, Nguyễn Thị Quối, who was holding their newborn baby. Picking up a kerosene lantern, Kerr inspected the back room and noticed candlelight emanating from the family bunker. Kerr borrowed Townsend's .45—no one else was armed—and pulled a four-year-old boy from the bunker. "I just turned him loose, and he went to his papasan," stated Kerr, who, peering into the bunker again, spotted a girl, whom he dragged out. Liking what he saw, Townsend grabbed the girl—Tặng Thị Cúc, age fifteen—stripped off her pajama bottoms, and threw her onto a couch near the front door. Maxfield pried the girl's legs apart as Townsend unbuttoned his fly and then penetrated Cúc—whose name means "Chrysanthemum." The teenager reacted so violently that she and Townsend tumbled off the couch, whereupon Townsend clamped a hand over her mouth to muffle her cries and raped the struggling girl on the dirt floor. "My parents witnessed all this and screamed," Cúc later testified, whereupon, "they were beaten by the Americans . . . It appeared that the Americans were drunk as I smelled bad odor from their breathing."

Amid the commotion, another girl—Tạng Thị Minh, age fourteen—emerged from the bunker at Kerr's command. At that point, the father of the girls, having been punched and "[b]ecoming panic[ked]," as his awkwardly translated statement reads, "ran outside of the house and screamed, [that] my [oldest] daughter was still inside being raped. I shouted to the near by stationed Popular Force Troops. They were to[o] scared and dared not come [to help]."

Kerr, meanwhile, "was trying to run the mamasan out of the hootch," as he later testified. "[S]he was hollering and raising all kinds of commotion . . . I kept drawing [the .45] back like I was going to strike her, and I done that three or four times, and she finally went outside." With that, Maxfield and Kerr stripped Minh naked, whereupon Kerr held the girl down on a bed while Maxfield, already shirtless, "undone his britches," to quote Kerr, "and pulled them down to approximately his knees, and [then] he got between her legs."

Unable to get an erection under such circumstances, Lieutenant Maxfield shortly rolled off Tạng Thị Minh. "Well, I might as well get up," the platoon leader said to Kerr. "I can't do any good." Minh sat up at the edge of the bed, but Kerr wanted a turn, so Maxfield told the girl to lie back down. When she did not, the platoon leader pushed her back: "Goddamnit, bitch, lie down!"

Kerr recounted that "I got in between her legs, [but] I couldn't do anything, either," being only "half hard." The frustrated trooper stood up and, pulling Minh back to a sitting position by her hair, forced her to commit an act of oral sodomy. At some point during the assaults, Castro stepped into the hootch but "came out shortly," stated Eskowski, "and said that they had two nice looking girls inside." Eskowski entered the hootch but wheeled away when he saw what was going on and joined Castro, who was making tracks for the laager. Staff Sergeant Czinege also wanted nothing to do with acts that could land them all in the stockade: the last of the group to enter the hootch, he testified that he told Maxfield, Townsend, and Kerr, "Let's get out of here, you fools," then "ran down the road" and "caught up with Sergeant Eskowski and Spec Four Castro. We went back to the rear of the tank, and we started to drink beer again."

Some twenty minutes into the assault, Sgt. Henry T. Williams, a supply man with squadron headquarters, decided to investigate the screaming and headed into the ville with Spec Four Wilson and Pvt. Richard A. Hoopes, both of C Troop. Peering in a side window of the hootch, the three saw Maxfield and Kerr assaulting a naked girl; with that, they rushed inside through the front door. Hoopes tripped over Townsend, who was still raping Cúc. "I pulled her up by the arm, and gave her the clothes which I picked up from the floor," testified Hoopes. "Another girl [Minh] came running toward me [from the back room], and she did not have any clothes on. I took the girls halfway to the back door and told them to leave, and they did. I followed the girls outside and I lost sight of them." Upon rushing outside, Cúc stated that she and her sister "climbed onto the roof of the house, and hid there for the rest of the night."

Sergeant Williams shined a flashlight on Maxfield, Townsend, and Kerr. "I told the men to move out," stated Williams. "I told all of them to get out of the hootch . . . [T]hey were wrong for what they were doing over there. They had no business in that hootch at all." As Williams, Wilson, and Hoopes followed Maxfield outside, either the lieutenant or one of his cohorts fired a round from the .45 in their possession. If not an accidental discharge, the shot—and it was never determined who pulled the trigger—was probably an act of defiance by men upset that their fun had been interrupted. Williams and Townsend, in fact, exchanged sharp words on the way back to the laager, the supply sergeant intoning angrily that the men in the hootch had "disgraced the squadron."

An hour later, by which time a light rain was falling, flames could be seen flickering inside a hootch. Sergeant Williams and Spec Four Wilson, securing a fire extinguisher, again went to investigate. They found that Lieutenant Maxfield had returned to the ville with Czinge, Townsend, and a GI named Hooper. Maxfield's group was "tearing the place up," said Wilson. Williams testified that in addition to "kicking and pushing the furniture around," the lieutenant's group was "burning some substance on the floor at three places in the house." Wilson stated that Maxfield "claimed it was a VC hootch, and that there was nitro starch in some bags . . . I tasted the substance and found it to be rock salt. We extinguished the fire and told them to get out . . . Maxfield got a straw mat, rolled it, and took it with him when we left the house . . . "

Reaching the laager, Williams and Townsend again argued, so heatedly, in fact, that those gathered around the pair thought they were going to start throwing fists. They didn't, perhaps because Staff Sergeant Czinege barked at Sergeant Williams to "lay off my men" and sent Townsend back to his bridge tank. As Townsend left, Williams snarled, "I'll see you hang for this!"

In addition to being sexually assaulted, Minh had been relieved of a necklace, and Cúc a bracelet. Their father was robbed of an unknown amount of money. The investigation never pinned down who took the piasters and bracelet, but Castro apparently stole Minh's necklace. "The next morning, just before we were leaving, Castro came over and showed me and Sergeant Eskowski a necklace that was broken," testified Czinege. "I asked him where did he get it, and he said he got it last night. He put it back in his pocket and left." Eskowski added that "there was all kinds of talk [that morning] about what had happened the night before. Later on in the morning, we had a line-up. After the line-up, the CO of the 1st Cav got us together and chewed us out, and after that we were dismissed and sent back to our vehicles" for the return trip to Hill 29.

As described by Logan, Lawrence "got on the horn" with General Gettys while en route to Hill 29 and suggested that "we needed time to perform maintenance. Since we would be passing Chu Lai on the way home, and the beach was a good place to perform maintenance, wouldn't it be a great idea if the squadron could spend a night on the beach?" Gettys agreed, and the dragoons—afforded their first break after a year of combat—rolled onto the beach below the Americal Division Combat Center, where replacements received in-country training before being shipped to their units. "The first order of business was to pull maintenance," writes Logan. "It was probably the fastest motor stables ever performed. Then it was everybody into the South China Sea."

Thanks to Major Filbert's efforts to secure good chow, the "mess sections built fires on the beach and grilled steaks for every one," notes Logan. "To top things off, there was an Australian show at the Combat Center that evening. The whole squadron trooped up for the performance. Several of the officers commandeered an AVLB and drove it up to the amphitheater," continues Logan. "We watched the show from there. Afterwards, Lawrence made a few remarks, and then things got a little out of hand. The guys on the AVLB—all officers and gentlemen—had brought along a large supply of beer and not a few red and green star-cluster flares." The beer mostly finished, "someone suggested that a few flares would sort of round out the evening," notes Logan. "My memory of the events that followed is somewhat dim. Whether due to the passage of time or the number of beers consumed, all I can recall is a fire broke out in the Combat Center [from the flares], and there were reports that it burned to the ground."

Kaczor recalls that the commander of the Combat Center "wanted our heads," but that General Gettys intervened in the cav's behalf. "Morale was exploding," notes Lawrence. "The troops knew they could whip anyone."

Captain Albers described the events of September 16 in his journal:

> [P]layed a game of chess [with] Lt Jackson [at Son Long]—[then] packed up the pig & moved out to Chu Lai—loggered [sic] up on the beach—set up an aid station. Went swimming—dunked by Maj Filbert. Had steak & ice cream for supper. Floor show—very good—wiener roast on driftwood fire after the show—slept well—1-1 Cav—saviors of Tam Ky & Quang Ngai—damn near tore the combat center apart—soul brother dispute—Col Lawrence waxed eloquent. A nice 18hr stand-down R&R. Talked with most of my medics—all did an outstanding job. A good unit & great esprit—I'm proud to serve with them.

On September 17, Albers "[a]woke [early] to a beautiful sunrise with the fishing junks on the horizon. Walked in solitude on the beach, collected a few shells only to return them to the sea. Beer for lunch," he continued, then at noon "we pulled out for Hawk Hill . . . Bridge, jeep, [and] civilian bus blown up by mine north of Tam Ky—we took sniper rounds. Arrived Hill 29 about 1400 hrs—beau coup patients—worked until about 10 when the damn sirens blew—couple of mortar rounds—no casualties."

Upon the squadron's return to base camp, Lieutenant Maxfield's involvement in the Sơn Long incident was reported to Lawrence, and agents from the army's Criminal Investigation Division (CID) began taking sworn statements from both GIs and the Tạng family. In addition, line-ups were conducted in the day room of the 23rd MP Company, Americal Division, in Chu Lai. The parents of Cúc and Minh could not identify those who had violated their daughters—"Americans have the same face," said the mother—but Cúc and Minh fingered Maxfield and Townsend, as did Williams, Wilson, and Hoopes. The cooperation with authorities against fellow dragoons put a certain onus on the three GIs. While at division, Wilson, in fact, was asked point-blank by one of the investigating officers: "Has anyone threatened you before your testimony here this morning?" Wilson replied, "I've heard rumors from the hill that we would be had when we go back."

No charges were filed against Eskowski or Castro. Czinege and Kerr were granted immunity for their testimony, though only Kerr actually took the stand. Townsend pled guilty under a plea arrangement by which he would receive a dishonorable discharge but a reduced sentence—five years instead of eight—and thereafter testified at Maxfield's trial, conducted at Chu Lai in December 1968. Maxfield had originally offered to resign his commission in lieu of a court-martial. That was not to be, and Maxfield's defense—as expressed in a statement to the CID, for he apparently didn't testify in court—was that he had entered the ville to investigate the very screams that disturbed Williams, Wilson, and Hoopes, but by arriving first, his presence in the hootch in which Kerr and Townsend were violating the girls had been misinterpreted by Williams, Wilson, and Hoopes. It was a thin defense, and based on the testimony of Williams, Kerr, and Townsend, not to mention Tạng Thị Cúc and Tạng Thị Minh, 1st Lt. Lynn A. Maxfield of the 1st Squadron, 1st Cavalry, Americal Division, was duly found guilty of assault with intent to commit rape and sentenced to dismissal from the service and five years hard labor at the U.S. Disciplinary Barracks, Fort Leavenworth, Kansas.

Lieutenant Maxfield was returned to Chu Lai in May 1969, having been granted a new trial on several legalistic grounds, including that his original counsel had not sufficiently emphasized his fine character and exemplary combat service. As such, the officers of the second jury learned that Lynn Maxfield haled from Havre, Montana, the youngest of four sons born to an engineer with the Great Northern Railroad. One of the brothers also became a railroad engineer, while another was killed in World War II, and a third made a career in the U.S. Marine Corps. By all accounts a bright, cheerful, and energetic young man, Lynn Maxfield was an athlete and Eagle Scout during his high school years, worked summers with the Department of Agriculture, and was also active in the Junior Chamber of Commerce and Methodist Youth Fellowship. The leader of Maxfield's boy-scout troop, also a first sergeant in the National Guard, recruited him when he turned seventeen into E Troop, 2nd Reconnaissance Squadron, 163rd Armored Cavalry Regiment of the Montana Army National Guard.

Some hard times followed Lynn Maxfield's graduation from high school in 1963. For one, his father died. Next, he ran out of the money he had saved up after only a year at college and found himself in an unsatisfying job. Maxfield married in 1965, the same year he was commissioned a second lieutenant through National Guard OCS, but in April of '67, his young bride was killed in a car accident at Fort Knox, where Maxfield was attending the armor basic class. Soon thereafter, Maxfield, sick of his job, went on active duty with the intention of making a career in the army. Lieutenant Maxfield served originally with the 69th Armor at Fort Benning, where he earned efficiency reports marking him as a real hard-charger, and signed the paperwork to volunteer for Việt Nam.

Lieutenant Maxfield joined the dragoons in early July 1968 and, assigned to B Troop, impressed Captain Lewis as an "excellent" platoon leader. Now, it was true that Maxfield had been written up on August 15 when he and a regular army staff sergeant were caught drinking beer in an off-limits brothel in the shantytown adjacent Hill 29; warned to leave by the MPs, the pair was still there when the military police returned thirty minutes later. No matter, for on August 20, Maxfield won a Bronze Star when he dismounted with his infantry squad to pursue a group of Vietnamese who ran into a wooded area: ducking sniper fire, the squad claimed a prisoner and was returning to the tracks when three automatic weapons opened up, whereupon Maxfield led his riflemen in an attack on the VC. The enemy dispersed, and Maxfield reported finding a blood trail. Next, Maxfield earned two Purple Hearts during the Battle of Tam Kỳ.

Ironically, the medals were approved and awarded while Lieutenant Maxfield was sweating out the investigation that led to his first court-martial. In any event, the details of Maxfield's combat service were provided the jurors at the second court-martial, as was a letter sent by the first sergeant who had known the defendant in the Boy Scouts and National Guard. "[Maxfield's] character, his morals, and his dedication were of a nature to convince me that he is not capable of participating in any act of an unsavory nature," the first sergeant wrote. "That he would be a party of an act that would discredit his uniform is inconceivable."

Disagreeing, the jury at the second court-martial found Lieutenant Maxfield as guilty as the first, and he was returned to Fort Leavenworth.

Lynn Maxfield was paroled on March 4, 1970.

First Sergeant Williams—the former dragoon captured in the Hiệp Đức Valley shortly before Tết—died on or about September 18, 1968, in a miserable little guerrilla camp deep in the mountains west of Tam Kỳ. Of the handful of prisoners in the camp, a third of them—seven—were to die of disease and malnutrition. Williams and one of the men who had been captured with him, Cannon, also suffered from untreated wounds and were the first of the group to end up in unmarked jungle graves. By the time Williams died, the magnificent old soldier's spirit had long since been extinguished by the Việt Cộng.

The first sergeant, an old man among the prisoners at age forty-one, was a natural leader, big as a bull, but fatherly in attitude. One ex-prisoner would remember Williams as "the most influential man in camp," adding that "[w]henever someone had a question, they went to him."

The camp cadre wanted no leaders among the prisoners. Leaders might keep their spirits up, keep them from signing the propaganda statements the communists considered so important, keep them from defecting, as had one marine in the camp, an amoral, determined-to-survive-at-all-costs young private named Robert Garwood. As such, the cadre singled Williams out for harassment and criticism during the indoctrination classes the prisoners were forced to attend. Williams might have better withstood the onslaught had his fellow Americans not also participated. Uneasy about doing their captors' bidding, most of the prisoners softened the verbal blows they were ordered to direct at their leader. Not Garwood. "You have come here to kill innocent Vietnamese people, Williams," Garwood barked with real venom. "You think you know more than everybody else. I've always hated you. I spit on you, Williams!"

Finally, First Sergeant Williams was hauled into the camp commander's hootch, where he was ordered to write an apology for his sins. "At first, he wouldn't put in the strong stuff they wanted," recalls another ex-prisoner. "They made him write it thirty times. They hit his wounded hand, held a gun to his head, and threatened to shoot him."

Williams cracked. His strong baritone reduced to a squeak, the first sergeant stood in front of the next class and meekly apologized to the National Liberation Front. "He looked very old," recalls Dave Harker. "Old and tired. He had a runny nose and seemed as helpless as a little child. I remembered how he had kept fighting after he was wounded, how he pulled us through those first days after our capture. I hated the VC."

From then on, the first sergeant wrote whatever the communists wanted in exchange for the cigarettes he craved. Without Williams, an ex-boxer private who had no qualms about using his fists to impose his will, gradually emerged as the new decision-maker. The ex-boxer decided that the strong had no obligation to the weak, and that even the sickest prisoners would be responsible for gathering their own manioc—a starchy tuber—from the jungle and cooking their own rice. To make matters worse, a skin disease spread among the Americans. "The epidermis cracked open with water-blister-type sores that first ran clear serum and then pus," remembers Harker. "Scratching was almost sexual in its relief but only made the disease worse. The pus dried, gluing our pajamas to our backsides. The pain was horrible." Harker notes that at night, all the prisoners would be jammed together in their single rat-infested hut. "It was excruciatingly hot, but we had to sleep under our blankets to ward off hordes of mosquitoes. Men cried out at night, 'Kill me, I want to die!'" Harker adds, "[g]uys began to schiz out in the daytime by pulling blankets over their heads to shut out the world. The [skin] disease was combined with our growing dysentery and malaria. [Because men did not have the strength to reach the latrine,] the hootch smelled like a septic tank."

Cannon died first, after slipping into a coma. At that time, First Sergeant Williams "had a bad case of edema," notes an ex-prisoner. "The fluid had *swollen his testicles to three times their normal size, they were unreal, watery looking. His legs and stomach were swollen [too], and the fluid had begun to press toward his heart." There was an army doctor among the prisoners, Capt. Floyd Kushner, captured after his helicopter crashed into a mountainside. "If Kushner had had the simple diuretics available in any pharmacy, he could have saved his life," the ex-prisoner continues. "It was especially hard on him watching men die whom he knew he could save if medicines were available. But nothing was available, or if it was, the VC waited as usual until it was too late." Williams had become so weak that the ex-boxer had to carry him to the latrine, and other prisoners had to wash him, before the VC provided a can of condensed milk. "Kushner warned him not to drink it without diluting it because it was too sweet in concentrated form and would complicate his dysentery. By this time, however, Williams was practically incoherent. He drank it straight. One morning, several weeks after Cannon died, we awoke to hear Williams breathing strangely. In a couple of hours, he was dead."*

The deaths continued, one by one . . .

A week after returning to base camp from Quảng Ngãi City, Captain Albers noted in his journal that a "VC tried to booby trap our perimeter this afternoon—mine went off & blew a hole in his guts—[he was taken prisoner and] came in [to the aid station] with peritonitis—lived in the village next door[,] too."

The next major action, the battle of Núi Yon, was named for a hill mass on the south side of Route 533 eight kilometers out of Tam Kỳ, near the mouth of the valley leading to Tiên Phước. The hill mass, a chunk removed from the high ground to the south and west, rose from rice paddies flooded at the time by the monsoon rains. "Our mission was to conduct a tactical movement into a particular area near Núi Yon, and gain contact if an enemy was present," notes Lawrence. "As it turned out, we ran into a whole mess of NVA."

First contact was made by a platoon from B Troop on September 24. Foul weather notwithstanding, Lawrence and Logan directed air strikes from the command ship, after which the platoon launched an assault on the hill mass, only to lose a track to an RPG. Several troopers were wounded, one killed. Lawrence pulled the platoon back as the track burned—the dead man on board would be recovered the next day—and ordered the rest of B Troop to the area, along with Captain Kaczor and A Troop, aboard whose vehicles rode Capt. Barry D. Gasdek's D/4-21 Infantry of the 11th Light Infantry Brigade.

More air strikes were called in as the rains allowed, and a second assault was launched with A Troop pressing into the wooded fringes of the hill mass from the north, B Troop from the south. "We couldn't make a dent in 'em," recalls Kaczor, who lost three tracks to RPGs. "We'd get into the wool, make heavy contact, then back up, call in more TAC air, and hit 'em again from a different side. I had all three platoons spread out, trying to find a weak spot in the enemy's defenses, but they were very well dug in, and we just couldn't break into 'em."

Captain Kaczor was superficially wounded. Likewise, Captain Gasdek sported a bandaged leg as he dragged a wounded infantryman to the safety of a track across a hundred meters of wet paddy. As the melee continued, both of Gasdek's radiomen also became casualties, and the big, hard-driving commander of Company D ended up fighting the battle with one of the radios strapped on his own back. "The infantry went right in with us," recalls Kaczor, "because it was so thick in there, you needed protection right alongside your tracks so you didn't have somebody pop out of a hole you couldn't see and hit you with an RPG."

The weather made a mess of things. "I remember one tank in mud all the way up to its sponsons still blazing away at a hillside," writes Logan; with gunships and the command ship sometimes chased from the sky by heavy rain, he recalls Núi Yon as a "confusing, disjointed, and unsatisfying engagement." To make matters worse, Lawrence recalls that some enemy soldiers "had strapped themselves into trees, armed with RPGs. As we moved in, they were shooting down at us from the trees, and it was hard to elevate our .50-cal MGs to get at them. Instead, we were shooting with rifles, and even pistols, from the closest tracks, while vehicles at a distance trained their fires on the NVA above and away from them. It was touch and go for a moment, but the troopers stood their ground and killed almost everyone in the trees."

The squadron pulled back as darkness approached, set up a laager near Route 533, and, with one dragoon dead and thirty-one grunts and dragoons wounded, reported a seemingly exaggerated enemy body count of eighty-eight, to include those credited to the Blue Ghosts. The mood at ground zero was grim. "[T]hey kicked our ass today," Captain Albers confided to his journal. Memories are not perfect with regard to timing, but it was probably at the end of the first sour day of the battle that Captain Kaczor, while getting reorganized and resupplied—the troop was low on fuel and almost completely out of ammo—came upon an officer from another troop who was "cowering in his track. He just couldn't function. Things like that happen sometimes. His troop had gotten all shot to hell, and when I found him, he was in the fetal position at the bottom of his track. He was completely ineffective. I don't think he went to the field again."

It rained all night and was still raining on the gray morning of September 26 as A Troop and D/4-21 once again advanced on the wooded fringe of the hill mass from the south, while B Troop and two companies from the 1st of the 52nd Infantry moved in from the north. Despite prep fires, a rocket-propelled grenade nailed another one of Captain Kaczor's tracks as the assault line neared the wool. Kaczor called in more air strikes—the jets screamed through green tracers from a .51-cal—then swung to the right and pressed forward again, finally making it into the wool. "Once we broke into 'em, and got 'em disorganized, then we started takin' 'em apart piece by piece," notes Kaczor. The troop commander's track presently started up a slight incline. "I was just trying to pull up to a place where I could get a little high ground, and kind of see what the hell was going on around me," recalls Kaczor, who was still short of the crest when "all of a sudden, an RPG flew up over my head, hit the tree above me, and detonated, and I got splattered with frags. I caught a couple big pieces in my shoulder and arm. Thank God the guy with the RPG launcher fired high, *and* missed me and missed the ACAV."

Captain Kaczor picked up two more Purple Hearts at Núi Yon, as well as another Silver Star, cited, among other things, for personally "engag[ing] an enemy anti-tank team, killing four insurgents," as well as "refus[ing] evacuation and remain[ing] in command until the objective was secured." Kaczor's memory mirrors the citation: bandaged up, he stayed with his cavalrymen until the battle was over. On the other hand, Lieutenant Jackson recalls Kaczor getting him on the horn after being wounded the second time—"I'm being evacuated, *you got it.*"—and the senior platoon leader's own Silver Star for Núi Yon credits him with taking command of A Troop. Whatever the exact timing, Kaczor's evacuation was dramatic. "We were right overhead when [Kaczor was wounded], so we decided to use the C&C to dust him off," recounts Logan. "As if on cue, Helix 12, our forward air controller, came up on the net to tell us he had a Phantom with iron bombs to help keep the bad guys' heads down while we went in. This sounded like a good idea to us, so we told him to have at it." However, the Phantom did not release iron bombs but instead dropped a cluster bomb that exploded in a whirlwind of screaming pellets "directly in front of A Troop," continues Logan, "and close enough to the C&C to make us wonder if we would survive the Air Force's attempt at helping us. [The cluster bomb] did keep the NVA down while we went in and got Kaczor out... Since it was the fourth or fifth time he had been wounded, we offered him the job of assistant operations officer on the spot. He accepted."

Captain Gasdek banged on the side of Lieutenant Jackson's track and, holding up a loaded RPG launcher, shouted, "How do I disarm this thing?"

"Hell, I don't know! Just point it at the next enemy position and pull the trigger: that's the only way I know how to unload the damn thing!"

Captain Gasdek fired the RPG, then, despite a shrapnel wound in his back to go with his previous leg injury, aggressively led Company D through the bunker complex, earning the Distinguished Service Cross. "We would run over the enemy positions," recalls Jackson, "and the infantry would grenade all the spider holes and trenches to make sure that somebody wasn't going to pop up behind us." The grunts, three of whom were killed, eliminated numerous enemy soldiers at eyeball-to-eyeball range because "the NVA were pretty much holding their ground as we went through 'em," continues Jackson. "There was a bunch of 'em there, they were well dug in, and we were fighting pretty hard to eliminate 'em."

Two enemy soldiers, buried by a bomb blast, were captured when someone noticed a hand sticking out from the dirt. Unearthed, one of the NVA held up his fingers in the peace sign, begging for mercy. "They weren't coherent," recalls Jackson. "We evacuated them immediately." At some point in the action, Doc Johnston dismounted with their ARVN interpreter and, using his medic scissors, snipped enemy commo wire running across the ground. Something suddenly exploded, knocking both down. "The interpreter had a bunch of frag wounds in the leg, but he wasn't hurt bad: he was limpin' around." Johnston himself discovered a small shrapnel hole in his back. "The frag hit me square in the right shoulder blade. In fact, it cracked my shoulder blade, and damaged the muscle so I couldn't move my arm away from my body." The telegram sent to Johnston's parents indicated an RPG had wounded their son. The medic wasn't so sure. "The Blue Ghosts had spotted some dinks with AK-47s right around us, and made a rocket run through the area, and the fact of the matter is that the explosion might have been a rocket from one of the choppers. In any event, I wasn't in any pain, but I couldn't move my arm, which meant I was going to get out of the field, so I was kind of in a good mood."

Even as the last of the enemy in the wool were being eliminated, more revealed themselves to be occupying a circular island to the south by unleashing a barrage of rocket-propelled grenades. In response, Lawrence diverted air strikes onto the island, then brought B Troop and the 1st of the 52nd Infantry—which had secured the high ground without major incident—into position alongside A Troop to support an attack across the paddies by Company D. The tracks were at the edge of the woods, firing on the circular island, when a B-57 Canberra "came in low and dropped a 750-pound bomb," recounts Jackson. "There was a huge explosion, and the next thing I know, there was a great big *wham* on the front of my vehicle—the track actually shook—and I was covered with dirt." Thinking they had been hit by an RPG, Jackson realized instead that a chunk of dirt four feet in diameter, and weighing some fifty pounds, had been heaved across the paddies to land on his ACAV. "No one was hurt, but we were sure scared."

The infantry advanced while the dragoons provided supporting fire from the high ground, but the air strikes had done the job: the enemy had fled, leaving numerous bodies among the craters and upturned earth. "As I walked the area," writes Lawrence, "it looked like a moonscape, there was such destruction."

The prisoners taken at Núi Yon identified themselves as members of the 1st VC Main Force Regiment of the 2nd NVA Division and explained that their battalion had been providing a rear guard as the rest of the regiment slipped back into the mountains at the end of the Third General Offensive. The dragoons claimed a body count of 296 but reported capturing only seventeen weapons. In any event, Lawrence proudly submitted the 1-1 Cavalry for a Presidential Unit Citation for its heroic performance during the battles of Tam Kỳ, Quảng Ngãi, and Núi Yon. B Troop had already been included in the Presidential Unit Citation awarded the 2-12 Cavalry for the traumatic Quế Sơn Valley action, and the entire squadron had earned a Presidential Unit Citation of its own for Tết and the Tết Counteroffensive. As for the battles of the Third General Offensive, the 1-1 Cavalry eventually received a second-place Valorous Unit Award instead of another Presidential Unit Citation.

A Dull, Gray Time

OCTOBER–NOVEMBER 1968

THE FULL FURY OF the monsoon descended upon the dragoons on October 9. "It rained torrents for nine straight days," notes Lawrence. "Trafficability was miserable, particularly for armor. We reconfigured the squadron until the rains subsided, putting the tanks in temporary platoons to act as limited-mobility fire support for the lighter tracks that could still move around the soaked terrain. We thus continued to operate, albeit in a more limited fashion." The rains seemed to dampen enemy activities, too. "Our AO was as quiet as it had ever been since I took command," adds Lawrence, although "reports did begin to filter in again about a new threat to Quảng Ngãi City. We kept an eye on that because we felt sure that if the city was threatened, we would get the call."

From Captain Albers' journal:

The day has been a study in tedium—the rain unrelenting . . .

Ho, ho, the mildew season is here. Rained all night & all day again—the [aid-station] bunker is a sieve—walls beginning to cave in on medics bunker. Promises to be a joyful winter . . .

Bravo troop hit a mine west of Hill 74 [on October 18]—one killed & 3 wounded . . . Had a firefight outside the Vil[le] during med cap (Tu Cam) but our security drove them off . . .

> Couldn't sleep last night—had a mouse in my bed & he's been stealing & caching my crackers...
>
> Trooper shot himself in the leg today [October 21]—received an AR 15 [Article 15 non-judicial punishment, in lieu of a court-martial] on the pad while waiting for dust off. The Army sucks. I'm ready to chuck it.

There were better ways to escape the misery than putting a hole through one's leg and losing a stripe. For those so inclined, there were drugs—"[m]ore morphine stolen from A Troop," Albers wrote—and, more fashionably, booze. At the end of another gray, rain-soaked day, Albers wrote that "Albers, Venn, Del Judice, Reyer, Stenger, Hall, Sowards all drunk as skunks."

Lieutenant Jackson would later recall returning to his sleeping bunker from the officers club after having a few too many martinis. "The alert siren sounded about 0100, and I was still feeling no pain," he writes. "I pulled on my boots, but did not lace them, and my flak jacket, grabbed a helmet, and headed for my ACAV. I didn't even bother to put on my trousers, just my undershorts. About halfway to my track, I felt on my head, and suddenly realized that I had picked up the wrong helmet. There I was, running around, still blitzed, in my shorts and floppy boots, .45 in my hand, and an NVA pith helmet on my head. I must have looked like an NVA sapper, and it's a wonder I didn't get shot."

Lawrence had already conducted a reconnaissance and assured General Gettys that armor could operate in the sodden terrain west of Quảng Ngãi City, when the division commander called on the secure net on October 27 and ordered the 1-1 Cav to once again shield the province capital from an anticipated attack by the 3rd NVA Division. At the time, "we had all new troop commanders," notes Jim Logan, who'd recently been promoted to major, "and we figured if nothing else, [the defense of Quảng Ngãi City] would be a good shakedown for them."

Captain Albers described the mount-up in his journal:

> Whoops—got word at 1600 hrs that we're moving to Quang Ngai at 1700. Hurry up and collect my stuff and on the road at the appointed time. 5 hour drive over a washed out road [Highway 1] and the rain

coming down . . . NVA supposed to have a big push because of our elections. It's kind of spooky and sad to enter a beleaguered city at night. The streets were lined by silent and watchful people; each house had a kerosene lamp burning on its door step to provide some light for the defenders if Charlie got in. Passed under an ancient, gnarled tree and I felt vulnerable and insignificant—how many wars had that tree lived through?

The squadron laagered in an ARVN outpost, where a trooper was wounded, noted Albers, when a track "rolled up some barbed wire on the road which had a booby trap in it." Albers "[s]lept fitfully in a lawn chair I had brought along." Moving on at dawn on October 28, Albers noted that the dragoons set up their command post in the ruined Buddhist cemetery occupied the first time the squadron saved Quảng Ngãi City: "Spent a quiet day—no action—just getting ready to start S&D missions to flush out Charlie before he gets set up."

One mission that first day was of some psychological importance. "On a hilltop overlooking the area, and visible to many villages in the area, a VC flag flew from a high pole," explains Lawrence. "The flag had been placed there by the VC in defiance of the government to show that the area was under communist control. A Troop assaulted the hill under concentrated fire to seize the top and capture the flag. It was torn and shot up, and everyone in the vicinity was put on notice that there was a new sheriff in town."

After a miserable night of rain and mosquitoes, "the troops had just started out when one of our Blue Ghost choppers was shot down about 300 meters off our northern perimeter," Albers wrote on October 29. Since squadron headquarters was closer to the crash site than the line troops, Lieutenant Colonel Lawrence and Sergeant Major Ogas "grabbed two security ACAVs from our CP and went to get the downed pilots," writes Lawrence. "It was unknown territory for us, and there were enemy in the area, but we went in quickly, at least until stopped by a stream that was fairly wide and of unknown depth. Could we ford it? What was waiting on the other shore to shoot us when we got in the water?" In response, "Max Ogas was his usual fearless, taciturn self," notes Lawrence; without even pausing to ask permission, the sergeant major "jumped off the ACAV and into the water with his M16 to recon the opposite shore. Ogas was able to wade at chest level, and got across with us ready to rake the opposite shore with .50-cal MG fire if he took fire. Ogas conducted a quick recon, gave an all clear, and we raced across. When we got to the pilots, two helicopters were in the area for pickup. We let them go in under our over watch and pick up the pilots."

The area from which the fire came "received a good pounding with Redleg [artillery] and I could actually see the rounds passing over our position," wrote Albers. "The troops moved in then[,] but no Charlie." General Gettys arrived after lunch, continued Albers, as did both assistant division commanders—"[h]elicopters like to blow us away as they land & take off"—plus "beaucoup Cols[,] including Division Surgeon with his usual inanity. The command post came under sniper fire, and "Pat [Stenger] went on night patrol in the driving rain to check out the area from which the sniper fire came—they succeeded in getting thoroughly wet and blowing up an old [rice] pan with a grenade."

The operation dragged on without solid contact, though not without casualties, as recorded in Albers' journal:

> [While operating to either side of a wooded island,] Alpha and Bravo troop shot up each other today [October 31]. Col is pissed off. Casualties amounted to 3 soldiers with minor wounds. Couple of [new and inexperienced] troop commanders are going to get their ass chewed . . .
>
> First KIA today [November 6]—troops out all day without any contact—then coming in tonight received AK-47 sniper fire—sgt wounded in leg [with] fx [fractured] femur; trooper shot thru heart and died immediately. Sort of put a damper on everybodies [*sic*] day.

While the enemy proved elusive, the locals did not, flocking greedily to the command post, as described by Albers:

> Seems there was a whore on the hill last night—made between $125-300[,] but Awful Alpha robbed her pimp and threw them off the hill!!! . . .

Chapl[a]in discovered another whorehouse today while preparing to hold services for the troops . . . We told him he should have gotten in line just to see what the troops would do . . .

Gooks have been stealing us blind—basins, letters, shoes, equipment. Some of our guys have been retaliating by pouring garbage on them, beating them up, etc.

At its conclusion, Albers described the second trip south as "a frustrating, unproductive, irritable operation. No contact—officers all at each other[']s throats." Albers added that their senior NCO was actually "an ass profiterring [sic] on beer & soda[,] and has his finger in everybodies [sic] pie."

Frustrations were many. For one, the ARVN proved a nearly invisible ally, notes Lawrence, content to once again let U.S. troops carry the burden in the field. In addition, a tour of dirty, impoverished Quảng Ngãi City by Lawrence and his staff on November 7 left them a little raw. The MACV compound was "all whitewashed concrete buildings," Albers noted, with "a nice PX, library, church, hot showers, flush toilets, and even a handball court. War is really rough." Even rougher, noted Albers, were the accommodations of the province chief: "The Vietnamese general has a sprawling pagoda type house [with] formal gardens, beautiful lawns[, plus] regal peacocks and a tennis court."

Finally, word came that the squadron was going "Home to Hawk Hill!!!" as Albers jotted in his journal on November 8. "Had last guard so up early and had aid station all policed when call came over the radio for all troops to return to their [units] & be ready to move out by 1300. We were ready[,] believe me. Got everything loaded up and were sitting by the gate when a wrecker came roaring by and hit a Vietnamese on a bike." The man suffered a fractured femur "and probable cerebral laceration—had to give M-M [mouth to mouth resuscitation]—finally got him dusted off & we were on our way." The squadron had hardly departed Quảng Ngãi City, but "one of the towed tracks broke its cable[,] plowing off the road and into a hoo[t] ch[,] breaking a woman's leg. Then outside Chu Lai," continued Albers, "the 577 in front of us swerved off the road and hit a man," producing head and internal injuries. "Just about home when we received small arms fire and 2 guys fell off a track—both were drunk. Lt. Venn had steaks & beer [waiting] for us [upon finally reaching Hawk Hill]."

§

Major Logan wrote home on November 10 of the news received shortly before departing Quảng Ngãi City that Richard Nixon, narrowly embraced by his so-called Silent Majority, had been elected on a platform of Law and Order and Peace with Honor in Việt Nam. "Well[,] we have our republican president," jotted Logan. "Fine by me. We listened to it in the field. We even had a bottle of champagne to [open] with the election night returns. Last time we were in Quang Ngai in September[,] we had a bottle of Champagne and Charlie shot at us. This time he must have been listening to the radio[,] too[,] because he left us alone." Noting the recent bombing halt of North Việt Nam declared by the outgoing Johnson, Logan added, "it appears that a cease fire is close at hand. I hope not. We have been watching closely[,] and the VC/NVA are getting all set up for it . . . [W]hen they feel the time is right[,] they will go for a cease fire and the next thing will be that they control 75% of the country. They are busy as bees moving in cadre and little committees in all the villages. When a cease fire is agreed on," Logan continued, "they will most likely demand that everything remain as is[,] and [they] will have ready made governments in all the villages. So[,] we have to dispose of all these little groups before we agree to a cease fire or everything we have fought for goes down the drain."

Operation Daring Endeavor

NOVEMBER 10–20, 1968

ON NOVEMBER 10, TWO platoons from B Troop, reinforced by C/2-1 Infantry, assumed blocking positions at the north end of Barrier Island while a battalion landing team—the 2nd Battalion, 7th Marines of the 1st Marine Division—helicoptered ashore from U.S. Navy ships in the South China Sea. The cordon-and-search operation was codenamed Daring Endeavor. Unlike the army grunts with whom the dragoons had worked in the same general area two months before, the marines came on strong, "moving inland, systematically searching the area, and looking for VC," writes Lawrence. "I believe we kept a tight cordon, even at night, although some VC probably did get by us. The marines did make contact, and find stores and bunkers. The fighting was not prolonged. The VC were moving around, looking for a way out, but fighting if cornered."

Lawrence had choppered into the marine command post to coordinate with his counterpart on November 12 when the most intense firefight of the operation took place. The two lieutenant colonels were talking when "suddenly, behind us," writes Lawrence, "a corrugated tin cover buried lightly in the sand almost right in the middle of the CP flew in the air—and three VC, wearing loin cloths, and throwing grenades, jumped out of their bunker and ran for the perimeter." The grenades killed one marine. Even as the guerrillas who had spent the night quietly trapped among the marines made a break for it—and Lawrence could not recall if they made it or not—other VC who had crept in close "opened up with heavy rifle and machine-gun fire. The two actions may have been coincidence. Later, we found no evidence of any commo between the VC inside and those outside the perimeter. In any event, we all ran for the perimeter and jumped in a shallow ditch to return fire as best we could."

First Lieutenant Henry Susak—former dragoon platoon leader—was also in the ditch, having been attached to the marines as a liaison officer. "Susak was a great character," notes Logan, "and the best scrounger in the squadron. He had been born in Poland, and escaped from behind the Iron Curtain by going over the Berlin Wall." Lawrence recalls that Susak settled in New York City, where he acquired a wise-cracking persona, and that the sharp young lieutenant was "a hell of a brave and committed officer even though not Regular Army."

Lawrence used Susak's radio to summon the Blue Ghost commander, but "when he arrived," notes Lawrence, "he could not see our lines because of the heavy foliage in some spots, and was afraid to make any firing passes for fear of hitting us instead of the VC. He could see some VC running around, but could not get a fix on our position, and asked for smoke to mark our line so he could go to work." Lawrence asked his counterpart for smoke grenades and was stunned when the lieutenant colonel answered that he had none, such were the supply problems of the overtaxed, stretched-thin marines in Việt Nam.

Susak chimed in: he had smoke grenades in the little tent he'd rigged in the center of the CP. "Okay," replied Lawrence, "let's go get 'em."

Lawrence writes that he and Susak "took off running in a crouch with bullets whizzing past. At his tent, we loaded our hands full with smoke grenades, and started back. About ten yards from the ditch, I heard a low moan, and looked back: Susak had been hit in the leg, and had fallen forward, dropping his smoke grenades." Amid the continuing fire, Lawrence threw his own smokes into the ditch and then grabbed Susak's collar, pulled him into the ditch, and ripped open his bloody trouser leg to examine the wound. "Susak had a clean shot in his calf," notes Lawrence. "It was the perfect wound: no bone or artery hit, and a hole so clean I could stick my finger through it. I quickly patched him up, and we passed out the smoke grenades to the marines to mark our positions."

The gunships silenced most of the enemy, soon after which General Gettys attempted to land in the marine command post. Unable to warn the division commander or his pilots by radio that the command post was still receiving sporadic fire, Lawrence notes that "we tried to wave them off, but they did not see or understand. I finally jumped up and ran along the ditch, frantically waving. They were about fifteen feet from touching down when they got the message and quickly ascended." The situation soon calmed enough to allow the general to land, followed by medevacs from the ships offshore. "I helped put Susak on one of them," writes Lawrence. "He was in some pain, but being well taken care of by navy corpsmen. I later went to the hospital to see him. He was doing well, and on his way to Japan with his ticket home."

B Troop ran into more enemy that evening: a mine killed one trooper and wounded eight dragoons and marines, then a recoilless-rifle round through a track saw five more dragoons being lifted out aboard a medevac.

Contact dwindled thereafter, and Lawrence left on R&R pursuant to being reassigned to division headquarters. "Fred Filbert and I managed to take care of business," writes Logan, "without getting into too much trouble."

Before the mission folded up on its tenth day, the marines reported killing thirty-nine guerrillas and capturing thirty. According to the official marine history of the war, Battalion Landing Team 2-7 conducted no civic action during Operation Daring Endeavor because the population of Barrier Island was "considered to be hostile[,] and hard line psy ops [psychological operations] was used [instead]."

Specialists Fourth Class Joe Knopic and Nathan Hale, prisoner-of-war interrogators from division who often worked with the dragoons, were witness to the "hard line" methods used during Operation Daring Endeavor. Though both saw the same things, their interpretations differed. While Knopic was always to remain hawkish and stress that actionable intelligence needed to be obtained by whatever means necessary to save lives, his friend Hale—both were blue-collar guys from rural Pennsylvania—would later join the Vietnam Veterans Against the War and make public the brutal slides he'd taken on Barrier Island. "This is a group of detainees being brought in," Hale told the audience of the Winter Soldier Investigation in

1971. "This [next slide] just shows a typical Vietnamese who was bound. The ropes are really super-tight, and the idea is to make the prisoner or detainee as uncomfortable as possible."

The actual interrogations were carried out by members of the paramilitary Vietnamese National Field Police, supervised, said Hale, by a marine warrant officer. "At all times during these interrogations, there were officers present," said Hale. "At one time, there was a lieutenant colonel present."

The Field Police were infamous for their brutality, and as they worked over the detainees, said Hale, clicking to another slide, "These are all the marines sitting around, giving the various cheers." Hale was sitting in the sand, drying his boots and socks over a little fire, when one of the Field Police "came over, and put a tin spoon—it's a Vietnamese spoon, it's shaped like a scoop [with a flat bottom]—and he put it in my fire." When the spoon was scorching hot, the Field Police "grabbed my sock, wrapped it around [the handle], and [as can be seen in the next slide] he's burning the skin off of the back of [a detainee's] neck." Next slide. "This is after he burned his neck. The man's still not giving the correct information." Next slide. "And, finally, the man, in fear of his life, admitted that at one time he had given tax to the VC[.]"

Though offering no photographic evidence, both Knopic and Hale stated that the Field Police separated two military-age males from the rest of the detainees and, claiming them as confirmed VC, strung rope around their necks and hung them from a tree until dead. "[T]he marines used a lot of CS on this particular operation," continued Hale, showing a slide of a middle-aged Vietnamese in black pajamas, face and clothes discolored by the residue of smoke and tear-gas canisters. "[T]his particular man wouldn't come out of the hole [he was hiding in], and they threw two CS grenades at him [plus smoke grenades]." Neither tear-gas nor smoke was designed to be lethal, but in this instance, claimed Hale, the detainee's lungs were so polluted that he could not regain normal breathing. "I personally escorted this man back to division, and he died. So, if [tear] gas doesn't kill, I don't know what killed [the prisoner]." Knopic shed no tears himself, noting that any Vietnamese who refused to budge from his hiding place essentially confirmed his status as an enemy combatant: "That older guy was definitely hardcore. If I'm not mistaken, he was actually NVA."

§

Regarding interrogations, Nathan Hale told a reporter after his testimony at the Winter Soldier Investigation that "I preferred the friendly approach of giving prisoners cigarettes to gain their friendship. Whether or not I got brutal depended on how cooperative they were." Having turned against the war about halfway through his tour, Hale says that he was still willing to physically abuse prisoners for information because he was "afraid of being busted for not performing my job. This was my main motivation at the time. But while I was doing it, I thought I was wrong, that I was betraying myself."

According to Hale, the first time he was sent to Hill 29 to assist the dragoons, the S2 of the 1-1 Cav informed him that he could use any means possible to illicit information from prisoners, so long as he didn't get caught. "What he meant was I could beat these people, I could cut 'em," Hale testified at the Winter Soldier Investigation, but just not "in the presence of a non-unit member . . . That's someone like a visiting officer, or perhaps the Red Cross[.]" Hale added that as an interrogator, he was always monitored by the military police, who were to ensure that prisoners were treated according to the Geneva Conventions. Hale's testimony gave the impression that the rear-echelon MPs at Chu Lai went by the book but that despite their over-watch, "this doesn't mean you can't kick prisoners under the table. We used to take knives into the interrogation huts, and use the guy's hands as a means of terror."

Hale further gave the impression that the field MPs at Hill 29 had a sterner attitude about captured VC. "I was monitored by an MP sergeant at Hill 29," stated Hale, "who often helped me in my interrogations—he and his squad . . . I personally used clubs, rifle butts, pistols, [and] knives, and this was always done at Hill 29." According to Hale, there was a see-no-evil-hear-no-evil-speak-no-evil attitude about interrogations up the chain of command. In one incident at Hill 29, Hale stopped a number of ARVN who were savagely kicking a prisoner during an interrogation. When the prisoner died the next morning from his injuries, Hale stated that the S2 of the 1-1 Cav, "instead of going through the necessary paperwork, had [the dead Vietnamese] put in a large rice sack, and the troops took him out that day and dumped him [in the field]. He was added to the previous day's body count [as if killed in combat]."

§

Joe Knopic always considered Nathan Hale's testimony during his days as an anti-war veteran a bit over the top. For one, he doubted that a decent, intelligent guy like Hale really bashed prisoners with the butt of his .45, or plied a knife between a prisoner's splayed fingers. "I think the worst Nate ever did," opines Knopic, "is smack a prisoner on the back of his head to keep him focused."

Knopic's own testimony on the subject is shaded in gray. On one hand, he emphasizes that however roughly prisoners might have been treated in the field—and many showed up well bruised—they were handled with kid gloves from the time they arrived at the interrogation center in Chu Lai until transferred to the permanent POW compound in Đà Nẵng. The Red Cross ensured that prisoners had regular meals, rest periods, etc., and were otherwise treated humanely. Knopic recalls that most of the prisoners across the desk from him in his plywood-and-screen interrogation cubicle—they usually ignored the chair and squatted on the floor, smoking the cigarettes and munching on the candy offered them—claimed they were innocent civilians who had been detained at random and beaten into confessing involvement with the VC. Those who admitted to being combatants insisted that they were privates who simply followed orders, knew nothing of their unit's plans, and were captured in their first firefight. In most cases, Knopic jotted these lies on his clipboard, wheedled a bit of intelligence from the more unwary, trusting, or weary among the prisoners, and had them returned to their cells without a hair out of place.

On the other hand, Knopic admits that he sometimes bent the rules to get a prisoner talking. They had information that could save American lives, and after seeing row upon row of wounded GIs in the hospital at Chu Lai, Knopic was determined to get whatever information he could from these captured VC. "You couldn't feel sorry for them," says Knopic, who recalls the hard cases to whom "you might take a field phone, and attach it to their genitals, and crank it a few times. There were a couple times that happened. I can testify to that. They weren't puppy dogs. They were taught to resist, and sometimes you had to get their attention. You couldn't always just give them M&Ms."

Despite calling "bullshit" on the systematic brutality Hale claimed took place at division headquarters, Knopic's own descriptions of field operations actually mirror his anti-war buddy's in detail, if not context. For example, Knopic recalls accompanying a patrol from the 1-1 Cav that had a wounded prisoner in tow who promised to lead them to a weapons cache. The prisoner was limping on his bandaged leg as the patrol filed down a dike. The prisoner's guard finally removed the rope leash around his neck to allow him to walk more comfortably, but when the guard turned to say something to another trooper, the supposedly disabled VC bound like a rabbit in the direction of a small hamlet about fifty meters away. "We went down there, and looked all over," says Knopic, "but couldn't find the guy. We had the Blue Ghosts hovering overhead. They tore the place up, but they couldn't find him, either." Given the complicity of the villagers in hiding the escaped guerrilla, the officer in charge of the patrol—"I don't want to put him on the spot, but I think it was the squadron S2"—decided some punishment was in order: "That night, they artillery'd the hell out of that ville." As an anti-war veteran, Hale would have decried the incident as a war crime. Not Knopic: "They were the enemy. We were always losing men to mines while walking down roads in populated areas, and it gets to the point where you say, dammit, let's just go through and teach 'em a lesson."

Along the same lines, Knopic recalls those times when he was sent to Hill 29 to assist the dragoons with interrogations, only to end up sitting in a lawn chair atop a bunker, reading magazines and working on his tan, because "a pilot had gotten shot in one of those little scout helicopters, and when that happened, there weren't going to be any prisoners coming back for me to interrogate. Everybody the Blue Ghosts saw for the next several days was going to be a KIA. If one of their own was killed or wounded, everybody they saw, they shot, whether they were innocent or not. That's just the way it was."

Regarding those cheerful, fearless, and bloodthirsty aviators, Knopic recalls, "there was a couple times that we delivered detainees back to their little villages, and I might just add that maybe the helicopter wasn't on the ground when they disembarked." Indeed, affirms Knopic, some of the detainees in question were shoved out at "high enough altitude to break 'em," which is to say kill them. "I remember one time, we took 'em out, and we dropped 'em off right outside their coastal village. Unfortunately, the pilot might have made a mistake, and he was above the ocean instead of the land. Hope they were good swimmers."

Finally, Joe Knopic discusses that minority of prisoners—the fanatically uncooperative and those so damaged during field interrogations "that you did not want them showing up at division where the Red Cross might ask questions"—who were turned over to the ARVN to keep them out of the system. "We'd turn 'em over, and our jeep probably wasn't out of the district chief's compound and they were already dead." And why not? The Vietnamese had picked their sides and fought a war without mercy against each other, explains Knopic: "The other side weren't altar boys. The district chief had a price on his head from the VC. It was a kill-or-be-killed situation. You couldn't just slap their wrist and let 'em go because they'd come back and kill you."

End of an Era

NOVEMBER–DECEMBER 1968

DURING LAWRENCE'S R&R, the squadron, like all units in the war zone, underwent its yearly Command Maintenance Management Inspection, at which time all records and equipment were to be examined just like the 1-1 Cav was back at Fort Hood. "It was a *peacetime* inspection," recalls Tom Jackson, then serving as executive officer of A Troop. "I mean, these guys flew in from the United States in fresh-pressed greens. It was ridiculous." In no mood for such "army chickenshit," Jackson recalls that when the CMMI team was about to land on Hill 29 in a CH-47 Chinook, the dragoons "initiated a Mad Minute and announced on the radio that we were taking incoming fire. The pilot pulled pitch, went up to about five thousand feet, and took off back to Chu Lai. General Gettys himself got on the squadron net the next day as the team flew back up, and informed us that 'There *will* be no incoming fire!'"

The dragoons greeted the spit-and-polish inspection team with icy contempt. "CMMI team with snotty [lieutenant colonel] was around inspecting today," Captain Albers jotted in his journal, "but he got nowhere with me."

Albers did have some fun during the inspection, though, as noted in a later entry: "Scared hell out of [A Troop's first sergeant] by mentioning his hiding [an unauthorized] water trailer in front of the CMMI people at lunch[!]"

As executive officer, Lieutenant Jackson was responsible for vehicle maintenance, and the inspection team wanted to see his logbooks.

"Well, they're over in this footlocker here."

"Lieutenant, these haven't been filled out every day."

"Well, no, sir, most of our vehicles don't last more than about three months before they're blown up, so we really don't bother with the log books."

"You're *required* to fill them out."

Jackson was also taken to task because many of the tank and track drivers did not actually have military-issue driver's licenses; they had arrived in-country without having earned them only to pick up the necessary skills in the field.

One of the inspectors disassembled an M60 on a scout track to check its cleanliness and operation, and was chagrined when the weapon's broken firing pin fell out in two pieces. The inspector said the weapon would have to be deadlined and turned over to the troop armorer for repair, "and my guy looked at him like he was nuts," recalls Jackson, "and said, 'You think I'm going out there without my machine gun!? We can't get extra firing pins, and if you put this one together real careful like this, it stays together and works just fine.'"

Lawrence had returned by the time the CMMI team finished its troop-by-troop, vehicle-by-vehicle inspection and, having failed the squadron, scheduled a debriefing in the officers club. "The lieutenant colonel in charge of the team stood up," recalls Jackson, "and looked at Lawrence, and started his briefing with, 'Colonel, we understand your problems'—and Lawrence stood up and said, 'That's your problem, you *don't* understand our problems, and I think you need to get the hell off my firebase now.' Lawrence didn't let the other lieutenant colonel debrief. He didn't let him do anything. He just sent him away. The inspection was after Tam Kỳ and Quảng Ngãi and Núi Yon," continues Jackson. "We had this combat record that was unbelievable—and they wanted us to deadline every one of our vehicles. It was very surrealistic, and we just kind of told 'em: 'Go away, we don't care what you have to say. The general's not going to stop using us because we didn't pass inspection, we're not going to stop fighting, so what you have to say has no bearing on anything.'"

§

The dragoons definitely considered themselves a breed apart. There was the evening, for example, that Lieutenants Ginz and Jackson crashed a party at the officers club of the 2nd Surgical Hospital. "We wanted to dance with some American girls," recalls Jackson, and since the Blue Ghosts often spoke of the wondrous nurses at Chu Lai, he and Ginz decided to see for themselves. When they showed up, there were numerous doctors and warrant-officer pilots already at the party. "We went in, and the doctors took exception to us crude, rude, and socially unacceptable cavalrymen dancing with their nurses," recalls Jackson. "They asked us to leave, and we allowed that if we had to leave, there wouldn't be anything left in the building, but they insisted that we leave—so we started throwing doctors and furniture out the windows and doors." By the time Ginz and Jackson jumped in their jeep, one step ahead of the military police, "every doctor and every piece of furniture that had been in the officers club was outside on the ground. Anyway, we did things like that. That was just part of the morale of the Cav: we were better than everybody else, and we knew it."

Lawrence had served almost five months on the line when General Gettys, highly impressed by his feats with the dragoons, selected the intense firebrand as his operations officer. Such was the most prestigious position on the division staff, and a plum for an officer on the fast track. Lawrence was, in fact, to retire with three stars, "and he earned every one of 'em," says Jackson. The squadron held a farewell party for Lawrence on November 24. "[S]everal nice speeches & introductions all around for the new people," wrote Albers. The party was interrupted when the phone rang, recalls Jackson, "and Lawrence all of a sudden got real serious—'yes, sir, yes, sir, we can be on the road in thirty minutes, sir'—it was Gettys on the line—and we were halfway out the door before Lawrence hung up and said, 'It's okay, guys, it was a joke.' Gettys knew we were having a going-away party, and was pretending he had one more mission for Lawrence." According to Albers' journal, the division commander actually let the dragoons sweat a little before dropping the punch line: "[G]ot a phone call [during the party] that we were on 10 min alert for Quang Gnai [sic] [again]. Was loading up the pig when we got mortared—put on flak vests & helmets & continued to load. Finished & then got a stand-down. Damn division anyway."

Lieutenant Colonel Bolté, senior advisor at Tam Kỳ and another academy graduate, arrived at Hill 29 on November 27, having extended his tour to get a command. Lawrence formally passed the squadron standard to Bolté on December 1. "Nice ceremony," wrote Albers, "[with] pass in review of [tracks], tanks & Blue Ghost."

Logan writes of Bolté's assumption of command: "We had worked well together while he was at Tam Kỳ, and like Lieutenant Colonel Lawrence, he was a thoroughly professional cavalryman. We never missed a beat."

During Bolté's first day in command, seven Alpha Troopers were wounded in two separate mine incidents. On the new commander's third day, Albers wrote: "[G]ot an emergency call from the TOC—one of their people had walked into the tail rotor of a helicop[t]er. Took off a piece of scalp & fractured his skull—nice way to begin the day. Sick call was brisk. Col Bolté came down for a briefing and stayed about 30 mins—had a nice chat & drank a cup of coffee."

Bolté was indeed a fine officer, but comments about a smooth transition aside, the squadron was actually in something of a funk at the time of the change of command. The rains had been endless, encounters with mines too frequent, enemy body counts—which were great for morale—too rare as the VC and NVA disappeared into the mountains to regroup after the Third General Offensive. Albers' journal notes from the beginning of December mention pent-up, overly aggressive young troopers acting out in their frustration:

> [U]p at 0730 this AM for a boy whose buddy had thrown a knife through his foot . . .
>
> [Treated] a troop who was in a [fist]fight & sustained a skull fracture and is blind!
>
> After lunch had to examine 2 Vietnamese females who had reportedly been raped by the Cav. The 16 y.o. had been raped[,] but the 18 y.o. managed to fight them off with multiple bruises & abrasions[,] but no permanent damage. Always some damn thing going on around here to upset me.

Albers also wrote that more morphine was stolen from his medical supplies and that he "[h]ad to have a father-son talk [with] one of my medics who has been smoking pot & frequenting the whore house."

On December 14, four days after the rains finally petered out, Captain Albers and one of his young Vietnamese medics were holding a medcap when combat casualties and frantic villagers began arriving from another hamlet in the vicinity. "Seems a helicopter had received some sniper rounds & proceeded to shoot the hell out of a vil[le]," Albers wrote. Whatever the fate of the enemy sniper, three villagers had been killed outright in the barrage of machine-gun and rocket fire. Albers carefully listed in his journal the wounded who were brought to him: a baby with fragment wounds in the back, a little girl with "legs peppered," an "old papasan" hit in his hands and forearms, an "old lady" with chest and hip wounds, a pregnant woman with wounds to her thorax, another pregnant woman whose chest had been ripped open, a comatose young woman with a hole in her skull, and, finally, a "[l]ittle girl [with] frag in brain [and] multiple frags of arms & amp[utation] of left leg at knee . . . For 4 hours we worked[,] resusitating, [sic] stopping bleeding, aspirating chest, etc.—finally got them all off to the hospital—all alive—probably half will die[,] but we did our best."

Albers was deeply shaken that the Blue Ghosts had wreaked such havoc over a few incoming rounds of small-arms fire: "[The w]ar has changed—lashing out blindly at innocents—how in hell can you win their hearts & minds?"

Days later, Albers—missing his family terribly as Christmas approached—vented on a wider scale: "[T]o hell with the Army and the war and all this other shit—may the time come when we don't need such things."

"Christmas in Vietnam," Albers wrote on December 25. "[S]o lonely." He opened the presents sent from home and "wrote some thank you notes, saw some more patients . . . [T]oo many drunks around today—I want to go home."

Luckily, Albers was scheduled to leave for R&R on December 30, planning to meet his beloved wife in Hawaii. The squadron sergeant major and operations sergeant met the doc on the helipad at Hill 29 to have a goodbye drink of scotch before he departed aboard a chopper for Chu Lai. There, Albers hooked up with several dragoon lieutenants and captains who were also taking leave, or otherwise had business in the rear, as well as Major Logan, whose tour was actually over and who was bound for the air base at Cam Ranh Bay. The whole gang of them sauntered into the officers club of one of the marine jet fighter squadrons at Chu Lai. "[G]ood show," wrote Albers, adding that after the dragoons imbibed a fair share of champagne, they "had to fight some Marines." After that, they went over to the officers club of their own division but "got thrown out," whereupon they stumbled back to the transit barracks where their gear was stashed and hit the sack. The next morning, Albers, who had recently received an accelerated promotion to major based on his prior experience as a civilian doctor, asked Logan for a set of his gold oak leaves to wear when he met his wife. Logan cheerfully gave him a set just before they boarded the C-130 that would ferry them to Cam Ranh Bay, where they would catch civilian airliners, Logan for the United States, Albers for a blessed week in Hawaii. The flight took fourteen hours, but Albers was "too excited to sleep."

The war that waited on the other side of the New Year would remain the same war—of mines, snipers, quick ambushes, and the occasional big battle—that the dragoons had fought under Harrington, Cousland, and Lawrence. In retrospect, though, Lawrence's departure marked the end of an era, for as the war dragged on in the months and years ahead, the sacrifices being demanded of the draftee troops would make increasingly less sense to those riding the tanks and tracks. Since the cultural divides of the home front blossomed in the war zone, too, there was to be less unity of purpose, less respect for authority, less willingness to die in a war the country had turned against. The nihilism and Wild West attitude toward the Vietnamese that had marked the squadron's first aggressive days in combat would eventually turn inward, until the ills of many units in the latter dog days of the war—heroin, fraggings, combat refusals—would also tarnish the proud reputation of the First Regiment of Dragoons.

Still, the courage of the individual trooper would never falter.

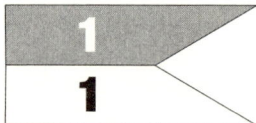

EPILOGUE

Home from War

Dick Albers

Returning from leave, Major Albers began running medcaps from an isolated outpost designated Fiddler's Green—named for that fabled place between heaven and hell where cavalrymen rendezvous after death—that had been built during Operation Hardin Falls. Conceived by Lawrence, and put into effect by Bolté, Hardin Falls was supposed to bring government control to the hamlets of Phước Âm village, located between Highway 1 and Barrier Island north of Hill 29, a safe haven to liberation fighters since the war with the French.

The intrusion was not well received. The dragoons, supported by militia troops, ran over mines and were harassed by snipers during their daylight patrols. At night, the communists mortared Fiddler's Green and fired on the position with AK-47s, RPGs, and a captured M79. One night, a guerrilla wiggled close enough through the concertina to take out a guard post with a grenade. Other nights, the guerrillas would shout to the cavalrymen from the dark: "We're gonna get you! We're gonna get you, GI!"

The medcaps were not immune. In one incident involving incoming mortar and automatic-weapons fire, Major Albers was compelled to draw a .45 himself and help return fire. In another, the Huey dispatched to pick up the surgeon's team came under heavy fire upon landing at Fiddler's Green. "[W]e loaded up quick," Albers wrote in his journal, "but had to leave [a medic, and the squadron operations sergeant, who took cover with the garrison] since fire was so heavy." In the confusion, Pat Stenger "threw himself over me—valorous[,] but unnecessary—I will recommend him for a bronze star [with] V . . . Continued to take sniper fire till clear of F.G.—no casualties in the chopper."

Those locals who obeyed curfew and spent the night in the resettlement village built adjacent to Fiddler's Green were targeted by communist mortar crews. Those who did not were assumed by the cavalrymen and government troops—including the ruthless PRUs—to be in league with the guerrillas, and Albers noted in his journal that treatment could get rough: "Saw 8 VC prisoners—old men, women & children at F.G. today—beaten and humiliated—we'll never win this war—we're fighting the people and it's their country."

There were many reasons for doubt. On January 31, 1969, Albers filled out the casualty card for another dead dragoon, Spec Four Charles W. Richardson of B Troop, killed during a stream crossing west of Hawk Hill. Mine sweepers had cleared the crossing site, and the first two vehicles across gained the high ground on the other side without incident. Slipping in their muddy tread marks, Richardson, driving the third track in line, veered slightly to one side to gain some traction, only to hit a mine that flipped the vehicle over. An after-action report noted that so many other tracks had encountered mines at the crossing site that the scattering of ripped metal made it impossible to properly sweep the area. "This area should not be crossed except in extreme tactical emergency," the report concluded, essentially conceding the uselessness of the squadron's latest fatality. Albers also had something to write about the incident, noting in his journal that he had spoken with Richardson "on several occasions & he was a fine young man[,] too . . . Sometimes I have difficulty reconciling the purpose of this war & the death of these young men."

The war continued, endlessly repeating the same scenes. "Charlie hit the hamlet west of us at 0130 this AM [February 3]," Albers wrote of yet another incident of communist terrorism; the enemy "killed 5 [with] grenades—brought 4 people here—papasan [with] face blown away and skull cracked like an egg—no hope . . . dead in a matter of minutes. Young man [with] frag thru eye—throat wound—sucking chest wound . . . He will probably not live." Two little boys were also evacuated to Albers' aid station, one with "multiple small frag wounds," the other with his "nose &

cheek blown away... Finally to sleep at 0330—very exhausted—couldn't get up this AM—angry, depressed."

On February 21, the Blue Ghosts delivered to Hawk Hill two prisoners with light wounds and a third who "was shot all to hell," as Albers wrote: right arm missing at the shoulder, right leg riddled with bullets. The third prisoner was in "[b]ad shape[,] but we got him resuscitated," noted Albers, who got "pissed off at some troopers who were [standing in the doorway of the aid station and] taunting me to kill him—chewed them out but good."

On February 28, Albers treated a prisoner with a minor scalp laceration. The captive, taken away for interrogation, was dead two hours later with "boot prints on his chest & abdomen," recorded Albers. "[B]ody 'fell out' of helicopter—one more added to [the] body count."

Having already received an accelerated promotion to major based on his years as a civilian doctor, Albers pinned on silver oak leaves soon thereafter on the same principle. There being no room for two lieutenant colonels in the squadron, Albers got his replacement settled in before being reassigned as the deputy division surgeon. "Party at the NCO club in my honor," Albers wrote on March 5. "[T]hey said nice things about me—I got drunk—Indian wrestled several people—turned the jeep over—no damage... I was presented with a pair of hippie sunglasses for my beach parties in Chu Lai, a nice plaque and a new butane ronsoon [sic] lighter. I was touched & pleased & humble."

Dick Albers had noted several times in his journal that he wanted to stay with the cav, where the hardships were leavened by purpose and camaraderie, and the surgeon found the spit-and-polish world of division headquarters dreary indeed. "Division sucks!" he told his journal, noting that there was "no direction, too many people for too little work, back stabbing[,] and always the little power struggle intrigues [among the career officers]."

In sum, "[m]y attitude has become more & more FTA," wrote Albers, borrowing the draftee acronym for Fuck the Army. "I'm ready to go home and forget the war, the poverty, the futility." No matter his own pride of service, and the awe in which he held the courage of the young troopers he had tended in the cav, the patriotic volunteer ultimately concluded that "War is useless, degrading, a black smear on the countenance of the world."

Three days before going home, Lieutenant Colonel Albers was awarded an end-of-tour Bronze Star and an Army Commendation Medal for his service as a dragoon, to complement the Vietnamese Cross of Gallantry already received for the Battle of Tam Kỳ. The medals were presented during a steak cookout that served as "my get out of town party," wrote Albers. "[G]ood time was had by all." The next morning, Albers showered, shaved, cleaned out the desk in his office, gave away what he didn't need, finished packing, signed off on the last of his out-processing paperwork, and then, without fanfare, threw his luggage in a jeep heading down Highway 1 for Cam Ranh Bay. The night was spent at the air base, whereupon, after a mostly idle day (June 4), the surgeon was directed aboard the bus that took him to the flight line. "[G]ot on the Freedom Bird and took off at 2000 hrs," he recorded. "Goodbye Vietnam."

The flight went by quickly: four hours to Tokyo, eight hours to Anchorage, Alaska, then three hours to McChord Air Force Base near Seattle. "[T]hrough customs and then a taxi ride to Ft Lewis," wrote Albers; with the processing center closed for the evening, the doctor "walked around till I found BOQ billeting and finally bedded down for the night! The Army still sucks but I'm back in the good old USA and soon I'll be with my loved ones."

"Finis to a year of sorrow . . . and terror in Vietnam."

Richard Brummett—1970

The war ended for each soldier when he died or finished his year in the Nam. No one even wanted to think about the maimed. Most went home and resumed their lives as truck drivers, loggers, factory workers, farmers, or students. Many wished to forget the war; many could not.

A dark hole was left in the families of those who were killed. The sadness was quietly endured by their loved ones and other family members who would have loved to have known their relatives but never did. The widows, the mothers, fathers, sisters, and brothers, had and still have a sense of the lost life, what could have been and never was. The void also reaches deeply into the young children and grandchildren of those who were too young to remember or never even knew their loved ones but who still have a deep sense of pride for the dragoons who served so bravely. Staff Sergeant Elwood Houston, who was killed on A-35 tank, left behind a wife and young children who barely had a memory of their father. Houston's grandchildren wonder what he was like, and what kind of man he was. Patrick Scognamilio and Brandt Neubacher's families and friends have written fond messages to their lost soldiers on memorial websites. The sadness of loss still lingers. John Hasford's mother wrote a letter begging for a scrap of hope about her son who she thought was missing in action, a letter never answered.

Brummett's story is perhaps the most telling; Guzik calls him the "conscience of the Cav." The Việt Nam war has disturbed, infected, and literally haunted him; it may never leave his thoughts.

Richard Brummett left Việt Nam on July 10, 1968. He had several months left on his army enlistment, which were spent playing soldier in the Sixth Cavalry in Maryland. The army, which was in many ways more burdensome than the war, finally finished with Spec Five Brummett in March of 1969.

That summer of '69 Brummett spent in Europe with Peter Dovi, formerly the track commander of A-30. Together, Dovi and Brummett had dug land mines out of the dirt highways of Việt Nam. Now they rode about the peaceful countryside of Europe on two motorcycles, sleeping beside the road and experiencing several adventures. Some of which were less advisable than others.

Both of these men entered college that fall thinking they were home and the war was over. The war, of course, did not end either literally or psychically in 1968.

In addition to now-distant armies still clashing in the tropic heat there was the issue of Scognamilio. Back at LZ Baldy in April of '68 the Bear had given Brummett the responsibility to train Scog to be a tank driver. The new guy was an armored scout and had never touched a tank before being assigned to A-35. So, one PFC, long in-country, was in charge of another PFC's tank education. Scognamilio would on July 5 become Brummett's replacement in the driver's compartment of that medium tank.

The problem was that Scognamilio, despite being very thoroughly killed in Quảng Nam on July 6, 1968, followed Brummett to college in Poughkeepsie. His spirit dropped by at night in the small hours. In Brummett's dreams he suggested he could use a hand replacing the left track on A-35. Brummett was damn sure Scog didn't need help with that track, and he knew what Scognamilio really wanted. Brummett had been responsible for only one other person in Việt Nam, and he had not completed his obligations to him, so he made plans to return to Việt Nam for the summer vacation of 1970.

It was not common for a college student to head off to a war zone without a green suit and government sponsorship, but it could be done. A letter of accreditation from his college newspaper was written (by himself), the passport with the entry stamps of European communist countries was replaced with a fresh one, a visa from the RVN consulate in New York was obtained, and a one-way ticket on Pan Am to Sài Gòn was purchased. Brummett did not have enough money for the round-trip airfare but, with the foolish optimism of youth, trusted that something would turn up in Sài Gòn to provide the funds to get back for the fall term at Marist College. Scognamilio was calling him, and Scog would not accept a promise for some vague, future year.

"A promise made is a debt unpaid," and all that.

The spring semester ended late in May, and Brummett took off, telling his parents he was going to do the standard college-student-hitchhiking-to-California summer tour.

Just about anyone could fly into Sài Gòn in 1970. Having the run of the war was another matter, which is what the letter from *The Circle* was supposed to accomplish. Brummett had read of an Ivy League type doing this sort of thing, but Marist College and its student newspaper did not make the cut with the military press office in Sài Gòn. To be accredited as a freelance photographer (Brummett's cover story), he needed letters from two genuine news organizations who would swear they were acquainted with Brummett, knew of his professional work, and planned to purchase photographs from him in the future. He was given a list of the names and addresses of all such news groups in Sài Gòn and shown the door. The *Baltimore Sun* turned him down, but Horst Faas at *AP* took a chance on him based on his being fluent in U.S. Army English and his combat experience. Brummett's time in the Big Red One seemed to be the clincher. The letter from the *AP* was all it took to convince the next journalist, Kevin Buckley at *Newsweek*, to write a letter as well. Within the hour Brummett was back at the press office where a surprised navy lieutenant commander issued him his accreditation cards on June 1. To his delight, Brummett found that he now had the "Assimilated rank of major in the U.S. Army!" Yip, yip! Spec Five to major in one easy step!

The war was now wide open for Brummett.

Brummett faced a small quandary as to communication with his parents back in New York. This he solved by snagging a stray picture postcard depicting Singapore he found on the airliner heading into Sài Gòn. About halfway through the summer he asked a journalist's wife who was going that way to drop it in a mailbox in that city. He wrote his parents he'd had a change of plans and would be spending the summer vacation in East Asia.

It was not until early July that Brummett got to the point of the journey to Việt Nam: Scognamilio.

On July 11 he went to Hill 29, where he explained to Lt. Col. Richard G. Graves, squadron commander of the 1-1 Cav, what he wished to accomplish. The colonel took Brummett out in his personal helicopter, found the wreck of A-35, noted its coordinates, and delivered him to A Troop, which was maneuvering in the vicinity of Square Lake. There he rode with Capt. George K. Williams, who graciously deflected his planned course to the coordinates provided by Lieutenant Colonel Graves.

There it was. A-35. Hull upside down, sixteen-ton turret separated and flung off several yards, engine off in the other direction, rubber burned off the track blocks, a land-mine crater so big the tank could have been placed in it. The ground speckled with bleached white fragments of bone. The remains of men.

A stillness was in the air. All the tracks had cut their engines. The men of A Troop 1970 were looking at their own from A Troop 1968.

On M48A3 tanks there is a hingeless escape hatch under the driver's seat. A lever drops the hatch straight down and free of the vehicle. This hatch was found inside the driver's compartment. It had either been blown inward by the mine blast or fallen there when the hull distorted from the intense heat during the hours the diesel fuel burned.

This was fortunate, since it allowed access to the inside of the driver's compartment. There, Brummett found his friend and replacement, Patrick Scognamilio. Much of him was present, as well as his dog tags, which were still at his feet. Soldiers in some units threaded those tags into their bootlaces. The theory was that if your legs got blown off, your face could identify you. If you had the tags around your neck and you caught an RPG dead in the chest, you would lose your dog tags as well as your face.

So, there he was from about the chest down. Two years behind the wheel. A pile of bones. The troopers gently removed Scognamilio and placed him and his dog tags in a small hole dug nearby. The grave was quickly covered, and a trooper appeared with a set of tank road wheels blown off A-35. He set them down, a soldier's grave marker. A moment of silence, a salute, and then A Troop had to be off on its mission.

Brummett had thought beforehand about this moment. He had attended a funeral in Brooklyn in 1968 for Scognamilio, and it was an emotion-drenched Italian drama including a grandma who tried to open the casket. Brummett made the judgment that the family did not need to go through that once again. He relied on the presence that July day in 1970 of a U.S. Army captain on the ground and a lieutenant colonel in the air overhead to correct him if they felt otherwise.

Leaving the site of the wreck of A-35 was stressful for Brummett. He was feeling guilty for luring an armored cavalry troop into a place where an enormous land mine had killed five of their predecessors. It accomplished Brummett's mission, which put him at ease with Scognamilio, but what if more men died there? Thus primed with anxiety, Brummett jumped out of his skin when the signature hollow boom and shock wave of exploding ordinance hit the command track.

Captain Williams did not feel it necessary to tell Brummett he had ordered his men to gather up and blow the unexploded 90mm rounds found near A-35. Brummett never did find out if it was a deliberate prank played on the outsider or simply happenstance. He was certainly relieved when the armored column put sufficient distance between itself and Square Lake to make any fresh disaster someone else's responsibility.

Everyone agreed it was odd the VC did not police up those rounds two years previously, but there they were.

In those three summer months of 1970, Brummett grew into his cover story of a photojournalist. Bringing back to Sài Gòn not just the photos but accurate stories earned him just enough money to buy a plane ticket home, arriving the day before the fall semester started.

Back at Marist College, Brummett felt moved on October 27 to write to Secretary of Defense Melvin Laird concerning the actions of Capt. David

Earl Roesler and Platoon Sgt. Charles Nathan Boyd in 1968. A two-year-long CID investigation was launched that stirred up a great deal of muck and upset any number of people. Due to a lack of back-up testimony from those who witnessed the incidents of rape and pillage, charges were said to be unfounded. "Man thrown in well" was "substantiated," but Boyd's commanding officer declined to prefer charges.

In that season, Brummett joined the Vietnam Veterans Against the War and participated in one of their marches in Washington, DC. Being oddly attached to the trinkets of his service in a pointless war, he could not bring himself to toss his medals over the White House fence.

Chuck Donaldson
Captain Donaldson attended the armor advance course after his combat tour, then was assigned for three years to the ROTC detachment at his alma mater, the University of California at Berkeley. The college was, of course, famous for anti-war activism, and "a couple of us used to put on our uniforms," recalls Donaldson, "and walk through the middle of campus just to see whether anybody had courage enough to actually confront you." Most of the baby-killer slurs always seemed to be muttered anonymously from behind Donaldson and his fellow officers. Other students, though certainly against the war, "were rational, reasonable people who would engage you in open discussion," notes Donaldson. "I sort of enjoyed the back and forth."

When the dragoons had originally deployed to combat, remembers Donaldson, "the war was still considered a matter of fighting the communists on freedom's doorstep and all of that." The waters had become so muddied since that time that Donaldson was able to meet the most virulent of the protesters halfway, as evidenced during the geopolitics course that he taught. The class was open to all students at the insistence of the academic senate, "and I went into my first class one semester," notes Donaldson, "and on one side of the room were all our ROTC cadets, and on the other side were all of the students from the Students for a Democratic Society. I looked at that, and kind of said, 'Well, let's start off with some ground rules: I think by now we've all concluded that Vietnam was a bad idea. I think what we probably disagree on is how we got there: honest miscalculation or sinister plot. I'm on the honest miscalculation side, but let's put that aside for awhile and just go on with this course.'"

Richard Brummett—1971

The previous summer vacation in Việt Nam had been like a drug. A drug that quieted the worst effects of post Việt Nam combat stress. But it only worked when Brummett was actually in Việt Nam, so he went back for another dose in 1971.

His first return to Việt Nam had been done quietly, since he did not know if it would be a success. In '71 he invited select members of *The Circle* staff to accompany him for a three-month guided tour of the real world of contemporary warfare. To no great surprise, everyone turned him down with greater or lesser thanks, including Bill O'Reilly. The last rejection was the most baffling, since Bill was the only *Circle* journalist at Marist College to approve of the war.

The consensus at *The Circle* seemed to be that Brummett was completely crazy.

"Odd how some minds work," thought Brummett.

Alone and without obligations to anyone,.Brummett decided this time to make an unconventional entrance, so he went to Việt Nam by bus. Well, he did fly to London but then proceeded east by bus, train, and ferry boat. Across England, France, Italy, Greece, Turkey, Iran, Afghanistan, Pakistan, and India. He had to fly into and out of Burma because the insecure borders were closed, as they are to this day. From Bangkok there was a train (ThaiTrac) to the Laotian border, then a ferryboat across the Mekong to the capital, Vientiane. Finally, the delicate matter of that last frontier between Laos and Việt Nam. Land travel was not advisable without your own personal armored cavalry squadron, so an Air Việt Nam DC-4 to Sài Gòn it was, and Brummett was back home to the war in August 1971.

The ARVN Cambodian Invasion was underway in September, but it was not the focus of his trip to Việt Nam. However, since it was there, he just had to go and see it. A minor affair for him, the tail end of that operation still gave Brummett the experience of being pinned down in the bunker line at LZ Pace with an 8-inch howitzer battery. Stir-crazy GIs were exposing themselves to enemy fire, the 8-inch howitzers fired point blank over his head into the tree line, and Brummett's forehead caught a tiny fragment as an RPG detonated against the chain-link fence in front of the bunkers.

There was a cranky helicopter pilot who did not want to be photographed after crash landing and a near mutiny when some grunts really did not want to go out into the jungle.

Usual late war stuff.

Mostly, Brummett was again in Việt Nam to keep an eye on the 1-1 Cav. What he found in 1971 was the Cav still burning villages wholesale. The only difference from 1968 was that either American infantrymen or Ruff Puffs who rode along on the ACAVS for that purpose did the actual act of putting the zippo to the thatch. Deniability.

Also, there was a certain camera shyness about the act. Brummett has many photographs of burning hootches from that era but not of the soldiers igniting them. There seemed to be a direct, mechanical connection between his camera rising up and the soldier's zippo arm dropping down.

Being in-country again seemed to be an odd antidote to Brummett's nightmares. He never seemed to be tormented by the war while he was actually immersed in it. Not something one can keep doing indefinitely, but good for short-term relief.

What could not be found was another Guzik. Recreating the camaraderie of his time in the 1-1 Cav was just not going to happen. Guzik, having sworn off both camping and jungles, was no longer available. Brummett tried luring Dovi to Việt Nam but got the expected laughter.

Doing well enough as a photographer, Brummett skipped college that fall but flew home for the Christmas break and then back again to Việt Nam in January 1972.

Richard Harrington

Lieutenant Colonel Harrington had commanded the 1-1 Cavalry since March 1966; he brought the squadron to the war from Fort Hood in August 1967 and ended his command at Hill 29 on New Year's Day 1968. He spent the rest of his tour behind a desk at MACV HQ at Long Bình. During his command of the Cav, he was awarded a Silver Star.

Harrington had started his career as a U.S. Army Air Forces Flexible Aerial-Gunner in bombers in the skies over Nazi Germany. During that time he earned two Bronze Stars and the Legion of Merit. After three years as an enlisted man, he received a Regular Army commission in the Armor Branch in 1945.

Harrington retired after thirty-three years of service as a full colonel in 1975. He died in 1980 in San Antonio, Texas, and is buried in Fort Sam Houston National Cemetery.

Mike Cousland

Lieutenant Colonel Cousland returned from Việt Nam wearing the Silver Star with oak leaf cluster, the Legion of Merit, the Distinguished Flying Cross, the Bronze Star Medal with V, the Air Medal with V and seven oak leaf clusters, and the Purple Heart. Cousland subsequently commanded a brigade in the 1st Armored Division and served as assistant division commander of the 25th Infantry Division before retirement as a brigadier general in 1983. Cousland moved with his wife to an old farmhouse in the foothills of Virginia and was enjoying the life of a country squire when diagnosed in 1988 with inoperable cancer. Mike Cousland died less than three months later and was buried at Arlington National Cemetery in Arlington, Virginia.

Butch Saint

Promoted to lieutenant colonel, Saint returned to Việt Nam for a 1970–1971 tour split between command of his old 1-1 Cavalry and service as the operations officer of the 23rd Infantry Division. The upward trajectory of his subsequent career included command of the 11th Armored Cavalry Regiment, the 1st Armored Division, and III Corps at Fort Hood, Texas.

Retiring in 1992 as a four-star general and commander of the United States Army Europe, Saint now lives with his wife on a horse ranch in Alexandria, Virginia.

Wade Medbery

Remaining on active duty after the war, Wade Medbery retired fourteen years later as a lieutenant colonel. After a varied career in the civilian world—including consulting work, becoming general manager of a diesel-remanufacturing corporation, and traveling the world for two years to install panels as part of a space-shuttle experiment—Medbery retired on social security in 1992. He presently lives with his wife in Burkburnett, Texas.

Dick Lawrence

Lieutenant Colonel Lawrence earned two Silver Stars, the Legion of Merit, and fourteen Air Medals in Việt Nam. His distinguished career subsequently included service as a brigade commander, commanding general of the 1st Cavalry Division, and commandant of the Army War College before he retired with three stars in 1986. Now a sculptor, he lives with his wife in Austin, Texas.

Jim Logan

The former squadron operations officer's pride in having served honorably in combat was such that when news of the Mỹ Lại massacre broke, he removed the Americal patch from his right shoulder and replaced it with that of the 1st Armored Division. Logan eventually retired as a colonel and became an executive in the automotive industry. He presently lives with his wife in Alexandria, Virginia.

Fred Filbert

The well-liked squadron executive officer served as the commander of an armor battalion before retiring as a lieutenant colonel in 1984. He and his wife now live in Monument, Colorado.

Phil Bolté

After serving as Quảng Tin Province senior advisor through most of 1968, Lieutenant Colonel Bolté extended the length of his tour when offered command of the 1-1 Cavalry by the Americal Division commander. During his six months of command, he added an oak leaf cluster to the Silver Star and Purple Heart he had been awarded in Korea.

Upon his return to the States, he attended the Army War College. Subsequent duties included command of the 1st Armor Training Brigade and program management assignments on the Abrams tank and Bradley fighting vehicles. He retired in 1980 as a brigadier general and worked as a consultant and writer in the combat vehicles area. Bolté and his wife ultimately settled in West Union, South Carolina.

Richard Brummett—1972

Brummett saw the last of the 1-1 Cav on its final day in the field in Việt Nam. It was a hot day in March 1972 as the Cav patrolled the familiar Việt countryside. By that late date, the land was overlaid with the detritus of several years of war. Everywhere the troopers looked they saw wreckage: dead ACAVs, Sheridans, Hueys, helmets, shell casings, wicked-looking cast-steel fragments from various-sized howitzer rounds, shards of bone, bomb and shell craters, rice paddy dikes destroyed by tank treads, burned-out villages, untended graves, and abandoned rice fields.

Apparently, after years of effort, the Cav had convinced at least some of the farmers to pack it in and head for a city until the war was over.

Wearied from years of struggle, the Cav had collectively kept its head down and got through its last five months in the Nam without a single KIA.

A very old and worn-out war. Not a trace of élan on the faces of the troops or even officers. That last mission complete, the unit headed up Highway 1 to Đà Nẵng. Soon, the members of the unit were afflicted by a VNAF Huey repeatedly buzzing the armored column with its skids at mid-antenna level. The troops figured the Việts were sorry to see them go home.

Touching.

Before long, the 196th Light Infantry Brigade band played and the Cav stood down.

It was over.

At the very end of that March, the Easter Offensive burst upon South Việt Nam in yet another communist bid to end the war and bring themselves to power in Sài Gòn. Brummett got an assignment to accompany a correspondent for the *New York Times* to the front at the DMZ. Just north of Đông Hà on April 6 the correspondent, Brummett, and Nguyễn Ngọc Lương, the paper's interpreter, waited for a possible tank battle between an ARVN M48 unit and the NVA tanks seen approaching from the west. Instead, they were caught in an iron storm of the usual 82mm mortar fragments fired from who knows where.

Brummett snagged several particles of Chinese cast iron in his hand, leg, and face—the common cold of Việt Nam. Unable to run or have the full use of his hands, Brummett decided he was no longer a combat photographer, so he called it a war and went home.

Chris Conrad

Following his combat tour as a troop commander, Chris Conrad's distinguished career included command of an armored cavalry squadron and an infantry brigade, plus duty at the National Training Center, before retiring as a colonel and starting a new career in the business world.

Dave Staley

For his pains in the Quế Sơn Valley and elsewhere, Staley earned two Silver Stars, the Distinguished Flying Cross, and three Purple Hearts. Recovering from his wounds in the United States, he tried to get back to Việt Nam, but there was an excess of armor officers with similar ideas.

Staley finished college and went on to become the chief of the U.S. military mission to Liberia for three years during their civil war. He left Liberia in 1990 and reported to Somalia during yet another civil war, again as chief of the U.S. military mission.

He retired as a full colonel in 1993 to Tucson, Arizona. Staley was in poor health and very much in pain for many years as a result of his grievous Việt Nam injuries. He finally succumbed to his wounds in 2008.

Walter Reed

Reed returned to Việt Nam in 1972, serving as a staff advisor to a Vietnamese infantry regiment. When the American share of the conflict ended in 1973, he was assigned to the Four Party Joint Military Commission as a logistics officer. For sixty days, his major duty was to ensure that the forty-eight North Vietnamese soldiers stationed in Pleiku were well fed and had adequate shelter.

Reed left the Army as a major in 1977 to work with General Dynamics on the M1 Abrams tank project. He retired as the director of marketing for customer support after twenty-four years with General Dynamics.

He and his wife have returned to his boyhood home in Clarklake, Michigan.

Michael Prothero

His time in the cavalry earned Captain Prothero two Silver Stars, the Legion of Merit, two Bronze Stars, and a Purple Heart. He later graduated from the National War College and was a full colonel and administrative chief of the Inter-American Defense College when he retired in 1990. Prothero died in 2002 of Lou Gehrig's disease.

Dave Roesler

For his service with the dragoons, Captain Roesler was awarded, among other decorations, the Silver Star, a Bronze Star Medal with V, an Army Commendation Medal with "V" device, and three Purple Hearts. He retired in 1993 as a colonel, went to work for an engineering firm, and presently lives with his wife in East Huntsville, Alabama.

Following major heart surgery in 2001, Roesler awoke to discover large blanks in his memory, to include, he writes, most of what he did in Việt Nam.

Bob Kaczor

Considered one of the squadron's best troop commanders, Captain Kaczor left Việt Nam with a Silver Star with two oak leaf clusters, a Bronze Star with "V" device and two oak leaf clusters, an Air Medal, an Army Commendation Medal, a Purple Heart with three oak leaf clusters, and the Vietnamese Cross of Gallantry with Silver Star.

Stacks of ribbons and great efficiency reports aside, Bob Kaczor nevertheless resigned his commission in 1971. "The Army had changed quite a bit from the time I came on active duty," explains Kaczor, noting the accelerated promotions and lowered standards brought on by the Việt Nam War. "The level of professionalism of both superiors and subordinates made an Army career no longer an attractive life." Highly successful in the real-estate business, Kaczor, now retired, lives with his wife outside of Medford, Oregon.

Jim Dickens

Following his initial combat tour, Dickens went on to serve for a twenty-year military career, retiring as a lieutenant colonel after a second tour in Việt Nam, tours in Europe and Canada, and various U.S. assignments, including a final assignment in the Pentagon.

After a successful corporate career with companies like General Electric and the Ogden Corporation, he started his own company, Dickens & Associates, and purchased another established company.

He started a third company building and operating restaurants in the Atlanta metro area.

In response to a call to move from success to significance, he sold his three companies and went into non-profit leadership with a faith-based non-profit focused on the revitalization of impoverished inner-city communities. Jim is currently the president and chief executive officer of Action Ministries, Inc., a non-profit that deals with hunger, homelessness, and addiction across the state of Georgia.

He and his wife live in Atlanta and enjoy their three children and three granddaughters, who also live in the Atlanta area.

Jim Lindsey

Lindsey left the army in 1969 after his return from Việt Nam to go back to his previous career in advertising and marketing.

He became the director of advertising for Cummins Engine Company and then a partner and director of marketing and strategic planning for a large national advertising agency.

Over the years he has managed and directed the work for many great American brands, such as Frigidaire, Daisy BB guns, Maker's Mark bourbon, Mossberg shotguns, Winchester, NASA, McDonalds, AMF, Berkley fishing tackle, and many more.

Lindsey is now semiretired and runs a consulting company, runs a publishing company, and acts as director of marketing for Schmitt Sohne USA, a large European wine company.

Chuck Donaldson

Following twenty-six years on active duty and command of a tank battalion, Chuck Donaldson retired as a colonel to the Pacific Northwest in 1991, where he immediately went to work for the Oregon Department of Environmental Quality. He is presently the manager for the department's emergency response program. Donaldson is also a family man with an active interest in scuba diving and old railroad locomotives.

George Norton

After his combat tour, George Norton, an academy graduate, climbed the career ladder up to command of an armored cavalry squadron in

Germany and then retired four years later as a lieutenant colonel.

Norton lives with his wife in Hope Mills, North Carolina, and works for a consulting company that teaches people leaving the service how to find work in the private sector as part of the U.S. Army Career and Alumni Program.

Ray Mahoy

Mahoy returned for a second tour in Việt Nam from April 1970 through April 1971. He was assigned to MACV Advisory Team 87 in III Corps and served as an advisor to an armored cavalry troop in the 18th ARVN Infantry Division located at Xuân Lôc. Mahoy arrived just in time to participate with the ARVN's incursion into Cambodia, which he says was a great experience. He completed the remainder of his tour as the assistant G3 air advisor.

After returning to the U.S., Mahoy was released from active duty in April 1972 as a result of the reduction in force at the end of the Việt Nam conflict. He resigned his commission and entered the Army National Guard as a staff sergeant.

In 1980, Mahoy was recommissioned in the rank of captain and became a battalion logistical officer. He progressed to the role of property book team chief within the division property book office, and, in 1985, he was promoted to major and became the division property book officer. Mahoy retired in 1988 from active duty with twenty-six years of service. During the above time he completed both the field artillery and quartermaster officer advanced courses at the Command and General Staff College.

Ray Mahoy's awards include the Silver Star with oak leaf cluster, Bronze Star, Purple Heart with oak leaf cluster, Meritorious Service Medal, Air Medal, Army Commendation Medal, Army Achievement Medal, Good Conduct Medal, Armed Forces Reserve Service Medal with three oak leaf clusters, National Defense Service Medal, Vietnam Service Medal with seven battle stars, Humanitarian Service Medal, Vietnam Campaign Medal with 1960 device, Vietnamese Cross of Gallantry with gold star, Vietnamese Staff Service Medal, Indiana Commendation Medal with oak leaf cluster, and Indiana Long Service Medal.

After retirement, he was employed in the areas of law enforcement and loss prevention until reaching age sixty-two, when he retired for the final time.

Mahoy is presently enjoying old age, spending time with seven grandchildren, and working on family genealogy where he has traced his ancestors back to 1786. As an interesting side note, there has been a Mahoy in every major conflict since the War of 1812.

Tom Jackson

Tom Jackson returned from Việt Nam with a Silver Star with one oak leaf cluster, the Bronze Star with "V" device and two oak leaf clusters, and the Purple Heart. While on active duty he earned his master's degree in systems management from USC. He remained on active duty until retiring as a lieutenant colonel in 1987.

After retirement, Jackson went on to have a successful career as a computer consultant, owning his own company. After selling the consulting company to his partner, he retired to the Texas hill country and now lives outside of New Braunfels, Texas.

Dave Miller

After his time as a platoon leader in both E and A Troops of the 1st Cavalry, Miller spent only eight months stateside before returning for another tour. The second time around he was the commanding officer of C Troop and later the night shift G3 at 23rd Division Headquarters. Feeling a need to stay connected to the real business of the war, Miller took some time off from his office duties to visit his marine engineer brother in Đà Nẵng. The brothers started each day by digging up a few land mines on Highway 1 and dodging the odd sniper round.

Two years of willfully throwing himself into various dangerous situations netted Miller a Silver Star, three Bronze Stars, and two Purple Hearts. Ouch.

Completing his second year in Việt Nam, Miller then sampled life on the other side in the Officer Advance Course at Infantry Hall at Fort Benning.

The war over, Miller left the army in 1973 and enjoyed several successful decades in business. After his wife, Beth, died in 2006, Miller retired to his childhood home in upstate New York. He spends his days hunting, fishing, golfing, and visiting with his three brothers, including the marine of land mine fame.

Dan Guida

Originally drafted upon flunking out of college, Lieutenant Guida, having finished his three years of service, returned to college and became a certified public accountant. Married before going to Việt Nam, he divorced after coming home. He is now remarried and is a family man living in St. James, New York.

Chris Noble

After completing his military service obligation as a noncombat arms officer, Noble left with two Bronze Stars, a Purple Heart, the Việt Nam Cross of Gallantry with Gold Star, and the Combat Medics Badge.

Noble entered into a business career that led him to the Arabian American Oil Company in Dhahran, Saudi Arabia. There he managed multimillion-dollar budgets in the creation of the Saudi Consolidated Electric Company–Eastern. He then became the director of operations and business manager to an independent school in upstate New York. He saved this school from bankruptcy and claims this as his proudest accomplishment to date. Noble joined the Peace Corps as a business specialist and was sent to assist East Europeans of the former Soviet Bloc countries in learning Western business practices. He did his Peace Corps time in the Ukraine.

Recently, Noble wrote a memoir about parallel wars that details his experiences in the medical platoon of the 1-1 Cavalry, for the year 1968.

Noble lives with his family in Marion, Massachusetts, in a home that is a four-minute walk from the beach, where he enjoys playing with his grandchildren.

Nate Boyd

After retiring from the army in 1973 as a first sergeant, Nate Boyd spent the next twenty-four years as a long-distance trucker, driving coast to coast and border to border. Boyd now lives with his wife in his hometown of Mount Vernon, Ohio, where he gives talks at the local high schools about the Việt Nam War.

Herman R. Jessie

Retiring from the army as a command sergeant major, Herman Jessie returned to his native Texas and started a second career with the U.S. Postal Service. He recently died of natural causes.

Ken Bouche

With a wife and two children, Staff Sergeant Bouche opted not to reenlist for a third time in the U.S. Army and instead went into the grocery business after Việt Nam. Now retired and a grandfather three times over, he lives with his wife in Brea, California.

Jim Hammerbeck

Following retirement as a master sergeant, Hammerbeck started a second career with the U.S. Postal Service and lives with his wife in Colorado Springs, Colorado.

Bob Schlagel

Having made sergeant in combat, Bob Schlagel also earned two Bronze Stars with V, in addition to a third end-of-tour award, plus two Purple Hearts and the Vietnamese Cross of Gallantry with Bronze Star. Reenlisting with thoughts of a military career, Schlagel married a German girl in Berlin. The marriage did not last. Nor did Schlagel's enthusiasm for the army in the demoralized phase brought on by the war in Việt Nam; he left the service in 1973 as a staff sergeant. Returning home to Indianapolis, where he soon remarried, Schlagel quit his construction job to attend the police academy and is presently a detective sergeant with the sheriff's department.

Tom Andersen

The draft originally scooped Tom Andersen up when he was working on the floor of the New York Stock Exchange on Wall Street. Returning from the war, Andersen took some time off to enjoy life, then called his old boss, got his job back, and spent the next thirty years working on the Street. "I hated every minute of it," he says. "I think I liked Vietnam better than working on Wall Street. High-pressure is putting it mildly. You've got the pressure, plus somebody always trying to put a knife in your back. Literally. People would threaten you. If a trade went bad, people would want to meet you outside to fight. It was just incredible, a real dog-eat-dog atmosphere. I finally retired to Florida."

Jerry Anderson

Following a long recuperation for his wounds, Jerry Anderson, graduate of a two-year electronic tech school, returned to his prewar job at the White Sands Missile Range in New Mexico. Subsequently earning a bachelor's degree in engineering, Anderson presently works for the National Aeronautics and Space Administration, performing test firing for space-shuttle engines and the international space station. Divorced twice after the war, he lives with his third wife in Las Cruces, New Mexico.

Wayne Byrd

Having gotten drafted after flunking out, Wayne Byrd returned to North Carolina State after the war to earn a degree in poultry science, only to find that the poultry business was infamous for long hours and poor pay. Switching careers, Byrd, who married a schoolteacher, subsequently made his living as a loan officer and real estate appraiser while rising to the position of deacon in his church. Byrd and his wife are recently retired and live in Graham, North Carolina.

Tom Bursott

Earning a college degree after the war, Tom Bursott returned to his hometown of Olney, Illinois, where he is now an independent insurance adjuster. Bursott is not one to make a big deal of his status as a veteran: "I never really thought that the Vietnam veterans should get anything more than the Korean or the World War II veterans, a little placard on the courthouse steps and go on about your business. I don't think we deserve any more attention than anybody else."

Wally Colligan

Proud to have served and still hawkish about the war, Sergeant Colligan returned from Việt Nam with both the Bronze Star and Army Commendation Medal with V, plus three Purple Hearts. Since his discharge, Colligan has been in construction work, including employment as a general foreman working on nuclear reactor installations. He presently lives with his wife in Bristol, Connecticut.

Ron Decktor

Lacking only a year of credits when drafted, Decktor returned to college after the war to finish his education. He married the next year, although still a bit in the wilderness because of Việt Nam. "I had some problems from PTSD [post-traumatic stress disorder, originally designated Post-Vietnam Syndrome], and all that," recalls Decktor. "You can't help it. I mean, I didn't want to be around people. I drank. I drank a lot, I guess, but my wife straightened me out. It took awhile, but I eventually got my head screwed on straight." Decktor did quite well thereafter, making his fortune in the restaurant and liquor business before turning the works over to one of his two sons and retiring with his wife to Cedar Crest, New Mexico. He spends much of his time now out on his sailboat. He is also active in the squadron's association, noting, "I'm happy to talk about the war because I'm proud of what we did in Vietnam."

David Eady

No worse for the wear, David Eady, the laidback draftee, returned to his prior life after the war, working for General Electric in small-town Indiana. He retired after rising to the level of inspector, never married, and is still an amiable and untroubled soul. "I like to travel," he says. "I like hanging out with friends and family."

Mike Esmond

Drafted in 1966 out of Philadelphia while working for the Philadelphia Naval Air Engineering Center, Esmond ended his army service as a spec five combat medic. He returned home with a Silver Star, two Bronze Stars with V, and two Purple Hearts.

After marrying in 1971, a daughter and two sons were born, and now there are two grandchildren. Esmond and his wife were together for thirty-eight years until her death in 2008.

He followed up his army introduction to medicine and became a licensed physical therapist with a P.T. degree from Temple University.

Esmond continues to work as a physical therapist in his New Jersey practice and is also the director of physical therapy at St. Francis Medical Center in Trenton, New Jersey.

Ronnie Fortner

After returning from Vietnam in 1968, Fortner worked as a deputy sheriff in Lee County, Virginia, for four years; drove coal trucks for several years; then operated heavy equipment on surface coal-mining operations until retirement after heart bypass surgery in 1998.

Fortner now enjoys his retirement in Dandridge, Tennessee, where he lives with his wife of forty years, his daughter, and his grandson.

Larry Gaydon

The former draftee medic married a year after the war and went to work for an electric utility company. The father of two grown sons, Gaydon recently retired and lives with his wife in Portland, Oregon.

Larry Graham

Seriously wounded by the land mine that killed Matchett and Rodgers, Graham's war ended on January 19, 1968. He had been raised in a family of World War II veterans where it was assumed that every generation would have its war. Việt Nam was Graham's, and his main regret was that his father did not live to see his son take up the quarrel with the foe.

With the support of a wonderful wife these past forty-four years, Graham has struggled with his disability while working full time. The Grahams raised four children to maturity and now are enjoying their five grandchildren.

Despite his obvious injuries, it took Graham forty years to get the Veterans Administration to do the right thing and compensate him for the suffering he endured for our nation.

Graham is proud to have served his country but does not begrudge those who chose not to fight. He still has fond memories of his platoon sergeant, Nate Boyd, and says, "He was the best . . . I would have followed him anywhere!!"

John Guzik

Home from the war, John Guzik climbed back behind the wheel of the bread truck he'd been driving when drafted and soon married his fiancée. They had three children before the marriage ended in divorce. Guzik, who now owns a small trucking company, has since remarried and lives in

Blackwood, New Jersey. Having given the big picture no thought when he was a young soldier, Guzik has since come to see the war as a mistake—his politics are liberal ethnic Democrat—but he remains free of bitterness and, in most regards, is the same funny, level-headed, hard-working soul that his comrades remember from the 1-1 Cavalry.

Gene Hotchkiss

Married shortly before going to war, Hotchkiss, the father of two, remains with his wife over four decades later and lives in his hometown of Hertel, Wisconsin. He originally worked in a factory and as a drapery installer after the war, but things did not work out, and he finally found himself on 100 percent disability for PTSD. "I couldn't figure out for years what the hell was wrong," says Hotchkiss, "but I'd go through my periods. I'd go for walks and stuff, and, anyway, the fella in the VA [Veterans Administration] hospital kind of tricked me along; he kept telling me he wanted to get me some help, and I fought him every step of the way, telling him to stick his welfare up his ass. I was stubborn like all of us are from Wisconsin."

Bob Johnston

Following his three-year enlistment, Bob Johnston left the army a specialist fifth class with the Silver Star, two Bronze Star Medals with V, and three Purple Hearts. Recognized as one of the squadron's most decorated medics, Johnston shrugs off the honor. "Awards and decorations are kind of funny," says the soft-spoken ex-medic. "When you really put yourself out there, and do something that might be deserving of an award, nobody's looking; but when you do what is second nature under fire, somebody turns around and hands you a cotton-pickin' medal. That's how I got my Silver Star."

Unscathed mentally by the war, and his interest in medicine piqued by Doc Albers' lessons in the squadron aid station, Bob Johnston used the GI Bill to attend a two-year junior-college course that trained him to be a physician's assistant in the field of orthopedics. He has been in that field ever since, divorcing once along the way, marrying again, and having four children.

Johnston is active in the squadron's organization, though he is hardly as hawkish as most of those who still wear the unit insignia and unfurl the old guidons. In fact, he has become something of a pacifist over the years, leery of U.S. involvement in El Salvador, Nicaragua, and Iraq. Still, the adventurous side of the war of his youth still tugs at him, and as idiotic as he has since concluded the Việt Nam War to have been, he cannot turn away from the 1-1 Cavalry. "It was the best and worst of times," he explains. "We did the job that we were asked to do, and professional and draftee alike, we did it damn well, particularly under the circumstances. The courage of the guys was amazing. To me, the reunions are about a shared experience, shared history, not politics."

If pressed into a political corner, Johnston will offer that having sided with corrupt Sài Gòn over the unrelenting nationalists in Hà Nội, the United States could not have expected to win such a war by conventional force of arms. Even to try was to do more harm than good. "The Vietnamese are so much better off when we finally fuckin' left them alone," opines Johnston. "What do they give a shit about what flag is flying while they till their rice fields? It was really Sài Gòn's war to win or lose, and they just plain blew it. With all the chances that we gave 'em that they squandered, they didn't deserve to win. Quite frankly, between the NVA and the ARVN, the better man won."

Unbedeviled by demons from the war, Bob Johnston engages in good-natured banter with those who are and, because they are, feel the need to justify the war in Việt Nam. "So many of the guys are still pissed off at Jane Fonda," laughs Johnston. "Aw, Jesus Christ, guys, grow up! She was a flake then, she's a flake now, so what?! A lot of my peers," he continues, growing more serious, "their whole identity is wrapped up in being a veteran. It's their whole social life. It's their whole identity. Part of who or what I am is marked by what I experienced in the war, but mostly—I can't believe I even went through all that."

Max Pryor

After returning home, Pryor, who says the war matured him and settled him down, took over his father's souvenir business from 1970 until selling it in 1986. During that time, he became a workaholic who drank whiskey by the quart, smoked three or four packs of cigarettes a day, and gave himself a heart attack by age forty-four. Pryor was also dealing with the ghosts of Việt Nam. He had terrible dreams about the war and one night found himself choking his wife in his sleep as she frantically fought back. Pryor eventually was to receive a 20 percent disability for PTSD to go with his Bronze Star with V, as well as 30 percent for the wounds that earned him three Purple Hearts.

Pryor and his wife had two daughters after his return from the war, one of whom is a certified public accountant married to a university basketball coach, the other a registered nurse married to a doctor. Still possessed of a devilish streak, Pryor jokes about the time he greeted one of his daughter's prom dates at the door with a 13-inch pistol and asked him who the hell he was and what the hell he wanted. Laughing, he recalls that his unamused daughter wouldn't talk to him for two weeks.

Now semiretired from various business ventures and a cancer survivor, Pryor enjoys drinking beer, smoking cigars, and fishing; identifies himself as a Fox News Republican; and lives with his wife in Wildwood, Missouri.

Rich Rensi

Upon returning home to Ohio, Rensi worked for a trucking company for three years. In 1973 he ran for and was elected sheriff of Harrison County, where he served the county's citizens until his retirement in 1997. The next five years were spent with a NASCAR team. Rensi does keep busy in his retirement as a member of the Harrison County Republican Central Committee.

Rensi has been married for forty-eight years and has two sons.

He does not think about Việt Nam much and has tried to forget about it entirely. "Life has been good to me."

Arvin Schoep

Ever the good, uncomplaining soldier, Arvin Schoep came home with sergeant stripes and the Bronze Star Medal with V. He soon married the girl he had been dating before being drafted and picked up right where he'd left off: working on the family farm in Minnesota. Soon thereafter, "my two younger brothers took over the farming," recalls Schoep, "and I went into gravel construction with my brother. That was another family business. I also started a trucking business on the side. In my family, we grew up kind of poor, and we all grew up with that determination not to be poor, and so we were all very driven."

Under the surface, however, the war was gnawing at Schoep. It was gnawing, too, at those buddies he kept in contact with after Việt Nam. He learned that one had been committed to a mental institution. Two others were killed in incidents involving drinking and driving. Another fell off the radar screen altogether. The last of the bunch, a tank driver evacuated with terrible head injuries after running over a mine, "is divorced, of course," notes a rueful Schoep, "and on lots of medications. He still has blackouts. Just a very unhappy individual."

Arvin Schoep was an unhappy individual himself, a good marriage and paycheck notwithstanding. "As I say, we were driven to succeed financially," notes Schoep, "so it was very unsettling coming back, and all of a sudden these things just didn't mean anything anymore. It just didn't matter how much money I made or how many things I acquired. To give you an example," continues Schoep, "I got into that trucking business, and I love trucks and love driving and stuff like that, and, aw, I thought, if only I could afford one of those nice, big, new tractor-trailers with the long nose on the front and the sleeper on the back. Well, I finally did. I bought one." Schoep was on the road night and day with his new baby for a month. "I was coming home one night," he recalls of another day of work in 1974, "it was about four in the morning, and I said to myself, you know, this isn't it, either—and I just started crying—it was just so heartbreaking. I was really struggling emotionally at that time. I realized somewhere along there that I just wasn't the same person as when I left. I think priorities had changed for me, and I was just very, very restless."

At that point, Schoep decided he wanted to go into the ministry, which meant, to begin with, four years of college, an intimidating prospect given his sketchy academic background as a farm kid who was absent as much as he showed up for high school. Schoep nevertheless earned a degree in philosophy, graduating with honors. Before going to seminary to do his graduate work, he stayed behind the wheel of his truck to afford his wife the time to finish her college degree, too, and next obtain a law degree. While she worked as an attorney, Schoep completed his graduate work and became pastor of a church in Hudson, New York. He was finally exactly where he wanted to be.

Despite some lingering issues of depression from the war, Arvin Schoep and his wife have made a good life for themselves. Their son grew up to be a corrections officer, their daughter a medical doctor. Now a grandfather, Schoep finally retired after twenty years as a pastor to four acres in the hills just north of the Catskill Mountains. "The quiet and nature is good for us," he reflects. "The war served as a defining lesson, or a defining event, in how I lived my life," he continues. "I just learned to look at life a different way. I believe God put us here to take care of one another and to help those who are less fortunate. When the Iraq war started, I spoke out very vehemently against it. The Bible tells us that if you have an enemy, you feed him—and I think we would just be so much better off if we'd skip the fighting. If someone has a need, then you fill that need, and you'll build a friend instead of making an enemy."

Richard Brummett—2006

Thirty-four years had passed since Brummett last walked the paddy dikes of Việt Nam, but he, like many veterans of the war, could not let it go. One incident in particular ate at him: The day he froze up and did nothing while Charles Nathan Boyd threw an old man down a well.

One morning in 2004 as he awoke he knew what he needed to accomplish to perhaps, maybe, put this matter to rest. He would go back to Việt Nam and visit that village, learn the name of the old man, burn incense at his grave, and ask his forgiveness.

Brummett retired in the spring of 2005 from the U.S. Postal Service, having been a small-town postmaster for the previous sixteen years. Retirement gave him the time to turn his attention again to Việt Nam.

So, in May 2006 he went back to Mậu Hoà, the village of the Old Man in the Well. A village elder, Huỳnh Điểu, told Brummett he had witnessed the incident. The old man now has a name, even if he was not as old as the twenty-year-old Brummett had surmised. He was Trần Văn Ưu, and he was fifty-eight on the day Boyd murdered him. His eldest son, Trần Văn Phố, still misses him.

Together, Brummett and Phố went to the grave. Brummett took out nine incense sticks, Phố lighted them, and Brummett stuck the sticks in the sand-filled urn before Ưu's grave.

Richard Sears

Being a former high-school athlete, Sears says he was "devastated" by the injuries he suffered in the Quế Sơn Valley. "I was upset that I could no longer play sports. I was really made aware of my limitations."

To be specific, Sears lost his left eye completely and, in place of his right arm, was left with a prosthetic limb and a metal hook. Fortunately, the vision in his right eye, though blurry, recovered to the point that he can read a little and recognize faces when the light is right. Married and divorced after the war, the father of two lives on his veteran's disability and resides on the twelve acres his family owns in his hometown of Danvers, Massachusetts.

Despite his injuries, or because of them, Richard Sears has developed a hard-line attitude about the war and finds his political voice best expressed by commentators like Sean Hannity, Rush Limbaugh, Oliver North, and Michael Savage. To Sears, the war was a worthwhile effort to stop communism. The patriotic stepped up to do their duty, while the cowardly hid behind peace banners and the leaders of the anti-war movement treasonously made common cause with Hà Nội. Sears blames the fall of Sài Gòn on the Jane Fondas, John Kerrys, and Ted Kennedys, those politicians who got "cold feet" because of the protesters, and left-wing journalists who harped on the negative. "Any idiot can point out a mistake that's been made," opines Sears, who doesn't believe the press should be allowed to cover military operations. In the end, says Sears, the anti-war movement forced a disgraceful U.S. retreat from Southeast Asia, which led, in turn, to the imposition of a Stalinist tyranny in South Việt Nam and full-scale genocide in Cambodia. "The protesters were so sure of themselves," says Sears, "but in the end, they were fools who have to pretend that they aren't responsible for the blood baths that took place after we left."

Sears' hatred for the left's anti-militarism is unbounded. "If it wasn't for the United States military, there wouldn't be a country, and without a country, there wouldn't be a Constitution—and without a Constitution, these little bastards wouldn't have the right to protest or do anything else that they do. You lose the country, you lose everything—and what keeps the country from falling is the military and those who serve in it. You can't say you support the troops, but not the mission. You can't have it both ways."

Sears continues: "I often say I'd like to have another civil war in this country—liberals against conservatives—winners stay, losers leave. I say it tongue in cheek, but I know who would win. It would be a walk over."

"I'm not bitter," Sears concludes. "I'm a happy person. I'm bitter about the political aspects of the war, but I don't blame anybody for what happened to me. I was just a casualty of the war—and there were a lot of people who got hurt a lot worse than me."

Dick Taskey

Returning home after the war, Dick Taskey, soon to be married and the father of two, also returned as a lumberjack to the forests of northern Michigan. He worked as a logger until 2000. "By then, I was wore out," says Taskey. "I had circulation problems in my legs from the cold weather. I couldn't feel my legs, so I figured it was a good time to get out. My two boys were old enough by then to take over the business. All I do is nothin' now."

While still working, and not long after being discharged, Taskey sought help at the VA. "My mind wasn't working good when I came back," he explains, "and I had a lot of problems with alcohol. Back then, though, they didn't care. Matter of fact, one of the doctors told me I was wasting his time and mine. That really ticked me off, and I guess I've been mad ever since. The impression was that the VA was against you back in those days."

Taskey's anger had terrible consequences: nightmares, drinking, bar fights, even a year in jail. "I'd flip out," he says. "It didn't take a whole lot to get me crazy. I couldn't even talk to people. I pretty much had to work alone."

Finally retired from logging, Taskey returned to the VA in 2002.

Sonny Webster

The product of an abusive childhood, Webster found himself slipping, like his parents before him, into alcoholism and violent outbursts after returning from the war. His hurts were many, not the least of which was the lack of appreciation, respect, or understanding afforded Việt Nam veterans in the years immediately after the war. "That was the killer," he says. "It was the first black war this country fought, and because it was so unpopular, the poor guys who fought over there got the butt end of a lot of resentment. That we were spit on is in the hearts and minds of most Vietnam veterans, and it's the one thing that makes them want to lash out at their family and everybody else around them. You know, you told me I had to go do this or go to prison," Webster continues, "and now I'm a fucking jerk for having done what I was told. Not a pretty picture. You go to church as a kid, and learn that thou shalt not kill. Then you're told to kill, and you do kill, and you come home, and you're supposed to shut up about everything and behave—and your head gets spun around in all those directions before you're even twenty-one."

Webster went to work for General Electric in upstate New York, from where he originally hailed, and, marrying in 1970, eventually had two boys and a girl. The marriage ended in divorce in 1984, a victim of Webster's alcoholism. Finding an anchor in God, Webster finally stopped drinking in 1991 and began seeking out counseling at the VA in 1998; he presently receives a 30 percent disability for PTSD. Webster retired in 2002 and lives now in an apartment in Fountain Hills, Arizona. By talking about the war in counseling, Sonny Webster has mostly made peace with his demons. "I had to, or I was probably going to kill myself or somebody else," he explains. "You need to face the shit you've been through, or it owns you. I didn't want to walk around wounded in my mind like a lot of Vietnam veterans." It's difficult for Webster to relive the war, "but I also know that the most important thing a person can do is to know the truth and say it. It's very important. Otherwise, your past gets very diluted, and you really don't know who you are because what you went through isn't real anymore." In general, "this country wants to make that war not real," Webster reflects. "We want to make the experience not real. We don't want to bring all that stuff back up and talk about it—but you have to. I've come to terms with all kinds of things. I have an ex-wife and three kids today who know who I am today because I'm not afraid to tell 'em and own what I did and who I am."

Bottom line, says Sonny Webster, "I feel like a survivor."

Richard Brummett—2007

Although the trip to Việt Nam in 2006 went far better than Brummett had expected, there were still some unanswered questions. And some questions he thought were not answered with the full truth. So, in May 2007 he again traveled to Việt Nam.

This time he stopped at the government office that administered Mậu Hoà and spoke with the officials there. The chairman of the People's Committee for the Bình Định District of Quảng Nam Province, Nguyễn

Đình Thiệp, was thirteen years old on that terrible day of March 18, 1968. He said he was hiding from the Americans but could see Mr. Ưu's front yard confrontation with Sergeant Boyd. His account of the incident closely followed that of Guzik, Brummett, and Điểu.

He did, however, have more of the back story. It was true that Ưu was a rice farmer, but not exactly a simple rice farmer as his son had declared in 2006. It seems that Ưu was otherwise employed as the head of Việt Cộng military intelligence for the district.

So, Charles Nathan Boyd had splashed a VC S2 officer. It is likely that Captain Kaczor, our own S2 back at Hill 29, would have enjoyed squeezing data out of his counterpart, but that was not to be. Boyd may have murdered the "right" man, but it was not for being a VC that Ưu died. He perished at the intersection of pointless pride and death-fueled fury. If Ưu had not been so defiant and Boyd not so angry, then Ưu might have lived through that day. Boyd could perhaps have let pass the incomprehensible singsong scolding, but the bony finger wagging in his face was too much.

Thiệp related other stories: As one might expect in a civil war, it turns out the Trần family had its own internal divisions. Trần Văn Phổ, who claimed to be the eldest but was actually the second son, spent much of the war as an artilleryman with the Army of the Republic of Việt Nam, our allies.

The actual eldest son, Trần Văn Ty, died for his country on September 30, 1969. Ty's gravestone in the Việt Cộng military cemetery near Châu Xuân 2 attests to his status as Liệt Sĩ: Revolutionary Martyr.

Huỳnh Điểu, who witnessed the incident at the well, also has a story. He had served with the Regional Forces, aka Ruff Puffs, the militia of our allies. His war ended when the man in front of him on patrol stepped on and detonated a small VC land mine. Điểu was looking down and caught the blast in his face, and that is why he is known today as the Old Blind Man.

Divided families, divided villages.

Brummett took some time in 2007 to ride about the countryside alone on a rented motorcycle. Hill 29 is still an army post and closed to tourists, but he went to other places of interest. Those three Chàm red brick tower ruins south of Hill 29 along Highway 1 could be examined closely and at leisure. Carvings on the foundation stones indicate a pre-Vietnamese

Hindu culture dating from the eleventh and twelfth centuries.

An Sơn, just to the west of Hill 29 turned out to be a Catholic ville, and, as such, the people were fiercely anticommunist during the war. In light of these facts, two rice farmers, Hoãng Trí Hāi and Võ Lự, asked Brummett why he tried to kill them, since they distinctly remember a tank main gun round zipping past their ears in 1968. Brummett was sure they were mistaken because if it had been A-35 with Guzik behind the sights, they would not have lived to complain about it in 2007.

The lesson learned is that if you go about the countryside killing people at random, you will find yourself killing your enemies, your friends, as well as more or less innocent bystanders.

The wreck of A-35 is now gone. In the past few years, the Vietnamese have managed to remove the last of the heavy war debris from their countryside.

LZ Goat is totally overgrown in tropical vegetation.

The railroad that passed in rusted silence west of Hill 29 in 1968 is now an active line. Brummett rode the rails from Đà Nẵng to Tam Kỳ and back just for the novel fun. The trains run on time.

Brummett watched with amusement as a unit of very sharply uniformed VA grunts (formerly NVA) stumbled about in a training exercise beside the road to Hill 29. As Guzik would later comment: "They've lost the edge we gave them."

Cigar Island, so tough to get to with an M48 in 1968, is now an easy motorcycle crossing on any one of several small bridges that connect it with the mainland. Brummett parked his bike and walked the beach, examining the wicker-and-tar boat hulls.

He savored the peace.

However, despite all his efforts to put the past to rest, Brummett knew he was too deeply stained to ever feel the last of Việt Nam this side of the grave.

"I'll never get this country and its war out of my soul."

APPENDIX A

Those Who Died

1st Squadron, 1st Cavalry Regiment
Republic of Việt Nam

KIA: killed in action
MIA: missing in action
BNR: body not recovered
DOW: died of wounds
PFOD: presumptive finding of death
* Trooper who came over from Fort Hood on the *General Walker*.

SEPTEMBER 5, 1967
1LT Garland D. Whitmore II*   A Troop   KIA
SGT Charles H. Gobble   A Troop   KIA   3-16 Artillery FO

SEPTEMBER 13, 1967
PFC Lawrence M. Svobodny*   C Troop   KIA

SEPTEMBER 20, 1967
PFC David E. Gossard*   C Troop   Cooking stove fire

OCTOBER 10, 1967
PFC George H. Winkempleck* A Troop Drowned

OCTOBER 21, 1967
PFC John L. Jones*   A Troop KIA
PFC David P. Kusy*   A Troop KIA
PFC David E. Ward*   A Troop KIA

OCTOBER 27, 1967
PFC Bruce W. Dudley Jr.*   A Troop KIA   DOW 1/23/1968
PFC Edward A. Moldavan*   B Troop KIA
PFC Francis P. Schmautz*   B Troop KIA

OCTOBER 29, 1967
SP4 Ralph W. Plummer III* A Troop KIA

NOVEMBER 8, 1967
SP4 Thomas L. Scott*   B Troop KIA

NOVEMBER 9, 1967
SSG David H. Wainscott*   B Troop KIA
PFC Jerry W. Gentry*   B Troop KIA
PFC Robert F. Nitz   B Troop KIA

NOVEMBER 28, 1967
PSG Hillard E. Williams   C Troop Friendly fire

DECEMBER 3, 1967
SSG Coleman G. Hillman*   C Troop KIA
PFC Richard C. Balukonis   C Troop KIA

DECEMBER 5, 1967
PFC David S. Kossowski*   A Troop Self-inflicted   DOW 7/30/1968
                                    gunshot

DECEMBER 10, 1967
PFC Michael J. Saunders*   C Troop   KIA

DECEMBER 21, 1967
SFC Thomas R. Kisner*   A Troop   Drowned
PFC Eugene Manigo   A Troop   Drowned

JANUARY 7, 1968
CPT John L. Barovetto*   B Troop   KIA

JANUARY 19, 1968
SP4 L. David Matchett*   A Troop   KIA
PFC John A. Rogers   A Troop   KIA

JANUARY 31, 1968
SGT Edgar L. Bolding*   C Troop   KIA
SGT Jack R. Lockridge   C Troop   KIA

FEBRUARY 15, 1968
SP4 Herbert C. Davis*   A Troop   KIA

FEBRUARY 19, 1968
SSG Michael W. Elben*   C Troop   Accidental shooting

FEBRUARY 22, 1968
SGT Robert B. Selby*   B Troop   KIA

MARCH 5, 1968
SP4 Richard E. Saldana*   C Troop   KIA   DOW 3/6/1968

MARCH 6, 1968
SSG Arlie Terry   C Troop   KIA
SP4 Jere D. Farnow*   C Troop   KIA

MARCH 11, 1968
PFC Joseph C. Carvajal   C Troop   KIA
PFC Henry B. Williams Jr.*   C Troop   KIA

MARCH 14, 1968
SP4 Earl C. Minard   B Troop   KIA
PFC David F. Cosby*   B Troop   KIA

APRIL 2, 1968
SP4 Bruce L. Badger   C Troop   KIA
SP4 Robert H. Rassel*   C Troop   KIA
PFC George J. Kohlmeir III   C Troop   KIA

APRIL 10, 1968
1LT Ronald J. Wojtkiewicz   C Troop   KIA
SP4 Kimmey D. Hobbs   C Troop   KIA   Medic
SP4 Quillard F. Lyons   C Troop   KIA   DOW 4/13/1968

PFC Willie E. Glover   C Troop   KIA
PFC Allen D. Hanlan   C Troop   KIA

APRIL 13, 1968
SGT Richard A. Renfro*   B Troop   KIA
SP4 August T. Battaglia*   B Troop   KIA

APRIL 29, 1968
SP4 James W. Powers Jr.   C Troop   KIA
PFC Harold Henasey   C Troop   KIA

MAY 5, 1968
PFC Stephen M. Lashinsky Jr.   C Troop   KIA

MAY 7, 1968
1LT Donald J. Mattaro Jr.   B Troop   KIA

SSG Aaron Hartness*   A Troop   KIA
SP4 Alonso Aragon Jr.   A Troop   KIA
SP4 Roger D. Cauley   A Troop   KIA

MAY 8, 1968
PFC Donald W. Pickering   B Troop   KIA

MAY 15, 1968
PFC George H. Coppage III C Troop   KIA   Medic

MAY 23, 1968
SP4 Richard I. Cullen   B Troop   KIA
PFC Florian A. Bugni Jr.   B Troop   KIA

MAY 28, 1968
PFC Walter M. Powell   A Troop   KIA   Medic

JUNE 18, 1968
SP4 Peter F. Fonda   B Troop   KIA
SP4 Stephen F. Turner   B Troop   KIA

JULY 6, 1968
SSG Elwood L. Houston   A Troop   KIA
SP5 John L. Hasford Jr.*   A Troop   KIA
SP4 Brandt S. Neubacher   A Troop   KIA
SP4 Patrick J. Scognamilio A Troop   KIA
SP4 John L. Roberts   A Troop   KIA

JULY 11, 1968
SP4 Ronald J. Tebbe   B Troop   KIA
PFC John L. Adams   B Troop   KIA

JULY 23, 1968
SP4 Kenneth A. Butler Jr. C Troop   KIA

AUGUST 5, 1968
SGT Steven C. Blossom   A Troop   KIA
SP4 Michael N. Hoban   A Troop   KIA

AUGUST 23, 1968
SSG Edward S. Stewart   C Troop   KIA
PFC Richard L. Rowland   C Troop   KIA

AUGUST 24, 1968
PFC William N. McMurtrey   C Troop   KIA
PFC Donald R. Pyrant   C Troop   KIA

AUGUST 25, 1968
SGT William A. Swoveland   C Troop   KIA
SP4 Steve O. Nussbaumer   C Troop   KIA   Medic
SP4 Jeffrey T. Cramer   A Troop   KIA

AUGUST 27, 1968
1LT Bruce W. Brown   B Troop   KIA   DOW 9/12/1968
PFC David U. Fritz   B Troop   KIA

AUGUST 28, 1968
PFC Charles D. Champion   C Troop   KIA
PFC Robert L. Coonrod   C Troop   KIA

AUGUST 30, 1968
SGT Maurice J. Haas   C Troop   KIA

SEPTEMBER 9, 1968
SGT Raymond Powell Jr.   HQ Troop KIA

SEPTEMBER 13, 1968
PFC Samuel L. Akins   A Troop   KIA

SEPTEMBER 15, 1968
SGT Leon D. Bullock   A Troop   KIA

SEPTEMBER 24, 1968
PFC Mario P. Estrada   B Troop   KIA

OCTOBER 1, 1968
SP5 Ronald E. Pochron   A Troop   KIA

OCTOBER 18, 1968
PFC Danny L. Rose   B Troop   KIA

NOVEMBER 6, 1968
SP5 Joel Vruggink   B Troop   KIA

NOVEMBER 12, 1968
SP4 Doyle W. Clark   B Troop   KIA

JANUARY 3, 1969
CPT Charles E. Heine   HQ Troop KIA
PFC Peter Binstock Jr.   A Troop   Crushed by falling sling-loaded water tank

JANUARY 23, 1969
SP4 Gerald J. Budbill   C Troop   Accidental homicide

JANUARY 31, 1969
SP4 Charles W. Richardson   B Troop   KIA

FEBRUARY 7, 1969
SGT Peter C. Hurlock   A Troop   Vehicle crash

FEBRUARY 25, 1969
SP4 Francis W. Cody   B Troop   KIA   Medic
PFC James E. Scott   B Troop   KIA

MARCH 11, 1969
SP4 Larry A. Jackson	C Troop	KIA
SP4 Larry Strahan	C Troop	KIA
PFC Perry L. Bozeman	C Troop	KIA
PFC Paul W. Shrewsbury	C Troop	KIA

MARCH 18, 1969
PFC Ray R. Jowers	B Troop	KIA

MARCH 25, 1969
SP4 Homer L. Gleaton	A Troop	KIA

APRIL 11, 1969
SFC Neil P. Farmer	B Troop	KIA
SP5 Peter E. Reece	B Troop	KIA
SP4 Robert L. Knight Jr.	B Troop	KIA
SP4 Stephen M. Lewis	B Troop	KIA
SP4 Robert H. Smart	B Troop	KIA

APRIL 15, 1969
SP4 Stephen W. Cummings	C Troop	Vehicle crash

APRIL 21, 1969
SFC Dwane G. Howard	B Troop	Accidental homicide

APRIL 29, 1969
SP4 Richard J. Fisher	A Troop	KIA

MAY 2, 1969
SP4 Dennis R. Rank	C Troop	Accidental burns	DOW 5/11/1969

MAY 12, 1969
SP4 Marloye K. Halgrimson	C Troop	KIA
PFC Randy T. Kendle	C Troop	KIA

PFC Edsel W. Steagall   C Troop   KIA
PFC Darrell C. West   C Troop   KIA

MAY 13, 1969
CPT Cordell B. Rogers   C Troop   KIA   DOW 5/27/1969

MAY 14, 1969
SP4 Michael K. Fultz   A Troop   KIA
SP4 Robert M. Higginbotham   A Troop   KIA

MAY 21, 1969
PFC Harry D. Ashcraft   HQ Troop Vehicle crash

MAY 28, 1969
PVT William J. Thornhill   A Troop   KIA

MAY 29, 1969
SP4 Rudy A. Carnley   A Troop   KIA

JUNE 23, 1969
SSG Homer D. Thick   C Troop   Vehicle crash
SP4 Gary Freeman   C Troop   Vehicle crash

JULY 21, 1969
PFC Raymond J. Palandro   C Troop   Drowned

JULY 25, 1969
SP4 Ronnie L. Herriman   A Troop   KIA

AUGUST 12, 1969
1LT Lawrence D. Greef   C Troop   KIA
SGT David O. Haake   C Troop   KIA
SP5 James A. Cabral Jr.   C Troop   KIA
SP4 Donald G. Dillard   C Troop   KIA   Medic

SP4 James L. Johnson   C Troop KIA
PFC Eugene P. Clark   C Troop KIA
PFC James Linder Jr.   C Troop KIA
PFC Bradley J. Simmons   C Troop KIA

AUGUST 13, 1969
SSG Robert A. Washington   B Troop KIA
PFC Kenneth R. McDaniel   B Troop KIA

SEPTEMBER 2, 1969
SP4 John A. Futo   A Troop KIA
SP4 Brent B. Nauss   A Troop KIA
PVT William E. McCormack   A Troop KIA

SEPTEMBER 16, 1969
PFC Eliseo Vergara   C Troop KIA

SEPTEMBER 29, 1969
SP4 Jimmy Kuhlenhoelter   C Troop KIA

NOVEMBER 21, 1969
PFC Ernest J. Davis Jr.   A Troop KIA

NOVEMBER 30, 1969
1LT Donald L. Kingery   B Troop Friendly fire

DECEMBER 14, 1969
PFC Chester L. Hughey   B Troop KIA

DECEMBER 27, 1969
SFC Donald I. Pringle   A Troop Suicide

JANUARY 7, 1970
SP4 Reid C. Henningsen   A Troop KIA

JANUARY 12, 1970
SGT Daniel E. Eckenrode   B Troop   KIA

FEBRUARY 2, 1970
SP4 Fred J. LeBlanc   A Troop   KIA
PFC Richard H. Miller   A Troop   KIA

FEBRUARY 26, 1970
SP4 John M. Wike   HQ Troop   Fall out of guard tower   Medic

MARCH 18, 1970
SP4 Douglas L. Shortley   A Troop   KIA
SP4 William J. Swartz   A Troop   KIA
PFC Jesse James Onishea   A Troop   KIA
PFC Hugh J. Ronneberg   A Troop   KIA

MARCH 19, 1970
SGT Atilano U. Tovar   B Troop   KIA
PFC Larry A. Branam   B Troop   KIA
PFC Galen G. Ludwig   B Troop   KIA
PFC Phillip W. Meador   B Troop   KIA
PFC Benny D. Sloat   B Troop   KIA

APRIL 2, 1970
SP4 Dale A. Gronsky   C Troop   KIA

APRIL 3, 1970
PFC William A. Miller   A Troop   KIA

APRIL 8, 1970
SP4 William A. Sharpe Jr.   C Troop   KIA
PFC Thomas C. Smith Jr.   A Troop   KIA

APRIL 26, 1970
SP4 Randall L. Crabtree   A Troop   KIA

MAY 7, 1970
SSG Neal A. Lord Jr.   A Troop   KIA

MAY 11, 1970
2LT David M. Kozak   A Troop   KIA   1-82 Artillery FO

MAY 20, 1970
PFC Kenneth M. Gray   C Troop   KIA   Medic
PFC David L. Vigil   C Troop   KIA

MAY 22, 1970
SSG William F. Duffner   A Troop   KIA

MAY 27, 1970
SP4 Gary C. Eaton   A Troop   KIA
SP4 Larry A. Rippe   A Troop   KIA
PFC Charles G. Floyd   C Troop   KIA
PFC Alan H. Parks   A Troop   KIA

MAY 30, 1970
1LT Dominick L. Cuccia   C Troop   Accidental cannon discharge

JUNE 9, 1970
SP4 Sarkis Dervishian   B Troop   KIA

JUNE 17, 1970
SGT Charles D. Maloney   C Troop   KIA

JUNE 18, 1970
SSG Robert C. Dawson   A Troop   KIA

JULY 18, 1970
SSG James L. Fore   A Troop   KIA
PFC Randall T. Baer   A Troop   KIA
PFC Michael E. Baum   B Troop   KIA   Medic

AUGUST 9, 1970
CPT David T. Maddux	A Troop	KIA
SP4 Kirk O. Barkley	A Troop	KIA
SP4 Gary W. Walker	A Troop	KIA DOW 8/18/1970
PFC Ivery L. Baxter	A Troop	KIA
PFC Joe Reyna Jr.	A Troop	KIA

SEPTEMBER 5, 1970
SP4 Jack M. Baker	A Troop	Malaria

SEPTEMBER 23, 1970
PFC John D. Bass	C Troop	KIA

OCTOBER 4, 1970
SSG Dennis L. Mikolajczyk	B Troop	KIA
SP4 Gary P. Formica	HQ Troop	KIA
SP4 Steven E. Grove	HQ Troop	KIA Medic
PVT Mark T. Sorci	B Troop	KIA

OCTOBER 6, 1970
SP4 James M. Kelso	A Troop	KIA

DECEMBER 7, 1970
SP4 Joe E. Crenshaw	C Troop	KIA
PFC Thomas L. Lafferty	C Troop	KIA
PFC Carmine A. Macedonio	C Troop	KIA

DECEMBER 20, 1970
PFC Sazin D. Fabacher	B Troop	KIA

DECEMBER 31, 1970
PFC Ronald E. Gerten	HQ Troop	KIA Medic
PFC Ira E. Gibbs	HQ Troop	KIA Medic

JANUARY 20, 1971
SGT James R. Garten　　　　A Troop　KIA
PFC Ronald D. Stephenson　A Troop　KIA

MARCH 5, 1971
SP5 Marcus E. Stoen　　　B Troop　KIA　DOW 3/14/1971
SP4 Larry P. Johnson　　　B Troop　KIA
PVT Frankie G. Baker　　　B Troop　KIA

MARCH 6, 1971
SGT Thomas Valerio　　　　C Troop　KIA　DOW 5/7/1971
SP5 Stephen W. Burgdorfer　C Troop　KIA
SP4 Horace L. Burton　　　C Troop　KIA

MARCH 7, 1971
LTC Sheldon J. Burnett　　HQ Troop　MIA　Remains repatriated 10/4/2004

MARCH 10, 1971
PFC Dale M. Mozdzen　　　B Troop　KIA

MARCH 15, 1971
SP5 Philip R. Jamrock　　　C Troop　KIA

MARCH 18, 1971
SSG John R. Champlin　　　B Troop　KIA

MARCH 19, 1971
PFC Thornton L. Woolridge　B Troop　KIA

MARCH 20, 1971
PFC Vincent C. Mauro, Jr.　B Troop　KIA

MARCH 21, 1971

SGT Claudius A. Small   C Troop   Accidental discharge
PFC Alan E. Davis   C Troop   KIA

MARCH 22, 1971
SP4 Larry D. Leamon   B Troop   KIA
SP4 Jerome E. Leroy   B Troop   KIA

MARCH 23, 1971
PFC Manasseh B. Warren   C Troop   KIA

MARCH 25, 1971
SSG R. D. McDonell   B Troop   MIA   BNR
PFC Manuel R. Puentes   B Troop   MIA   PFOD 9/6/1978
PFC Richard J. Rossano   B Troop   MIA   BNR
PFC Randall A. Thompson   B Troop   KIA

MARCH 26, 1971
SGT Martin R. Huart Jr.   C Troop   KIA
SP4 Gerald Zlotorzynski   C Troop   KIA
PFC Otto T. Wieben   C Troop   KIA

MARCH 29, 1971
SGT Andrew R. Steward Jr.   HQ Troop Vehicle crash

MARCH 30, 1971
PFC Terry L. Bosworth   C Troop   Accidental cannon recoil

MAY 2, 1971
PFC Lawrence L. Wiesendanger   HQ Troop KIA

MAY 3, 1971
SP4 Robert H. Royer   B Troop   KIA
MAY 12, 1971
SP5 Edelmiro L. Garcia Sr.   C Troop   KIA

MAY 17, 1971
SP4 Larry L. Robinson   A Troop   Drowned

JUNE 21, 1971
SP4 Raymond R. Mays   C Troop   KIA

JULY 8, 1971
SP5 Marion T. Griffin   C Troop   KIA

AUGUST 5, 1971
SP4 Robert D. Severson   B Troop   KIA
SP4 Rodrick Troup   B Troop   KIA

AUGUST 9, 1971
SFC Loy W. Pierce   B Troop   KIA

AUGUST 20, 1971
SSG Johnny E. Jones   B Troop   KIA

AUGUST 26, 1971
SSG Robert N. Vennik   B Troop   MIA Remains repatriated   6/27/2000
SGT John P. Hoffman   B Troop   KIA
SP4 Daniel A. Brancheau B Troop   KIA
SP4 George A. Chapman   B Troop   KIA
SP4 Curtis C. Kastler   B Troop   KIA
SP4 Rodolfo Valdez   B Troop   KIA

AUGUST 27, 1971
SP4 Robert F. Gartner   B Troop   KIA

SEPTEMBER 15, 1971
PFC George A. Floyd   B Troop   KIA

OCTOBER 4, 1971
SP4 Sidney A. Cottrell   A Troop   KIA

Losses by Troop

A Troop	73
B Troop	77
C Troop	86
HQ Troop	11

Losses by Year

1967	23
1968	69
1969	55
1970	53
1971	47
1972	0

Losses by Rank

LTC	1
CPT	4
1LT	7
2LT	1
SFC	5
PSG	1
SSG	18
SGT	21
SP5	10
SP4	84
PFC	91
PVT	4

Losses by Cause

Killed in action	119

Vehicle crash	7
Drowned	5
Friendly fire	5
Equipment malfunction	3
Accidental shooting	3
Accidental self shot	1
Suicide	1
Malaria	1
Falling water tank	1
Fall out of guard tower	1

Losses by Specialty

Radio operator (05B)	1
Infantryman (11B)	53
Indirect fire infantryman (11C)	13
Armor reconnaissance specialist (11D)	85
Armor crewman (11E)	48
Infantry operations and intelligence specialist (11F)	1
Infantry direct fire crewman (11H)	1
Cannon fire direction specialist (13E)	1
Field communications electronics equipment mechanic (31B)	1
Turret artillery repairman (45G)	2
Armament repairer (45K)	1
Mechanical maintenance helper (63A)	1
Light-wheel vehicle mechanic (63B)	1
General vehicle repairman (63C)	9
Recovery specialist (63F)	2
Medical corpsman (91A)	7
Medical NCO (91B)	5
Food service specialist (94B)	2
Field artillery unit commander (1193)	1

Tank unit commander (1203)	4
Armored reconnaissance commander (1204)	8

Losses by State

Alabama	4
Arizona	2
Arkansas	2
California	25
Colorado	2
Delaware	1
District of Columbia	1
Florida	9
Georgia	6
Illinois	12
Indiana	10
Iowa	2
Kansas	1
Kentucky	5
Louisiana	4
Maryland	8
Massachusetts	5
Michigan	20
Minnesota	7
Mississippi	2
Missouri	4
Montana	1
Nebraska	1
Nevada	1
New Hampshire	4
New Jersey	7
New York	14
North Carolina	8

North Dakota	1
Ohio	13
Oklahoma	2
Oregon	2
Pennsylvania	17
Puerto Rico	1
South Carolina	2
Tennessee	10
Texas	13
Utah	1
Vermont	1
Virginia	7
Washington	2
West Virginia	1
Wisconsin	6
Total Squadron Losses 1967–1972	247

APPENDIX B

Squadron and Troop Commanders

1st Squadron, 1st Cavalry Regiment
1967–1968

Squadron

Lt. Col. Richard H. Harrington	August 1967–January 1968
Lt. Col. Walter C. Cousland	January 1968–July 1968
Lt. Col. Richard D. Lawrence	July 1968–December 1968
Lt. Col. Philip L. Bolté	December 1968–May 1969

A Troop

Capt. J. Christopher Conrad	August 1967–December 1967
Capt. David E. Roesler	December 1967–May 1968
Capt. G. Robert Kaczor	May 1968–October 1968
Capt. Earl V. Shackelford	October 1968–February 1969

B Troop

Capt. David H. Staley	August 1967–November 1967
Capt. John L. Barovetto, KIA	November 1967–January 1968

Capt. Walter R. Reed   January 1968–June 1968
Capt. Wayne J. Lewis   June 1968–October 1968
Capt. Kenneth W. McCarley   October 1968–December 1968
Capt. Thomas L. Beale   December 1968–May 1969

C Troop
Capt. Ralph P. Brown   August 1967–January 1968
Capt. Michael B. Prothero   January 1968–May 1968
Capt. Jerry D. Frost   May 1968–October 1968
Capt. Kenneth R. Lamison   October 1968–April 1969

APPENDIX C

MACV Wallet Card

THE ENEMY IN YOUR HANDS
AS A MEMBER OF THE US MILITARY FORCES, YOU WILL COMPLY WITH THE GENEVA PRISONER OF WAR CONVENTIONS OF 1949 TO WHICH YOUR COUNTRY ADHERES. UNDER THESE CONVENTIONS:

YOU CAN AND WILL
DISARM YOUR PRISONER
IMMEDIATELY SEARCH HIM THOUROUGHLY
REQUIRE HIM TO BE SILENT
SEGREGATE HIM FROM OTHER PRISONERS
GUARD HIM CAREFULLY
TAKE HIM TO THE PLACE DESIGNATED BY YOUR COMMANDER

YOU CANNOT AND MUST NOT
MISTREAT YOUR PRISONER
HUMILIATE OR DEGRADE HIM
TAKE ANY OF HIS PERSONAL EFFECTS WHICH DO NOT HAVE SIGNIFICANT MILITARY VALUE
REFUSE HIM MEDICAL TREATMENT IF REQUIRED AND AVAILABLE

ALWAYS TREAT YOUR PRISONER HUMANELY

KEY PHRASES

<u>**ENGLISH**</u>   <u>**VIETNAMESE**</u>

English	Vietnamese
Halt	Đứng lại
Lay down your gun	Buông súng xuống
Put up your hands	Đưa tay lên
Keep your hands on your head	Đưa tay lên đầu
I will search you	Tôi khám ông
Do not talk	Đừng nói chuyện
Walk there	Lại dàng kia
Turn Right	Xây bên phải
Turn Left	Xây bên trái

"The courage and skill of our men in battle will be matched by their magnamimity when the battle ends. And all American military action in Vietnam will stop as soon as aggression by others is stopped."

21 August 1965   Lyndon B. Johnson

APPENDIX D

Chiêu Hôì Leaflet

Front and back of Chiêu Hôì leaflet found at the side of Provincial Highway 533 by the driver of A-35 immediately after that tank was damaged by a land mine on June 23, 1968.

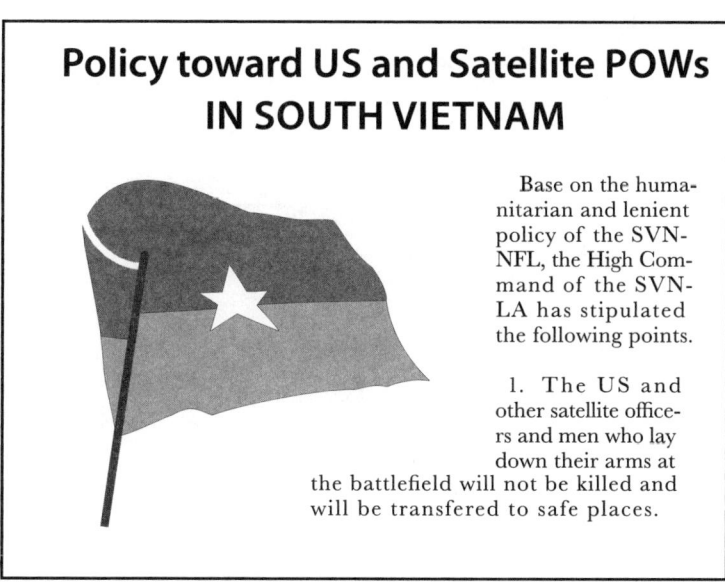

2. POWs will be well-treated – will not be tortured or insulted and will be given medical care in case of sickness.

3. All their personal belongings such as : money, gold-watches, pens and other private souvenir will not be deprived

4. POWs are allowed to communicate news and write to their families and friends.

5. The wounded left in the battlefield will be banadged and cured if possible by the LA medical-men.

6. The dead left in the battlefield will be given proper funeral and their graves taken care of.

The High Command of the
SVNLA

APPENDIX E

Fiddler's Green
(The Cavalrymen's Poem)

Author Unknown

Halfway down the trail to Hell,
In a shady meadow green
Are the Souls of all dead troopers camped,
Near a good old-time canteen.
And this eternal resting place
Is known as Fiddler's Green.

Marching past, straight through to Hell
The Infantry are seen.
Accompanied by the Engineers,
Artillery and Marines,
For none but shades of Cavalrymen
Dismount at Fiddler's Green.

Though some go curving down the trail
To seek a warmer scene,
No trooper ever gets to Hell
Ere he's emptied his canteen,

And so rides back to drink again
With friends at Fiddler's Green.

And so when man and horse go down
Beneath a saber keen,
Or in a roaring charge of fierce mêlée
You stop a bullet clean,
And the hostiles come to get your scalp,
Just empty your canteen,
Put your pistol to your head
And go to Fiddler's Green.

APPENDIX F

Where Are Those Things Now?

Forty years on, some of the icons of the Việt Nam War are still in active use in the U.S. military, such as the B-52 heavy bomber, C-130 transport airplane, CH-47 transport helicopter, M2 machine gun, and M113 armored vehicle. Some of the other vehicles have faded away or disappeared outright.

M48A3 Medium Tanks

The late-war Vietnamization program included giving M48A3 tanks to the Army of the Republic of Việt Nam (ARVN) to augment their original M41s.

Most of the M48A3s that survived the war in U.S. possession were converted to M48A5s, which involved swapping the 90mm main gun for the British-designed 105mm. The new cannon had a reverse twist to the lands and grooves compared to every other weapon in the U.S. arsenal except for the .45 pistol. The old-time tankers at Fort Knox were not informed of this English eccentricity, which caused no end of puzzlement when they tried to figure out why they couldn't zero the rounds flying down range.

So few purely M48A3 tanks remained that when the curators at the Patton Museum of Cavalry and Armor at Fort Knox wanted to honor Spec Five Dwight H. Johnson, the only tank driver who won the Congressional Medal of Honor in Việt Nam, they had trouble locating an unaltered M48A3.

M113A1 Armored Cavalry Assault Vehicles

Many M113s left in Việt Nam at the end of U.S. involvement in ground combat were also turned over to ARVN. The M113 family of combat vehicles are still popular with the militaries of many allied nations and remain in use in 2010. Soldiers of various armies have given local names to this vehicle. In the Norwegian army, for example, it is known as the "Vietnam Dumpster."

A certain quantity of worn-out M113s found their way into coastal waters as the foundations for artificial reefs. Thus some of the weapons of the Việt Nam War are now nurturing life.

USNS *General Nelson M. Walker*

The *General Walker* was built in Alameda, California, and originally commissioned in 1945 as the USS *Admiral H. T. Mayo*, after Adm. Henry Thomas Mayo, the commander in chief of the Atlantic Fleet during World War I.

Decommissioned by the navy in 1946, it was assigned to the Army Transport Service and renamed the USAT *General Nelson M. Walker* to honor Brig. Gen. Nelson Macy Walker of the 8th Infantry Division, who had been killed in action at Normandy in 1944. Transferred back to the navy in 1950 but not recommissioned, it retained its army name but with the prefix changed to USNS (United States Naval Ship).

In 1997, Art and Lee Beltrone salvaged 150 canvas bunks (and some bed frames) from the *General Walker* to preserve the graffiti scrawled on the undersides by soldiers and marines as they made the three-week journey across the Pacific Ocean to Việt Nam in 1966 and 1967. This became the basis for a traveling exhibit, "Marking Time: Voyage to Vietnam." A CD of the same name includes interviews with some of these troops, and a companion book, *Vietnam Graffiti: Messages from a Forgotten Troop Ship*, collects over 130 images of the graffiti.

The ship itself was broken up for scrap in 2005.

USS *Iredell County*

Built in Ambridge, Pennsylvania, the ship was commissioned in December 1944 as an LST-542-class tank-landing ship and served in late World War II as LST-839. In 1955, all surviving LSTs, including those in the mothball fleet along with 839, were named after U.S. counties; Iredell County is in west central North Carolina.

Placed back into service in 1966, the USS *Iredell County* served on the Đà Nẵng–Chu Lai run and elsewhere in Việt Nam from October 1966 until July 1970.

Decommissioned in 1970 and loaned to Indonesia under the terms of the Security Assistance Program, the ship was renamed the KRI *Teluk Bone*. In 1979 the thirty-five-year-old ship was struck from the Naval Register and sold to Indonesia outright.

Although still active in the Indonesian navy as of 2002, it was no longer on the rolls of that navy in 2010. Present disposition is unknown.

APPENDIX G

Healing

Việt Nam and America are bound by the peculiar ties that connect people who have engaged one another in bloody combat. As long as men and women from both sides still live who have stalked each other with mortal intent, there will be a lingering trail of pain and anger. For many veterans of the war, there is simply no forgetting. Nor should there be.

Việt Nam and the Vietnamese people have, on the surface, recovered from the long, terrible war fought in their land. The roads are no longer a string of mines and mine craters. The bridges are new and graceful. The stick and thatch huts have been replaced with sturdy masonry homes. Power pylons march across the countryside bringing electricity to all but the temporary villages of the nomadic Hill People. Dams in the foothills linked to the lowland rice paddies via concrete-lined irrigation ditches allow for dry-season crops and a prosperous peasantry.

A former U.S. cavalryman in 2010 has nothing to fear while traveling alone and unarmed through the Việt countryside on a motorcycle. In some villages he might even be invited in for tea.

What do American veterans owe, if anything, the people of Việt Nam? Do we owe them a simple apology for destroying their homes and killing their families? Would that do?

What do we owe ourselves?

How do we put the war where it belongs? We certainly ought not to forget what happened nor forget the savage emotions it brought forth. To forget those things is to invite the evil back. Perhaps the key is to forgive the Vietnamese and offer them an opportunity to forgive us. And, if we dare, to forgive ourselves.

Sometimes it does work. A former Việt Cộng told one American veteran that although he would have enthusiastically killed him long ago, he was pleased to see him in Đà Nẵng alive and well in 2007. They then went together with a former ARVN, some younger Vietnamese, and a Swedish woman to do a water assessment in a Quảng Nam village.

One U.S.-based non-governmental organization, the East Meets West Foundation, has done much to atone for our violent thrashing about in the Việt countryside. As of mid-2009, their Đà Nẵng office is now installing two village water systems per month in Quảng Nam Province. These systems include sealed wells drilled to a depth below the rice paddy water table, purification towers with storage tanks, and webs of delivery pipes with metered service to the front door.

Pure water, symbolically the very essence of life, is a fitting counterbalance for the lead and iron dished out to the villagers of Quảng Nam in the spring of 1968.

East Meets West involves the people of a village in the water projects from the start. The first step is an assessment: Do the people of the village feel they have a water problem? Are they willing to contribute labor to dig the trenches for the pipes and then back-fill them later? How many đồng per month is pure water piped to their homes worth to them? Are they able to appoint a meter reader, pay the monthly fees, and administer the maintenance of the system?

At least one former member of the 1-1 Cavalry is monitoring this process with hope. Mậu Hoà, the village in which an older Việt was thrown down his own well and murdered in 1968, seemed to be a symbolically fitting locale for an American-sponsored water system in 2008, but the people of Mậu Hoà proved to be uncooperative, so there will be no water system there anytime soon.

The village of Phước Âm welcomed a new water system. It was there on March 19, 1968, that the 1st Platoon of A Troop worked out its rage and fear after losing a tank and a much-admired platoon sergeant to a five-hundred-pound land mine. Officially, only four Vietnamese were killed in retribution for the mine near their village. It is possible that the number is that low because the locals had long since come to associate an American loss with their own demise. Those who were quick made it to a place of relative safety; the slow fell to 1st Platoon's machine guns.

In 2006 the East Meets West Foundation installed a safe water system in the Phước Âm hamlet of the Bình Triêu Commune of the Thăng Bình District of Quảng Nam Province. Today 1,864 people in 466 households in that ville enjoy the benefits of healthy water. Children no longer miss so many days of school due to waterborne diseases, and achieving the age of five will now be a routine accomplishment.

Another non-governmental organization, the Veterans Việt Nam Restoration Project, is also striving to mend the wounds of war. This group takes small teams of veterans to Việt Nam about once a year where they work with the Vietnamese on projects. Small primary schools, housing for disabled veterans, medical clinics, and a solar electricity system for a hospital are examples of their work. VVNRP has also done some of its good deeds in conjunction with East Meets West.

They are always looking for a few good veterans.

These are just two examples of NGOs at work today in Việt Nam. There are many others. A mom-and-pop NGO in Đà Nẵng, Bread of Life, specializes in running a small bakery and café where young deaf Việt people are taught useful trades, making them employable and independent.

Although the help the veterans contribute to these projects is appreciated by the Vietnamese, the benefits largely accrue to the veterans. One veteran said he would never have thought that going back to his war zone would bring him such peace.

APPENDIX H

If You Go Back

Age is revered in the East, and since Westerners turn gray sooner, we have an advantage. You will look older than you are to a Vietnamese, so you will be treated with greater respect.

The Việt custom is to give or receive an object from someone with both hands. This is often awkward, but if you make this small effort, you will be rewarded with smiles.

Never, ever touch a Việt on the head, not even a child. Extremely bad manners. Even the shoulders are chancing it. Elbows and forearms are fair game during a conversation between good friends.

The Vietnamese generally need more than one syllable in an American name so that it makes sense to them. "Ed" or "Sue" will frustrate them, so go with the full version of your name. You will be Mister Edward or Misses Susannah. Never call a Vietnamese by his or her name alone unless you are very close friends, and then only in private.

Vietnamese do not go by their family names, which are spoken first. This is partly modesty and partly privacy. We are all minor and passing manifestations of the great family we are born into. To claim that name as your very own is a bit presumptuous. Also, if someone asks your name and you simply say: "Mister Thomas," it gives you a certain bit of anonymity. Many guys named Thomas are out there. So, Nguyễn Ngọc Lương would be known as Ông Lương. The Nguyễns had been a line of kings, a source of pride to a Vietnamese, but he would not flaunt it. A married woman named

Tạng Thị Minh would be addressed as Bà Minh. A maiden's title is Cô.

The trains are slow, but they run on time, and the fares are fair. But the most flexible way to see the old AO is to rent a motorcycle and head out with your topographical map and a GPS device (a GPS is also handy for breaking the ice with old VC guys). Smile and wave. In 2007, a new Honda 110cc Trail Bike could be rented in Hội An for five dollars a day plus gas. No insurance or helmet required. Drive carefully. Getting onto Hill 29, currently a VA facility, has not been possible so far. Reactions of the guards vary from a polite refusal to drawn AKs. It is not an open post.

Vietnamese seem to have no problem with photography, and they act honored that you are taking the trouble. Traveling with a portable, battery-powered, dye-sublimation printer will make you a big hit in a village. Handing out 4x6 color prints on the spot to the elders will be appreciated. Exception: Do not photograph at airports or the outside of government or military installations. Unless you are still a good runner.

Even knowing a very small bit of Vietnamese will help. Just being able to say hello—"Chàu Ông" (Hello Sir) or "Chàu Bà" (Hello Ma'am)—will open doors. One former cav trooper approached an extremely wrinkled old man and a middle-aged guy leaning on his motorcycle. He greeted the elder first with a friendly "Chàu Ông," which caused the younger Việt to guffaw; closer examination revealed an extremely wrinkled old *woman*.

Hội An is a good base camp for exploring the old 1st Cav AO. It is a tourist town with fine hotels. There are many shopping opportunities, so if your spouse is not one to follow you out into the wool, you may leave her behind happily occupied. Tam Kỳ is closer, but it is dusty and rundown. One driver hired by an American couple did not want to stop there due to a recent government crackdown on covert protestant missionaries. He was afraid his passengers' Western faces would draw unwanted official attention because of the religious tensions. A better recommendation is the Bình Minh beach resort at Hà Bình on Barrier Island.

When out in the countryside, stay on the trails. There is still a lot of unexploded ordinance in the bushes, and farmers die every year from picking up old hand grenades. Go with an open mind, and don't expect to see your old bunker or the crippled tank you abandoned under fire. They are gone.

Glossary

A-1E: USAF, USN, and USMC single-engine propeller bomber—"Skyraider" aka "Spad"
A-6A: USAF, USN, and USMC two-engine jet bomber—"Intruder"
AC-47: USAF two-engine propeller gunship—"Puff the Magic Dragon," aka "Spooky"
ACAV: armored cavalry assault vehicle—an M113A1 with extra machine guns and shields
ACR: armored cavalry regiment
AH-1G: helicopter gunship—"Cobra," aka "Snake"—replaced the "Huey" gunships in 1968
AK-47: Avtomat Kalashnikova Model 1947—7.62mm VC and NVA full-automatic infantry assault rifle
Americal: American, New Caledonian Division, aka 23rd Infantry Division
AO: area of operations
AP: Associated Press
APC: armored personnel carrier—an ACAV or M113A1
Arc Light: bombing mission by B-52s
ARVN: Army of the Republic of Việt Nam, pronounced *Arvin*
B-52: USAF eight-engine jet heavy bomber—"Stratofortress"
B-57: USAF two-engine jet light bomber—"Canberra"
bàu: lake
BB: battleship hull designation—USS *New Jersey* is BB-62
Big Red One: 1st Infantry Division
black can: 90mm canister round with one thousand cylindrical slugs
blivet: rubberized bag used for transporting and storing diesel fuel

blue line: river or stream (on a map)

body bag: rubberized bag used for transporting dead soldiers

Blooper: M79 40mm grenade launcher

BOQ: batchelor officers quarters

C-3: plastic explosive—older, less stable version of C-4

C-4: plastic explosive

C-7: USAF two-engine STOL transport—"Caribou"

C-47: USAF and USMC two-engine propeller transport—"Skytrain," aka "Dakota"

C-130: USAF four-engine propeller transport—"Hercules"

CAR15: 5.56mm rifle, short version of M16 for officers

CBU: cluster bomb unit

C&C: command and control—a colonel's or general's helicopter

CH-21C: light transport helicopter—"Shawnee," aka "Flying Banana"

CH-34: light transport helicopter—"Choctaw"

CH-47: heavy lift helicopter—"Chinook"

CH-54B: heavy lift helicopter—"Tarhe," aka "Skycrane"

Chiêu hồi: "I surrender!" Once a Việt Cộng does so voluntarily, he becomes a hồi chánh

CID: Criminal Investigation Division—U.S. Army detectives

CMH: Congressional Medal of Honor

CMMI: Command Maintenance Management Inspection

CN: tear gas—phenacyl chloride—"mace"

CO: commanding officer

CO: conscientious objector

CP: command post

CS: tear gas—2-chlorobenzalmalononitrile

CV-2: USA two-engine STOL transport—"Caribou"—surrendered to the USAF in 1966

CWO: chief warrant officer

DEROS: date eligible for return from overseas

DOA: dead on arrival

DShKM (ДШКМ): Degtyaryova-Shpagina Krupnokaliberny ("M" for modernized 1946 version) .51-caliber (12.7x108mm) heavy machine gun, NVA and VC—known as "Dushka," Russian for "Sweetie"

dust-off: medical evacuation by helicopter

Dại Úy: captain

EM: enlisted man—private through specialist fifth class

F-4D: USAF, USN, and USMC two-engine jet fighter-bomber— "Phantom II"

F-100D: USAF single-engine jet fighter-bomber—"Super Sabre"

FAC: forward air controller—flying an O-1E or an O-2A

FO: forward observer—usually a second lieutenant from an artillery unit

FSB: fire support base

FTA: "Future Tankers of America," "Fun Travel and Adventure," and "Fuck the Army"

giang: stream

green can: 90mm Flechette or "Beehive" round containing 8,500 darts

grunt: infantryman

HE: 90mm high explosive

HEAT: 90mm high explosive anti-tank

HEP: 90mm high explosive plastic

H&I: harassment and interdiction—artillery fired at speculative targets

hồi chánh: a Việt Cộng who has rallied to the RVN side

HQ: headquarters

I Corps: northernmost military division of South Việt Nam— pronounced *Eye Core*

IO: information office

IPW: interrogator of prisoners of war

jarhead: U.S. Marine Corps member

Kalashnikov: *see AK-47*

Katyusha: 122mm rocket—name is Russian version of "Katie"

KIA: killed in action

klick: kilometer, one thousand meters

liệt sĩ: revolutionary martyr—dead Việt Cộng

LOH: light observation helicopter, OH-6A, OH-13, or OH-23— pronounced *Loach*

LST: landing ship, tank

LT: lieutenant, first or second

LZ: landing zone

M2HB: .50-caliber (12.7x99mm) Browning heavy machine gun—"Ma Duce"

M3A1: .45-caliber sub-machine gun—"Grease Gun"

M14: 7.62mm semi-automatic infantry rifle

M16: 5.56mm full-automatic infantry rifle

M29: 81mm mortar

M41: twenty-four-ton light tank—"Walker Bulldog"

M48A3: fifty-two-ton medium tank—"Patton"

M55: multiple machine gun carriage—"Quad .50"

M60: 7.62mm light machine gun

M60A1 AVLB: fifty-six-ton bridge tank (armored vehicle-launched bridge) "Swatter"

M72 LAW: 66mm light anti-tank weapon

M73: 7.62mm tank coaxial machine gun

M79: 40mm grenade launcher—"Blooper"

M88: fifty-six-ton medium recovery vehicle, aka VTR (vehicle, tracked, recovery)

M103: sixty-five-ton heavy tank

M107: thirty-one-ton, 175mm, self-propelled, long-range bombardment gun

M110: thirty-one-ton, 8-inch, self-propelled howitzer

M113A1: eleven-ton scout or infantry track—an ACAV—"Green Dragon" (VC name)

M114: seven-ton scout track—failed its Việt Nam test

M114: 155mm towed howitzer

M125A1: eleven-ton, 81mm mortar track

M132A2: twelve-ton flame-thrower track—"Zippo"

M548: six-ton tracked cargo carrier—unarmored fuel- or ammo-carrying tracks

M577A1: thirteen-ton command track

M578 LVR: twenty-six-ton light recovery vehicle

M1911A1: .45-caliber semi-automatic pistol

M1943: 82mm Soviet mortar used by VC and NVA—also Chicom Type 53

MACV: Military Assistance Command, Vietnam—the advisors

MEDCAP: medical civil action program

medevac: medical evacuation

MG: machine gun

MIA: missing in action

MOS: military occupational specialty—a person's job in the army

   11B: infantryman (grunt)

   11C: indirect fire infantryman (mortarman)

   11D: armor reconnaissance specialist (armored scout)

   11E: armor crewman (tank crewman)

   63C: general vehicle repairer (field mechanic)

   91A: medical corpsman (field medic)

   1204: armored reconnaissance unit commander (cavalry platoon leader, and cavalry troop, squadron, and regimental commander)

MP: military police

NCO: noncommissioned officer—corporal through command sergeant major

núi: mountain

NVA: North Vietnamese Army

O-1E: USAF single-engine propeller observation aircraft—"Bird Dog"

O-2A: USAF two-engine propeller observation aircraft—"Skymaster"

OCS: Officer Candidate School

OH-6A: light observation helicopter—"Cayuse," replaced the OH-13 in 1968

OH-13: light observation helicopter—"Sioux"

OH-23: light observation helicopter—"Raven"

Pan Am: Pan American World Airways—a defunct airline

PF: Popular Forces, *see Ruff Puffs*

POW: prisoner of war

PRUs: Provincial Reconnaissance Units—ARVN Special Ops

quad .50: four .50-cal machine guns mounted on an M55 carriage

ROTC: Reserve Officers' Training Corps

RF: Regional Forces, *see Ruff Puffs*

RPD (РПД): Ruchnoy Pulemyot Degtyaryova—VC and NVA 7.62mm light MG

RPG (РПГ): Ruchnoy Protivotankoviy Granatomyot—VC and NVA anti-tank weapon—"rocket propelled grenade" is a backronym

RPK (РПК): Ruchnoy Pulemyot Kalashnikova—VC and NVA 7.62mm light MG

RTO: radio telephone operator

Ruff Puffs: Regional Forces/Popular Forces—RVN militia

RVN: Republic of Việt Nam

S1: personnel officer

S2: intelligence officer

S3: operations officer

S4: logistics officer

S5: civil affairs officer

S&D: search and destroy

short-timer: a soldier whose time in Việt Nam is nearly over

sông: river

STOL: short takeoff and landing

SVNLA: South Việt Nam Liberation Army—Việt Cộng

SVN-NLF: South Việt Nam National Liberation Front—political arm of the Việt Cộng

tac air: tactical airpower—support from fighter-bombers rather than heavy bombers

TC: tank commander or track commander

Tết: Lunar New Year

Thiệu Úy: second lieutenant

TOC: tactical operations center

track: an ACAV—APC—M113A1

Trung Úy: first lieutenant

Type 36: 57mm Chicom recoilless rifle—VC and NVA—copy of U.S. M18A1

Type 52: 75mm Chicom recoilless rifle—VC and NVA—copy of U.S. M20

Type 53: 82mm Chicom mortar—VC and NVA—copy of Soviet M1943

UH-1B: gunship "Hueys," replaced by the AH-1G in 1968

UH-1C: similar to the UH-1Bs

UH-1D: standard utility helicopter—"Iroquois," aka "Huey" or "Slick"

UH-1F: similar to the UH-1Ds—used for C&C and heavier lifting than the "D" model could accomplish
UPI: United Press International
USAF: United States Air Force
USARV: United States Army Vietnam—logistical support command
USAT: United States Army Transport
USMA: United States Military Academy, West Point, New York
USNS: United States Naval Ship
USS: United States Ship
VA: Vietnamese Army—since 1975
VC: Việt Cộng
VNAF: Việt Nam Air Force, pronounced *Vee Naff*
vũng: bay
VVA: Vietnam Veterans of America
VVAW: Vietnam Veterans Against the War
WIA: wounded in action
WO: warrant officer
World, The: anywhere other than Việt Nam
WP: white phosphorous
XO: executive officer

Bibliography

Books

Beltrone, Art and Lee. *Vietnam Graffiti: Messages from a Forgotten Troopship.* Charlottesville, VA: Howell Press, 2004.

Emerson, Gloria. *Winners and Losers: Battles, Retreats, Gains, Losses, and Ruins from the Vietnam War.* New York: Random House, 1976.

Goff, Stanley C. *Brothers, Black Soldiers in the Nam.* Novato, CA: Presidio Press, 1982.

Herr, Michael. *Dispatches.* New York: Alfred A. Knopf, 1977.

Kelly, Michael P. *Where We Were in Vietnam: A Comprehensive Guide to the Firebases, Military Installations and Naval Vessels of the Vietnam War 1945–1975.* Central Point, OR: Hellgate Press, 2002.

Sheehan, Neil. *A Bright Shining Lie: John Paul Vann and America in Vietnam.* New York: Random House, 1988.

Spector, Ronald H. *After Tet: The Bloodiest Year in Vietnam.* New York: The Free Press, 1993.

Stanton, Shelby L. *Order of Battle: A Complete Illustrated Reference to the U.S. Army Combat and Support Forces in Vietnam 1961–1973.* Mechanicsburg, PA: Stackpole Books, 2003.

Westmoreland, William C. *A Soldier Reports.* Garden City, NY: Doubleday and Company, 1976.

Periodicals

"Death Valley." *Newsweek*, January 29, 1968, p. 29.

Documents

The Coffelt Database (The Comprehensive Vietnam KIA Project) found at: www.virtualwall.org/docs/vwdbase.htm

Congressional Medal of Honor citation for James A. Taylor
Distinguished Service Cross citation for Charles Nathan Boyd
Distinguished Service Cross citation for Steve O. Nussbaumer
Distinguished Service Cross citation for William A. Swoveland
"Daily Staff Journals: 1st Squadron, 1st Cavalry," August 1967–December 1968
CID report of investigation No. 70-CID052-06312, December 2, 1971
General court-martial of 1st Lt. Lynn A. Maxfield (CM 421442)

Interviews*
1st Squadron, 1st Cavalry
HQ Troop

Gen. Crosbie E. Saint (Ret.); Lt. Gen. Richard G. Lawrence (Ret.); Brig. Gen. Philip L. Bolté (Ret.); Col. Charles W. Donaldson (Ret.); Col. James A. Logan (Ret.); Lt. Col. Frederic J. Filbert (Ret.); Lt. Col. Wade E. Medbery (Ret.); Maj. Karl Steinmetz (Ret.); Chief Warrant Officer Clifford L. Dunn, Sr. (Ret.); Command Sgt. Maj. Max B. Ogas (Ret.); Richard K. Albers, MD; Philip H. Davis, MD; Robert C. Kelly; Christopher Noble

A Troop

Col. J. Christopher Conrad (Ret.); Col. David E. Roesler (Ret.); Lt. Col. Thomas H. Jackson (Ret.); Lt. Col. George E. Norton (Ret.); 1st Sgt. Charles Nathan Boyd (Ret.); Thomas M. Andersen; Jerry L. Anderson; Gary R. Bakewell; Richard H. Brummett; Thomas M. Bursott; Bobby R. Butler; Wayne L. Byrd; Alfred V. Cognetti; Michael F. Dolan; David L. Eady; Ronnie Fortner; G. Robert Kaczor; Larry L. Gaydon; Thomas M. Ginz; Lawrence W. Graham; Daniel J. Guida; John Guzik III; Robert Johnston; David L. Miller; A. Leon Palatas; Richard P. Rensi; Robert W. Schlagel; Arvin W. Schoep; Larry A. Scull; Dick L. Taskey

B Troop

Col. David H. Staley (Ret., now deceased); Lt. Col. James A. Dickens (Ret.); Maj. Raymond H. Mahoy (Ret.); Maj. James A. Taylor (Ret.); Command Sgt. Maj. Gary L. Boggs (Ret.); Master Sgt. James O. Hammerbeck (Ret.); Kenneth L. Bouche; Ron Decktor; Michael D.

Esmond; Gene R. Hotchkiss; James S. Lindsey; Walter R. Reed; Richard J. Sears; Robert D. (Sonny) Webster

C Troop
John Ahrenberg; Kevin Brawley; Michael A. Colicchio; Wallace (Wally) Colligan; John Max Pryor; Dean E. Wingrove

INFORMATION OFFICE, AMERICAL DIVISION
Cary S. Sklaren

INTERROGATION SECTION, MILITARY INTELLIGENCE DETACHMENT, AMERICAL DIVISION
Joe Knopic

A/123RD AVIATION BATTALION
Dennis DeWine

A/1-35TH INFANTRY
Col. Charles W. Chapinski, Jr. (Ret.); Richard J. Arnold

FAMILY MEMBERS
Carol Cousland Weyand, widow of Brig. Gen. Walter C. Cousland; Michele Nussbaumer Johnson, sister of Spc. 4th Class Steve O. Nussbaumer, DSC

RESEARCH ASSISTANCE
Richard J. Arnold; Mary B. Chapman; Brian Eugene Gunn; Leslie Hines; Thomas H. Jackson; George Lepre; Marilee P. Meyer; Carolyn Miller; Tom Pike; Bob Skwaryk; Clifford L. Snyder

HEALING RESOURCES
East Meets West Foundation: www.eastmeetswest.org
Veterans Việt Nam Restoration Project: www.vvrp.org

*Ranks given only for those who retired from service.

In Memoriam

Keith W. Nolan, who authored this book, died on February 19, 2009, after enduring a fourteen-month siege of lung cancer. Keith devoted his entire working life to recording the stories of the soldiers who fought in the war in Việt Nam. Although he was not of military age during that conflict, he has shown a great love and understanding for those who struggled with the near impossible task of fighting in an unpopular guerilla war at the side of lukewarm allies amid an indifferent-to-hostile population.

Over the course of his twenty-six-year writing career, Keith evolved from an uncritically patriotic eighteen-year-old to a middle-aged man somewhat saddened by what the war had done to its soldiers. And by what some of its soldiers had done to themselves and to the hapless innocents caught in the middle of a vicious war.

Keith had also grown weary of hearing grandfathers still using disparaging terms for East Asian people. In his mind's eye, he saw us as dynamic twenty-six-year-olds, just back from a great adventure. Now he was seeing some of us as having learned too little from that adventure.

Keith leaves behind a nine-year-old daughter, Anna Britt, whom he loved more than any words can express. He also leaves behind twelve books of history on the American War in Việt Nam. Books that will stand upon library shelves for decades hence and will be reached for by subsequent generations of Americans who wish to know what "that" was all about.

Richard Brummett
Bellingham, Washington
May 2009

Index

1st Air Cavalry Division, 81, 82, 95, 99, 102, 164, 185, 186
3rd Brigade, 36, 81, 95, 102, 136, 164
    7th Cavalry Regiment, 34, 81, 82, 85, 86, 89
        1st Battalion, 81, 82, 85, 86, 89
        5th Battalion, 81, 85
    9th Cavalry Regiment, 85, 104, 108, 133
        1st Squadron, 81, 85, 104, 108, 133
        B Troop, 81, 85, 108, 133
    12th Cavalry Regiment, 6, 81, 134, 135, 149, 156, 158, 164
        1st Battalion, 6
        2nd Battalion, 6, 81, 95, 134, 135, 149, 151, 153, 156, 158–161, 322
            A Company, 153
            C Company, 149, 153, 160
            D Company, 151
1st Armor Training Brigade, 355
1st Armored Division, 11, 12, 23, 35, 41, 136, 168, 354, 355
    1st Cavalry Regiment, 1st Squadron, 1, 2, 5–8, 11–16, 18–20, 23, 27, 35, 41, 44, 45, 72, 73, 75, 81, 86, 93, 96, 100, 118, 130, 136, 147, 160, 168, 178, 181, 195, 231, 232, 248, 249, 255, 258, 290, 302, 311–313, 322, 324, 333, 335, 337, 349, 353–356, 361, 362, 368

A Troop, 13, 15–18, 25, 28, 30, 32–34, 44, 46, 49, 55, 71, 73, 81, 82, 84, 86, 88, 90, 91, 113, 116–118, 137, 138, 140–142, 169, 175, 179, 181, 187, 189, 197, 201, 215, 218, 219, 225, 226, 228, 231, 235, 239–241, 249, 253, 259, 260, 265, 268, 271, 276, 278, 281, 289, 318–321, 324, 325, 337, 349, 350, 361
    1st Platoon, 13, 16, 54, 74, 83, 91, 141, 159, 180, 193, 195, 197, 198, 201, 202, 215, 268
    2nd Platoon, 49, 54, 55, 63, 64, 69, 71, 82, 87, 104, 116, 139, 179, 171, 231, 216, 259, 269
    3rd Platoon, 71–73, 83, 87, 104, 115, 172, 175, 180, 187, 188, 193, 196–198, 202, 208, 215, 216, 226, 249, 276
B Troop
    1st Platoon, 107, 163
    2nd Platoon, 58, 63, 307
    3rd Platoon, 58, 63, 66, 268, 269
C Troop, 178–180, 182, 218, 219, 265

1st Cavalry Regiment, 3rd
    Squadron, 35
1st Tank Battalion, 12
1st Constabulary Squadron, 12
1st Aviation Brigade, 17th Cavalry
    Regiment, 7th Squadron, C
    Troop, 78
1st Infantry Division, 5, 172
    4th Cavalry Regiment, 172
1st Marine Division, 40, 329
    7th Marine Regiment, 329
        2nd Battalion, 329
2nd Armored Cavalry Regiment, 5
2nd Surgical Hospital, 339
3rd Armored Cavalry Regiment, 5
3rd Armored Division, 6
    12th Cavalry Regiment, 6
        3rd Squadron, 6
3rd Marine Division, 5
4th Infantry Division, 44
    1st Cavalry Regiment,
        2nd Squadron, 27, 44, 267,
        268, 269, 280, 282, 329
5th Infantry Division, 6
    12th Cavalry Regiment, 6
        4th Squadron, 6
6th Armored Cavalry Regiment, 5
10th Cavalry Regiment, 17
11th Armored Cavalry Regiment, 5,
    36, 354
    2nd Squadron, 36
14th Armored Cavalry Regiment, 5
67th Evacuation Hospital, 131
69th Armor Regiment, 314
163rd Armored Cavalry Regiment,
    2nd Reconnaissance Squadron,
    E Troop, 314
Americal Division (23rd Infantry
    Division), 69, 81, 95, 136, 164, 167,
    195, 200, 237, 248, 301, 302, 307,
    311, 313, 355
4th Infantry Division, 3rd Brigade,
36, 95, 136
35th Infantry Regiment, 99, 104, 200
    1st Battalion, 99, 104, 109
        A Company, 104, 109
        B Company, 200
    8th Cavalry Regiment, 253
        F Troop (Blue Ghosts), 78, 121,
        137–139, 175, 178, 180, 202, 213,
        218, 237, 239, 248, 253, 254, 257,
        260, 268, 269, 272, 278, 279, 302,
        319, 321, 325, 330, 335, 339–341, 345
11th Light Infantry Brigade, 136, 200,
    214, 231, 267, 302, 318
    3rd Infantry Regiment, 214
        4th Battalion, 214
            B Company, 214
    20th Infantry Regiment, 200,
        215, 219
        1st Battalion, 200, 215, 219
            C Company, 200, 215
            D Company, 219
    21st Infantry Regiment, 118, 119,
        267, 272, 275, 278, 282, 318, 319
        3rd Battalion
            B Company, 118, 119
        4th Battalion, 267, 272, 275,
        278, 282, 318, 319
            B Company, 267, 272, 275,
            278, 282
            D Company, 318, 319
16th Field Artillery Regiment,
    3rd Battalion, 50
23rd MP Company, 313
26th Engineer Battalion, 307
101st Airborne Division, 36, 40, 95,
    100, 118, 185, 186
    1st Brigade, 36, 40, 95, 118
        327th Infantry Regiment, 40
            1st Battalion, 40
    123rd Aviation Battalion, HQ
Company, 109, 110
    196th Light Infantry Brigade, 36,

46, 63, 118, 136, 139, 149, 164, 267, 356
  1st Infantry Regiment, 267
    2nd Battalion, 63, 267
      B Company, 267
      C Company, 63
    21st Infantry Regiment, 118, 119, 161, 163, 210–212
      3rd Battalion, 16, 118, 119, 161, 163, 210–212
        A Company, 163, 210–212
        B Company, 118, 119
        D Company, 161
        E Company, 16
    31st Infantry Regiment, 118–120
      4th Battalion, 118
        B Company, 118
        C Company, 119
        D Company, 118–120
    198th Light Infantry Brigade, 118, 136, 225
      52nd Infantry, 1st Battalion, 319, 321
24th Infantry Division, 16
  21st Infantry Regiment, 16
    E Company, 16
25th Infantry Division, 19, 35, 354
  4th Cavalry Regiment, 3rd Squadron, 19
I Corps, 1, 36, 172, 177, 194, 199
II Corps, 44, 179
III Corps, 35, 36, 172, 354, 360
Task Force Barker, 214
Task Force Oregon, 36, 39, 40, 44, 69
Tiger Force, 40, 199

4th ARVN Cavalry, 180, 259
18th ARVN Infantry Division, 360

2nd NVA Division, 95, 118, 133, 149, 181, 237, 258, 282, 321
  1st Main Force VC Regiment, 149, 181
  3rd Regiment, 118, 133
  21st Regiment, 149
3rd NVA Division, 302, 324
  95th Regiment, 302

A Shau Valley, 186
AH-1G Cobra, 253, 254, 304
AK-47, 56, 63, 81, 85–87, 98, 109, 113, 130, 138, 140, 152, 154, 162, 164, 170, 190, 202, 203, 210, 219, 227, 254, 261, 263, 274, 279, 304, 321, 326, 343
Alcatraz Island, 28
Alexandria, Virginia, 354, 355
Americal Division Combat Center, 311
An Sơn, 181, 386
Arc Light, 135, 149
Arlington National Cemetery, 354
Arlington, Virginia, 354
Armor School, 15, 100
Army War College, 355
Asheboro, North Carolina, 30
Atlanta, Georgia, 359
Austin, Texas, 24, 355
B-17 bomber, 19
B-52 bomber, 135, 160
B-57 Canberra, 321
Barrier Island, 7, 218, 256, 301, 329, 331, 343
Battalion Landing Team 2-7, 331
Bàu Bàng, 82
Bay Bridge, 28
Bergstrom Air Force Base, 24, 35
Berkeley, California, 221
Berlin Brigade, 286
Berlin, Germany, 286, 363
Biên Hòa Air Base, 181
Big Red One, 194, 202, 348
Bình Định District, 375

Bình Tây, 215
Bình Yên, 86, 88
Blackwood, New Jersey, 367
Blairsville, Georgia, 191
Blandensville, Illinois, 285
Boeing 727, 27
Boyd's Bastards, 17, 30, 31, 46, 58, 115–117, 121, 137, 169, 172, 188, 193, 196–198, 205
Bradley fighting vehicle, 355
Brea, California, 363
Bristol, Connecticut, 364
Brooke General Hospital, 173
Broomfield, New Jersey, 30
Browning automatic rifle (BAR), 16
Büdingen, Germany, 194
Burkburnett, Texas, 354
C-130 Hercules, 35, 342
Cam Ranh Bay, 251, 255, 341, 342, 346
Camden, Delaware, 7
Camden, New Jersey, 7, 32
Camp Kaiser, Korea, 17
CAR15 Colt Commando, 112, 134, 158, 195, 254
Cedar Crest, New Mexico, 365
CH-47 Chinook, 68, 120, 123, 267, 337
Châu Chanh, 222
Châu Xuân 2, 375
Chicago, Illinois, 32, 256, 285
Chicoms, 130, 153, 202
Chu Lai, 36, 37, 41, 44, 45, 50, 51, 68, 71, 110, 118, 121, 130, 141, 158, 167, 173, 181, 189, 213, 251, 254, 257, 263, 276, 279, 290–292, 296, 298, 311–314, 327, 333, 334, 337, 339, 341, 342, 345
Cigar Island, 2, 7, 71, 81, 85, 90, 92, 96, 111, 121, 138, 169, 170, 187, 200, 218, 376
Clarklake, Michigan, 357

Claymore mines, 45, 134, 244
Colorado Springs, Colorado, 363
Command and General Staff College, 148, 360
Craterville, 253, 278, 279
Đà Nẵng, 36, 38, 41, 43, 74, 181, 334, 356, 361, 376
Dandridge, Tennessee, 366
Danvers, Massachusetts, 372
DC-4, 352
Decatur, Indiana, 32
Detroit, Michigan, 32, 251
Dhahran, Saudi Arabia, 362
Diện Biên Phu, 37, 177
Dink Valley, 63, 69, 235
Đông Hà, 356
Đông Mỹ 1, 222
Đức An 1, 253
Army National Guard, 314, 360
East Huntsville, Alabama, 358
El Paso, Texas, 207
Esopus, New York, 194
Fat City, 36, 45–47, 49, 53–55, 63, 121, 148, 167, 212, 233–235, 286, 305
Fiddler's Green, 343, 344
First Regiment of Dragoons, 7, 12, 110, 148, 172, 194, 283, 342
Fort Benning, 160, 314, 361
Fort Hood, Texas, 11, 14, 15, 23, 24, 26, 27, 31, 32, 35, 51, 60, 100, 118, 121, 168, 191, 214, 255, 337, 353, 354, 373
Fort Knox, Kentucky, 15, 89, 160, 194, 237, 314
Fort Leavenworth, Kansas, 148, 223, 313, 315
Fort Lee, Virginia, 233
Fort Sam Houston, Texas, 286, 354
Fountain Hills, Arizona, 374
Fourth Cavalry, 194
Gallup, New Mexico, 299
Galveston, Texas, 24

INDEX 433

Grafenwöhr, Germany, 236
Graham, North Carolina, 364
Green Berets, 37
Hà Nội, 5, 36, 39, 40, 132, 165, 185, 219, 237, 254, 368, 372
Hà Tây, 86, 87, 89
Harrisonburg, Virginia, 51
Havre, Montana, 314
Hawk Hill, 7, 75, 78, 111, 115, 119, 233, 265, 267, 291, 292, 294, 297, 298, 313, 327, 344, 345
Headquarters Troop, 25, 35, 41, 86
Hertel, Wisconsin, 367
Hiệp Đức Valley, 96, 149, 161, 315
Highway 1, 36, 45, 75, 81, 82, 93, 113, 137, 178, 179, 214, 302, 324, 343, 346, 356, 361, 375
Hill 29, 7, 36, 73, 75, 77, 78, 81, 92, 93, 116, 118, 141–143, 167, 178, 180, 187, 188, 190, 196, 200, 207, 210, 212, 220, 231, 234, 244, 249, 251–254, 256, 259, 260, 262, 263, 266, 272, 276, 277, 279–282, 286, 287, 293, 295, 302, 307, 311, 313, 314, 333, 335, 337, 340, 341, 343, 349, 353, 375, 376
Hill 34, 210, 211, 213, 222
Hill 35, 36
Hill 54, 36, 55, 57–62, 74, 93
Hill 63, 118, 119
Hill 74, 323
Hill X, 118, 119
Hồ Chí Minh, Pres., 38
Hồ Chí Minh Trail, 39, 254, 256
Hội An, 301
Hope Mills, North Carolina, 360
Hopedale, Ohio, 30
Houston, Texas, 286
Hudson, New York, 370
Huế, 181, 185, 186
Huey, 68, 78, 88, 102, 106, 108, 109, 152, 254, 262, 272, 286, 303, 343, 356

Hương Mỹ, 170
Hussars, 7, 8
Indianapolis, Indiana, 363
Infantry Hall, 361
Inter-American Defense College, 358
Jefferson Barracks, Missouri, 12
Jungle Operations Course, 20
Khâm Đức, 237
Khe Sanh, 177, 186
Las Cruces, New Mexico, 364
Lee County, Virginia, 366
Liberia, 357
Loaches, 78
London, England, 286, 352
Long Bình, 148, 181, 287, 353
Los Angeles, California, 32
Luzon, Philippines, 12
LZ (landing zone) Baldy, 81, 82, 95, 96, 121, 200, 229, 347
LZ Goat, 6, 239, 241, 244, 245, 251, 376
LZ Leslie, 149, 151
LZ Pace, 352
LZ Ross, 96, 97, 108, 133, 149, 155, 156, 158, 160
M1 Abrams tank, 357
M3 grease gun, 253
M14 sniper rifle, 14, 190, 270
M16, 14, 54, 74, 83, 86–88, 103, 107, 112, 117, 118, 124, 128, 135, 139, 151, 152, 155, 162, 167, 188, 192, 201–203, 206, 208, 210, 235, 260, 264, 273–275, 304, 326
M48 tank, 78, 87, 90, 99, 108, 123, 130, 153, 180, 194, 251, 356, 376
M48A3 tank, 8, 13, 30, 41, 59, 87, 349
M55 Quad-50, 135
M60 light machine gun, 13, 45, 67, 86–88, 98, 102–104, 108, 121, 128, 135, 142, 150, 155, 157, 164, 169, 171, 187, 191, 201, 227, 235, 242, 261, 263, 269–271, 275, 279, 286,

303, 304, 338
M60 tank, 12, 13
M79 grenade launcher, 14, 45, 56, 78, 82, 86, 114, 117, 135, 138, 150, 155, 157, 161, 162, 182, 188, 190, 190, 218, 221, 264, 275, 343
M88 tank retriever, 41, 54, 72
M113A1 armored personnel carrier, 12, 41, 75, 82, 86
M114 scout vehicle, 12
M125 mortar track, 41
M577 command track, 41, 75, 86
Ma Duce, 13
Mad Minutes, 135, 150, 244, 337
Marble Mountain, 43
Marion, Massachusetts, 362
Marist College, 348, 350, 352
Marist Novitiate, 194
Mậu Hoà, 7, 215, 371, 374
McChord Air Force Base, 255, 346
Mechanical Mule, 115
Medford, Oregon, 358
Medical Field Service School, 286
Mekong Delta, 181, 352
Monument, Colorado, 355
Mosin Nagant rifle, 124
Motor Bear, 220
Mount Vernon, Ohio, 362
Mỹ Khê 4, 215
Mỹ Lại 4, 215, 355
National Training Center, 357
National War College, 357
Navy Seabee, 31, 77, 92, 132, 179, 180
New Braunfels, Texas, 361
New York, New York, 32, 194, 209, 330, 348, 349
Ngok Ta Vak, 237
North Carolina State, 30, 364
Núi Yon, 317–322, 338
Oakland, California, 27
Oceanside, California, 17
Officer Candidate School (OCS), 15, 17, 21, 51, 100, 175, 231, 314
OH-13, 98, 108
Ohio State University, 247
Okinawa, 33, 34, 194, 207
Olney, Illinois, 30, 364
Panamá, 20, 147
Paris, France, 219, 237, 286
Peace Corps, 362
Pearl Harbor, 69
Peoria, Illinois, 77
Phantom, 261, 320
Philadelphia Naval Air Engineering Center, 365
Philadelphia Navy Yard, 33
Phước Âm 3, 217, 343
Pineapple Forest, 2, 93, 123, 124, 126, 131, 201, 213, 235, 257–260, 265, 267, 272, 275, 278, 280
Pleiku, 357
Porterville, California, 73
Portland, Oregon, 366
Provincial Reconnaissance Unit, 182
Quảng Nam Province, 7, 95, 301, 347, 375
Quảng Ngãi City, 302, 305, 306, 317, 323–325, 327, 328
Quảng Ngãi Province, 36, 39, 200, 214, 302
Quảng Tin Province, 7, 36, 95, 355
Quế Sơn Mountains, 95, 96, 149
Quế Sơn Valley, 2, 81, 95, 118, 133, 149, 153, 210, 322, 357, 371
Qui Nhơn, 121, 131, 140
Reserve Officer Training Corps (ROTC), 15, 17, 148, 160, 239, 247, 351
Rome, Italy, 286
Route 533, 225, 228, 317, 318
Route 535, 81, 96, 97, 163
Ruff Puffs (Regional Forces), 71, 72, 182, 353, 375
Sài Gòn, 5, 19, 35–37, 39, 40, 148,

165, 177, 178, 181, 194, 220, 237, 282, 297, 348–350, 352, 356, 368, 372
Samoa, California, 100
San Antonio, Texas, 173, 354
San Francisco, California, 27, 28, 35, 255
Schofield Barracks, Hawaii, 136
Seattle University, 239
Seattle-Tacoma Airport, 255
Seattle, Washington, 255, 346
Sheridan, 356
Sixth Cavalry, 347
Sơn Long, 305–307, 312, 313
Sơn Trà 1, 163
Sông Lý Lý, 119
Square Lake, 249, 349, 350
St. Francis Medical Center, 365
St. James, New York, 362
Surprise, Arizona, 274
Swatter, the, 195
Tam Kỳ, 7, 36, 93, 112, 126, 131, 167, 175, 179–183, 190, 201, 225, 235, 242, 258, 265, 281, 282, 288, 297, 301, 303, 306, 312, 313, 315, 317, 322, 338, 340, 346, 376
Tân Sơn Nhất Airbase, 181
Temple University, 32, 365
Terryville, Connecticut, 264
ThaiTrac, 352
Thăng Bình District, 178, 182
Thompson submachine gun, 124
Thôn Hai 2, 98, 99, 101, 104, 110
Thôn Hai 3, 190
Tiên Phước, 225, 228, 231, 240, 317
Tiger Force, 40, 199
Travis Air Force Base, 35
Trenton, New Jersey, 365
Trường Giang, 71, 82, 83, 85, 90, 138, 140, 142
Tucson, Arizona, 357
Tuscumbia, Missouri, 31, 62

U.S. Army Air Forces, 19, 353
U.S. Disciplinary Barracks, 313
U.S. Special Forces, 225, 237
University of California at Berkeley, 17, 19, 351
University of Kentucky, 18
Vân An, 178
Vienna, Austria, 8
Vientiane, Laos, 352
Vietnamese National Field Police, 332
Vĩnh An, 138
Virginia Military Institute, 247
Võ Lự, 376
Vũng Tàu, 35
Washington, DC, 351
West Point, 15, 17–21, 55, 96, 111, 137, 147, 172, 210, 247, 253
West Union, South Carolina, 355
White Beach Naval Facility, 33, 34
White Sands Missile Range, 364
Wildwood, Missouri, 369
William Beaumont Army Hospital, 207
Xuân Lôc, 360
Xuân Quê 5, 153, 154, 159

Index of Names

Names in italics are of those known to have died during the war years.

Abrams, Gen. Creighton C., 249
Ahrenberg, Pfc. John E., 274
Albers, Capt. Richard K., 254, 257, 265, 276, 279–281, 285–299, 302, 305, 312, 317, 319, 323–327, 339–346, 367
Albers, Dolly, 285, 286
Ames, Sgt. Roy, 274
Andersen, Pfc. Thomas M., 187, 226–228, 363
Anderson, Pfc. Jerry L., 114, 192, 193, 201, 203, 205–207, 364

Bacon, Staff Sgt. Nicky D., 272–275, 282
Bakewell, Sgt. Gary R., 202, 205
Barnard, Staff Sgt. Marvin W., 189, 190
Barovetto, Capt. John L., 19, 100, 103, 104, 106, 108, 109, 134, 135, 152–154, 156, 159, 160
Beltran, Pfc. William R., 103
Bennett, Staff Sgt. Davis, 216
Black Hawk, Chief, 11, 12
Blossom, Sgt. Steve, 254
Boggs, Staff Sgt. Gary L., 154–156, 160
Bolding, Sgt. Edgar L., 180
Bolté, Lt. Col. Philip L., 180, 182, 340, 343, 355
Bouche, Staff Sgt. Kenneth L., 25, 86, 106, 107, 150, 151, 164, 178, 179, 255, 363
Boyd, Platoon Sgt. Charles Nathan, 16, 17, 23, 30, 31, 43, 44, 46, 53, 58, 77, 83, 84, 91, 92, 111, 113–117, 119, 121, 122, 131, 137, 140–142, 169–172, 181, 188, 190–193, 195–198, 201, 204–206, 215–217, 351, 362, 366, 371, 375
Brooks, Sgt. (first name not available), 54
Brown, 1st Lt. Bruce W., 280
Brown, Capt. Ralph P., 14, 15, 17, 22, 35, 36, 54–56, 93, 123, 126, 127, 167, 180, 203–205
Brummett, Spc. 4th Class Richard H., 172, 173, 187, 193–198, 208, 216–218, 220–223, 229–231, 241, 244, 245, 249, 251–253, 346–353, 356, 371, 374–376
Buckley, Kevin P., 348
Bursott, Pfc. Thomas M., 17, 24, 25, 30, 31, 34, 44–47, 50, 57, 62, 75, 78, 81, 115, 116, 118, 141, 142, 169, 201, 202, 205–207, 219, 243, 255, 364
Butler, Staff Sgt. Bobby R., 202, 203, 205
Byrd, Pfc. Wayne L., 30, 51, 92, 116, 117, 120, 176, 179, 255, 364

Castro, Spc. 4th Class (pseudonym), 307–311, 313
Chaisson, Brig. Gen. John R., 179
Chamberlain, Spc. 4th Class James, 88
Chaplinski, Capt. Charles W., 99, 107–109
Cognetti, Pfc. Alfred V., 33, 46
Colicchio, Pfc. Michael L., 128, 131
Colligan, Spc. 4th Class Wallace M., 264, 265, 278, 282, 364
Conrad, Capt. J. Christopher, 14, 15, 17, 18, 20, 22, 27, 34–36, 51, 71–73, 82–84, 86, 88, 137, 357
Cosby, Pfc. David F., 214
Cousland, Lt. Col. Walter C., 147, 148, 176, 181, 202, 205, 210, 211, 225, 233, 237, 240, 242, 247, 248, 287, 289, 342, 354
Cramer, Spc. 4th Class Jeffrey T., 268
Czinege, Staff Sgt. (pseudonym), 307, 308, 310, 311, 313

Davis, Spc. 4th Class Herbert C., 191, 192
Davis, Spc. 4th Class John A., 129
Davis, Capt. Philip H., 193, 235, 236, 287
Decktor, Spc. 4th Class Ron, 100, 110, 135, 150, 151, 153, 155, 156, 160, 164, 178, 213, 214, 255, 365
DeWine, Warrant Officer Dennis M., 261–263
Dickens, 1st Lt. James A., 14, 15, 21, 47, 58, 64–69, 100, 158–160, 255, 358
Dolan, Spc. 4th Class Michael F.
Donaldson, 1st Lt. Charles W., 18,

INDEX 437

20, 21, 51, 71–73, 78, 82, 86, 90, 91, 181–183, 351, 359
Dovi, Spc. 4th Class Peter J., 241, 347, 353
Dunn, Chief Warrant Officer Clifton L., 21, 24, 111, 234
Durst, Staff Sgt. Donald W., 54, 125, 180, 204, 205

Eady, Spc. 4th Class David L., 32, 73, 115, 175, 188, 195, 216, 223, 244, 245, 255, 365
Eisenhower, Pres. Dwight D., 37
Eskowski, Sgt. (pseudonym), 307–311, 313
Esmond, Spc. 4th Class Michael D., 33, 65, 66, 87, 88, 102, 105, 109, 255, 365

Faas, Horst, 348
Filbert, Maj. Frederic J., 237, 248, 281, 282, 302, 312, 331, 355
Fortner, Sgt. Ronnie, 44, 116, 117, 137, 142, 170, 171, 173, 255, 366
French, Staff Sgt. Kenneth B., 88
Frost, Capt. Jerry D., 260, 261, 264, 265, 272, 273, 275, 280, 302, 303

Garwood, Pvt. Robert R., 315, 316
Gasdek, Capt. Barry D., 318, 320
Gaydon, Spc. 4th Class Larry L., 84, 116–118, 138, 182, 217, 255, 366
Gellhorn, Martha, 38
Gentry, Pfc. Jerry W., 104–106, 109
Genus, Pfc. David J. (pseudonym), 106
Gettys, Maj. Gen. Charles M., 311, 312, 324, 326, 331, 337, 339
Gilliam, Platoon Sgt. Donald L., 102, 109
Ginz, 1st Lt. Thomas M., 259, 260, 268, 269, 278, 279, 339
Gobble, Sgt. Charles H., 50

Goff, Pfc. Stanley C., 269, 270, 282
Gomez, Pfc. Jorge, 157, 160
Gossard, Pfc. David E., 62
Graham, Pfc. Lawrence W., 28–31, 44, 46, 51, 53, 57–60, 62, 74, 77, 79, 82–84, 117, 139, 142, 143, 169, 171, 173, 364, 366
Graves, Lt. Col. Richard G., 349
Gregory, Lt. Col. Bob L., 134, 153, 164
Gudanov, Spc. 4th Class Dmitri I. (pseudonym), 230
Guida, 2nd Lt. Daniel J., 137, 138, 141, 142, 169–171, 173, 225, 255, 362
Guzik, Spc. 5th Class John, III, 32, 73, 118–121, 187, 188, 195–197, 216–218, 220–223, 229, 243, 244, 251, 252, 255, 347, 353, 366, 367, 375, 376

Haeme, 1st Lt. Richard A., 82–84
Hale, Spc. 4th Class Nathan, 331–335
Harker, Dave, 162, 163, 316
Harrington, Lt. Col. Richard H., 11, 12, 19, 20, 23, 24, 27, 35, 36, 41, 44, 55, 75, 86, 88, 91, 97, 109, 111, 342, 353, 354
Harrington, Col. Tracy B., 19
Hammerbeck, Staff Sgt. James O., 60, 65, 100–102, 363
Hardin, Gerald, 116
Hasford, Spc. 5th Class John L., 250, 251, 347
Henspeter, Spc. 4th Class Gary L., 127, 128, 131
Hillman, Staff Sgt. Coleman G., 124, 126, 128
Hoãng Trí Hãi, 376
Hô Chí Minh, Pres., 38, 39
Hoban, Mike, 254
Hobbs, Spc. 4th Class Kimmey D., 226
Hooper, Pfc. (first name not

available), 311
Hoopes, Pvt. Richard A., 310, 313
Hoover, Spc. 5th Class Richard J., 116, 171, 207
Hotchkiss, Pfc. Gene R., 89, 90, 100, 104–106, 108, 110, 150, 154, 157, 160, 255, 367
Houston, Staff Sgt. Elwood L., 216, 217, 222, 223, 243, 245, 249–251, 346, 347, 354
Huáng Đình Thơ, Lt. Col., 180
Humphrey, Sen. Hubert H., 256
Huỳnh Điểu, 371, 375

Iervolino, Pfc. Robert R., 106

Jackson, 1st Lt. Thomas H., 249, 250, 253, 254, 261, 263, 268–271, 282, 303, 304, 312, 319–321, 324, 337–339, 361
Jessie, Platoon Sgt. Herman R., 15, 16, 32, 90, 91, 115, 118–120, 187, 188, 194, 196, 219, 229, 362
Johnson, Pres. Lyndon B., 38, 110, 219, 220, 286, 328
Johnston, Spc. 4th Class Robert E., 226, 227, 231, 232, 240, 245, 261, 269–272, 279, 282, 295, 303, 320, 321, 367, 368

Kaczor, Capt. G. Robert, 228, 239, 240, 243, 244, 248, 250, 253, 254, 268, 269, 272, 275, 289, 302–304, 312, 318–320, 358, 375
Kennedy, Pres. John F., 37
Kennedy, Sen. Robert F., 237
Kerr, Pfc. (pseudonym), 307–310, 313
Kimmel, Lt. Col. Robert G., 99, 108, 109
King, Rev. Dr. Martin Luther, Jr., 237
Kisner, Sgt. 1st Class Thomas R., 139
Knopic, Spc. 4th Class Joe, 331, 332, 334–336
Kolstad, Spc. 4th Class Arlen, 197, 198
Kossowski, Pfc. David S., 120, 121
Koster, Maj. Gen. Samuel W., 69, 159, 168, 215, 225
Kushner, Capt. Floyd, 317

Laird, Sec. Def. Melvin R., 350
Lawrence, Lt. Col. Richard D., 28, 247–250, 253, 254, 256, 257, 259–268, 270, 272, 275, 278–283, 289, 296, 301–303, 305–307, 311–313, 317, 318, 321–325, 327, 329–331, 337–340, 342, 343, 355
Leroy, Catherine, 96
Lewis, Capt. Wayne J., 267, 279, 280, 302, 306, 307, 314, 346
Lindsey, 1st Lt. James S., 18, 59, 69, 85, 96–100, 102, 103, 106, 109, 110, 255, 359
Lockridge, Sgt. Jack R., 180
Logan, Capt. James A., 248, 256, 257, 259, 268, 272, 277, 278, 281, 282, 302, 303, 305, 306, 311, 312, 317, 318, 320, 324, 328, 330, 331, 340–342, 355
Lundquist, Maj. Donald C., 20–22, 27, 29, 55, 100, 109, 110, 142, 148, 228, 233–237, 283

MacArthur, Gen. Douglas, 39
Mahoy, 2nd Lt. Raymond H., 87, 96, 97, 101–104, 106, 109, 110, 154, 157, 160, 200, 360, 361
Martin, Staff Sgt. Beverly A. (pseudonym), 73
Matchett, Spc. 4th Class Leslie D., 170, 171, 173, 366
Mattaro, Donald, 211, 212
Maxfield, 1st Lt. Lynn A., 307–311, 313–315

McCarthy, Sen. Eugene J., 256
McGuinn, Pfc. James E., 137
McKenna, Col. James O., 102
McKinney, Spc. 4th Class Bill, 206, 207
McPherson, 1st Sgt. William, 114, 115, 120, 122, 141, 228, 229
Medbery, Maj. Wade E., 147, 148, 225, 228, 233, 242, 354
Miller, 1st Lt. David L., 230–232, 243, 244, 256, 257, 361
Montoya, Staff Sgt. Gabino, 126
Moses, Spc. 5th Class Frank, 156, 158, 160
Motin, Spc. 4th Class Charles L., 129

Neubacher, Spc. 4th Class Brandt S., 221, 229, 250, 251, 347
Newland, Pfc. Michael D., 128, 129
Nguyễn Đình Thiệp, 375
Nguyễn Ngọc Lương, 356
Nguyễn Thị Quối, 308
Nguyễn Văn Thiệu, Pres., 282
Nitz, Pfc. Robert F., 101, 109
Nixon, Pres. Richard M., 220, 256, 328
Noble, 1st Lt. Christopher, 189, 193, 235, 241, 242, 262, 265, 271, 282, 287, 294, 362
Norton, 1st Lt. George E., III, 21, 24, 37, 86, 88–91, 93, 111, 114, 115, 193, 226, 228, 236, 237, 359, 360
Nowicki, Pfc. James E., 157, 160
Nussbaumer, Spc. 4th Class Steve O., 273, 282, 283

Ogas, Cmd. Sgt. Maj. Max B., 248, 259, 325, 326
O'Reilly, William James "Bill," Jr., 352

Palatas, Pfc. A. Leon, 90, 116, 255
Peeler, 2nd Lt. Ronald (pseudonym), 63, 64, 65, 68, 69
Phụ, Sgt. (family name not available), 188
Plummer, Spc. 4th Class Ralph W., III, 90
Preston, Pfc. William, 140
Prothero, Capt. Michael B., 210, 211, 242, 357, 358
Pryor, Staff Sgt. John Max, 24–26, 29, 31, 32, 34, 54–57, 61, 62, 93, 94, 124–132, 167, 168, 175, 182, 183, 186, 187, 189, 190, 193, 201, 203, 204, 208–211, 213, 255, 368, 369

Reed, Capt. Walter R., 22, 35, 91, 92, 100, 160, 178, 211–213, 357
Rensi, Sgt. Richard P., 30, 50, 51, 82, 84, 255, 369
Richardson, Spc. 4th Class Charles W., 344
Ridgway, Gen. Matthew B., 37
Roberts, Spc. 4th Class John L., 250, 251
Robinson, 1st Lt. Dennis L., 104, 109
Roesler, Capt. David Earl, 35, 137–139, 169–173, 175, 189, 195, 197, 202, 203, 205, 206, 216, 218, 222, 223, 240, 351, 358
Rogers, Pfc. John A., 172, 173
Ross, Lt. Col. Collier M., 96, 97, 99, 108, 133, 135, 149, 151–153, 155, 156, 158–160, 163, 229, 230

Saint, Maj. Crosbie E., 20, 21, 27, 35, 47, 54, 55, 66–68, 71, 72, 75, 85–89, 111, 112, 147, 354
Saunders, Pfc. Michael J., 131
Schell, Jonathan E., 39, 40
Schell, Orville H., III, 39, 40
Schlagel, Staff Sgt. Robert W., 243, 244, 269, 276, 282, 363
Schmidt, Pfc. Barry J., 152

Schneider, Spc. 4th Class Herman W., Jr., 218
Schoep, Spc. 4th Class Arvin W., 30, 31, 58, 61, 191, 198, 255, 369–371
Scognamilio, Spc. 4th Class Patrick J., 229, 230, 249–253, 347–350
Scott, Spc. 4th Class Thomas L., 99, 109
Sears, Spc. 4th Class Richard J., 33, 89, 100, 134, 135, 151, 154–158, 160, 371–373
Selby, Sgt. Robert B., 200
Sheehan, Neil, 39
Sherburne, Capt. Thomas N., 172
Snyder, 2nd Lt. Ronald L., 188
Staley, Capt. David H., 14, 15, 17–19, 22, 23, 25, 27, 35, 36, 45, 47, 63–69, 85–89, 96–100, 109, 110, 357
Steinmetz, Capt. Karl, 22, 24, 35
Stenger, Spc. 5th Class Patrick, 298, 299, 324, 326, 344
Stewart, Staff Sgt. Edward S., 257
Susak, 1st Lt. Henry, 330, 331
Svobodny, Pfc. Lawrence M., 55
Sweet, Lt. Col. Richard S., 158, 159
Swoveland, Sgt. William A., 273, 283

Tạng Kỳ Sơn, 308
Tạng Thị Cúc, 308, 313
Tạng Thị Minh, 309, 313
Taskey, Spc. 4th Class Dick L., 31, 118, 141, 193, 198, 199, 201, 202, 205, 208, 218, 255, 373
Taylor, 1st Lt. James A., 21, 25, 86, 96, 99, 100, 102–106, 109, 110
Thompson, Hugh, 215
Tinker, Staff Sgt. Curtis J., 101, 106, 109, 152, 157, 160

Townsend, Spc. 5th Class (pseudonym), 307–311, 313
Trần Văn Phú, 371, 375
Trần Văn Ty, 375
Trần Văn Uu, 371

Venn, 1st Lt. David, 288, 324, 327
Võ Lự, 376

Wainscott, Staff Sgt. David H., 107, 109
Wallace, 2nd Lt. George N., III, 34, 83, 138, 139, 255, 264
Webster, Sgt. Robert D. "Sonny," III, 105, 106, 109, 110, 152, 209, 210, 212, 255, 373, 374
Westmoreland, Gen. William C., 1, 38, 39, 177, 179, 185, 186, 220
Wheeler, 1st Lt. William L., 87, 88, 96, 99, 100, 103, 105, 106, 109, 155, 160
Whitmore, 1st Lt. Garland D., II, 49–51
Williams, 1st Lt. Gary D., 260–262, 265, 268
Williams, Capt. George K., 349, 350
Williams, Sgt. Henry T., 310, 311, 313, 315–317
Williams, Platoon Sgt. Hillard E., 126
Williams, 1st Sgt. Richard F., 129–131, 161–165
Wilson, Spc. 4th Class Peter F., 307, 310, 311, 313
Winkempleck, Pfc. George H., 73
Wojtkiewicz, 2nd Lt. Ronald J., 126, 226